Lecture Notes in Artificial Intelligence 6967

Subseries of Lecture Notes in Computer Science

Michael Beigl Henning Christiansen
Thomas R. Roth-Berghofer
Anders Kofod-Petersen Kenny R. Coventry
Hedda R. Schmidtke (Eds.)

Modeling and Using Context

7th International and Interdisciplinary Conference
CONTEXT 2011
Karlsruhe, Germany, September 26-30, 2011
Proceedings

Springer

Series Editors

Randy Goebel, University of Alberta, Edmonton, Canada
Jörg Siekmann, University of Saarland, Saarbrücken, Germany
Wolfgang Wahlster, DFKI and University of Saarland, Saarbrücken, Germany

Volume Editors

Michael Beigl
Hedda R. Schmidtke
Karlsruhe Institute of Technology, Germany
E-mail: {michael.beigl, hedda.schmidtke}@kit.edu

Henning Christiansen
Roskilde University, Denmark
E-mail: henning@ruc.dk

Thomas R. Roth-Berghofer
University of West London, UK
E-mail: thomas.roth-berghofer@uwl.ac.uk

Anders Kofod-Petersen
Norwegian University of Science and Technology (NTNU), Trondheim, Norway
E-mail: anderpe@idi.ntnu.no

Kenny R. Coventry
Northumbria University, Newcastle upon Tyne, UK
E-mail: kenny.coventry@northumbria.ac.uk

ISSN 0302-9743 e-ISSN 1611-3349
ISBN 978-3-642-24278-6 ISBN 978-3-642-24279-3 (eBook)
DOI 10.1007/978-3-642-24279-3
Springer Heidelberg Dordrecht London New York

Library of Congress Control Number: 2011936632

CR Subject Classification (1998): I.2, F.4.1, H.4, J.3, J.4

LNCS Sublibrary: SL 7 – Artificial Intelligence

Typesetting: Camera-ready by author, data conversion by Scientific Publishing Services, Chennai, India

Printed on acid-free paper

Springer is part of Springer Science+Business Media (www.springer.com)

Preface

Fourteen years after the first conference in 1997, the 7th International and Interdisciplinary Conference on Modeling and Using Context (CONTEXT 2011) set out to extend foundational research on context and to evaluate the status and consequences of context research, as well as to address new questions for the field. CONTEXT, the oldest conference series focusing on context, is unique in its emphasis on interdisciplinary research. Previous conferences have been held in Rio de Janeiro, Brazil (CONTEXT 1997), Trento, Italy (CONTEXT 1999, LNCS 1688), Dundee, UK (CONTEXT 2001, LNCS 2116), Palo Alto, USA (CONTEXT 2003, LNCS 2680), Paris, France (CONTEXT 2005, LNCS 3554), and Roskilde, Denmark (CONTEXT 2007, LNCS 4635). Each of these brought together researchers and practitioners from a large range of fields to discuss and report on context-related research and projects.

CONTEXT 2011 was held during September 25–29, 2011 at the Karlsruhe Institute of Technology, Germany. During the first two days, four workshops focussing on specific topics within the area of context research and a doctoral consortium took place. The main conference included paper, poster, and video presentations, as well as system demonstrations. The conference invited researchers and practitioners to share insights and cutting-edge results from the wide range of disciplines concerned with context, including: the cognitive sciences (linguistics, psychology, philosophy, computer science, neuroscience), the social sciences and organizational sciences, and all application areas. Moreover, CONTEXT 2011 featured a special track—*Commercialising Context*—to reflect both the fact that context research has found numerous successful applications in recent years and the fact that context itself has become a product that can be sold.

This volume contains the papers and posters presented at CONTEXT 2011 as well as invited papers from our keynote speakers Ruth Kempson and Paul Holleis. Overall there were 54 submissions to the full paper track. The Committee decided to accept 17, that is, 33%, after a careful and highly selective review process to be presented as full papers at the conference. Another seven were accepted as short papers. Moreover, this volume further contains abstracts of the posters that were selected to be shown at the conference.

We thank the keynote speakers Jerry Hobbs, Ruth Kempson, and Paul Holleis for their inspiring talks and contributions. We are grateful to the members of the Program Committee and the additional reviewers for their efforts and hard work, which led to the high quality of the program. Special thanks go to the people at TecO, Predrag Jakimovski, Markus Scholz, Matthias Berning, Yong Ding, and Verena Noack for local organization. Moreover, we are grateful to KIT for hosting the conference.

We thank the Workshop Chair, Robert Ross, as well as the organizers of the four workshops and their Program Committee members for preparing the workshops, and we thank Klaus David and Robert Ross for their work toward a successful video, demo, and poster track. We are grateful to all authors who submitted their work to the conference. We thank the Steering Committee for their advice, guidance, and practical help to make this conference possible.

The submission process was organized using the EasyChair system. We thank Springer for their continued support in publishing the proceedings of CONTEXT.

September 2011

Michael Beigl
Henning Christiansen
Thomas R. Roth-Berghofer
Kenny R. Coventry
Anders Kofod-Petersen
Hedda R. Schmidtke

Conference Organization

General Chairs

Michael Beigl	Karlsruhe Institute of Technology, Germany
Henning Christiansen	Roskilde University, Denmark
Thomas R. Roth-Berghofer	University of Hildesheim, Germany

Program Chairs

Hedda R. Schmidtke	Karlsruhe Institute of Technology, Germany
Anders Kofod-Petersen	SINTEF ICT, Norway
Kenny R. Coventry	Northumbria University, UK

Workshop Chair

Robert J. Ross	Dublin Institute of Technology, Ireland

Video/Demo/Poster Chairs

Klaus David	Kassel University, Germany
Robert J. Ross	Dublin Institute of Technology, Ireland
Yong Ding	Karlsruhe Institute of Technology, Germany
Markus Scholz	Karlsruhe Institute of Technology, Germany

Local Organization

Hedda R. Schmidtke	Karlsruhe Institute of Technology, Germany
Predrag Jakimovski (Location)	Karlsruhe Institute of Technology, Germany
Markus Scholz (Publicity)	Karlsruhe Institute of Technology, Germany
Matthias Berning (Finance)	Karlsruhe Institute of Technology, Germany
Irina Schierholz (Secretary)	Karlsruhe Institute of Technology, Germany

Steering Committee

David Leake (Chair)	Indiana University, USA
Varol Akman	Bilkent University, Turkey
Paolo Bouquet	University of Trento, Italy
Patrick Brézillon	University of Paris 6, France
Henning Christiansen	Roskilde University, Denmark
Anind Dey	Carnegie Mellon University, USA

Chiara Ghidini	FBK-irst, Italy
Fausto Giunchiglia	University of Trento, Italy
Boicho Kokinov	New Bulgarian University, Bulgaria
Thomas R. Roth-Berghofer	University of Hildesheim, Germany
Roy Turner	University of Maine, USA

Program Committee

Agnar Aamodt	Norwegian University of Science and Technology, Norway
Michael Beigl	Karlsruhe Institute of Technology, Germany
Thomas Bittner	University at Buffalo, USA
Patrick Brézillon	University of Paris 6, France
Jörg Cassens	Norwegian University of Science and Technology, Norway
Henning Christiansen	Roskilde University, Denmark
Kenny R. Coventry	Northumbria University, UK
Klaus David	University of Kassel, Germany
Jérôme Euzenat	INRIA Grenoble Rhône-Alpes and INP University of Grenoble, France
Babak A. Farshchian	SINTEF, Norway
Jacqueline Floch	SINTEF, Norway
Christian Freksa	University of Bremen, Germany
Valentin Goranko	Technical University of Denmark, Denmark
Pierre Grenon	The Knowledge Media Institute, UK
Odd Erik Gundersen	Verdande Technology, Norway
Athanasios Karapantelakis	KTH, Sweden
Anders Kofod-Petersen	Norwegian University of Science and Technology, Norway
Kun Chang Lee	SKK Graduate School of Business, Korea
Bjørn Magnus Mathisen	SINTEF, Norway
Takashi Miyaki	Karlsruhe Institute of Technology, Germany
Aaron Quigley	The University of St. Andrews, UK
Robert J. Ross	Dublin Institute of Technology, Ireland
Thomas R. Roth-Berghofer	University of Hildesheim, Germany
Hedda R. Schmidtke	Karlsruhe Institute of Technology, Germany
Roy Turner	University of Maine, USA
Emile Van Der Zee	University of Lincoln, UK
Kristof Van Laerhoven	Technische Universität Darmstadt, Germany
Vaninha Vieira	Federal University of Bahia, Brazil
Rebekah Wegener	Macquarie University, Australia
Diedrich Wolter	University of Bremen, Germany

Reviewers

Atencia, Manuel
Bhatt, Mehul
Chaves Steinmacher, Ana Paula
Chung, Namho
Dostal, Jakub
Duckham, Matt
Dylla, Frank
Grineva, Maria
Klein, Niklas
Kreutzmann, Arne
Kwon, Ohbyung
Lambert, Dave
Lau, Sian Lun
Molina, Jose M.
Nacenta, Miguel
Novák, Peter
Özcep, Özgür
Pool, Mike
Ruge, Lukas
Sauer, Christian Severin
Schmid, Falko
Schmitt, Felix
Schultheis, Holger
Serafini, Luciano
Steinmacher, Igor
Stevenson, Graeme
Sørmo, Frode
Trojahn, Cassia
Tøndel, Inger Anne
Valcheva, Donika
Van De Ven, Jasper
Wienhofen, Leendert W.M.

Table of Contents

Modelling Context-Dependence: Ellipsis in Conversational Dialogue *(Keynote Talk)* 1
Ruth Kempson

Providing Generic Context for Mobile Games on Phones *(Keynote Talk)* 5
Paul Holleis, Alireza Sahami, and Albrecht Schmidt

A Peer-Based Approach to Privacy-Preserving Context Management 18
Wolfgang Apolinarski, Marcus Handte, Danh Le Phuoc, and Pedro José Marrón

Classical Planning and Causal Implicatures 26
Luciana Benotti and Patrick Blackburn

Contextualization of Scientific Workflows 40
Patrick Brezillon

Intelligible TinyOS Sensor Systems: Explanations for Embedded Software 54
Doina Bucur

Business Context Information Manager: An Approach to Improve Information Systems 67
Hamdi Chaker, Max Chevalier, Chantal Soulé-Dupuy, and André Tricot

Communicative Inferences and Context of Interests 71
Marco Cruciani

Enabling Privacy-Preserving Semantic Presence in Instant Messaging Systems 82
Anca Dumitrache, Alessandra Mileo, Antoine Zimmermann, Axel Polleres, Philipp Obermeier, and Owen Friel

Towards Context-Based Explanations for Teacher Support 97
Anneli Edman, Jenny Eriksson Lundström, and Narin Akrawi

An Experiment in Hierarchical Recognition of Group Activities Using Wearable Sensors 104
Dawud Gordon, Jan-Hendrik Hanne, Martin Berchtold, Takashi Miyaki, and Michael Beigl

Global Peer-to-Peer Classification in Mobile Ad-Hoc Networks: A Requirements Analysis 108
Dawud Gordon, Markus Scholz, Yong Ding, and Michael Beigl

Towards a Multi-perspectival Approach of Describing Context 115
Thomas Grill and Manfred Tscheligi

The Emotion Ontology: Enabling Interdisciplinary Research in the Affective Sciences 119
Janna Hastings, Werner Ceusters, Barry Smith, and Kevin Mulligan

Autodoxastic Conditional Reasoning: The Monotonic Case 124
Haythem O. Ismail and Aya S. Mahfouz

Delayed Synapses: An LSM Model for Studying Aspects of Temporal Context in Memory 138
Predrag Jakimovski and Hedda R. Schmidtke

Modelling with Problem Frames: Explanations and Context in Ambient Intelligent Systems 145
Anders Kofod-Petersen and Jörg Cassens

Enhancing Alignment Based Context Prediction by Using Multiple Context Sources: Experiment and Analysis 159
Immanuel König, Christian Voigtmann, Bernd Niklas Klein, and Klaus David

Buy, Sell, or Hold? Information Extraction from Stock Analyst Reports 173
Yeong Su Lee and Michaela Geierhos

WPT: A Toolkit for Publishing a Web-Based Lifelog 185
Takuya Maekawa, Yasue Kishino, Yutaka Yanagisawa, and Yasushi Sakurai

Smart Phone Sensing to Examine Effects of Social Interactions and Non-sedentary Work Time on Mood Changes 200
Aleksandar Matic, Venet Osmani, Andrei Popleteev, and Oscar Mayora-Ibarra

Monitoring for Digital Preservation of Processes 214
Martin Alexander Neumann, Till Riedel, Philip Taylor, Hedda R. Schmidtke, and Michael Beigl

Promoting Personalized Collaborative Distributed Learning through i-Collaboration 3.0 221
Eduardo A. Oliveira, Patricia Tedesco, Thun Pin T.F. Chiu, and Viviane Aureliano

A Real-Time Living Activity Recognition System Using Off-the-Shelf Sensors on a Mobile Phone 226
Kazushige Ouchi and Miwako Doi

An Empirical Study on Web Search Behavior through the Investigation of a User-Clustered Query Session 233
Hyun Kyu Park, In Ho Cho, Sook Young Ji, and Joong Seek Lee

Indoor Localization Using Audio Features of FM Radio Signals 246
Andrei Popleteev, Venet Osmani, Oscar Mayora, and Aleksandar Matic

SenST: Approaches for Reducing the Energy Consumption of Smartphone-Based Context Recognition 250
Maximilian Schirmer and Hagen Höpfner

Distributed Spatial Reasoning for Wireless Sensor Networks 264
Hedda R. Schmidtke and Michael Beigl

Mental Models of Ambient Systems: A Modular Research Framework ... 278
Felix Schmitt, Jörg Cassens, Martin Christof Kindsmüller, and Michael Herczeg

LiCoRMS – Towards a Resource Management System Based on Lifecycle and Content Information 292
Axel Schulz, Benedikt Schmidt, and Heiko Paulheim

Entropy of Audio Fingerprints for Unobtrusive Device Authentication 296
Stephan Sigg, Matthias Budde, Yusheng Ji, and Michael Beigl

A Context-Based Approach to Detecting Miscreant Behavior and Collusion in Open Multiagent Systems 300
Larry Whitsel and Roy Turner

A Notion of Event Quality for Contextualized Planning and Decision Support Systems 307
Leendert W.M. Wienhofen, Davy Preuveneers, Andreas D. Landmark, Pieter J. Toussaint, and Yolande Berbers

An Architecture and a Prototype for Querying and Visualising Recorded Context Information 321
Erqiang Zhou, Bing Wu, Jianfeng Wu, and Yi Ding

Author Index 335

Modelling Context-Dependence: Ellipsis in Conversational Dialogue*

(*Keynote Talk*)

Ruth Kempson

King's College London

Despite recognition that context dependence is endemic to natural language, arguably one of its core properties, standard grammar formalisms remain poor vehicles for expressing this. Grammars are standardly defined in terms of principles underpinning structures inhabited by sentence strings to yield a concept of sentence wellformedness, these being defined independently of any attribute of performance; and all data not characterisable in these terms are seen as in some sense peripheral, requiring grammar-external explication. Phenomena displaying context dependence all pose problems for this methodology, context dependence being no respecter of sentence boundaries. Ellipsis poses this challenge in a particularly acute way. A reasonable goal for accounts of ellipsis might be seen as one providing formal explication of the informal insight that ellipsis constitutes the license for expressions to be omitted if recoverable from context, with ellipsis data taken as a window on the requisite concept of context for language construal. But such a goal isn't even addressed as a desideratum in current accounts. Ellipsis is seen as falling into two major types: sentence-internal and discourse ellipsis; and even within the former type, there is further bifurcation into those types of ellipsis characterisable as semantically grounded (Dalrymple et al 1991) and those requiring syntactic characterisation with a number of discrete structural types (Merchant 2009). And, with a pragmatic remainder falling outside grammar-based characterisation (Stainton 2006), the phenomenon is seen as irreducibly "fractally heterogeneous" (Ginzburg and Cooper 2004).

Elliptical effects of conversational dialogue dramatically add to this challenge. In conversational exchanges, participants can extend what is said, either by themselves or by others, with switch of speaker/hearer roles at any point in a conversational exchange, taking some partially specified contribution and extending it with some fragment construed relative to their own assumptions.

(1) Gardener: I shall need the mattock.
Home-owner: The...
Gardener: mattock. For breaking up clods of earth.[BNC]

* This talk reports results from collaborative work with Patrick Healey, Matthew Purver, Wilfried Meyer-Viol, Eleni Gregoromichelaki, Arash Eshghi, Graham White, Ronnie Cann and Yo Sato on the ESRC RES-062-23-0962 "DynDial" project on The Dynamics of Conversational Dialogue. We are grateful to the ESRC for their support and to many other colleagues who have provided helpful feedback.

M. Beigl et al. (Eds.): CONTEXT 2011, LNAI 6967, pp. 1–4, 2011.

(2) A: I've just got back
B: from...
A: Finland
B: with Peter, I presume
A: Not this time, possibly in January.

With such speaker-hearer switches, interlocutors apparently work together in a highly coordinated activity, the output of some partial generation activity feeding seamlessly into the activity of parsing, and vice versa. It might seem that the purpose of such exchanges is to determine some agreed content as in (1)-(2), each participant contributing fragments that are only interpretable relative to the unfolding context. Yet, despite some cases displaying self-consciously collaborative activity, contributors to such *split utterances* may diverge from any shared intention, using the provided context for their own means:

(3) A and B (arguing):
A: What this shows is
B: that you are completely wrong.

Furthermore, any syntactic dependency whatsoever can be split across the participants so that the fragment uttered may be wellformed only relative to the emergent structure as a whole, with this structure moreover representing content derivable from the string and not the string itself:

(4) A: Did you hurt..
B: Myself?
(5) A: D'you know whether every waitress handed in
B: her tax forms?
A: or even any payslips?

What such data display is participants' reliance on a highly structured and incrementally evolving concept of context, a concept for which current grammars provide no basis, lacking as they do the vocabulary for articulating the incremental unfolding of structures in real time. The consequence for current formalisms is that unless some account of these data are provided, no syntactic/semantic phenomenon will be given complete characterisation, as a subset of the data for each syntactic phenomenon will remain as a performance dysfluency resisting explanation, despite its systematicity.[1]

With a grammar articulated as a set of principles that underpin how interpretation is built up relative to context, the picture is transformed. We can define an integrated account of ellipsis despite the diverse forms of interpretation: divergency of interpretation types is explicable from an integrated basis yielding strict/sloppy readings of stripping/VP ellipsis, gapping, antecedent-contained ellipsis. There is no need to invoke a dichotomy between sentence-internal and discourse ellipsis; and split utterances emerge as a subcase of the more general phenomenon of how elliptical fragments are construed in context. Ellipsis

[1] 20% of the DynDial corpus data are split utterances (Purver et al 2009).

becomes subject to formal explication as the recovery of interpretation from what context makes available, matching the folk intuition about ellipsis directly (Purver et al 2006, Cann et al 2009, Kempson et al 2011). This success is ensured by defining context and content in dynamic structural terms, with growth of information reflecting real-time dynamics as the core syntactic notion.

The framework in which this account is expressed is that of Dynamic Syntax (DS: Kempson et al 2001, Cann et al 2005). In DS, syntax itself is defined as growth of representations of content, with concepts of underspecification and update as the core concepts of syntax. On this view, a grammar is a set of principles (lexical and general actions) whereby representations of content can be progressively built up reflecting the incremental processing of language in real time (Cann et al 2005). There is no concept of syntax independent of this. Both context and syntax (determining the emergent representations of content) are defined in the same terms of mechanisms inducing growth of representations of logical formulae (Purver et al 2006); and context is defined as a record of how this process takes place, recording words, partial trees representing the monotonically accumulating representations of content, and the actions used to build such structure up (Cann et al 2007). The system is neither domain-specific (phonology apart), nor is it encapsulated, so, despite the articulation of such principles of tree growth as a grammar formalism, pervasive interaction between pragmatics and syntax is licensed as appropriately triggered. In using these mechanisms, both speakers and hearers build up interpretation relative to their own cognitive context, hearers in response to the trigger provided by the words uttered, speakers by checking that any such constructive step is commensurate with some richer *goal tree* that corresponds to what they are trying to communicate. As I shall sketch, different forms of ellipsis and their respective syntactic constraints turn on whether participants rely on (i) representations of content recoverable from context, (ii) structures provided by context, (iii) actions whereby such structures are built up. This range matches exactly the dynamic structural concept of context defined in the DS framework: hence the matching of formal specification with the intuitive correspondence between ellipsis construal and context. With both speakers and hearers making use of the same mechanisms, split utterances emerge as an immediate consequence, since the switch involves nothing more than shifting from the progressive construction of a structured representation of content relative to a subsumption check with some goal tree (for the speaker) or not (for the hearer). The shift is thus predicted to be seamless, a bonus over all conventional sentence-based grammar formalisms.

Such split utterances are of considerable significance for pragmatic theory too, since speaker intentions may emerge during the course of such exchanges, in part determined as a result of such exchanges. But in these exchanges then, there may be no fixed propositional content intended by the speaker which the hearer has to grasp. On all current approaches to pragmatics, such exchanges would not be characterisable as successful acts of communication, since these, by definition, involve grasping that propositional content which the speaker either has or could have in mind (Grice 1989, Sperber and Wilson 1986, Recanati

2004 etc). Yet such exchanges give every appearance of being successful communicative exchanges in virtue of such interactions rather than despite them. So I shall argue in closing that though recognition of the content of the speaker's intention may be presumed as a goal by both speaker and hearer, it is not a necessary condition for effective communication to take place. Instead, we suggest, successful utterance interpretation involves interaction between participants relative to dynamic and evolving concepts of content and context (Gregoromichelaki et al 2011). Thus, I shall conclude, grammars of natural language constitute a specification of mechanisms for conversational interaction.

References

1. Cann, R., Kempson, R., Marten, L.: The Dynamics of Language. Elsevier, Oxford (2005)
2. Cann, R., Kempson, R., Purver, M.: Context and Well-formedness: the Dynamics of Ellipsis. Research on Language and Computation 5, 333–358 (2007)
3. Cann, R., Kempson, R., Purver, M.: Semantics: Meaning in Language. Cambridge University Press, Cambridge (2009)
4. Dalrymple, M., Shieber, S., Pereira, F.: Ellipsis and higher-order unification. Linguistics and Philosophy 14, 399–452 (1991)
5. Ginzburg, J., Cooper, R.: Clarification, ellipsis, and the nature of contextual updates in dialogue. Linguistics and Philosophy 27, 297–365 (2004)
6. Gregoromichelaki, E., Kempson, R., Purver, M., Mills, G., Cann, R., Meyer-Viol, W., Healey, P.: Incrementality and intention-recognition in utterance processing. Dialogue and Discourse 2(1), 199–233 (2011)
7. Grice, H.P.: Studies in the Way of Words. Harvard University Press, Cambridge (1989)
8. Kempson, R., Gregoromichelaki, E., Howes, C. (eds.): The Dynamics of Lexical Interfaces: Collected Papers on Dynamic Syntax. CSLI Publications, Chicago University Press (2011)
9. Kempson, R., Meyer-Viol, W., Gabbay, D.: Dynamic Syntax: The Flow of Language Understanding. Blackwell Publishing, Malden (2001)
10. Merchant, J.: Ellipsis. In: Alexiadou, A., Kiss, T., Butt, M. (eds.) Handbook of Contemporary Syntax, 2nd edn., Walter de Gruyter, Berlin (2009)
11. Purver, M., Cann, R., Kempson, R.: Grammars as parsers: meeting the dialogue challenge. Research on Language and Computation 4, 289–326 (2006)
12. Purver, M., Howes, C., Gregoromichelaki, E., Healey, H.: Split utterances in dialogue: a corpus study. In: Proceedings of SIGDIAL 2009: the 10th Annual Meeting of the Special Interest Group in Discourse and Dialogue, pp. 262–271 (2009)
13. Recanati, F.: Literal Meaning. Cambridge University Press, Cambridge (2004)
14. Sperber, D., Wilson, D.: Relevance: Communication and Cognition. Blackwell Publishers, Oxford (1986)
15. Stainton, R.: Words and Thoughts: Subsentences, Ellipsis, and the Philosophy of Language. Oxford University Press, Oxford (2006)

Providing Generic Context for Mobile Games on Phones
(Keynote Talk)

Paul Holleis[1], Alireza Sahami[2], and Albrecht Schmidt[2]

[1] DOCOMO Euro-Labs
Landsberger Str. 312
80687 Munich, Germany
[2] University of Stuttgart
Pfaffenwaldring 5a
70569 Stuttgart, Germany
holleis@dococmolab-euro.com,
{alireza.sahami,albrecht.schmidt}@vis.uni-stuttgart.de

Abstract. Mobile phone games are played in context. Although such information has been used in several prototypes, very few context-aware games have made it beyond the research lab. In our research, we investigate how the development of context-aware games needs to be changed such that their commercialization is more feasible and they can be deployed more easily. Based on the findings of the creation and evaluation of a context-based game called *ContextSnake*, we developed a platform named *Gatherer* which frees the developer from the burden of collecting, preprocessing, storing, and interpreting raw sensor data. We introduce the novel concept of generic context which enables the use of context in mobile applications without having detailed information about the actual environment in which the system will be deployed. In order to preliminarily validate the platform, a second game called *ContextInvaders* developed on top of this platform is described.

Keywords: Generic context, context-awareness, mobile games, mobile phone.

1 Introduction

Mobile phones have become ubiquitous and a widely adapted powerful computing platform with multimedia and network capabilities. They offer various options for creating sophisticated user interfaces and implementing different types of applications such as games. Built-in cameras, microphones, and color displays as well as different types of sensors can provide information about the status of the devices and the context in which it is used. One popular example is using accelerometer sensor data on the phone to control motions in games.

In order to make games on mobile phones more valuable, they have to be usable in the users' everyday situations. The following points distinguish some important differences to traditional games (i.e. board games or digital games on a PC):

- As mentioned in [13], "killing time is a killer application". Therefore, the time for playing is often short; a typical scenario is waiting for public transports where people typically spend between 1 and 20 minutes [16].

M. Beigl et al. (Eds.): CONTEXT 2011, LNAI 6967, pp. 5–17, 2011.

- Mobile games are played at different locations in the real world. It is common to start a game in one place and resume playing somewhere else.
- Mobile phone games are played as 'filler', and interruptions occur frequently, e.g., when an incoming call is received.

Several projects have looked at mobile gaming, but many of these approaches assume physically very active users (e.g., running around a city and chasing other players [7]) or users that are disconnected from real world activities (e.g., immersed in the game only). The initial experience shows that these are not mainstream mobile gaming scenarios as most people are physically not very active when playing mobile games [16]. In our research, we focus on using contextual information on mobile phones to develop games that work everywhere and motivate people to exploit their context. We evaluate the feasibility of such applications by developing two mobile context-based games and introduce a platform for mobile phones that manages and provides contextual information to simplify developing such context-based applications. The paper makes the following main contributions:

- Introduction of the concept of generic versus absolute context
- Overview of the design space and development requirements for generic contextual games
- Introduction of context-action-tables as a way of describing the semantics of context-aware games
- A platform for developing contextual mobile games

The structure of this paper is as follows: after providing an overview of related work, we describe how context information can be used in mobile games. We provide definitions for the distinction between absolute and generic context. In order to show the feasibility and to examine the requirements for the development of generic context-aware applications, we introduce a game called *ContextSnake*. Based on the findings during its development and the subsequent evaluation, we describe the design and implementation of a context-aware platform called *Gatherer*, which organizes context information available on mobile phones and presents it to developers in an easy-to-use way. Finally, we show the applicability of the development platform by describing a second game called *ContextInvaders* built on top of this platform.

2 Related Work

In the process of growing competition and search for novel features for mobile applications, developers have explored the benefits of being able to sense contextual information such as location information in designing applications. The "Backseat Gaming" prototype [5] is a mobile game in which the player has to find virtual objects related to the real world by pointing with the mobile device towards these objects. In [4] "Tycoon", a market-based distributed resource allocation system is introduced where GSM cell information is used to define the positions of the resources in a trading game. "Feeding Yoshi" is another game in which Yoshis (small creatures) must be fed with fruits growing in different locations, defined by the availability of wireless networks in urban environments [2].

The variety of information described in early research in context-awareness [19] has not been used to a great extent. Most games and applications making use of contexts other than location have not made their way into products on a large scale. In "Fizzees", motions are used to allow young children to care for a virtual pet [14]. Since the Tamagotchi[1] boom in 1996 proved that people are willing to nurture virtual pets, further games and devices have been developed in this area, e.g., DigiPets[2]. We expect that by introducing the notion of generic contexts and by providing a platform which includes self-learned generic contexts, we can make the use of context types beyond location easier and more approachable for developers.

Besides, the mobility of people makes way for other types of applications that interweave with everyday life [2]. This concept is brought further by the idea of persuasive technology. This includes applications trying to influence users' behavior in the real world. The two games we introduce in this paper based on generic context follow this line of thought. We refer to the book by Bogost [3] for a thorough treatment of persuasive games. Less game-like examples are the "UbiGreen Transportation Display" [8], a mobile application prototype that semi-automatically senses and reveals information about the transportation behavior to encourage green transportation habits by using mobile phones and the remote control that helps people spend less time watching TV, as well as the exertion interfaces by Mueller et al. [12].

Researchers also have explored some ways to facilitate the development of context-aware applications on mobile devices. In order to reduce the efforts of common tasks and to help developers focus on the application-specific components, various frameworks with different aims for individual mobile platforms (such as Symbian, Windows Mobile, etc.) have been introduced. Recent examples can be found in [10,11,15] which encapsulate certain functionalities and provide services for other applications. However, none of them focuses on capturing and providing generic context to the developers.

3 Absolute vs. Generic Context

Although context-aware applications have been the focus of many research projects, up to now, only very few have matured into commercial services. In location-aware and mobile gaming, one common approach is to create specific, absolute contexts, such as absolute positions, that are meaningful within the application. Such games are fixed to a predefined context and are only economically viable if the number of potential users is high (e.g., in a large museum). Creating context-aware games or context-aware applications that work independent of a location, specific time, etc. is a challenge that needs to be addressed.

3.1 Absolute Context

Definition: *An absolute context is a context that is tied to a specific situation such as a location described in absolute terms. This implies that an absolute context is independent of the history of the user or device.*

---

[1] http://en.wikipedia.org/w/index.php?title=Tamagotchi (accessed May 2011)
[2] http://www.digipet.com/ (accessed May 2011)

Examples for absolute contexts are a location defined by absolute coordinates or the proximity of a device characterized by a specific id. This has traditionally been used in context-aware applications: most existing tourist and museum guides running on mobile devices offer support for a specific setting and location. Either the location of an interesting site has been fixed or the mobile application reacts on the proximity of a specific device attached to an artifact. These applications are difficult to migrate to different scenarios, as it requires at least the redefinition of the absolute context parameters. To overcome this issue, we define generic contexts that do not depend on absolute specifications.

3.2 Generic Context

Definition: *A generic context is a context that can be described without referencing to a specific or absolute property. Hence, a generic context can specifically be related to the history of the user or device.*

In the example of a museum guide, there are several levels between absolute and generic context. Let's say a mobile application reacts when the user is close to a specific location (i.e. position in a specific room) and looks at a specific artifact. When removing the restriction of location, the employed context applies to all copies of that particular artifact. This can be even more generalized by abstracting this to only one type of artifact defined by properties such as date, value, size, usage, etc. Then one instance of a most generic context is the one that does not restrict itself to any specific components at all but relies on the history of the user contexts. Examples for such generic contexts are a new place the device has never been before or the proximity of a set of devices that already have been encountered before (see **Fig. 1**).

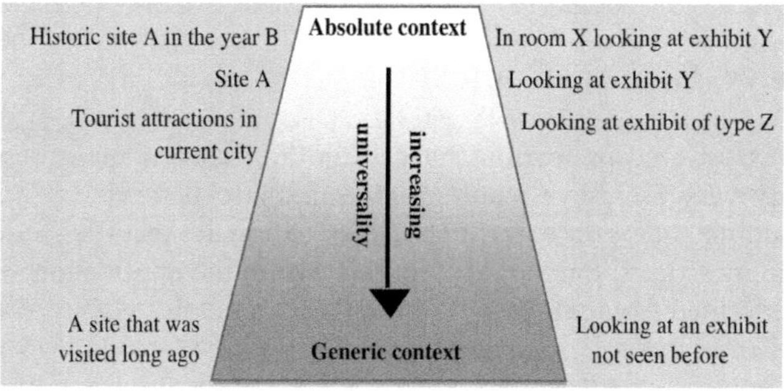

Fig. 1. Examples of absolute vs. generic context

Generic contexts have the advantage that they can be learned (unsupervised) during usage. A generic context-aware application, once developed, can work in any environment without manual tweaking. Hence, from a production point of view, they can be produced to suit a global mass market without additional efforts in creating specific context descriptions.

4 ContextSnake

To investigate the usage of context information in mobile games, we developed a context-aware game called *ContextSnake*. This development led to the understanding and refinement of requirements for the context toolkit we describe afterwards. In this initial phase we deliberately use a very simple game to explore the impact context can have. We believe that if we can show that even simple games benefit from generic context this is a strong indicator that this may also be true for more complex games.

4.1 Concept and Design

We decided to use the straightforward and well-known game *Snake* in which a user controls a snake moving through a scene and turn it into a context-aware application. This had the advantages that it simplifies the task of introducing users to the application and offers great potential for including contextual parameters. We focused on using simple learning algorithms and statistics to acquire further information about the context (e.g. finding out the favorite places a user plays in with statistics over the acquired cell IDs) and storing contextual parameters persistently. This last requirement is directly connected to fact that people often play mobile games in short breaks and persistently storing and learning of contextual and conventional game parameters enables a longer game experience.

For the use of contextual parameters we focused on acquiring the information about battery power (bat), network signal strength (rss), GSM cell ID (cID), and system time (t). In comparison to other parameters (e.g., environmental noise, light condition, Bluetooth devices in vicinity) these parameters are very easy and fast to acquire. Additionally, they are very robust and rely little on the way the user is handling the device. Furthermore, for all sensor values a history is kept and we use functions to abstract the values into higher-level contexts (e.g., frequency of cell changes, estimated activity of the user).

4.2 Context-Action-Table

To design such games, we suggest using context-action tables. A context-action table describes the mapping between the sensed parameters and abstracted contexts to the parameter influenced in the game (appearance, logic, functionality). In **Table 1**, the context-action table for the prototype is shown. In each row a context, expressed by a function on raw context data over time, is described. The values used as input parameter to the function are typically sensor data, values calculated from sensor data, and a history of data. Each column reflects behavior in the game. Marks in the intersections between rows and columns denote a functional dependency. The more dots in a row, the more often this context is used to influence game parameters; the more dots in a column, the more dependent on contexts is this game parameter. Functions then describe the actual mapping, i.e., the semantics of the connection between context and game content.

The benefit of using such a form of description is that the relationships can be easily observed and further options for potential new mappings become apparent. In our prototype, these mappings are selected at the design step and reflect the design choices of the game's developers. However, it is feasible to have these mappings modeled as functions, too. This makes changes during runtime possible, adding another dimension of options for dynamic and customizable game play.

Table 1. Context-Action-Table for the ContextSnake game

	$f_0(rss_t)$	$f(rss_t,\ldots, rss_{t-n})$	$f(bat)$	$f(cID_t, \ldots, cID_{t-n})$	$f(cID)$
color of the snake					•
color of the background					•
color of the food					•
size of the field	•				
size of the snake	•				
the speed of the snake			•		
the size of food items		•		•	
growth of the snake per food		•		•	
points earned for a food item				•	
time before new food appears		•		•	

Without going into too much detail, some of the mappings between the contextual parameters and the game shown in **Table 1** are as follows:

- Low signal strength increases difficulty (larger snake and smaller field size).
- Battery-level roughly proportional to snake speed.
- Quicker changes in signal strength / cell IDs increases size of a food item
- Visiting an unknown cell ID provides more and more valuable food items
- Cell ID defines the background color (other colors are calculated to ensure contrast).

Overall, the mappings for the prototype have been chosen to be a first attempt to create a compelling and more diverse gaming experience. The rationale of the mappings is mainly due to the way the designers want users to play the game. Even with a restricted set of contextual parameters a large set of relations to the real world can be included.

4.3 Game Implementation

ContextSnake is realized as a Python script using the Nokia Series 60 Python SDK. The development was iterative and tests have been conducted throughout the development using the Series-60 Emulator running on the PC (included in the C++ SDK) as well as in the runtime environment on different phones. The implementation of the *ContextSnake* game is based on the example provided with the SDK (snake.py). A class allows accessing to required system parameters such as GSM information extended the example. Additional functionality was added to store and access recorded information (e.g., contextual parameters) and game status information (e.g., score) persistently in the phone using a database. Changes in the status are also directly written to the external database to ensure that all changes are recorded even if the program is terminated or interrupted. The current implementation was tested and

(a) Playing at home... | (b) ... while waiting for a train... | (c) ... while on the bus... | (d) ... at the favorite café.

run with good performance on the Nokia 6630 and Nokia N90 and can be run easily on newer models supporting Python development.

4.4 Evaluation

To evaluate the game concept and the prototype, we conducted a study including two parts with ten people, four females and six males, aged between 13 and 32 years. In the first part, we used general questions to find out about mobile phone usage and frequency of playing games on mobile phones. During the second part, participants played the game and explored its features. For this, we observed the participants during play and discussed their experiences. With the questions in the interview the participants could express their agreements on a 5-point Likert-scale.

Based on the results, all participants were experienced in using mobile phones. Nine had experience playing games on the phone (one user once per week and eight users about once a month). Situations in which they played games were mainly on public transport or while waiting; only two persons stated that they played mobile phone games at home. Furthermore, all users understood the concept of *ContextSnake* and in general the idea of contextual gaming. All participants agreed (three users) or strongly agreed (seven users) that the game becomes more interesting when it is context dependent. Nine out of ten agreed or strongly agreed that they would play the game at more locations and different places to get a higher score. Besides, all participants were confident that the game becomes considerably less predictable when contextual parameters are used and can thus remain more interesting in the long term.

Fig. 2 shows some examples of the game screen and its use in various everyday situations: playing longer at the same location becomes less rewarding as food gets scarce, see setting (a). Places with little or no signal strength (e.g., at an underground station) render the food larger and easier to get, see setting (b). This can turn the waiting time for a train into a more positive experience. Travelling provides many location changes and hence a lot of food. The game also motivates users to sometimes explore different routes as otherwise less food will be available, see setting (c). Setting (d) shows a specific café where food never becomes scarce; such a game could be a giveaway of a company that has interest that you come back onto their premises.

One important finding is that contextual games are a reason to encourage people exploring their real world environment more (eight participants agreed or strongly agreed). All participants agreed that *ContextSnake* is more interesting than the conventional snake game. Overall, we received as feedback that using contextual parameters is an intriguing way to make games more interesting. Comments from five participants included that detecting encounters (e.g., Bluetooth, WLAN) could be another exciting contextual parameter.

5 Gaming in Context

Generic real-world locations can be linked to a mobile game and provide the stage that reaches from the real world into the virtual environment, creating the game canvas. Consider, for instance, a virtual pet game: in order to eat, the pet has to be in a supermarket, for exercise it has to be in a forest, etc. This pervasive feature adds physicality, as players have to move to certain locations in order for the pet to feel well.

Generic context opens several additional opportunities. Continuing the location example, the game can force the players to seek out new locations or, reversely, the game only makes sense in a location where they spend most of their time. These design parameters allow the game designer to induce certain behavior – in the real world – to the player. This has obviously severe implications on the player's behavior in the real world and hence includes ethical issues, e.g., what is more desirable, to create a game that makes people stay at home or that makes people go and play in places where they meet others?

Further to location, investigations in context and context-awareness in previous projects such as [18] show that there is a great set of information that can be taken into account. Examples of real world contexts and a sample way of estimating whether this context applies at the current situation we found to be important include:

- being in a place that a user has never visited before (unknown GSM base station)
- being in a place that is minimally populated (seeing only one GSM base station)
- being in a very quiet environment (based on the noise level from the microphone)
- being outside in daylight (based on images captured from the phone camera)
- being in a crowded place (several other Bluetooth devices visible)

Although the use of context is gaining importance with an increasing number of pervasive computing applications, it is still a challenge to enable applications to make use of context information. This is especially true for mobile applications, as they are not bound to specific context but rather generic ones. Learning from implementing *ContextSnake*, we see the strong requirement for a platform on a system level that provides not only real-world context information but also aggregates, abstracts, and interprets raw data and translates the abstract context data to a more generic one. Specific requirements are:

- **A history** on which generic context and many algorithms (e.g. profiling) rely on
- **Supporting generic context** and not only absolute context information
- **Extensibility**: a modular platform should easily accept new types of sensors etc.
- **Interoperability**: an open platform should accept different data formats
- **Independent** of any sensor network or infrastructure for enabling context-awareness

By using such a platform, developers should be enabled to create games that are dynamic, context-aware, learn about their environment and users' mobility, and behave differently in different situations so that they are consistent in their reaction to the environment without being fully predictable.

6 Framework: The Gatherer

To fill the gaps and fulfill the requirements described in the previous section and to enable mobile applications to access different types of contextual information, a platform called *Gatherer* was implemented running on top of existing infrastructure in a mobile phone. The *Gatherer* enables developers to access context information and frees them from developing the whole process chain of collecting raw sensor data, preprocessing, storing, and interpreting it. Developers can treat the *Gatherer* as a black box, which provides various context data and they need only focus on designing their applications. It not only assists in the creation of context-aware applications but also supports rapid prototyping as it provides various data formats, hence, developers do not need to take care of accessing and processing information.

The *Gatherer* platform is a Python-based application running as a background process (server) on mobile phones and handles the whole process of sensing, preprocessing, storing, interpreting, and formatting context data. This system can be installed and used on mobile phones that include the Python interpreter such as Nokia Symbian phones. In the design stage, it was decided to separate the sub-processes of the platform due to easy maintenance and expansion. Thus, a modular microkernel-like design was chosen for the software architecture. This speeds up the development process and new features can be easily added to the system. The system is divided into four layers:

- **Device Abstraction Layer:** the actual sensing mechanism, pulling data from available sensors on the phone, preprocessing (aggregating / smoothing) and storing them. Supported sensors include: physical (e.g. accelerometer); infrastructural (GSM cell ids, battery level, nearby Bluetooth enabled devices); informational (incoming / outgoing text messages / calls).
- **Persistency Layer (database):** produces the context history by storing sensed context data. In accordance with Dey et al. [6], we use a name-value tuple as the main data type for the context-aware applications.
- **Context Conversion Layer:** includes all data access methods and processes all requests from client applications and produces a collection of tuples.

- **Formatting Layer:** formats the data retrieved from the Context Conversion Layer based for specific requests. Currently provided are XML, JSON, and simple CSV.

On the other side, context-based applications (clients) which want to use the *Gatherer* platform simply establish a connection to a specific port on the localhost of the mobile phone and send requests. In the requests, the required context information and data format are specified. The clients can then extract the information from the responses.

7 ContextInvaders

In order to explore how the usage of context information in combination with traditional games can change the compelling and fun part of a game experience, another game called *ContextInvaders* was developed. In addition, it served as an example to evaluate the *Gatherer* platform. *ContextInvaders* is based on the Space Invaders game[3] – one of the first arcade shooting games released in 1978. In contrast to the original game, it uses context information to modify the game's parameters. The mission of the player is to save the earth from an alien invasion by shooting their spaceships before they reach the earth using a laser cannon. As the aliens also shoot the player, one can take cover behind defense bunkers placed between the player and the aliens.

Table 2 shows the context-action table for the *ContextInvaders* game. As the *Gatherer* platform handles context acquisition, representation, interpretation, and provides more generic data, the table can now be written with more generic and understandable descriptions. The table explains what kind of information provided by the *Gatherer* is used within the game logic:

- Average movement (by accelerometer) modifies the player's speed
- Current GSM cell ID and duration spent in a location influences game parameters (e.g. number of lives, number of spaceships, …)
- Current time modifies background and spaceship's color (simulating day / night)
- Battery level information changes the amount of the player's shots

7.1 Preliminarily User Study

The *ContextInvaders* game was evaluated with ten participants, five males and females (age range 19-24), who all had a gaming background on mobile phones. The game and the *Gatherer* framework were installed on a Nokia N95. The users played both the classical Space Invaders and *ContextInvaders* for three days in a row and provided feedback through a questionnaire.

Although all users understood the concept and meaning of context-aware games, not all were able to find out how the sensed context information changed the game. The main reason might have been the lack of context parameters visualization in the game as described in the previous prototype. Interestingly, just three of

---

[3] http://en.wikipedia.org/wiki/Space_Invaders (accessed May 2011)

the participants stated that this encouraged them to play the game at different locations in order to achieve more scores. This can be partially attributed to the fact that mobile games are mostly played when there is some time to kill between events of interest [13].

The question whether the context enhanced mode was more challenging to play than the normal mode divided the group into half. This is probably the result of the usage of context parameters, which makes the game harder or easier based on the phone's status. Another important factor can be the different gaming experiences the participants had. Some of the features are only available and more feasible when using the game for a longer period of time and thus experiencing more of the defined generic situations.

Table 2. Context-action table for the *ContextInvaders* game. LP (directly proportional) means an increase in context parameter value leads to an increase in the game's parameters; IP (inversely proportional) means an increase in context value leads to a decrease in the game's parameters.

	Battery level	*Time of day*	*Location familiarity*	*Enter new location*	*User activity*	*Crowdedness*
player movement speed					LP	
color of the background		●				
number of aliens spaceships			IP	LP		
number of player's lives			LP	IP		
number of player's shots	LP					
number of bunkers			IP			
number of points			IP	LP		
color of spaceships		●				

8 Discussion and Conclusion

Playing in context is a reality as users already play games with mobile devices in a variety of everyday situations. So far, most games are still ignorant of the actual physical environment. We have assessed how mobile gaming can benefit from the mobile usage model and investigated what opportunities arise in the domain of contextual gaming. Introducing the concept of generic context, we showed that interesting contextual elements can be added without the effort of specifically designing applications and games for a specific environment.

To validate the concepts, we implemented a context-aware version of the popular Snake game available on most mobile phones. Beyond using the current context, we saw that using statistics over context histories as parameters for the game is also promising as a parameter. For visualizing the mapping between context information and the parameters in a contextual game, we introduced the context-action table. Our evaluation of the game based on interviews and the users playing the game provides evidence that making games context-aware will make them more interesting – and this applies even to very simple games. The game can receive a more realistic touch and become much more intriguing over time when physically moving around has a direct impact on the game.

From implementing and evaluating the relatively simple game, we learned and discussed requirements for creating a platform on the system level for the development of such applications. Especially when using parameters that rely on context-histories (e.g., how familiar is this place / has the user ever been here before?), a common contextual gaming platform is beneficial for game developers. The *Gatherer* platform was introduced to give developers access to context information by taking care of the whole process chain of collecting raw sensor data, preprocessing, storing, interpreting, and providing more generic data. Based on its flexible core and system structure, this platform can be easily extended and run on various platforms. A second game, *ContextInvaders* was then developed on top of the *Gatherer* platform. It is a context-aware variant of the well-known Space Invaders game. The game's logic uses different types of context information provided by the *Gatherer* to modify the parameters.

One main advantage of using generic contexts is that the developers do not need to know the actual location and context of deployment; hence, applications built on this concept are easier to deploy and maintain. Using generic contextual parameters, game designers can create games that trigger people to interact with their environment and with others in novel and playful ways, enabling easier designs for Homo Ludens [9]. Games can be created to push the players towards a certain behavior, e.g. encourage people to explore their environments or to go to certain places.

9 Future Work

In this paper we focused on using generic context in games and showing the potential in this domain. Our experience so far suggests that the notion of generic context may also be useful for context-aware applications in general. To our knowledge, many context-aware applications do not make their way from the laboratory to the real world, as defining the absolute contexts required on a national or global scale is not practical. In future work we plan to assess how the concept of generic contexts can help to provide more context-aware locations in realistic environments.

A further dimension of future work evaluates how interaction with games and applications changes when the application logic is linked to generic contexts. We assume that when people learn that some of their actions have impact on the game, it may lead to a change of their behavior to maximize the benefit, without even reflecting on their behavior change, e.g., opting for the bus instead of the subway as the game is more exciting on the bus route. We plan to investigate if this can be used to take the concept of implicit interaction [17] to a new level where people are subconsciously influenced.

One promising domain is the creation of persuasive games. By providing incentives in the game that are linked to actions in the physical world we image many possibilities. Such an approach may have interesting implications in designing healthcare and wellness application but can be frightening at the same time if we think of possibilities in advertising.

References

1. Bell, D., Hooker, B., Raby, F.: FLIRT: Social Services for the Urban Context. In: Proc. HCI International 2003 (2003)
2. Bell, M., Chalmers, M., Barkhuus, L., Hall, M., Sherwood, S., Tennent, P., Brown, B., Rowland, D., Benford, S.: Interweaving Mobile Games with Everyday Life. In: Proc. CHI 2006, pp. 417–426 (2006)
3. Bogost, I.: Persuasive Games: The Expressive Power of Videogames. The MIT Press, Cambridge (2007)
4. Broll, G., Benford, S.: Seamful Design for Location-Based Mobile Games. In: Kishino, F., Kitamura, Y., Kato, H., Nagata, N. (eds.) ICEC 2005. LNCS, vol. 3711, pp. 155–166. Springer, Heidelberg (2005)
5. Brunnberg, L., Juhlin, O.: Movement and Spatiality in a Gaming Situation - Boosting Mobile Computer Games with the Highway Experience. In: Proc. INTERACT 2003 (2003)
6. Dey, A.K., Abowd, G.D., Salber, D.: A Conceptual Framework and a Toolkit for Supporting the Rapid Prototyping of Context-aware Applications. Human Computer Interaction Journal 16(2), 97–166 (2001)
7. Flintham, M., Benford, S., Anastasi, R., Hemmings, T., Crabtree, A., Greenhalgh, C., Tandavanitj, N., Adams, M., Row, F.J.: Where On-line Meets on the Streets: Experiences with Mobile Mixed Reality Games. In: Proc. CHI 2003, pp. 569–576 (2003)
8. Froehlich, J., Dillahunt, T., Klasnja, P., Mankoff, J., Consolvo, S., Harrison, B., Landay, J.A.: UbiGreen: Investigating a Mobile Tool for Tracking and Supporting Green Transportation Habits. In: Proc. CHI 2009, pp. 1043–1052 (2009)
9. Gaver, W.: Designing for Homo Ludens. I3 Magazine 12 (June 2002)
10. Kukkonen, J., Lagerspetz, E., Nurmi, P., Andersson, M.: BeTelGeuse: A Platform for Gathering and Processing Situational Data. IEEE Pervasive Computing 8(2), 49–56 (2009)
11. Linner, D., Kirsch, F., Radusch, I., Steglich, S.A.: Context-aware Multimedia Provisioning for Pervasive Games. In: Proc. ISM 2005, pp. 60–68 (2005)
12. Mueller, F., Agamanolis, S., Vetere, F., Gibbs, M.R.: A Framework for Exertion Interactions over a Distance. In: Proc. SIGGRAPH 2009, pp. 143–150 (2009)
13. Nielsen, J.A.: WAP Field Study Findings (December 10, 2000), `http://www.useit.com/alertbox/20001210.html`
14. Page, A., Cooper, A.: Fizzees (Physical Electronic Energisers), `http://archive.futurelab.org.uk/projects/fizzees`
15. Raento, M., Oulasvirta, A., Petit, R., Toivonen, H.: Context-Phone: a Prototyping Platform for Context-Aware Mobile Applications. IEEE Pervasive Computing 4(2), 51–59 (2005)
16. Rukzio, E., Schmidt, A., Hussmann, H.: Physical Posters as Gateways to Context-aware Services for Mobile Devices. In: Proc. WMCSA 2004 (2004)
17. Schmidt, A.: Implicit Human Computer Interaction Through Context. Springer Journal on Personal and Ubiquitous Computing 4(2/3), 191–199 (2000)
18. Schmidt, A., Aidoo, K.A., Takaluoma, A., Tuomela, U., Van Laerhoven, K., Van de Velde, W.: Advanced Interaction in Context. In: Gellersen, H.-W. (ed.) HUC 1999. LNCS, vol. 1707, p. 89. Springer, Heidelberg (1999)
19. Schmidt, A., Beigl, M., Gellersen, H. W.: There is More to Context than Location. Computers & Graphics 23(6), 893–901 (1999)
20. Zeimpekis, V., Giaglis, G.M., Lekakos, G.: A Taxonomy of Indoor and Outdoor Positioning Techniques for Mobile Location Services. SIGecom Exch., 19–27 (2003)

A Peer-Based Approach to Privacy-Preserving Context Management

Wolfgang Apolinarski[1], Marcus Handte[1], Danh Le Phuoc[2], and Pedro José Marrón[1]

[1] Networked Embedded Systems, University of Duisburg-Essen, Germany
{wolfgang.apolinarski,marcus.handte,pjmarron}@uni-due.de
[2] Digital Enterprise Research Institute, Galway, Ireland
danh.lephuoc@deri.org

Abstract. Providing adequate support for context acquisition and management is a non-trivial task that complicates application development. To mitigate this, existing middleware systems rely on a centralized context service that manages the context of all devices located within a certain area. However, in many cases, centralized context management impacts privacy as it requires users to share their context with a possibly untrusted device. In this paper, we show how this problem can be avoided by a peer-based approach to context management. To validate the approach, we have implemented it on top of the BASE middleware and used it extensively in the PECES European research project. The evaluation shows that given a customizable implementation, the approach provides high flexibility while being suitable for a broad spectrum of devices.

Keywords: Context Management, Peer-to-Peer, Privacy, Security.

1 Introduction

To provide seamless and distraction-free task support, ubiquitous computing applications must be able to perceive their context. To avoid repetitive development effort for context management at the application layer, existing middleware systems for ubiquitous computing provide context management support as one of their main building blocks. Thereby, they usually rely on a central system service that manages the context of all devices that are located within a certain physically limited area [2]. Sensors and other devices that are located within the area report their information directly to this service which can then provide a comprehensive view to interested applications. Such a centralized approach can considerably reduce the application development effort. Yet, if the number of devices increases, the central service may become a bottleneck.

While scalability issues can be countered by adding more resources, hierarchical [3] or decentralized context management [5,9], from a user's perspective, a more problematic issue resulting from centralization is privacy. Given that context information may reveal sensitive information, centralized context management is only viable in cases where users are willing to put a sufficiently high

M. Beigl et al. (Eds.): CONTEXT 2011, LNAI 6967, pp. 18–25, 2011.

degree of trust in the intentions and capabilities of the operator. While this might be appropriate for some scenarios such as smart class rooms or smart homes, it is clearly not the case when considering scenarios such as smart shopping malls in which shop owners might operate context management services for their customers. In this paper, we show how such privacy problems can be avoided by peer-based context management. To validate the approach, we have implemented it on top of the BASE [7] middleware and used it for application development in the PECES project. The evaluation shows that the approach provides high flexibility while being applicable to a broad spectrum of devices.

The remainder of this paper is structured as follows. In Section 2, we first outline our approach for context modelling. Then, in Section 3 we present the system architecture which we evaluate in Section 4. Finally, we conclude the paper in Section 5.

2 Context Model

As basis for a generic context model, we adopt OWL-based context modeling [3,6] since it facilitates autonomicity and interoperability. This enables the usage of an ontology to establish a common understanding among application developers and processing engines. Furthermore, it is possible to reuse existing ontologies such as SOUPA [4] or CONON [10] and it is easy to create extensions to support different application domains. In the following, we outline the underlying technologies and describe how they can be used to define and execute queries.

As OWL is a vocabulary extension of RDF[1], the atomic data element for context information is an RDF triple. Every piece of context information is implicitly or explicitly represented as a set of triples. To avoid inconsistency of RDF blank nodes in distributed settings, we do not use blank nodes to model context information. Assume there is an infinite set I (Internationalized Resource Identifiers IRIs) and an infinite set L (RDF literals). A triple (s, p, o)$\in$(I)$\times$(I)$\times$(I$\cup$L) is called a non-blank node RDF triple, where s is the subject, p is the predicate and o is the object. The assertion a triple states that some relationship, indicated by the predicate, holds between the subject and object. As examples for such triples consider statements such as 'user' 'has' 'name' or 'sensor' 'reads' 'value'. Conceptually, a set of triples can then be connected along the subjects to create a graph structure. The assertion of such an RDF graph accounts to asserting all the triples in it, so the meaning of an RDF graph is the conjunction (logical AND) of the statements corresponding to all the triples it contains. This enables the formulation of arbitrary expressions such as 'device' 'has' 'sensor', 'sensor' 'reads' 'value' which can then be used by means of complex queries.

As context information is represented as RDF triples, we naturally chose SPARQL query fragments as basis for defining queries. In order to be suitable for resource-poor embedded devices, however, we only include basic graph matching patterns as well as built-in conditions. Furthermore, we add simple geo spatial extensions to express nearest neighbor as well as range queries analog to

[1] `http://www.w3.org/TR/rdf-syntax/`

http://code.google.com/p/geospatialweb/. Informally, basic graph matching patterns allow us to formulate sequences of triples that may contain variables. Upon execution, the variables are bound based on the triples contained in the model. As a simple example, we might query sensors by specifying a pattern consisting of 'x' 'reads' 'y' and 'x' 'is a' 'sensor'. Using built-in conditions, we can restrict the binding of variables to particular values, e.g. 'y' is greater than 5.

Given this model, the query evaluation process is a state machine which can be presented as a query graph [8]. The query graph consists of operators that perform operations on their input data to generate output data. After decomposing a query process into smaller operators, it can be shown that all queries are composed from triple pattern operations. Therefore the minimum operators for building a state machine to execute a query is the triple pattern matching operator. Other operators such as $\bowtie$, $\cup$ and $\models$ can be optionally built as relational JOIN, UNION and SELECTION operators, if needed.

3 System Architecture

To avoid the inherent privacy issues of centralized context management approaches, we take a peer-based approach to context management in which each device is managing its own context that can then be shared with other devices on demand by executing remote queries locally. For spontaneous interaction between devices in the vicinity, we are using BASE as underlying communication middleware. BASE is structured as a minimal extensible micro-broker that is deployed on each device and mediates all interactions. This results in the layered system structure depicted on the left side of Figure 1. At the highest layer, application objects and middleware services interact with each other, either locally or remotely, through their local micro-broker. Usually, this interaction is mediated through stub objects that can be generated automatically from interface definitions. Underneath, the micro-broker takes care of providing a uniform interface for device discovery and interaction. To realize this, BASE utilizes an extensible plug-in architecture to abstract from different communication abstractions, protocols and technologies. So, each middleware instance can be configured with different sets of plug-ins and, at runtime, BASE takes care of automatically composing suitable communication stacks. We refer the reader to [7] for details. As indicated on the left side of Figure 1, the extensions to support peer-based privacy-preserving context management affect all layers of BASE.

The key storage takes care of establishing the identity of a device or a domain in a secure manner. It associates each device with a unique asymmetric key pair that represents its identity as well as a certificate that is signed by a particular domain. Thereby, domains may either represent individual devices as well as individual users or even larger corporations, e.g. by means of hierarchically signed certificates. Avoiding a central point of trust, individual trust levels are associated to the certificates and stored in the key storage to model trust relationships between devices/domains. The certificate's trust level recursively covers the whole tree spanned by the certificate which reduces configuration effort. The

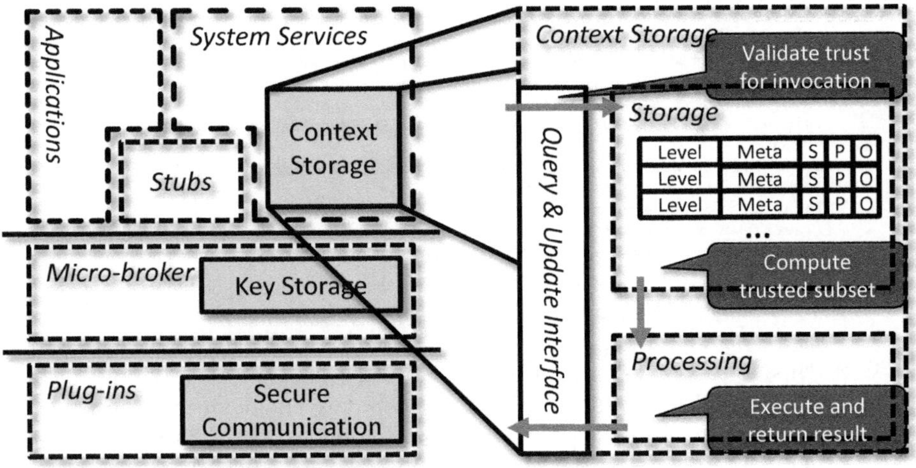

Fig. 1. Overall Architecture

trust levels are only valid for a particular device which enables users to model trust individually. At the same time, it enables the definition of uni-directional relationships. Regarding the trust levels, the key storage does not prescribe a particular semantic. To automate the evaluation of trust relationships, the key storage assumes transitivity such that a higher level of trust includes lower levels. Consequently, the two extremes are **full trust** and **no trust**.

The extensions for secure communication are verifying and enforcing the sharing according to the trust relationships. Due to the cost of asymmetric cryptography, the certificates contained in the key store are not suitable to secure interactions. Therefore, a key-exchange plug-in negotiates a secure symmetric key using the asymmetric keys. Thereby, the correct trust level is determined by exchanging certificate chains. Once a symmetric key is established and the trust level is evaluated, it is cached to secure all further interactions. This key can then be used by a second plug-in which ensures authenticity, integrity and optionally secrecy. For authenticity and integrity, an HMAC is attached to the transmitted messages. Encryption can be added additionally, e.g. by using AES.

With the extensions described previously, the task of the context storage service is reduced to ensure the generation of query results that adhere to the given trust level. As shown in Figure 1, a query and update interface is responsible for accepting incoming queries and update requests. Besides, it is responsible for determining the trust level of the incoming request. For this, it interacts with the key storage to determine the context of the call. The storage part is responsible for storing the context in a generic way that can be supported by resource-constrained devices. As discussed in Section 2, we rely on the triple representation defined by RDF, stored internally in the quoted string representation. To restrict the sharing of context on the basis of trust, each triple is extended with a trust *level*. In addition, each triple may contain further *meta* information to allow the decentralized validation as described in [1].

```
Q1: select ?device where{ ?device rdf:type device:Coordinator }

Q3: select ?device where{ ?device rdf:type device:Member.
    ?device device:hasAccessory ?accessory.  ?accessory rdf:type device:Screen.
     ?accessory device:hasResolution ?resolution.  ?resolution device:width.
     ?width ?resolution device:height ?height. FILTER (width>=240 && height>=320)}

Q5: select ?device where{ ?device smartspace:hasContext ?locCxt.
    ?locCxt smartspace:relatedLocation ?location.
    ?location spatial:within(53.27 -9.05 53.275 -9.055).
    {{?device service:provides data:printingService}
    UNION {?device  service:provides data:otherService} }}
```

Fig. 2. Excerpt for Classes of Queries

Given this context representation, a caller may add/remove triples with the associated level and meta information to manipulate the device's context. In our implementation, the addition of level information as well as the triple generation for a particular context type is done statically as part of a sensor implementation. When executing a query, the update and query interface uses the attached level information to determine the relevant triples. It selects all triples whose level is lower or equal to the caller's level and forwards them together with the request to the processing engine. The processing engine then executes the query over the set of triples. Since the context that is used during query evaluation is restricted already, the result can be passed directly to the caller.

4 Evaluation

We implemented the described architecture and used it as basis for two application prototypes in the PECES European research project. Next, we first discuss our experiences before we present excerpts of an experimental evaluation.

To validate the applicability of the OWL-based model, we used it to model an ehealth and a traffic management application. Both scenarios shared a number of concepts such as different types of users, sensors, devices and smart spaces. To reduce the modeling effort, we developed a core ontology by combining and extending various established ontologies (FOAF, OWL-S, WGS-84, etc). On top of the core ontology we developed scenario specific extensions. While using the models, we found that even unexperienced application developers where quickly able to define static context characteristics and queries using Protege or SPARQL. Both scenarios also required the addition of intermediate trust levels which can be seen as an indicator for the need of a privacy-preserving approach. In the traffic management application, sharing the destination was necessary to automatically pay toll roads and parking lots. In the e-health application, the health-related sensor readings had to be shared with nurses and doctors. In both cases the definition of trust levels, certificates and relations was straight forward.

In contrast to centralized context management, peer-based management must be suitable for a broad range of heterogeneous devices. Thus, it is necessary that

Table 1. Query Latency in Milliseconds

Dataset	Implementation	Q1	Q2	Q3	Q4	Q5
S1	Embedded	49.06	42.01	3246.30	-	-
S1	Mobile	95.75	60.79	506.67	544.93	35.96
S1	Desktop	1.71	1.41	4.11	9.16	2.84
S2	Mobile	860.92	194.35	3589.34	2156.09	63.60
S2	Desktop	4.24	1.17	12.56	97.09	1.58

the concepts can be realized with little resources or that they can be tailored to the devices. To support a broad set of devices, we developed three interoperable context processors.

- **Desktop:** To support desktops that are for instance controlling patients homes, we developed a context storage using JENA and ARQ which supports processing and storage of thousands of triples and enables complex reasoning.
- **Mobile:** To provide a storage for less powerful devices such as the smart phones used by a driver or a patient, we created a stripped-down processor by removing unnecessary code from JENA and ARQ. Thereby, we chose a particular database backend which uses a B-Tree for indexing.
- **Embedded:** For embedded devices, such as the actuators in the traffic management scenario or on-body sensors of a patient, we created a minimal context storage without relying on existing libraries. The variant stores triples in-memory and performs an un-indexed query evaluation. It is suitable for 300-500 triples which turned out to be sufficient for our applications.

For the performance evaluation, several experiments were performed that measured the storage's response time with regard to different query types and data sets. As basis for this evaluation, we used a PC (AMD Opteron 250, 4GB RAM, Sun JVM 1.6) to test the desktop variant, a HTC Desire (CPU 1GHz, 576 RAM, Android 2.1) smart phone to test the mobile variant and a SunSPOT (CPU 180 MHz ARM920T, 512KB RAM, 4MB Flash, CLDC 1.1) to test the embedded variant. Based on the PECES applications, we generated 2 data sets and we identified 5 classes of queries with increasing complexity shown in Figure 2. The small set (S1) encompasses 350 triples with 50 devices and 2 smart spaces. The large set (S2) consists of 12000 triples with 2000 devices and 50 smart spaces. The first three queries, Q1, Q2 and Q3 are representative queries for all types of devices. The other two queries only appear on desktop type devices.

Table 1 shows the resulting latency. The implementation for embedded devices can easily handle Q1 and Q2. As a result of the non-indexed query processing, Q3's complexity increased the latency drastically. Given sufficient memory, it would be possible to decrease the latency significantly. The implementation for mobile devices can easily handle all queries in the small dataset (S1). In the medium dataset (S2), the latency rises which can be justified by the comparatively large size. The desktop machine can easily handle all queries on both set. Given these results as well as our experiences with application development in

PECES, we are convinced that our peer-based approach to context management can provide a suitable privacy-preserving alternative to centralized approaches.

5 Conclusion

Providing adequate support for context acquisition and management is a non-trivial task that complicates the development of ubiquitous applications. In this paper, we have presented a peer-based alternative to centralized context management which overcomes privacy issues by supporting a fine-granular device- and thus, user-dependent definition of sharing policies. Although, our current implementation enables a fine-granular protection of the user's context, the actual policy specification must be done statically upfront. However, in some cases the user's privacy goals may not only depend on the type of context but also on the actual context itself. To handle that, we are currently working on languages and tools to automatically adapt the sharing policy at runtime.

Acknowledgments. This work has been partially supported by CONET (Co-operating Objects Network of Excellence) and PECES (PErvasive Computing in Embedded Systems), both funded by the European Commission under FP7 with contract numbers FP7-2007-2-224053 and FP7-224342-ICT-2007-2.

References

1. Apolinarski, W., Handte, M., Marron, P.: A secure context distribution framework for peer-based pervasive systems. In: 8th IEEE International Conference on Pervasive Computing and Communications Workshops, pp. 505–510 (April 2010)
2. Baldauf, M., Dustdar, S., Rosenberg, F.: A survey on context-aware systems. Int. J. Ad Hoc Ubiquitous Comput. 2, 263–277 (2007)
3. Chen, H., Finin, T., Joshi, A.: Semantic web in the context broker architecture. In: 2nd IEEE Intl. Conference on Pervasive Comp. and Comm., p. 277 (2004)
4. Chen, H., Perich, F., Finin, T., Joshi, A.: Soupa: Standard ontology for ubiquitous and pervasive applications. In: Annual International Conference on Mobile and Ubiquitous Systems, pp. 258–267 (2004)
5. Dey, A.K., Abowd, G.D., Salber, D.: A conceptual framework and a toolkit for supporting the rapid prototyping of context-aware applications. Hum.-Comput. Interact. 16, 97–166 (2001)
6. Gu, T., Wang, X.H., Pung, H.K., Zhang, D.Q.: An ontology-based context model in intelligent environments. In: Communication Networks and Distributed Systems Modeling and Simulation Conference, pp. 270–275 (2004)
7. Handte, M., Wagner, S., Schiele, G., Becker, C., Marron, P.J.: The base plug-in architecture - composable communication support for pervasive systems. In: 7th ACM International Conference on Pervasive Services (July 2010)

8. Hartig, O., Heese, R.: The sparql query graph model for query optimization. In: Franconi, E., Kifer, M., May, W. (eds.) ESWC 2007. LNCS, vol. 4519, pp. 564–578. Springer, Heidelberg (2007)
9. Hofer, T., Schwinger, W., Pichler, M., Leonhartsberger, G., Altmann, J., Retschitzegger, W.: Context-awareness on mobile devices - the hydrogen approach. In: 36th Hawaii International Conference on System Sciences, HICSS 2003 (2003)
10. Zhang, D., Gu, T., Wang, X.: Enabling context-aware smart home with semantic technology. International Journal of Human-friendly Welfare Robotic Systems 6(4), 12–20 (2005)

Classical Planning and Causal Implicatures

Luciana Benotti[1] and Patrick Blackburn[2]

[1] NLP Team, Universidad Nacional de Córdoba, Argentina
benotti@famaf.unc.edu.ar
http://cs.famaf.unc.edu.ar/~luciana/
[2] Department of Philosophy, Roskilde University, Denmark
patrickb@ruc.dk
http://www.patrickblackburn.org/

Abstract. In this paper we motivate and describe a dialogue manager (called Frolog) which uses classical planning to infer causal implicatures. A causal implicature is a type of Gricean relation implicature, a highly context dependent form of inference. As we shall see, causal implicatures are important for understanding the structure of task-oriented dialogues. Such dialogues locate conversational acts in contexts containing both pending tasks and the acts which bring them about. The ability to infer causal implicatures lets us interleave decisions about "how to sequence actions" with decisions about "when to generate clarification requests"; as a result we can model task-oriented dialogue as an interactive process locally structured by negotiation of the underlying task. We give several examples of Frolog-human dialog, discuss the limitations imposed by the classical planning paradigm, and indicate the potential relevance of our work for other relation implicatures.

1 Introduction

In conversation, an important part of the content conveyed is not explicitly stated, rather it is *implicated*. However, Grice's [11] classic concept of *conversational implicature* (CI) is far from fully understood. Traditionally, CIs have been classified using the Gricean maxims: there are *relation CIs* (also known as relevance CIs), *quantity CIs*, *quality CIs* and *manner CIs*. In linguistics, the most widely studied CIs are quantity CIs, probably because they are the ones most obviously amenable to context-independent analysis; see [10] for a survey of the state of the art. Far less studied are relation CIs, but these are arguably the most interesting of all. For a start, relation CIs are the most obviously context-dependent type of implicature, so studying them is important if we want to understand contextual reasoning. Moreover, it has been argued that all other types of CIs can be viewed as relation CIs [23]. Whether or not this is correct, it is undeniable that the maxim of relation ("be relevant") collapses a mixed bag of implicatures, which differ mainly in the the kind of contextual "relation" driving the inference. So gaining a more precise understanding of relation implicatures is an important task, and this paper is a step towards their computational formalization. We shall analyze a kind of relation CI that we call *causal CIs* and we

M. Beigl et al. (Eds.): CONTEXT 2011, LNAI 6967, pp. 26–39, 2011.

will work in *task-oriented dialogues* where there is a clear notion of *task-domain causality*. Consider the following example:

Mary: The chest is locked, the crown is inside
Bill: Give me the crown
Bill causally implicated: Open the chest

To spell this out a little, in order to carry out Bill's request (giving him the crown) it is necessary to open the chest. Hence Bill is implicating, by trading on the domain causal relations (after all, the contents of a chest are not accessible unless the chest is open) that Mary is to open the chest. To put it another way, Bill has tacitly conveyed (by exploiting contextual knowledge of the task domain) that Mary should carry out an "open the box" subtask [21]. What are Mary's options once she has inferred this causal CI? There are two clear choices: to accept this subtask silently or to negotiate it. Mary might decide to silently accept it (that is, she might simply open the chest without further ado) because she has the key that unlocks the chest or knows how to get it; in such cases we say that Mary has constructed an *internal bridge* from the current task situation (the crown being inside the locked chest) to the proposal made by Bill (giving him the crown). On the other hand, Mary might decide that she has insufficient information to construct the internal bridge (perhaps she has no key, or sees that the lock is rusty) so she may make a *clarification request*, such as *But how can I open the chest?* We call such a subdialogue an *external bridge*. The internal process of bridging (silent acceptance) is often called *accommodation* [14] or (plain old) *bridging* [8]. The external process of bridging, on the other hand, constitutes an important part of conversation.

A real task-oriented dialogue situation is typically made up of a (seemingly effortless) interplay of internal and external bridging as the dialogue participants explore the task at hand. The main claims of the paper are that understanding causal implicature is crucial to understanding this "seemingly effortless" interactive process, and that the inferences required can (at least to a first approximation) be modeled computationally in the classical planning paradigm.

Our motivation is both theoretical and practical. On the theoretical side, we believe that it is crucial to explore CIs in real dialogue settings. Strangely enough (after all, Grice did call them *conversational* implicatures) this view appears to be novel, perhaps even controversial. In the formal pragmatics literature, CIs are often simply viewed as inferences drawn by a hearer on the basis of a speaker's utterance and the Gricean maxims. We find this perspective too static. CIs (especially relation CIs) are better viewed as intrinsically *interactional* inferences, arising from the dynamics of conversations and situated in changing contexts. As conversations progress, speakers and hearers switch roles, meaning are negotiated, and contexts are updated via a grounding process [22]. Moreover, even within a single turn, hearers are not restricted to simply drawing (or failing to draw) "the" CI; in fact, choosing between internal and external bridging is better viewed as part of a process of *negotiating what the CI at stake actually is*. As a result of the negotiation, inferred CIs are grounded in the evolving context. We believe that modeling the changing context, and the inferences drawn from it, is necessary to extend the theory of CIs beyond the relatively narrow domain of quantity CIs towards the more challenging problems posed by relation CIs. We also believe that the dialogue-centered approach we advocate may have practical consequences. In particular, we believe that modeling external bridging is an important step towards defining an incremental dialogue manager (DM) in the spirit of that sketched in [6]; such a DM would be able to handle clarification requests in a principled way. This explains our interest in classical planning [17]. If the causal inferences can be computed using the well-understood and computationally-efficient technology this paradigm offers, we are well on the way to having a practical tool for dialogue management . The rest of the paper presents the dialogue manager Frolog, which infers *causal* CIs in task-oriented dialogue; Frolog is intended as a proof-of-concept of the ideas just sketched.

The paper proceeds as follows. In Section 2, we motivate the study of causal CIs by showing that their inference is critical for dialogues situated in physical task situations. In Section 3 we present the computational model for inferring causal CI using classical planning that underlies Frolog. In Section 4 we examine in detail the kinds of external and internal bridging that Frolog can (and cannot) handle. Section 5 concludes.

2 Causal Implicatures and Physical Tasks

In this paper we focus on causal implicatures. There are two main reasons for this. First, we view talking as a special case of purposive behavior. And so did Grice; indeed, he even showed that his maxim of relation (the maxim governing relation CIs) was relevant to *physical* acts:

> *I expect a partner's contribution to be appropriate to immediate needs at each stage of the transaction; if I am mixing ingredients for a cake, I don't expect to be handed a good book, or even an oven cloth (though this might be an appropriate contribution at a later stage).* [11, page 47]

The maxim of relation is traditionally viewed as important but obscure (it simply says: "Be relevant"). But if we restrict our attention to causal CIs arising in dialogues situated in a task domain, we get a useful parallelism between talk and actions: both are purposive behavior, and both are governed by the same maxim. This gives rise to an informational interplay between the task level and the dialogue level that we can exploit computationally.

Second, causal CIs give us an *empirical* handle on CIs. It is not controversial that (in non-conversational activities) the causal relations between acts define the expectations of the interaction. But it turns out that the same holds when conversational activities are situated in a physical task: there too causal relations guide the interaction. We did an empirical study on a task-oriented dialogue corpus [5] and found that most CIs which were made explicit—by being externally bridged as clarification requests—could be explained in terms of causal CIs. Let us briefly review this work before introducing the Frolog dialogue manager.

2.1 Empirically Studying Implicatures Using the SCARE Corpus

For our empirical study, we annotated and classified clarification requests (CRs) that appear in the SCARE corpus [19]. This corpus consists of fifteen spontaneous English dialogues situated in an instruction giving task. It was collected using the Quake environment, a first-person virtual reality game.

In the corpus, one of the dialogue participants plays the role of the direction giver (DG), who gives instructions to the other participant, the direction follower (DF) on how to complete several tasks in the game world. The DF has no prior knowledge of either the world map or the tasks and thus must rely on his partner, the DG, to guide him in playing the game. The DG has a map of the world and a list of tasks to complete. As the participants collaborate on the tasks, the DG has instant feedback of the DF's location in the simulated world. So the corpus is a treasure trove of lengthy task-oriented dialogues set in a richly-structured and well-understood situation.

We randomly selected one dialogue; its transcript contains 449 turns. We classified the clarification requests according to the four-level model of communication independently developed by Clark [9] and Allwood [2]. We found 29 clarification requests (CRs). Of these, 65% indicated an obstacle in carrying out the act proposed by the source utterance, and thus belong to level 4 of the model. As for the rest, 31% belonged to level 3 (indicating an obstacle in reference resolution) while 4% belonged to level 2 (indicating acoustic problems).

We agree with Thomason's view [20] that CIs are added to the context in order to *eliminate obstacles to the conversation*. Therefore, as we argue in [4], when CIs cannot be internally bridged, they are made explicit as level 4 CRs. To put it another way: *CRs in level 4 make explicit the CIs that cannot be silently accommodated.* We then classified the CRs in level 4 using the Gricean maxims. We found that *all* of them made explicit relation CIs (no other kinds of CIs were found). Finally, we further classified the relation CI according to the kind of relation involved: causal relations, at 73%, were far and away the most frequent.

2.2 Computationally Studying Causal Implicatures Using Frolog

How do we infer causal CIs of the sort found in the SCARE corpus? And what kinds of mechanisms lead to their being made explicit in CRs? To investigate such questions, we designed a system that mimics the type of instruction giving found in the SCARE corpus. In our setup, the DF is a dialogue system that we call Frolog. The role of the DG is played by a human who we call "the player".

Let's start right away with a sample interaction: we'll walk through the example reproduced in Figure 1. Incidentally, the point of this first example is to show just how unnatural interactions can be if a dialogue participant *can't* internally bridge causal implicatures. In the example, Frolog is in a room with a locked door, sitting on a big couch. The player is asking Frolog to look around (turns (1) to (6)) when Frolog says that there is a golden key on a table in the room. Then (in turn (7)) the player tells Frolog "Unlock the door with the key." In order to be executed in the virtual world, the action "unlock" has several preconditions (specified in the definition of the action "unlock", shown in the upper right-hand side the figure). One precondition is that Frolog must be holding the instrument required by the action. But this does *not* hold in the current state of the virtual world (the key is on the table). The fact that there is an obstacle to carrying out the action is made explicit by Frolog, who verbalizes the failed precondition of the unlock action (turns (8) and (9)). So the player tries to overcome this obstacle by making the causal CI "take the key!' explicit in turn (10), only to find that another obstacle gets in the way: this time, the key is not accessible (turn (12)) because it is on the table and Frolog is sitting on the couch! Again the player is forced to externally bridge the intended CI, and so says "Stand up". Since all the preconditions of the "stand up" action hold, Frolog is able to do this (turn (15)) and so the context is changed with the effects of the action. Once Frolog is standing in the drawing room the key is accessible, and so the command "take the key" in turn (16) can be directly executed and the context updated with the effects of this action (turn (18)). Finally, all the preconditions of the action "unlock the chest with the key" hold and Frolog can execute this command (turns (19) to (21)) without inferring any CI.

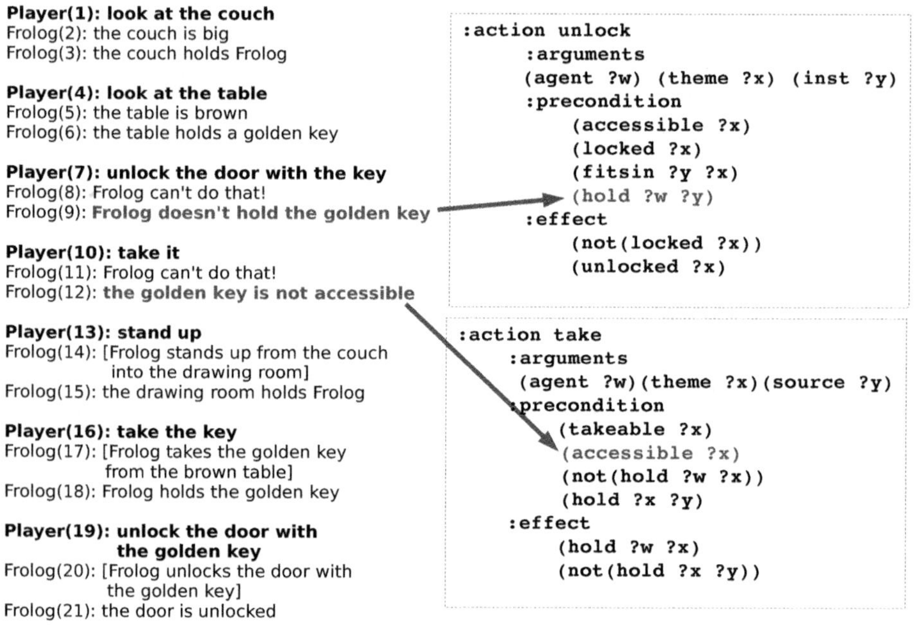

Fig. 1. Frolog *without* internal bridging

Much ado about nothing, and all to get a door unlocked! This example illustrates the (decidedly unhelpful) behavior of a dialogue system that does not internally bridge causal CIs. In such a situation we would expect a human conversational partner to simply stand up, take the key, and unlock the chest—no

Player(1): look at the couch
Frolog(2): the couch is big
Frolog(3): the couch holds Frolog

Player(4): look at the table
Frolog(5): the table is brown
Frolog(6): the table holds a golden key

Player(7): unlock the door with the golden key
Frolog(8): [Frolog stands up from the couch into the drawing room]
Frolog(9): the drawing room holds Frolog
Frolog(10): [Frolog takes the golden key from the brown table]
Frolog(11): Frolog holds the golden key
Frolog(12): [Frolog unlocks the door with the golden key]
Frolog(13): the door is unlocked

```
:definition here
  (some hold player)
:definition accessible
  (or here
      (some (inv hold) here)
      (some (inv hold)
            (and accessible open)))
```

```
:action standup
    :arguments
     (agent ?a)(source ?s)(goal ?g)
    :precondition
        (hold ?s ?a)
        (seated ?a)
        (hold ?g ?s)
    :effect
        (not(hold ?s ?a))
        (hold ?g ?a)
```

Fig. 2. Frolog *with* internal bridging

muss, no fuss. Frolog, however, forces the player to do all the work: the player does all the bridging unaided.

This gives rise to a clear feeling of non-cooperativeness; it's as though Frolog is being willfully unhelpful. But Frolog is not malicious—he simply does not have the capabilities to bridge internally, as he lacks the ability to reason about the context in which he finds himself. So what happens if we give Frolog these capabilites? Figure 2 shows the result.[1]

Adding reasoning capabilities has resulted in a bright new Frolog who behaves more like a collaborative human partner. But what exactly are these capabilites, and how do they enable Frolog to use contextual knowledge to infer the appropriate causal CIs?

3 Causal Implicatures and Classical Planning

In a nutshell, Frolog uses classical planning to compute causal implicatures. That is, Frolog uses classical planning (a well-explored and reasonably efficient AI technique) to fill out the micro-structure of discourse (the bridging information required in the next interactional step).[2] In particular, Frolog uses the classical planner FASTFORWARD [12]. Like all classical planners, FASTFORWARD takes three inputs—the initial state, the goal, and the available actions—and outputs a sequence of actions which, when executed in the initial state, achieve the goal.

[1] Figure 2 also shows the definitions and action specifications which, together with those of Figure 1, complete the causal relations used in the example.

[2] Since we use AI planning, the work reported here is very different from the classical work on plan-based dialogue managers [18,1]. The classic work uses *plan recognition* (a computationally expensive task) to interpret utterances by inserting them into the plan the macro-structure (the global shape) of discourse.

These three inputs are the crucial pieces of contextual information that Frolog must keep updated in order to use classical planning to infer appropriate CIs. Let's see what the content of each one should be.

3.1 The Initial State

In Frolog, two types of information are recorded and maintained: complete and accurate information about the game world is kept in the *world KB*, and a representation of the common ground (the local context constructed during the interaction) is kept in the *common ground KB*. So: which KB should be used as the initial state? As it turns out, we need both.

To see this, let's modify our running example. Suppose that the golden key (last seen lying on a table) is taken by a thief without either Frolog or the player realizing it. As a consequence, in the common ground KB the key is still (incorrectly) recorded as being on the table, whereas the world KB (correctly) notes that the thief has it. Now suppose the player issues the command "Unlock the door with the golden key" in this scenario. If we included in the initial state the complete information recorded in the game KB, Frolog would automatically take the key from the thief (for example, by using the "steal" action) and unlock the door. But Frolog should *not* be able do this—after all, Frolog does not know where the key actually is! So Frolog should *not* be able to use the world KB in order to infer the appropriate CIs.

But what happens if we use the common ground KB instead? In this case, Frolog would decide to take the key from the table and use it to unlock the door. But this sequence of actions is *not* executable in the game world because the key is no longer accessible (the thief has it). That is, a sequence of causal CIs found by reasoning over the common ground KB might not be executable in the game world because the common ground KB may contain information inconsistent with respect to the world KB. Hence Frolog needs both KBs: he *infers* the actions intended by the player using the information in the common ground KB but he has to *verify* this sequence of actions on the world KB to check that it can actually be executed. The importance of the verification step is an instance of what we call the *Causality Clarification Principle (CCP)*:

> *Causal CIs become explicit when they cannot be carried out in the* context *in which the conversation is situated.*

Frolog implements this principle by attempting to execute the CIs in the virtual world KB which contains complete information. If the execution fails he will trigger the external bridging of the CI (for instance by saying *"The key is not on the table"*).

The CI inference step can also fail because Frolog does not have enough game experience. That is, he has not collected enough information (in the common ground KB) to enable him to devise, all on his own, a sequence of CIs that will modify the context so that the player's command can be successfully executed. In such cases, Frolog will start a process of external bridging in which all the required CIs will be explicitly negotiated. Section 4 explores the circumstances that make external bridging necessary in situated dialogue.

3.2 The Goal

In the Frolog dialogue manager, the goal of the planning problem is not given in advance, nor does it have to be inferred during the dialogue (as is the case in plan recognition approaches [15,7]). For in our approach it is not the whole dialogue that is a hierarchical plan, rather *each utterance can be interpreted as a plan that links the utterance to the context.* In order to come up with the appropriate CIs of an instruction, Frolog should simply act to make the preconditions of the instruction true. So we can define the goal as the conjunction of all the preconditions of the command uttered by the player.

3.3 The Actions

To complete the picture, the actions available to the planner are all the actions in the game action database. We assume that all the action schemes that can be executed, such as the ones in Figure 1 and Figure 2, are mutually known to Frolog and the player. Clearly, in order for bridging to be possible, it must be mutually known what the preconditions and the effects of the actions involved are. In our unlock the door example, if the player doesn't know that Frolog needs to be holding the key to use it to unlock the door, then the player cannot possibly implicate that Frolog should take the key by saying "Unlock the door with the golden key". The same goes, *mutatis mutandis*, for Frolog.

The assumption that the player and Frolog know the exact specification of all the actions that can be executed in the game world is clearly a simplifying assumption. We leave for future work the task of modeling how differing knowledge about actions gets coordinated through dialogue; computationally coping with such issues is still an open problem [16,13].

4 Negotiating Implicatures

We now present several detailed examples of how solutions to the planning problems introduced in the previous section can (and cannot) be used to perform internal bridging and trigger external bridging (when appropriate). Incidentally, Frolog's bridging ability can be activated or deactivated at will, making it simple to compare its behavior with and without inference.

In the example in Figure 3, the player issued the command *put the green frog on the table* while Frolog was sitting on the couch. The action *put* requires its *goal* parameter, namely *the table*, to be accessible, but in this context the precondition does not hold. When bridging is deactivated, Frolog will simply verbalize the failed precondition. But as soon as the bridging abilities are activated (in the same context) the same command is bridged and executed by Frolog. Frolog makes explicit its internal bridging process by verbalizing each action and its effects in order, which is not very natural but is useful to monitor Frolog's internal inferences.

It's worth noting that planning problems are generated on the fly each time a precondition does not hold. In the example shown in Figure 3, the state to

(bridging dis-activated)

Player(1): put the green frog on the table
Frolog(2): Frolog can't do that!
The table is not accessible

(bridging activated)

Player(3): put the green frog on the table
Frolog(4): [Frolog stands up from the couch into the drawing-room]
Frolog(5): the drawing room holds Frolog
Frolog(6): [Frolog puts the green frog on the table]
Frolog(7): the table hold the green frog

Player(8): look at the table
Frolog(9): the table is red
Frolog(10): the table holds the green frog, the yellow apple and the key

Player(11): eat the yellow apple
Frolog(12): [Frolog takes the yellow apple from the table]
Frolog(13): Frolog holds the yellow apple
Frolog(14): [Frolog eats the yellow apple]
Frolog(15): the yellow apple is gone

```
:action put
    :arguments
     (agent ?w)(theme ?x)(goal ?y)
    :precondition
        (hold ?w ?x)
        (container ?y)
        (accessible ?y)
    :effect
        (not(hold ?w ?x))
        (hold ?y ?x)
```

```
:action eat
    :arguments
       (ingestor ?p)(ingestible ?x)
    :precondition
       (edible ?x)
       (not(disgusting ?x))
       (hold ?p ?x)
    :effect
       (not(hold ?p ?x))
       (gone ?x)
```

Fig. 3. *Internal* bridging in Frolog

which the command "put the green frog on the table" is bridged to is different from the state to which "eat the yellow apple" is bridged to (in this last state the green frog is by the yellow apple on the table).

As we said in Section 3, bridges are *inferred* using the information in the common ground KB, while their execution is *verified* with respect to the complete and accurate state of the world (kept in the world KB). So Frolog distinguishes two ways in which internal bridging can fail: when there is no bridge, and when there is a bridge—but it's not executable in the game world. We illustrated the case of a non-executable bridge in Section 3.1. We now illustrate the "no bridge" case with the interaction in Figure 4 (which continues the interaction in Figure 3). Here Frolog has just entered a room (called the treasury) which has a white wall, when the player issues command (20), "take the wall". In this case, the precondition that fails is `(takeable wall1)`. In AI planning terms, we say that the predicate `takeable` is *static* because there is no action that modifies its extension. In simpler terms, this means that there is no way of making the wall takeable. Therefore, as `(takeable wall1)` is a precondition, the planner will report that no plan can be found, and Frolog verbalizes the failed precondition. This failed-precondition verbalization could actually be considered a triggering of external bridging, at least if we dropped our assumption of completely synchronized action schemes; after all, maybe the player can teach Frolog how to use magic powers (or the strength of the incredible Hulk) to make a wall takeable.

Instruction (29) is an example of an instruction that cannot be internally bridged but whose failed precondition involves an *irreversible action* (namely, killing) rather than a static predicate. In this case, the planner is invoked with the goal `(alive dragon1)` and the planner will not be able to find a plan: the

Player(16): go through the south exit
Frolog(17): [Frolog goes through the south exit into a treasury]
Frolog(18): the treasury hold you, a chest and a dragon
Frolog(19): the treasury has a white wall

Player(20): take the wall
Frolog(21): Frolog can't do that!
Frolog(22): **the wall is not takeable**

Player(23): look at Frolog
Frolog(24): Frolog is alive
Frolog(25): Frolog holds the sword, the worm and a golden key

Player(26): kill the dragon with the sword
Frolog(27): [Frolog kills the dragon with the sword]
Frolog(28): the dragon is dead

Player(29): kill the dragon with the sword
Frolog(30): Frolog can't do that!
Frolog(31): **the dragon is not alive**

```
:action take
    :arguments
     (agent ?w)(theme ?x)(source ?y)
    :precondition
        (takeable ?x)
        (accessible ?x)
        (not(hold ?w ?x))
        (hold ?x ?y)
    :effect
        (hold ?w ?x)
        (not(hold ?x ?y))
```

```
:action kill
    :arguments
       (agent ?w)(theme ?p)(inst ?x)
    :precondition
       (alive ?p)
       (accessible ?p)
       (hold ?w ?x)
    :effect
       (dead ?p)
       (not (alive ?p))
```

Fig. 4. *External* bridging in Frolog (world constraints)

dragon can be killed only once. Whenever the planner says there is no plan for all the preconditions in the goal, the planner will be invoked with each precondition separately. For at least one of these preconditions no plan will be found, and the first such precondition found will be verbalized. In our example, this results in Frolog saying *the dragon is not alive* in turn (31).

Now, it is not only when the predicate is static or the actions are irreversible that the planner will find no plan: it can also happen when Frolog has not acquired enough knowledge to infer the bridge. This is the case in instruction (37) in Figure 5. Here the player wants Frolog to open the chest—but Frolog does not know how to do this. In the screen-shot to the right you can see state of the common ground KB from turns (37) to (40). The player does not have information about what fits into the chest; this is why the planner is unable to find a plan that realizes the precondition `(unlocked chest1)` of the command "open the chest" in instruction (37).[3]

Let's take this example further. Frolog's behavior continues as expected until turn (48), when Frolog is again unable to bridge the command to open the chest. But at this stage it should clearly be mutual knowledge that the golden key fits into the chest, so why does Frolog not react appropriately? The problem is that the classical planning based architecture assumes that all the actions are *deterministic*, but actions that acquire information are *non*-deterministic: after the player tries to perform an unlock action with a key, he can end up either in a

[3] Instruction (39) fails as well, making the obstacle explicit. Incidentally, utterance (40) is an example of a CR caused by a "required but unknown" thematic relation filler (the second most frequent CR in level 4 in the SCARE corpus).

Player(32): look at the chest
Frolog(33): the chest is closed and locked and wooden

Player(34): look at Frolog
Frolog(35): Frolog is alive
Frolog(36): Frolog holds the sword, the worm and the golden key

Player(37): open the chest
Frolog(38): Frolog can't do that!
the chest is not unlocked

Player(39): unlock the chest
Frolog(40): Frolog can't do that!
Frolog doesn't know what fits into the chest

Player(41): unlock the chest with the golden key
Frolog(42): [Frolog unlocks the chest]
Frolog(43): the chest is unlocked

Player(44): lock the chest with the key
Frolog(45): [Frolog locks the chest]
Frolog(46): the chest is locked

Player(47): open the chest
Frolog(48): Frolog can't do that!
the chest is not unlocked

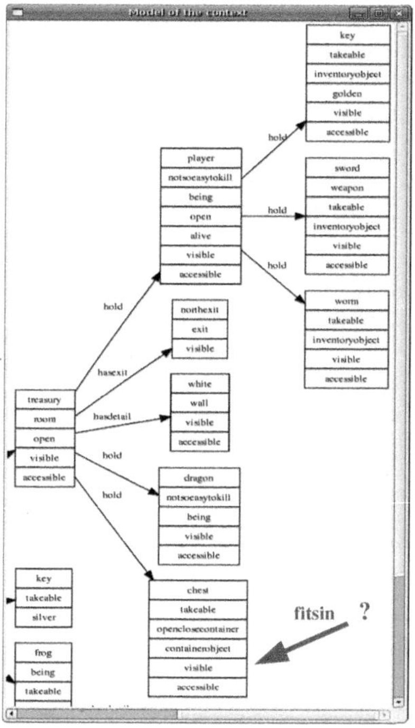

Fig. 5. *External* bridging in Frolog (knowledge constraints)

state where the key fits or one where it doesn't. That is, he must *learn* whether the key fits or not. Such learning cannot be modelled with deterministic actions.

In order to overcome this issue there are two options: (1) either we allow different sources to update the mutual information (thereby losing uniformity in the update process) or (2) we add non-deterministic actions. Here we describe option (1). Option (1) can be seen as a procedural version of "strict accommodation" (as defined in [3]). For a discussion of option (2), see [5].

The intuition behind the strict notion of accommodation is this: when the speaker utters a sentence, she is not only trying to achieve the obvious effects of the utterance, she is also conveying her image of how she takes the world to be. Crucially, the success of the utterance depends on letting this image "come into existence". Accordingly, we argue that the intention behind the utterance "unlock the chest with the golden key" in turn (41) is twofold. It is clear that the player wants to achieve the effects of the action (that is, she wants to have the chest unlocked). But the player also expects Frolog to recognize the assumptions she is making and on which the success of the utterance depends. In particular, she expects Frolog to recognize that she is assuming that the golden key fits into the chest's lock (this is why Frolog could coherently ask here: *but why do you think that the golden key will fit?*).

In particular, after the action (`unlock(door1 key1)`) is executed successfully, the player will believe that the assumption she made was confirmed by the

Player(1): unlock the chest
Frolog(2): Frolog can't do that!
Frolog doesn't know what fits-into the chest

Player(3): look at you
Frolog(4): you are alive
Frolog(5): you hold a golden key

Player(6): unlock the chest with the golden key
Frolog(7): [Frolog unlocks the chest with the golden key]
Frolog(8): the chest is unlocked
Frolog(9): **the key fits-into the chest**

Player(10): lock the chest
Frolog(11): [Frolog locks the chest with the golden key]
Frolog(12): the chest is locked

Player(13): look at the chest
Frolog(14): the chest is closed and locked and wooden

Player(15): open the chest
Frolog(16): [Frolog unlocks the chest with the golden key]
Frolog(17): the chest is unlocked
Frolog(18): [Frolog opens the chest]
Frolog(19): the chest is open
Frolog(20): the chest hold a golden crown

```
:action unlock
     :arguments
     (agent ?w) (theme ?x) (inst ?y)
     :precondition
         (accessible ?x)
         (locked ?x)
         (fitsin ?y ?x)
         (hold ?w ?y)
     :effect
         (not(locked ?x))
         (unlocked ?x)
```

```
:action open
     :arguments
     (agent ?w) (theme ?x)
     :precondition
         (accessible ?x)
         (closed ?x)
         (unlocked ?x)
     :effect
         (not(closed ?x))
         (open ?x)
```

Fig. 6. *External* bridging becomes *internal* as common ground accumulates

success of the action. This means that, when an action is executed, the common ground KB will be updated not only with the *effects* of the action but also with its *preconditions*. And those preconditions that were not in the common ground KB before will be verbalized as in turn (9) in Figure 6.

The rest of the interaction (from turns (10) to (15)) shows that once the proposition `(fitsin key1 chest1)` is added to the common ground KB, the action "open the chest" can be internally bridged, even when the chest is locked, because all the necessary information is in the common ground.

So what's the problem? This: the updates done during the execution of the actions no longer mimic those done when doing internal bridging. We have broken the symmetry of the update processes. And this means that solution (1) is only partial. Although Frolog can now learn during execution (as in Figure 6) he is not able to experiment to try and acquire information himself. For example, Frolog cannot decide on his own to try a key to see if it fits.

Solution (1) is able to model 78% of the causal implicatures observed in the SCARE corpus (see Section 2.1). For a more detailed discussion of cases beyond the scope of classical planning, see [5].

5 Conclusions

Causal implicatures are a kind of relation implicature (historically Grice's most obscure yet most crucial type) whose inference—we have argued—is essential to understanding how situated dialogue works. Causal relations certainly have a direct impact on the coherence structure of task-oriented dialogues (such as those in the SCARE corpus), but can their conversational effect be computed? Frolog was designed as a simple proof-of-concept to show that they can. How does it fare?

Rather well, we believe. On the practical side, our use of classical planning shows that a well-understood tool can be used to make inferences that model negotiations observed in human-human dialogue. Furthermore, the shortcomings of Frolog's inferential model are directly traceable to the restrictions build into classical planning; when more flexible partial planners become widely available, Frolog will be able to make use of them and the non-determinism they offer. But matters are more complex on the theoretical side. We believe our account shows what a genuinely interactive view of implicature could (and in our view, should) look like. But can we extend it from causal implicatures in task-oriented dialogues to other types of relational implicature in different dialogue settings? At present, this is unclear. The tight link between clausal implicatures and clarification requests in task-oriented dialogues makes empirical work relatively straightforward; implicatures in other settings can be much harder to analyze. Nonetheless, it is our belief that our approach will eventually throw further light on Grice's seminal work. In particular, it is our hypothesis that the following *Clarification Principle (CP)*—a generalization of the *CCP* noted earlier—will play a important role:

> *Relation Implicatures become explicit when they cannot be* grounded *in the context in which the conversation is situated.*

References

1. Allen, J., Allen, R.: Natural language understanding. Addison-Wesley, Reading (1994)
2. Allwood, J.: An activity based approach to pragmatics. In: Abduction, Belief and Context in Dialogue: Studies in Computational Pragmatics, pp. 47–80. John Benjamins, Amsterdam (1995)
3. Beaver, D., Geurts, B.: Presupposition. In: Handbook of Semantics, Walter de Gruyter, Berlin (in press)
4. Benotti, L.: Clarification potential of instructions. In: Proceedings of the 2009 SIGDIAL Conference on Discourse and Dialogue, pp. 196–205 (2009)
5. Benotti, L.: Implicature as an Interactive Process. Ph.D. thesis, Université Henri Poincaré, INRIA Nancy Grand Est, France (2010)
6. Buß, O., Schlangen, D.: Modelling sub-utterance phenomena in spoken dialogue systems. In: The 2010 Workshop on the Semantics and Pragmatics of Dialogue, Poznań, Poland (2010)
7. Carberry, S., Lambert, L.: A process model for recognizing communicative acts and modeling negotiation subdialogues. Computational Linguistics 25(1), 1–53 (1999)
8. Clark, H.: Bridging. In: Proceedings of the 1975 Workshop on Theoretical Issues in Natural Language Processing, pp. 169–174. ACL, Morristown (1975)
9. Clark, H.: Using Language. Cambridge University Press, New York (1996)

10. Geurts, B.: Quantity implicatures. Cambridge University Press, Cambridge (2011)
11. Grice, P.: Logic and conversation. In: Cole, P., Morgan, J. (eds.) Syntax and Semantics, vol. 3, pp. 41–58. Academic Press, New York (1975)
12. Hoffmann, J., Porteous, J., Sebastia, L.: Ordered landmarks in planning. Journal of Artificial Intelligence Research 22, 215–278 (2004)
13. Larsson, S.: Coordinating on ad-hoc semantic systems in dialogue. In: The 2007 Workshop on the Semantics and Pragmatics of Dialogue, Decalog 2007 (2007)
14. Lewis, D.: Scorekeeping in a language game. Journal of Philosophical Logic 8, 339–359 (1979)
15. Litman, D., Allen, J.: Discourse processing and commonsense plans. In: Intentions in Communication, pp. 365–388. MIT Press, Cambridge (1990)
16. Mills, G.: Semantic co-ordination in dialogue: the role of direct interaction. Ph.D. thesis, Queen Mary, University of London, supervised by Patrick Healey (2007)
17. Nau, D., Ghallab, M., Traverso, P.: Automated Planning: Theory & Practice. Morgan Kaufmann Publishers Inc., CA (2004)
18. Perrault, R., Allen, J.: A plan-based analysis of indirect speech acts. Computational Linguistics 6(3-4), 167–182 (1980)
19. Stoia, L., Shockley, D., Byron, D., Fosler-Lussier, E.: SCARE: A situated corpus with annotated referring expressions. In: Proceedings of LREC (2008)
20. Thomason, R.: Accommodation, meaning, and implicature: Interdisciplinary foundations for pragmatics. In: Cohen, P., Morgan, J., Pollack, M. (eds.) Intentions in Communication, pp. 326–363. MIT Press, Cambridge (1990)
21. Thomason, R., Stone, M., DeVault, D.: Enlightened update: A computational architecture for presupposition and other pragmatic phenomena. In: Presupposition Accommodation, Ohio State Pragmatics Initiative (2006)
22. Traum, D.: A Computational Theory of Grounding in Natural Language Conversation. Ph.D. thesis, Computer Science Dept., U. Rochester, USA (1994)
23. Wilson, D., Sperber, D.: Relevance theory. In: Handbook of Pragmatics, pp. 607–632. Blackwell, Oxford (2004)

Contextualization of Scientific Workflows

Patrick Brezillon

LIP6, University Paris 6 - UPMC
Paris, France
Patrick.Brezillon@lip6.fr

Abstract. Scientific-Workflow (SWF) management is similar to practice management. However, SWFs are stored in a repository as independent items that are reused by other actors after a complex process of contextualization, decontextualization and recontextualization. Conversely, practices are contextualized procedures applicable in different contexts. SWFs are collected in repositories in a flat way independently of each other, while practices can be organized in a uniform representation of elements of knowledge, reasoning and contexts. This paper shows that SWF management may benefit of the contextual approach used for representing procedures and practices. We propose a three-step approach, namely a support to scientist for finding the right SWF in the repository, a generation of all the possible SWFs in a situation, and the interactive development of SWFs. Thus, a SWF system will be flexible enough to acquire new knowledge incrementally and learn new ways for SWF building from scientists. A challenge for the short term is the possibility to model cooperation by the coupling of actors' task representation through a shared context.

Keywords: Decision making, Scientific workflows, Contextual Graphs, Contextualization, flexibility, cooperation modeling.

1 Introduction

Workflow is the automation of a business (dynamic) process, in whole or part, during which documents, information or tasks are passed from one participant to another for action, according to a set of procedural rules. Workflows represent declaratively the components or codes that need to be executed in a complex application, as well as the data dependencies among those components and people involved. Scientific workflows (SWFs) are concerned with the automation of scientific processes in which tasks are structured based on their control and data dependencies. SWFs are often described as knowledge intensive or "knowledge-rich workflow systems" (Gil, 2008). Knowledge intensive work is exploratory, loosely structured activities, flexible, non-repetitive and can, only to a limited extent, be specified in advance of execution. Thus, SWF management requires specific methods and tools. Artificial intelligence techniques can play an important role to represent complex scientific knowledge, to automate processes involved in scientific discovery, and to support scientists to manage the complexity of the hypothesis space.

M. Beigl et al. (Eds.): CONTEXT 2011, LNAI 6967, pp. 40–53, 2011.

Repositories contain SWFs successfully applied in specific contexts and published (implicitly) as "contextualized SWFs", although the complete trace of the contextualization process is not saved with the SWF. As a consequence, none SWF can be reused directly, and retrieving a SWF suppose to enter a difficult process of contextualization (identifying the published workflow that is close of the context at hand), then of decontextualization (extracting the part of the workflow model that can be reusable for in a relatively generic way), and finally of recontextualization (developing workflow instances adapted to the situation at hand).

Hereafter, we have organized the paper in the following way. Sections 2 introduces SWF management. Section 3 discusses of the SWF representation in terms of Contextual Graphs. Section 4 presents different ways to exploit a SWF presented in a contextual graph. Section 5 discusses the basis for a cooperation modeling in a SWF building, and we finally conclude on perspectives offered by this work.

2 Management of Scientific Workflows

A *Scientific Workflow (SWF) repository* is a shared database of various types of information about scientific artifacts produced, stored, retrieved and used by scientists. Information on each SWF includes SWF instances, data, results, origin, annotations, tags, associated documentation, etc. Such information concerns different contexts that are associated directly with SWFs, but in a flat way, and, as a consequence, a SWF repository generally cannot be structured and organized. The high-level focus of current SWF repositories is not directly related to SWFs.

Annotations associated with SWFs provide complementary information on SWFs, and eventually on relationships with few other SWFs (such as the SWF parent). They represent an external type of context that describes which contextual elements are considered (i.e. instantiated) for a given workflow. However, there are two main problems. First, annotations are attached to a specific SWF. Thus, it is not possible to rely stories on different SWFs (history, hierarchy, variants of a same solution in different contexts, etc.). Second, annotations make sense in the writer's context (where the SWF was successful), when readers interpret in their own contexts, which are different of the writer's context that is not made explicit to readers. Moreover, a SWF variant of the writer's SWF could be more interesting for a reader because the reader's context is closer of the SWF-variant context than the published-SWF context.

The problem of SWF repositories can be explained in the light of the well known ambiguity between procedures versus practices, task versus activity or logic of functioning versus logic of use (Brézillon, 2007). A procedure is the way in which the head of a company thinks that a problem must be solved, based on company policy and strategy. A practice is the way in which an employee will integrate personal (contextual) stuffs before to apply the procedure based on tactical and operational considerations. There are almost as many practices as actors and contexts for a given procedure because each actor tailors the procedure in order to take into account his particular and specific context.

In the SWF community, published SWFs in repositories implicitly are supposed to be procedures, while they are practices, i.e. resulting of a contextualization process (and thus cannot be reused directly). This contextualization process is partially represented in the SWF that is published as annotation in the repository. For example, it is not said that the scientist does not indicate a software piece because he knows that other scientists will use their own favorite software pieces. As a consequence, it is important to capture relationships between annotations for a better understanding of the links between SWFs, like practice representation in Contextual Graphs.

3 Representations of Scientific Workflows

A scientist is a decision maker that tries to gather first a maximum of contextual elements before to make his decision (and act after). We can illustrate this situation with an example of incident solving in subway area (Pomerol et al., 2002). Figure 1 shows the tree representation adopted for describing actor's reasoning during his decision-making process. Rectangles represent action (the building blocks at the chosen granularity) and circles correspond to chance nodes (the contextual elements) with exclusive values. We observe that actors gather a maximum of information for developing a mental representations of the problem before decision making. As a consequence, operators postpone most of the actions.

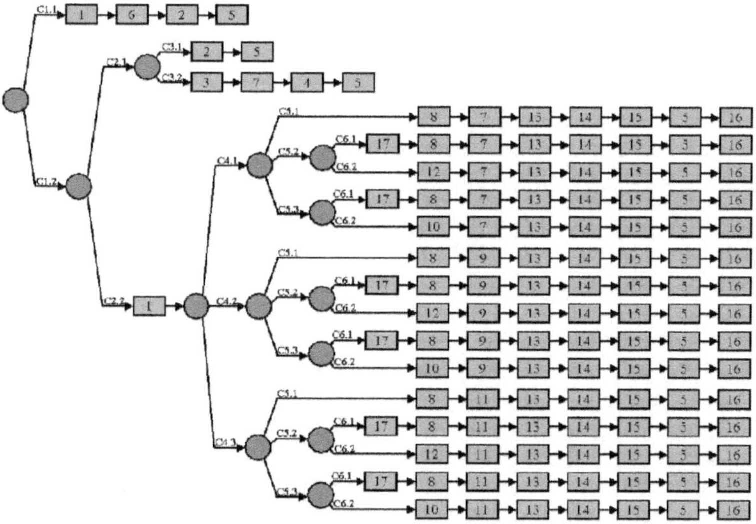

Fig. 1. Decision tree representation of an incident solving in the subway (Pomerol et al., 2002)

With respect to SWFs, we retain that there are (roughly) two parts in the decision tree represented in Figure 1. The left part is mainly composed of contextual elements, when the right part contains mainly macro-actions. This shows that decision making is a two-step process of contextualisation (Brézillon and Pomerol, 2010). The first step corresponds to the qualitative part of decision making levels (the diagnosis part). The second step corresponds to the quantitative part of decision making (the action part). SWF repositories deal with the quantitative part of SWFs (second step), not its qualitative part (first step). This is our motivation to introduce contextual graphs in SWF domain to propose a solution in SWF management.

The context-based tree representation evolved in a graph representation (see Figure 2) simpler than the tree representation (Figure 1). The contextual-graph formalism uses four building items: the action, the contextual element, the temporal branching and the activity (not represented in Figure 2). It is an actor-oriented representation for a logic of use, not a logic of functioning.

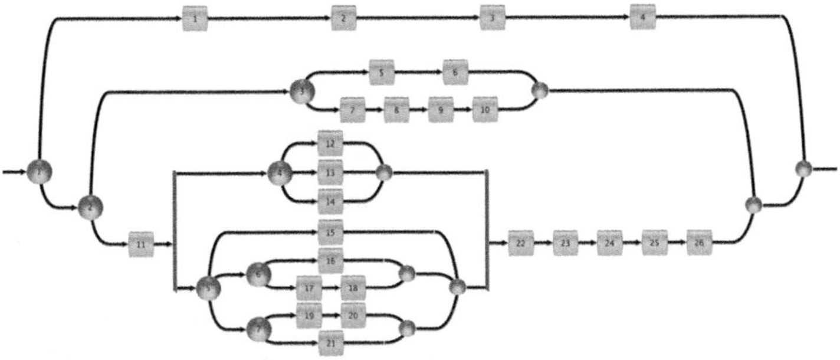

Fig. 2. Graph representation of an incident solving in the subway (Pomerol et al., 2002)

Thus, a contextual graph represented a problem solving at a given granularity and is applied in a known context. Each path in the contextual graph corresponds to a SWF building in a specific context. The contextual graph contains all the accumulated experience in a problem solving, and, thus, a description of SWFs in the Contextual-Graphs formalism will imply that a SWF repository may become a rich "experience base". Annotations could correspond to the ordered sequence of instantiated contextual elements leading to an item in the contextual graph, which we call the proceduralized context (Brézillon, 2005). Parallel between annotations of different SWFs and proceduralized contexts means that relationships between annotations are made explicit in a contextual graph and there is a possible reuse, say, for explanation purpose.

Now, SWFs in repositories are similar to the right part of the decision-tree representation given Figure 1. Representing SWF building in Contextual Graphs leads (1) to abandon the object-oriented view on SWFs for an actor-oriented view; and (2) to make a global view on SWF organization explicit in SWF repositories by proposing the explanation of the relationships between all the SWF instances.

4 Exploitation of Scientific Workflows in a CxG Representation

4.1 The Running Example

We continue now the discussion on a simple running example because context is always related to a concrete focus. The example concerns an activity-based workflow implementation[1].

---

1 http://thesis.romanofski.de/ch01s03.html

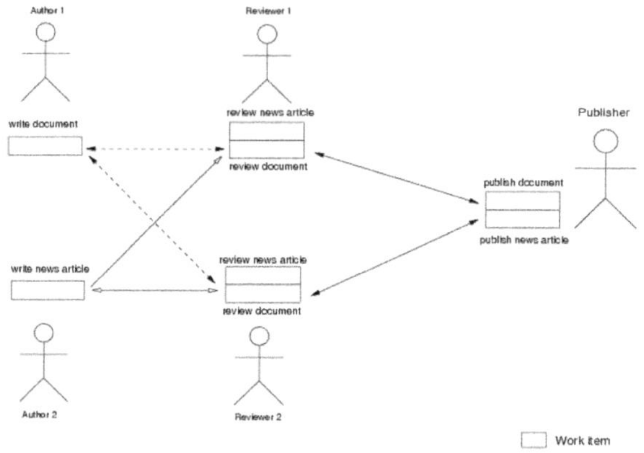

Fig. 3. Activity-based workflow implementation

Figure 3 represents the different steps in a submission process by which a paper is transformed through the process implying different activities realized by different actors (Joost, 2006). The submission process represents an author writing a document, two reviewers evaluating the document and finally the document being published by a publisher.

Each actor is responsible of an activity that modifies the content status: The author writes the paper, the reviewers require some changes, and the publisher put the document in the final format. The second observation is that the key actor in this process—the editor—is left implicit because he does not impact directly the content status. The third observation is that there is only one output (i.e. publication of the document). The real process is not so straightforward, e.g. some changes may be required or the paper may be rejected.

In the next section, we take an actor-oriented viewpoint instead of the activity-oriented view that is common in the SWF community. This allows to be more precise on the way in which that content can be modified directly, but we can go one step further by representing indirect modifications such as the rejection of the document and its eventual new submission.

4.2 SWF Process Modeling in Contextual Graphs

4.2.1 Step 1: Decision Support to Editors

According to the editor's viewpoint, activities describe in Figure 3 can be rewritten as: Receive a submission (from an author); Ask document review (at the two reviewers); Make a decision between (1) accept the paper (and send it to the publisher for publication), (2) Ask changes (to the author), and (3) Notify paper rejection. Figure 4 illustrates the corresponding representation, which is a kind of editor's behavior model.

A system using such a model can support other editors in the same task (essentially for more complex task, see after). In terms of SWF, the system would help the scientist in selecting a good SWF in the repository based on ways that other scientists

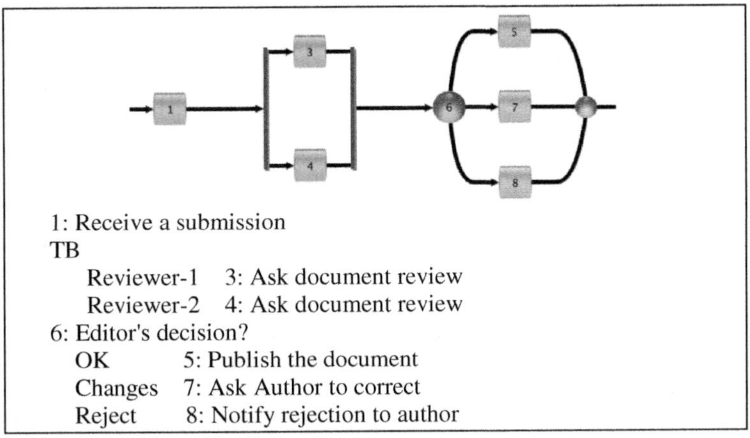

Fig. 4. Contextual graph of the activity-based workflow (editor's viewpoint)

did previously. This approach is useful when the problem is complex (each problem solving leading to a specific solution) and the repository contains a large number of SWF candidates. Such a system is only a support to the scientist and is particularly useful if the whole task realization cannot be planned in advance (not known or too complex) or needs to tackle too many contextual elements. Here, the main interest of Contextual Graphs relies on the capacity of the system to acquire incrementally new knowledge about the task and learn new practices from actors. The next section presents a possible automation of this support.

4.2.2 Step 2: Generating Static Alternatives

With a limited number of SWF variants, the system can reproduce automatically all the different solutions obtained by editors and, thus, generate (or compile) before any use all the SWF alternatives (Figure 5 shows the three possible workflows in Figure 4), put them in the repository, and thus other actors will be sure to select the right SWF for their task in the context at hand (given as an annotation). Conversely, the system can explore the repository in order to retrieve the potential candidates for the editor, based on editor's decision (the contextual element 6 in Figure 4). This supposes that all the contexts that can be encountered are known and described in advance.

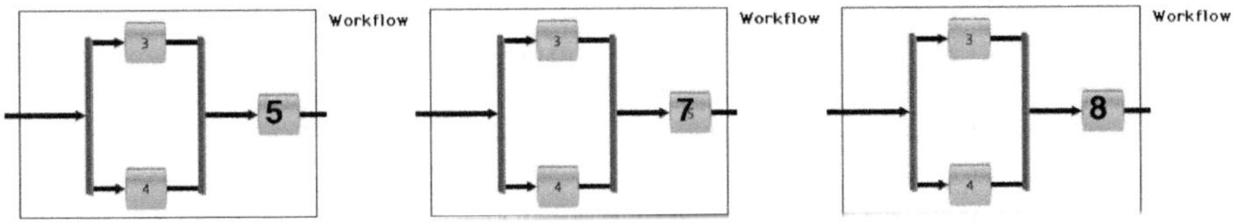

Fig. 5. Alternatives of the activity-based workflow in editor's viewpoint

Thus, knowing the right context, the system can act as the editor for exploring the repository. Such an approach can be useful for developing routines (i.e. workflows) automatically, when all is known in advance, especially the different contexts of use, although these contexts must be managed by the system apart.

4.2.3 Step 3: Dynamic Building of SWFs

Because a repetitive task is never accomplished strictly in the same context, the scientist is always obliged to adapt a SWF to the context at hand. Moreover, some contextual elements may be not reachable to the system directly. The third approach implies the use of the contextual graph as a SWF shell (i.e. with all the building blocks of SWFs) and the dynamical building of the workflow by interacting during the SWF execution with the scientist (see Figure 6 for the running example), the latter providing the context at hand when needed and thus the system selects the right activities to include in the SWF and, as a consequence, makes a dynamic compilation of a workflow "on the fly". The lessons learned here are: (1) the contextual graph is a macro-structure stored in the repository, (2) a contextual graph contains a solution (i.e. a SWF) and its alternatives in a meaningful way for a scientist looking for a SWF without knowing exactly the right context, and (3) a repository constituted of contextual graphs (for different task realizations) becomes an "experience base". Making context explicit in the repository, actors find more rapidly the right SWF for their specific tasks in their given contexts.

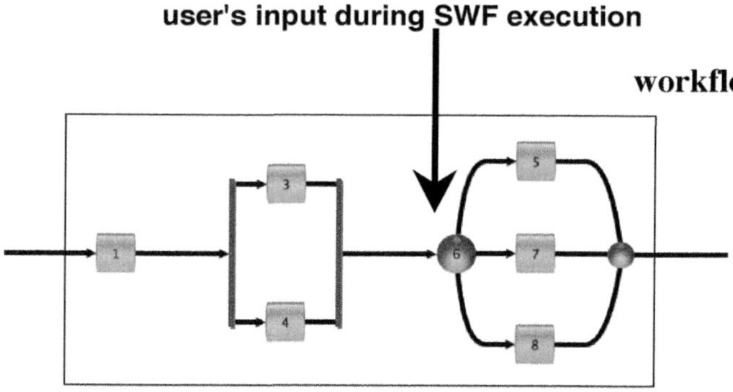

Fig. 6. Interactive building of the activity-based workflow in editor's viewpoint

Some researchers call such workflows ad-hoc workflows (e.g. see Huth et al., 2001) or weakly-structured workflows (van Elst et al., 2003) because they typically involve human coordination, collaboration or co-decision. However, these authors do not consider context explicitly. In our proposal, planning, decision making and action are intertwined. The task ordering and coordination decisions are made while the workflow is performed (e.g. see also Georgakopolous and Hornick, 1995).

4.2.4 Appraisal on the Three-Step Approach

The three-step approach can be combined or used independently to represent a larger spectrum of scientists' behaviors. The first step is relevant if scientists' activity is too complex to be represented in a unique workflow, especially when the task is ill defined (a usual situation for SWFs). This approach focuses on a model of the known practices developed by scientists previously for helping new scientists to do not forget important contextual elements and alternatives. At the second step, the same model of scientists' behavior can be used in two ways. First, the model is supposed an exhaustive description of the task realization (at least in the state of our knowledge) and thus it is possible to generate automatically all the possible workflows to be published in a repository. The second way is again a support to scientists by exploring the repository for retrieving workflows that fit the context at hand of the scientist. Thus, the system begins by a context matching its exploration of the repository. In both two ways, all the needed contextual elements and their instances are supposed known prior the system use. At the third step, the unit of reasoning is not the workflow, but the model of the task realization with all the possible practices (a kind of decontextualization process of SWFs). It is also supposed that the current context cannot be known in advance. Then, the solution consists of a joint building of the SWF by the system and the scientist (in a recontextualization process for a specific context).

Introducing CxG in SWF management brings a new insight on some problems in SWF domain like the lack of flexibility of scientific workflows. An interesting extension of SWF-building representation in a contextual graph (mainly through the choice of the actor's viewpoint) is the possibility to model a cooperation of actors through the contextual-graph representation of their task realization.

4.3 SWF Flexibility Expressiveness in Contextual Graphs

Business process flexibility is defined as the capability to yield to externally triggered changes by modifying only process parts that need to be changed and keeping other parts stable (Rosemann. and Recker, 2007). This allows to modifying the process partially without completely replacing it. In other words, a process is flexible if it can adapt itself to external unpredicted event by internal mechanisms. These internal mechanisms are to be defined either prior to the use of the applications or by modifying them manually.

Schonenberg (2008) defined flexibility as the actor-oriented ability to react to changes in actor's needs. Contextual Graphs offer a solution by focusing on practices developed by actors, not on procedures. For example, the definition of the editor's task as represented in Figure 4 can be enriched by considering first that the editor receives a submission or a revised version from the author (after a first loop in the process). The editor will behave differently in the two situations. Another development concerns a conflict management between reviewers' evaluation. In the following we discuss interaction between editor and reviewer tasks.

A context-based SWF system addresses this problem in two ways:

(1) The system knows all the solutions and their instances. The SWF system then can use the contextual graph as an input, selects paths according the way contextual elements are instantiated, assembles the "building blocks" of the SWF to be built. If the instances of some contextual elements are unknown, then the system enters in a phase of interaction with the scientist to acquire this instance.

(2) The system concludes on the selection of a wrong SWF. Then, the system asks the cooperation of the scientist to analyze the followed path step by step in

order to identify the step at which the scientist does not agree with the solution known by the system. Generally this concerns a contextual element that was not considered up to now because generally keeping always the same instance. Then, the scientist corrects the contextual graph by adding the missing contextual element and adding the needed action for his specific context. The SWF shell will be updated for future uses.

Thus, a SWF system becomes a context-based intelligent assistant system, drawing benefit of its interaction with the scientist to acquire knowledge incrementally and learns new practices

For example, starting from the contextual graph represented in Figure 4, interaction between the system and the editor leads to accumulate new practices developed by the editor facing different situations with authors and reviewers. Figure 7 represents a possible evolution of the initial contextual graph given in Figure 4, always along the editor's viewpoint.

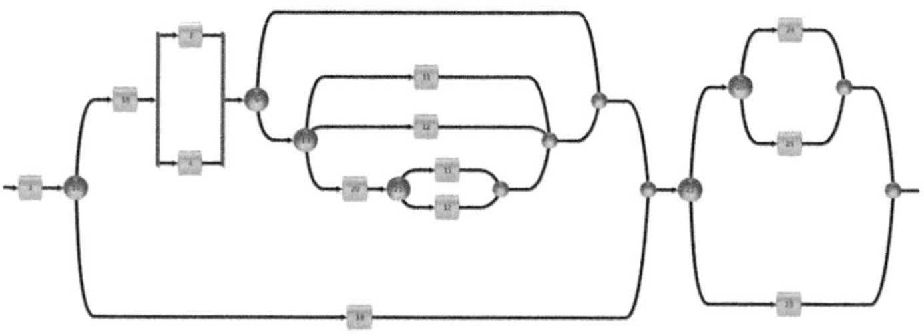

1: Receive a document
16: *Document_status*?
first submission
19: Find reviewers
2: Temporal Branching
Reviewer 1 3: Ask for review
Reviewer 2 4: Ask for review
9: *R_decision* conflict?
compatible evaluation
contradictory evaluation
10: Editor's choice?
Act as a reviewer 11: Make decision alone
external review 12: Ask for a third reviewer
join reviewers 20: Ask for an agreement
21: Editor's choice?
Act as a reviewer 11: Make decision alone
external review 12: Ask for a third reviewer
revised version 18: Compare requested and made changes
22: Editor's decision?
not accepted 26: *Changes*?
Possible 24: Ask author for changes
re-writing 25: Notify rejection
accepted 23: Send document to publisher

Fig. 7. Contextual graph of the editor's activity (extended version of Figure 4)

5 Cooperation Modeling for SWF Building

5.1 Making Shared Context Explicit for Describing SWF Interaction

The role played by an activity in a contextual graph concerns: (1) A part of the main task that actors find in different contextual graphs, or in the same contextual graph but on different paths; (2) The task of an actor is a subtask in the task of another actor; and (3) Two actors interact collaboratively in a problem solving, each having his own task and objectives, and need to interact punctually with the other to progress in his task execution. The same activity can appear on several paths of a contextual graph. We call occurrences the different copies of the activity (e.g. "Ask review" appears twice in Figure 7). An occurrence corresponds to the contextualization of the activity in a given context (the proceduralized context). For example, the editor can ask two reviewers to review a submission. Figure 8 gives a representation of a reviewer's task in the running example that must be combined with the editor's task presented in Figure 7 (supposing that the action "Ask to review" correspond to an activity).

The two contextual graphs share three contextual elements, namely Document_status, Changes and R_decision (contextual elements are in italics in Figures 7 and 8). Document_status is instantiated in the contextual graph representing author's activity (not given in this paper). The instantiation of the contextual elements R_decision and Changes are made in the reviewer's contextual graph (Figure 8) and used in the editor's contextual graph (Figure 7). We discuss this point in the next section.

The contextual graph representing a task realization is applied in a context containing all the contextual elements appearing in the contextual graph. These contextual elements have known values. For example, "Document_value" has the values "1st submission" and "revised version". When the task execution starts, all the contextual elements are instantiated to one value. For example, the instantiation of the contextual element "Document_value" corresponds to the selection of "1st submission" or "Rvised version". Otherwise, the instance will be ask to the actor or obtain as explained in Figure 8.

When we deal with two tasks, contextual graphs representing them are considered in their own contexts. The two contexts may be independent (there is no contextual element appearing simultaneously in the two contexts), but more generally, if the tasks are interdependent as discussed here (e.g. reviewer's activity ascribed in editor's activity), their contexts have a non empty intersection, either they share some contextual elements or one context may be included in the context of the other. In the running example, the shared context is composed of the three contextual elements Document_status, Changes and R_decision (as shown in Figures 7 and 8). The shared context contains all contextual elements that belong to both contextual graphs representing actors's tasks. These contextual elements often are instantiated by one actor and used by the other. Instantiation of such a shared contextual element plays a role of synchronization between different parts of a (global) task realization. For example, the editor makes a decision on the submission only once he gets the two (compatible) reviews. This is a way to represent a cooperation between different actors.

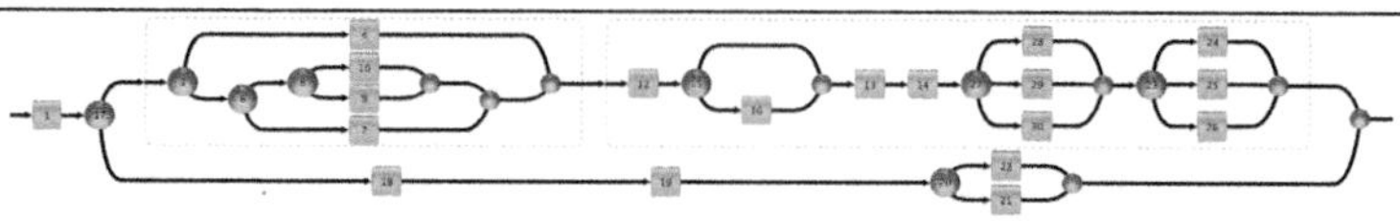

1: Receive a request
17: *Document_status*?
1st submission
2: Acceptance
Branch 3: Is subject interesting?
Yes 4: Accept
No 6: Can I refuse?
No 8: Time for reviewing?
Yes 10: Accept
No 9: Refuse
Yes 7: Refuse
11: Review process
12: Browse the paper for a general feeling
15: Authors known?
yes
no 16: Find information on Web
13: Print the paper for analysis
14: read and comment the paper
27: Change evaluation?
Small 28: *Changes* : small
Important 29: *Changes* : important
total revision 30: *Changes* : re-writting
23: Decision?
Accept 24: *R_decision* : Accept
Changes 25: *R_decision* : Ask revision
Refuse 26: *R_decision* : Reject
Revised version 18: Retrieve comments made
19: Compare to changes in new version
20: Revision status?
Satisfying 22: *R_decision* : Accept
Insufficient 21: *R_decision* : Reject again

Fig. 8. Contextual graph of a reviewer's activity

5.2 Modeling Cooperation through Shared Context

In the framework of Contextual Graphs, the shared context is the medium of interaction. The next step is to analyze cooperation mechanisms through shared context management (we do not want to discuss here the difference between cooperation and collaboration). In the previous section, we point out that instantiation of shared contextual elements is a way to synchronize actors' tasks and, thus, actor cooperation. In the running example (see Figure 9), the editor will resume his activity once he will have received the reviewers' decisions.

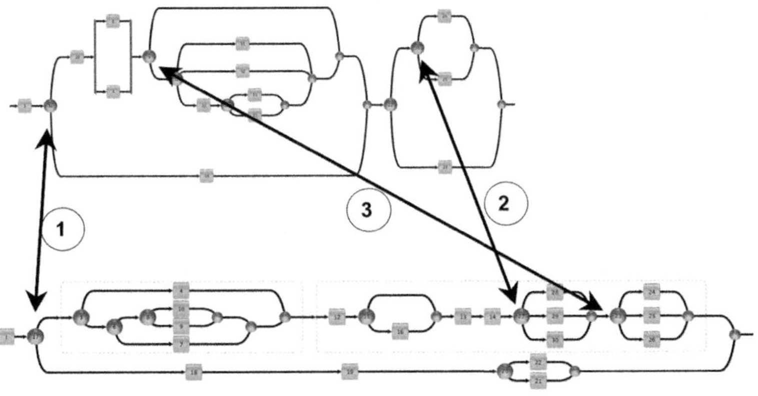

Fig. 9. Definition of the shared context between two actors' tasks

We also show that interaction between actors appears through the notion of activity in Contextual Graphs (through its occurrences). We identify three roles of activities in contextual graphs that correspond:

1. Interaction at the task level. Actors have independent tasks, but the realization of one task depends on the realization of the other task. This type of cooperation is limited to coordination of actors and of their tasks (e.g. editor's task and publisher's task).
2. Interaction at the actor level. An actor contributes to the task realization of another actor by an activity in the task realization of this actor. It is a weak cooperation because the goal belongs to a unique actor (e.g. the editor's task and the reviewer's task).
3. Interaction at the team level. Suppose that actors are in a team, the focus is on the team task. In this type of collaboration, the shared context must be the larger as possible and updated very frequently by all the team members. This is a strong cooperation because even the focus is on an actor, other actors must coordinated themselves according to the actor "in the focus". It is the situation of the tasks of the editor, of the reviewers and of the publisher with respect to a focus on maintaining a high quality of the journal at a strategic level.

For summing up, an effective cooperation supposes that actors share contextual elements and update frequently contextual elements they share, i.e. maintain their shared context updated. The more a shared context will contain contextual elements, the more the cooperation will be efficient. The more the shared context is large and regularly updated, the more the team is an efficient and powerful unit in its environment.

There is also an indirect cooperation when practices of different actors accomplishing the same task are stored in the same contextual graph. Any new actor using the contextual graph will benefit of the experience accumulated by all the actors in a logic of use far from the initial logic of functioning. Here, there is more a sharing of experience than of context.

6 Conclusion

Gil (2008) claimed that a related and important area of future research building on the knowledge level is learning from workflow usage in order to improve and adapt the behavior of the workflow system. Rather than expecting users to define reusable templates by hand, a system could learn reusable workflow templates from observing regularities and generalizing traces of workflows executed by a community of users. This paper makes a parallel between Scientific Workflow (SWF) management and practice management. Practices are efficient contextualization of a procedure in specific contexts, like SWF are successful workflows in specific contexts. A major difference is that practices are organized in structures called contextual graphs while SWFs are introduced in a repository in a flat way. We address in this paper the challenge of structuring SWF repositories through Contextual Graphs in a similar way to practices. We propose for that the notion of contextual graph to define SWF in repositories.

A first result is a change for a actor-oriented view that is deeper than the document- or activity view. A second result is a more efficient management of SWFs, thanks to an effective process of contextualization (extraction of a SWF), decontextualization (establishment of a SWF model) and recontextualization (generation of SWF instances). A third result is the proposal of a context-dependent three-step approach of SWF management, that is, an editor's task modeling, an automatic generation of related SWFs for repositories, and the development of a SWF shell in which compilation and execution of SWFs are intertwined. A fourth result concerns the explicit representation of SWFs based on the notion of occurrences of an item that are contexualized version of the item in a contextual graph.

Thus, a SWF repository can be structured by contextual graphs and such a repository will become a “base of experiences”, when usual SWF repositories behaves more as “case-based reasoning system” up to now. This leads to expressive "structured workflow graphs" more at a level closer to actors than formal approaches. Beyond these three approaches, the Contextual-Graphs representation addresses some problems like the lack of flexibility of workflows and the description of the cooperative realization of a task.

References

Brézillon, P.: Task-realization models in contextual graphs. In: Dey, A.K., Kokinov, B., Leake, D.B., Turner, R. (eds.) CONTEXT 2005. LNCS (LNAI), vol. 3554, pp. 55–68. Springer, Heidelberg (2005)

Brézillon, P.: Context modeling: Task model and practice model. In: Kokinov, B., Richardson, D.C., Roth-Berghofer, T.R., Vieu, L. (eds.) CONTEXT 2007. LNCS (LNAI), vol. 4635, pp. 122–135. Springer, Heidelberg (2007)

Brézillon, P., Pomerol, C.-J.: Framing decision making at two levels. In: Respicio, A., Adam, F., Phillips-Wren, G., Teixeira, C., Telhada, J. (eds.) Bridging the Socio-Technica Gap in Decision Support Systems. Challenges for the next Decade, pp. 358–368. IOS Press, Amsterdam (2010)

Georgakopolous, D., Hornick, R.: An Overview of Workflow Management: From Process Modeling to Workflow Automation Infrastructure. Distributesd and Parallel Databases 3, 119–153 (1995)

Gil, Y.: From Data to Knowledge to Discoveries: Scientific Workflows and Artificial Intelligence. Scientific Programming 16(4) (2008)

Huth, C., Erdmann, I.,Nastansky, L.: GroupProcess: Using Process Knowledge from the Participative Design and Practical Operation of ad hoc Processes for the Design of Structured Workflows. In: Hawaii International Conference on System Sciences, 34th Annual Hawaii International Conference on System Sciences (HICSS-34), vol. 9, p. 9041 (2001)

Joost, R.: Feasibility study on a graphical workflow editor based on the workflow management system "AlphaFlow". Ph.D. Thesis, University of Applied Sciences, Köthen, Anhalt (2006)

Pomerol, J.-C., Brézillon, P., Pasquier, L.: Operational knowledge representation for practical decision making. Journal of Management Information Systems 18(4), 101–116 (2002)

Rosemann, M., Recker, J.: Context-aware Process Design: Exploring the Extrinsic Drivers for Process Flexibility. In: Regev, G., Soffer, P., Schmidt, R. (eds.) Proceedings of the CAISE*06 Workshop on Business Process Modelling, Development, and Support BPMDS 2006, Luxemburg, June 5-9 (2007); 2006 CEUR Workshop Proceedings 236 CEUR-WS.org 2007

Schonenberg, M.H., Mans, R.S., Russell, N.C., Mulyar, N.A., van der Aalst, W.M.P.: Process flexibility: A survey of contemporary approaches. In: Dietz, J., Albani, A., Barjis, J. (eds.) Advances in Enterprise Engineering I. LNBIP, vol. 10, pp. 16–30 (2008)

van Elst, L., Aschoff, F.-R., Bernardi, A., Maus, H., Sven Schwarz, S.: Weakly-structured workflows for knowledge-intensive tasks: An experimental evaluation. In: 12th IEEE International Workshops on Enabling Technologies (WETICE 2003), Workshop on Knowledge Management for Distributed Agile Processes: Models, Techniques, and Infrastructure (KMDAP 2003) (2003)

Intelligible TinyOS Sensor Systems: Explanations for Embedded Software

Doina Bucur

Innovation Centre for Advanced Sensors and Sensor Systems (INCAS[3]), The Netherlands
doinabucur@incas3.eu

Abstract. As embedded sensing systems are central to developing pervasive, context-aware services, the applications running on these systems should be intelligible to system programmers and to users. Given that sensor systems are programmed in low-level languages, manually writing high-level explanations about their decision model requires knowledge about the system architecture, and is error-prone. We explore the possibility of extracting explanations which are small and expressive, but still preserve bit-level accuracy when needed. We contribute a tool which automatically and soundly generates compact, graphical explanations from sensor software implementation at compile-time. We base our algorithm on the techniques of (i) finite-state machine model extraction from software as used in model checking, and (ii) abstraction of program execution traces. We experiment with extracting explanations from heavyweight, low-level TinyOS applications for a mainstream sensor platform.

1 Introduction

Embedded sensor applications are inherently *context aware*; like other pervasive systems (surveyed in [1]), they most often implement a deterministic *rule-based decision logic* to trigger an output actuation out of a set of input events from the environment. For example, the classical TinyOS [2,3] sensor application signals its state on LEDs, and outputs a network message every set number of samples read from an on-board sensor. The control flow of such an application consists of a main thread and a set of *event handlers* to which context may be switched to at any time (i.e., a timer has fired, a new sensor sample is available, a network message has finished sending); the main thread and each event handler are implemented essentially as a series of `if/else` statements.

On the other hand, the programming of these sensor applications is done close to the hardware; programmers of microcontroller compiler suites avoid higher-level languages, since C is as an inherently powerful and efficient system programming language. A natural consequence is that this efficiency in programming limits expressivity and consequently *intelligibility* of the resulting application. This last fact explains why embedded software engineering is still in the domain of professional programmers; intuitive programming abstractions

M. Beigl et al. (Eds.): CONTEXT 2011, LNAI 6967, pp. 54–66, 2011.

and middleware [4] for embedded systems are still in their infancy, and research on *end-user software engineering* [5] for embedded systems is yet to develop.

To partly reconcile the need for high-level intelligibility with the low-level programming of embedded context-aware applications, one needs tools for software analysis which would automatically (i) document the program for users, and (ii) provide feedback to programmers, either during or post-development. Such tools may, e.g., automatize the task of collecting relevant information about the program logic from program source, for the purpose of program maintenance (as motivated by [6]). In particular, these analysis tools should automatically extract *explanations* about the context-awareness decision logic, with explanation types as categorized by e.g. [7,1]. We focus on this latter task.

We make the technical distinction between extracting explanations about the program context-aware behaviour either statically (i.e., offline at compile-time, from program source), or at runtime (i.e., during the sensor application's execution, in the field). Given their definition, some of the explanation types from [7,1] suit mostly a static approach, e.g.: 'What are the environmental *Inputs* to this system?', 'What are the *Outputs*?, '*How to* drive this system into reaching this Output?', and '*What* would the Output be *if* this were the Input?'. On the other hand, other explanation types suit a runtime approach (e.g., '*What* is the current state of the system?'), and the rest a combination. In this, we look at the static approach, and at extracting the four corresponding explanation types.

Our contribution. We show that program analysis algorithms and tools from the field of *software model checking*[1] are a solution to the problem of automatically and soundly generating explanations of context-aware behaviour from TinyOS application source. Our tool chain, *TOSExp*, takes as input a TinyOS application and information about the sensor platform, and:

- Generates *Input* and *Output* explanations [7], i.e., (i) that set of external events the application takes as inputs, and (ii) which system interfaces are used to output signals, respectively.
- Generates compact *What if* and *How to* explanations [7], i.e., state machines showing an abstracted model of program logic: the model shows (i) *what* happens in the logic *if* certain *Input* values are imposed, and (ii) *how to* reach certain *Output* values without dictating the *Inputs*.

The former is done through an inspection of the program for (a) functions which are registered as event handlers[2]—these point directly to the input events, and (b) those microcontroller peripherals[3] which are written by the application—these point to the program's outputs. For the latter, we make use of a tool suite

[1] Software model checking is also known as *formal software verification*.

[2] In operating systems, event or interrupt handlers are functions whose execution is triggered by an hardware interrupt. At the occurrence of an *interrupt request* (IRQ), the microprocessor switches context to the interrupt handler.

[3] Embedded systems are built around a microcontroller: a chip integrating a microprocessor, RAM memory and registers, and input/output ports. The latter are used to read from or command system components (on-board sensors or actuators) external to the microcontroller.

composed of: (i) a language translator from embedded C to ANSI-C from the previous TOS2CProver (TinyOS to CProver) tool [8], together with (ii) CBMC (C Bounded Model Checker) [9], a state-of-the-art verification tool for ANSI-C programs, from the CProver suite [10]. Embedded TinyOS applications are translated to ANSI-C by TOS2CProver, and *Input* values to the application may be specified. A *predicate* over the state of a program *Output* serves as a specification, and both program and specification are inputted to CBMC. The counterexample offered by CBMC is abstracted into a compact model of how input states lead to output states. We experiment with generating these types of explanations over standard TinyOS applications programmed in embedded C, as built from the nesC [11] source code by the TinyOS compiler; we include applications built for the mainstream TelosB [12] sensor platform.

In summary. In what follows, Section 2 gives background information on sensor platforms, embedded software, and on formal analysis techniques for C programs. Section 3 presents our algorithms, with a focus on generating *What if* and *How to* explanations, and exemplifies experimental results. Sections 4 and 5 overview related work and conclude, respectively.

2 Background: Sensor Platforms, Embedded Software, and Predicate Abstraction for C

2.1 Sensor Platforms and Embedded Software

A variety of platforms exist for wireless sensor nodes; TelosB [12] includes a MSP430 microcontroller [13], whose *input/output pins* connect to the on-board three LEDs, five sensors (some indirectly, through an analog-to-digital converter), and the radio and wired serial communication interfaces. These pins are mapped to registers, which form *peripheral ports*—e.g., microcontroller pins 48 to 50 connect to the three on-board LEDs, and are mapped to three bits in a register of peripheral port 5, P5OUT.

The software can access these peripherals by direct memory access; all on-board memory, including these ports, are mapped into a unique address space, with peripherals at low addresses, `0x10` to `0xFF`. Thus, for the case of software written in embedded C for the MSP compiler, `msp430-gcc` [14], the assignment `0x31 ^= 0x01 << 6;` toggles the yellow LED; this is because P5OUT resides at address `0x31` on this example microcontroller.

Finally, a C function declared with `__attribute((interrupt(..)))` is an interrupt handler. E.g., function `sig_ADC_VECTOR` is executed when a new sensor sample from the analog-to-digital converter is available.

2.2 TinyOS

For a complex embedded system such as TelosB, a programmer will program the microcontroller not in embedded C, but in a higher-level C dialect for a sensor operating system. For the mainstream TinyOS [2,3], the application is written in component-based *network embedded systems C*, nesC [15], as is the operating system itself. NesC is a more structured, I/O-centric, dialect of C, without memory allocation. Many system calls in TinyOS (e.g., sampling a sensor) are non-blocking; their completion is signalled to the application by an interrupt, whose handler may further post *tasks* to a *task queue* for further execution. Event handlers run with highest priority and may preempt tasks, which execute most of the program logic.

For an application, nesC components are wired together by the nesC compiler to form an OS-wide program; nesC is in fact designed under the expectation that a final, inlined embedded C program will be generated from all the necessary OS components. It is this inlined, OS-wide program for the TelosB platform that we analyze in this contribution.

2.3 Model Extraction from Software

Program analysis tools (such as model checkers) start by automatically extracting a mathematical *model* from the program given in input; this is essentially a nondeterministic finite-state machine consisting of a set of *states* and a set of *transitions* defined by a transition relation[4].

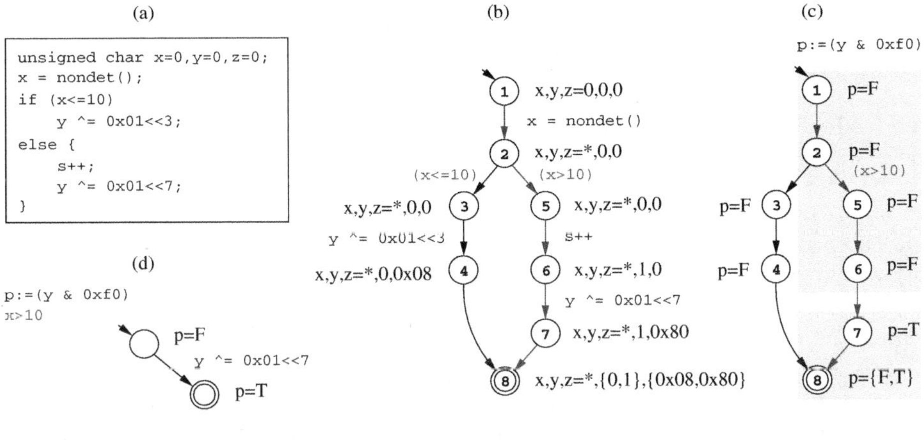

Fig. 1. Program fragment (a) with a bit-accurate model in (b). States are labelled with a valuation of the program's variables: in (b) state 7, **x** has a random value, **s** is 1, and **y** is 0x80; in (c) state 7, predicate **p** is true. Edges are labelled with corresponding C statements and conditions. (c) shows the truth values of the predicate **p** over the model's states, and (d) abstracts only that trace in whose final state **p** is true.

In the particular case of software model checkers, the state of the program is defined as the valuation of the program's variables, while a transition corresponds

[4] Allowing for nondeterminism in models of software is particularly relevant for the case of embedded software, in which inputs are assigned unknown values from the environment.

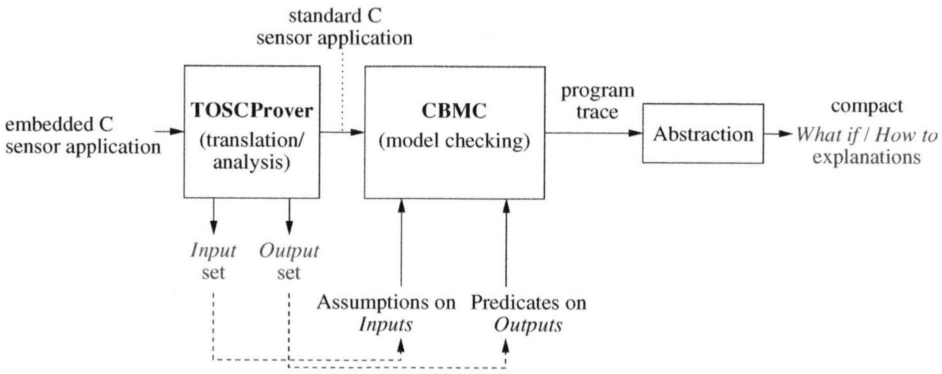

Fig. 2. The TOSExp tool chain. TOSCProver [8] analyses the sensor application for *Inputs* and *Outputs*, and further translates the program for use with CBMC. In order to obtain a *How to* explanation, we leave the *Inputs* nondeterministic; for *What if* explanations, the *Inputs* are given explicit values. Then, for both explanation types, we write a predicate over the values of *Outputs*, and run CBMC. The result is a program trace of input-output execution, which is finally abstracted into a compact form.

to one basic program assignment. An example is given in Fig. 1(b); it models the C fragment from Fig. 1(a). We use this state-machine syntax as the syntax for our explanations in what follows.

2.4 Model Checking and Abstraction

Model checking is a technique for exploring the states in a mathematical model for conformance to a given specification. Take again the example in Fig. 1(b) and the predicate `p := (y & 0xf0)` as a specification; a model checker (such as [9]) would return, as proof that the program can reach a final state in which `p` is true, the program trace including the `x>10` branch and excluding the `x<=10` branch, as in Fig. 1(c).

It is such program traces that allow us to extract *What if* and *How to* program explanations in what follows. A final step consists in *abstracting* the program trace for readability: by only tracking the change in value of relevant program variables, and removing other variables altogether from the model (as in Fig. 1(d)), a compact program model is possible.

3 TOSExp: TinyOS Explained

Fig. 2 overviews our program-analysis technique. TOSExp is based on our previous program translation and analysis tool, TOS2CProver [8], together with a C software model checker, CBMC [9].

An inlined, TinyOS-wide embedded C sensor application (as overviewed in the background Subsections 2.1 and 2.2) serves as input to the tool chain. In the following, we experiment on demonstrative applications provided with TinyOS;

Blink is a simple system-testing application which repeatedly toggles the state of the three on-board LEDs, with each toggle triggered by a timer alarm. *Sense* samples an on-board sensor, and displays part of the reading on the LEDs.

3.1 *Input* and *Output* Explanations

In order to obtain the sets of *Inputs*, the sensor application is searched by TOS2CProver for the set of functions registered as interrupt handlers; it is this which provides the *Input* set. For *Blink*, the only functional interrupt handler is `sig_TIMERB0_VECTOR`; this gives that the *Input* set is simply $\{\text{time}\}$. For *Sense* and *Oscilloscope*, the *Input* sets are $\{\text{sensors}, \text{time}\}$ and $\{\text{sensors}, \text{time}, \text{network}\}$, respectively. A dedicated hardware interrupt also exists to announce the software about a completed network send operation; thus, it is determined that the network is also an *Output* for *Oscilloscope*.

An application's other *Outputs* are also discerned through a TOS2CProver analysis step: out of all output peripheral registers characteristic to the TelosB platform, only some will be *assigned* values by the application, in the course of its execution after its booting and initialization phase. The three on-board LEDs are *Outputs* for *Sense* and *Blink*, as the three LED-controlling bits (bits 4, 5 and 6) [12,13] in the 8-bit peripheral register P5OUT are modified by the program following an input timer event or an event signalling the sampling of a sensor. The same reasoning would hold if the sensor node had an on-board actuator, which would be managed by the software through another peripheral port. Thus, for *Blink, Sense* and *Oscilloscope*, the *Output* sets are $\{\text{LEDs}\}$, $\{\text{LEDs}\}$ and $\{\text{LEDs}, \text{network}\}$, respectively.

This analysis step is sound: whenever an application does have an certain *Input* or *Output*, it will be included in the relevant set. On the other hand, whether or not the application does implement logic which makes effective use of a particular *Input* can only be determined by a *How to* explanation.

3.2 *What if* and *How to* Explanations: Assigning the *Input*

For a *How to* explanation (which essentially asks how the application's environmental inputs could hypothetically be given values in order for the application to then reach a particular output), the *Inputs* are not assigned—it is the *Outputs* which are dictated values. Input values are left nondeterministic, and the model checker will explore traces leading from every possible input value to the particular, relevant output state. If such a program trace exists, it will return this trace as proof of *How to* application behaviour.

For a $\{\text{time}\}$ *Input*, nondeterminism means that the main program will be interrupted by timer events, with each timer event arriving at an unpredictable point in time (i.e., for any local time on the system itself). This is again a sound approach: as TinyOS is not a real-time operating system, scheduling the timer to fire an interrupt every half second will have a result which only approximates the desired behaviour. Technically, local system time is implemented by a clock-tick count stored in the 16-bit timer register; time is thus made nondeterministic by assigning an 'any value' to the timer register, and allowing the program to be explored as it unfolds from any initial value.

For a *What if* explanation, on the other hand, which asks what would the application do given particular environmental inputs, it is the *Inputs* which are assigned explicit values, and subsequently all reachable *Output* values (and traces to these) should be identified by our analysis—the solution to the latter is discussed in the next subsection. In what regards this assigning of explicit values to inputs, CBMC allows adding *assumption* statements in the C program; for a {sensor} *Input*, assigning a value to a sensor reading incoming from the analog-to-digital converter is done with a statement such as:

```
assume(ADC12MEM == {0x0001, [..]})
```

3.3 *What if* and *How to* Explanations: Predicates on the *Output*

In order to extract both types of explanations using a model checker, we write boolean predicates over output values. For example, to find '*How to* turn LED 1 on' or '*What if* an amount of time passes' application behaviour, predicate `p`:

```
(P5OUT & 0x10) == 0      /* i.e., LED1 is on */
```

checks the value of bit 4 in P5OUT: a value of 0 in this peripheral bit turns this LED on. Predicates may be composed of any number of such basic predicates as the one above, composed with logical operators such as *and* or *or*.

This solution is generally correct also for both explanation types in that, for any given output's (range of) values, a predicate can be written—this is because all outputs are program variables, and a variable in software for the MSP430 microcontroller we use is (i) finite, and more, (ii) up to 16 bits long. The solution is especially fit for 'short' outputs, such as this 1-bit LED control.

This predicate is added to the program source in the form of an assertion, `assert(p)`; this then serves as a program condition against which CBMC is able to explore the program for behaviour leading to states in which the predicate holds[5]. If the predicate, on the other hand, can never hold, CBMC returns with this result and without a program trace; this signals that an explanation for this input-output situation does not exist, i.e. the situation is not possible in this application.

3.4 Abstraction and Results: *What if / How to* Explanations of Application Logic

We give two *How to* explanations in Fig. 3; these pertain to the *Blink* application, for which *Input*={time} and *Output*={LEDs}.

[5] On a technical note, the predicates we describe are then *negated* for use with CBMC, as the model checking algorithm will search for program traces leading to a *violation* of any such predicate. In the remaining of this section, for readability, we present our predicates before negation.

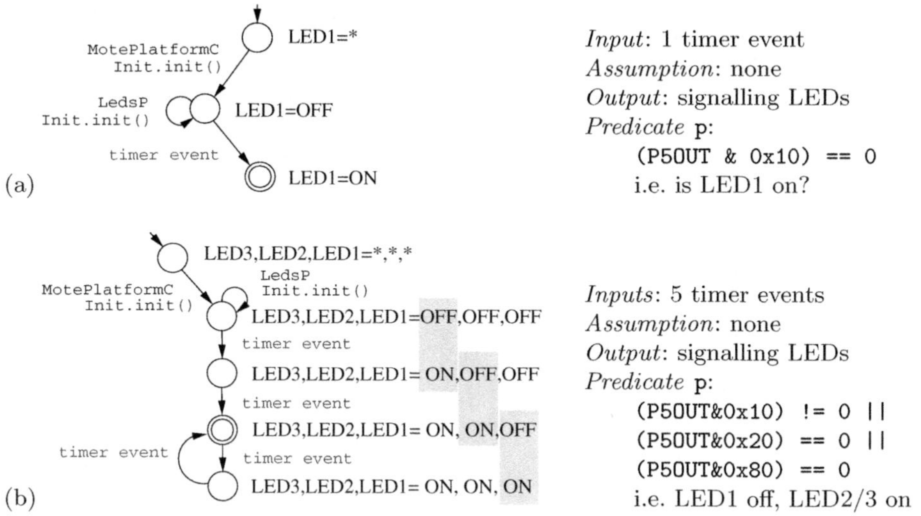

Fig. 3. *How to* explanations for *Blink*. In (a), the question posed is '*How to* have LED1 turned on?'. In (b), it is '*How to* have an off-on-on pattern on the three LEDs?'. For each example, we overview (on the right) the predicates used to generate the program trace, and we label the abstract states with valuations of the predicate (in (a)), and with valuations of each of the three subpredicates (in (b)). Edge labels are either input events (in red) or major internal program calls (in blue).

In Fig. 3(a), we ask: '*How to* have LED1 turned on?' i.e., including the boot process, system initialization, and main decision logic, what is the sequence of inputs leading to this LED state? For this, CBMC receives the program and the boolean predicate p asking whether LED1 is on, and returns one of the possible linear program execution traces leading to the desired state; initially, p has an unknown value, denoted by $*$. Similarly to the previous Fig. 1(b-d), we abstract the trace by organizing original states into fewer abstract states, one for each distinct value of a predicate, and present the result in the figure. We label the states with the corresponding predicate values, writing the predicate in full, for readability. We label the edges either simply with input events (highlighted in red), or also with adding checkpoints internal to the TinyOS implementation, which are relevant for programmers; for example, labelling an edge with the `Init.init()` interface command in the `LedsP` nesC component (in blue in the figure) signals that the LEDs are initialized at this point in the program.

To give an impression of the degree of compression in presenting this simple explanation, the *Blink* embedded source code is over 3000 lines of code; the program trace in this example contains 1192 states, which are abstracted into 3; the second abstract state subsumes almost 900 original program states.

Similarly, asking a slightly more complex question over how to obtain a particular lighting pattern on the three LEDs gives the answer from Fig. 3(b); for

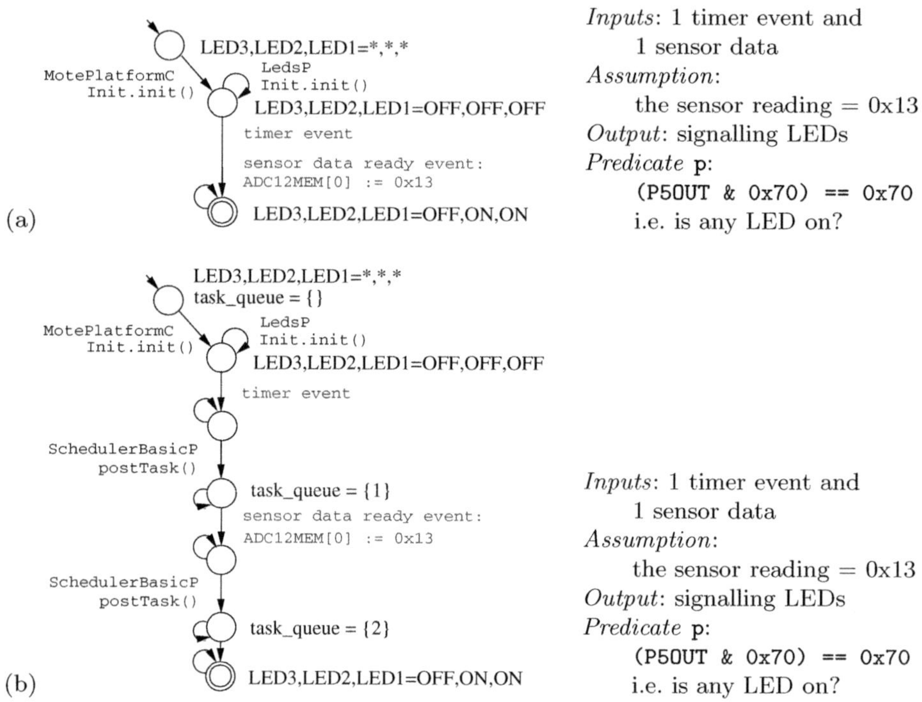

Fig. 4. *What if* explanations for *Sense*. In both (a) and (b), the question posed over *Sense* is '*What if* the voltage sensor reading would equal 0x13?'. An assumption over the ADC memory ADC12MEM implements this input value. The final state is determined by TOSExp to be an off-on-on LED pattern. In the explanation in (b), we allow more detail about the system's internal state, and thus include some of the values of the TinyOS scheduler's task queue (as in Subsection 2.2).

this, we label the states with individual truth values for each of the three sub-predicates in p. On a related note, an explanation to such *How to* questions may also *not exist*: asking TOSExp for the answer to the same question while allowing too few input events will return without a possible program execution trace.

Fig. 4 gives *What if* explanations for *Sense*; *Sense* has twice the number of *Blink* states. An assumption over the value of an incoming sensor reading is made, and the final output state depends on this: e.g., if we were assumed the data to be equal to 0x08 instead, the final state would be the existing state in which all LEDs are turned off.

3.5 Discussion: Efficiency and Limitations

Our technique does not suffer significantly from the expected efficiency issues related to the state-space explosion problem expected from model checking: all our CBMC runs terminate in under one minute. This efficiency is due to the fact that TOS2CProver already implements a sound state-space reduction technique, which we inherit in TOSExp.

However, a number of *limitations* remain for this approach to generating explanations. Specifically, a fair amount of knowledge on the internals of TinyOS is necessary for a programmer to experiment with generating new explanations; this, because both any assumptions on inputs and any predicate on outputs need to be written over low-level registers and peripherals, as seen in the examples above. This problem may be solved by also providing higher-level, pre-written templates for writing these assumptions and predicates.

Also, using bounded model checking as a program analysis method introduces one limitation in particular: with the method as is, it is difficult to recreate repetitive behaviour in the program—a program feature which may be of interest to programmers and users. This, because the method unwinds program loops of any size, effectively linearizing the explanation it extracts.

Furthermore, because our explanations are so precise to be bit-accurate and interrupt-accurate (as expected in the case of embedded systems, where precision of logic is key), when analysing large applications, a degree of user-friendliness in these models lacks: experimenting with input events which consist of a large number of repetitive interrupts (such as network events) crowds the model, and may require another degree of abstraction.

4 Related Work: Explaining Context-Aware Embedded Systems

4.1 Static Extraction of Explanations for Embedded Sensor Systems

The standard technique to explain a TinyOS application from source is with `nesdoc`, the documentation tool included in TinyOS. This documentation is targeted to the specialist programmer, as it only preserves the program structure (i.e. nesC components, their interfaces and wiring, as overviewed in Subsection 2.2). This cannot be a solution to the problem of extracting explanations of context-aware behaviour, as it does not document the program logic.

Similarly to TOSExp, *FSMGen* [16] extracts from the source code a visual, user-readable, high-level finite-state machine modelling part of the `nesC` program's logic. This is done with the aim of aiding the programmer's understanding of the program logic across the same OS-wide program source, and—while is uses symbolic execution as an analysis technique, it requires similar amount of time per analysis as TOSExp. The FSMGen models have a wider scope than our explanations, in that they represent all possible sequences of input transitions at once. However, unlike TOSExp, none of the inputs or outputs are quantified, a fact which precludes the extraction of the explanation types in [7]; the FSMGen models come closest to *How to* explanations.

Other program-analysis tools [17,18,19] for embedded sensor languages come from the validation and verification domain: they are designed to help the programmer detect if erroneous behaviour (e.g., standard programming errors such as memory violations) can arise in the application at compile-time, and provide a program trace (i.e., a *How to* explanation) of this behaviour. *T-Check* [17] and *KleeNet* [18] are based on model checking, testing, and symbolic execution; while, technically, the powerful analysis algorithms are eminently fitted to generate explanations out of program source (including at the level of a network of sensor nodes), they do not explicitly experiment with in this direction, or structure their program traces based on explanation types targeted at system users.

4.2 Explanations at Runtime

Runtime monitoring techniques for sensor systems, such as *Safe TinyOS* [20] and *NodeMD* [21] attempt to offer *What* and *Why* explanations to a user or programmer located remotely from the sensor testbed. SafeTinyOS is an extension of the `nesC` language and compiler, which enables the sensor node running the program to have its status monitored remotely in the event of an operational exception, i.e., to (wirelessly) send to a preprogrammed destination a compressed-status message explaining the state of the program wherever it is determined that the application has reached an 'unsafe' state. For remote testbeds, it is the monitoring safety more than of status which takes priority, thus these explanations do not cover the system's output state, but the system's internal state instead.

As argued in [22], it is important that the system explains itself also when nothing goes wrong; therein is where the tools above still lack.

4.3 Explanations for Other Context-Aware Systems

Tools such as the Intelligibility Toolkit [1], Enactor [23] or Panoramic [24] form the state of the art in explanation generators for rule-based, context-aware systems which are heavier-weight than our embedded sensor systems. Moreover, these tools are targeted at explaining the *inference of complex context* (such as the type of activity currently taking place involving devices, locations and people), instead of sensing-to-actuation program logic. The Intelligibility Toolkit thus covers a more extensive set of decision logics for context inferences and both static and runtime explanation types, yet has the single disadvantage that the application must be programmed using this toolkit in the first place—for embedded sensor systems, a domain in which high-level programming and macroprogramming are not yet mainstream and embedded C programming is the norm, the TOSExp approach in which the application itself needs no manual modification is more feasible.

5 Conclusions

In this contribution, we take the step of interfacing between (i) human-computer-interaction studies of *explaining* context-aware systems such as [7], and (ii) the area of embedded systems software analysis.

We experiment with automatically generating compact and readable input-to-output *Input, Output, What if* and *How to* explanations of rule-based sensor system logic, in a few degrees of detail, for sample TinyOS applications; these applications can thus be explained to users and programmers also in situations when the logic does not go wrong. We base our algorithm in known formal techniques for the extraction of mathematical models out of software, and model checking. TOSExp may make it easier for TinyOS programmers and the system's users to understand which behaviour the application can exhibit.

Besides addressing the current limitations of our algorithm (as overviewed in Section 3.5), future work includes user surveys to quantify the intelligibility of this style of explanations, and extending TOSExp to generate the remaining relevant types of explanations, e.g. *What, Why* and *Why not*; as these types require runtime generation, the difficulty resides less in the heavy-weight analysis, and more in efficiently instrumenting the application with status-logging mechanisms.

References

1. Lim, B.Y., Dey, A.K.: Toolkit to support intelligibility in context-aware applications. In: Proceedings of the 12th ACM International Conference on Ubiquitous Computing, Ubicomp 2010, pp. 13–22. ACM, New York (2010)
2. Hill, J., Szewczyk, R., Woo, A., Hollar, S., Culler, D., Pister, K.: System architecture directions for networked sensors. SIGPLAN Not. 35(11), 93–104 (2000)
3. Levis, P., Gay, D., Handziski, V., Hauer, J.H., Greenstein, B., Turon, M., Hui, J., Klues, K., Sharp, C., Szewczyk, R., Polastre, J., Buonadonna, P., Nachman, L., Tolle, G., Culler, D., Wolisz, A.: T2: A second generation OS for embedded sensor networks. Technical Report TKN-05-007, Technische Universität Berlin (2005)
4. Rubio, B., Diaz, M., Troya, J.M.: Programming approaches and challenges for wireless sensor networks. In: Proceedings of the Second International Conference on Systems and Networks Communications, ICSNC 2007, pp. 36–43. IEEE Computer Society, Washington, DC, USA (2007)
5. Ko, A.J., Abraham, R., Beckwith, L., Blackwell, A., Burnett, M., Erwig, M., Scaffidi, C., Lawrance, J., Lieberman, H., Myers, B., Rosson, M.B., Rothermel, G., Shaw, M., Wiedenbeck, S.: The state of the art in end user software engineering. Accepted for publication in ACM Computing Surveys (2011)
6. Ko, A.J., Myers, B.A., Coblenz, M.J., Aung, H.H.: An exploratory study of how developers seek, relate, and collect relevant information during software maintenance tasks. IEEE Trans. Softw. Eng. 32, 971–987 (2006)
7. Lim, B.Y., Dey, A.K.: Assessing demand for intelligibility in context-aware applications. In: Proceedings of the 11th International Conference on Ubiquitous Computing, Ubicomp 2009, pp. 195–204. ACM, New York (2009)
8. Bucur, D.: On Software Verification for Sensor Nodes. The Journal of Systems Software 84(10), 1693–1707 (2011)
9. Clarke, E., Kröning, D., Lerda, F.: A tool for checking ANSI-C programs. In: Jensen, K., Podelski, A. (eds.) TACAS 2004. LNCS, vol. 2988, pp. 168–176. Springer, Heidelberg (2004)
10. Kroening, D.: Formal verification (2010), `http://www.cprover.org/`

11. Gay, D., Levis, P., von Behren, R.: The nesC language: A holistic approach to networked embedded systems. In: ACM SIGPLAN Conference on Programming Language Design and Implementation (PLDI), pp. 1–11. ACM, New York (2003)
12. Moteiv Corporation: Telos. Ultra low power IEEE 802.15.4 compliant wireless sensor module. Revision B : Humidity, Light, and Temperature sensors with USB (2004), `http://www.moteiv.com`
13. Texas Instruments: MSP430x1xx family — user's guide (Rev.F) (2006), `www.ti.com.slau049f.pdf`
14. Underwood, S.: Mspgcc—A port of the GNU tools to the Texas Instruments MSP430 microcontrollers (2003), `http://mspgcc.sourceforge.net`
15. Gay, D., Levis, P., Culler, D.: Software design patterns for TinyOS. In: Proceedings of the ACM SIGPLAN/SIGBED Conference on languages, compilers, and tools for embedded systems (LCTES), pp. 40–49. ACM, New York (2005)
16. Kothari, N., Millstein, T., Govindan, R.: Deriving state machines from TinyOS programs using symbolic execution. In: Proceedings of the International Conference on Information Processing in Sensor Networks (IPSN), pp. 271–282. IEEE, Los Alamitos (2008)
17. Li, P., Regehr, J.: T-Check: bug finding for sensor networks. In: Proceedings of the 9th International Conference on Information Processing in Sensor Networks (IPSN), pp. 174–185. ACM, New York (2010)
18. Sasnauskas, R., Landsiedel, O., Alizai, M.H., Weise, C., Kowalewski, S., Wehrle, K.: KleeNet: discovering insidious interaction bugs in wireless sensor networks before deployment. In: Proceedings of the 9th International Conference on Information Processing in Sensor Networks (IPSN), pp. 186–196 (2010)
19. Mottola, L., Voigt, T., Österlind, F., Eriksson, J., Baresi, L., Ghezzi, C.: Anquiro: Enabling efficient static verification of sensor network software. In: Proceedings of Workshop on Software Engineering for Sensor Network Applications (SESENA) ICSE(2) (2010)
20. Cooprider, N., Archer, W., Eide, E., Gay, D., Regehr, J.: Efficient memory safety for TinyOS. In: Proceedings of the conference on Embedded Networked Sensor Systems (SenSys), pp. 205–218. ACM, New York (2007)
21. Krunic, V., Trumpler, E., Han, R.: NodeMD: Diagnosing node-level faults in remote wireless sensor systems. In: Proceedings of the International Conference on Mobile Systems, Applications and Services (MobiSys), pp. 43–56. ACM, New York (2007)
22. Kofod-Petersen, A., Cassens, J.: Explanations and context in ambient intelligent systems. In: Kokinov, B., Richardson, D.C., Roth-Berghofer, T.R., Vieu, L. (eds.) CONTEXT 2007. LNCS (LNAI), vol. 4635, pp. 303–316. Springer, Heidelberg (2007)
23. Dey, A.K., Newberger, A.: Support for context-aware intelligibility and control. In: Proceedings of the 27th International Conference on Human Factors in Computing Systems, CHI 2009, pp. 859–868. ACM, New York (2009)
24. Welbourne, E., Balazinska, M., Borriello, G., Fogarty, J.: Specification and verification of complex location events with panoramic. In: Floréen, P., Krüger, A., Spasojevic, M. (eds.) Pervasive Computing. LNCS, vol. 6030, pp. 57–75. Springer, Heidelberg (2010)

Business Context Information Manager: An Approach to Improve Information Systems

Hamdi Chaker[1], Max Chevalier[1], Chantal Soulé-Dupuy[1], and André Tricot[2]

[1] IRIT / D2S2u
Université Paul Sabatier Toulouse, France
[2] Cognition, Langage, Langue, Ergonomie (CLLE)
Université de Toulouse Le Mirail Toulouse, France
{Hamdi.Chaker,Max.Chevalier,Chantal.Soule-Dupuy}@irit.fr,
Andre.tricot@Toulouse.IUFM.fr

Abstract. In this paper we present a *business context information manager* based on a novel and generic interpretation of the context. This manager takes into account various contextual dimensions and acts as an intermediary between information system and contextual information. First, we discuss how the manager creates a snapshot of the context that is provided to the information system for different purposes. Then, we introduce a process (MES) that manages the various contextual dimensions using a rule set to create a unique situation at a moment *t*. These rules are part of the knowledge hold by the context manager. The situation inference is particularly related to the interactions between contextual dimensions. Thus the knowledge can evolve owing to an extracting and learning process which improves the context manager reliability.

Keywords: Contextual information, Context interpretation, Context information manager, Situation.

1 Introduction

Researches proposed a huge number of approaches to manage the context but the problem remains the same. The proposed context definitions are too specific and do not consider all available contextual dimensions. Therefore, Bazire and Brézillon [1] present and study 150 different definitions of context from different fields and observe the difficulty of finding relevant definition satisfying in any disciplines. *Thus, having a generic approach of the context is a great challenge.* The main problem in previous work is that they consider which dimensions of the context can be important and then which ones can be taken into account. So there is no general consideration in the characterization and the use of the contextual dimensions which are always specific to application fields.

On the contrary, we consider that a context manager must be based on a generic definition of the notion of context in order to take into account all that can be qualified as contextual dimensions. In this direction, we propose an approach to manage context by enabling any Information System (IS) to have access to a snapshot

M. Beigl et al. (Eds.): CONTEXT 2011, LNAI 6967, pp. 67–70, 2011.

of the past and present context. In contrast to classical approaches, the proposed Business Context Information Manager (BCIM) is based on an original interpretation of the context which assumes that the context information is dependent on each other. That is to say, the BCIM particularly focuses on the analysis of the interactions between contextual dimensions. Our approach is based on a set of rules and a specific process called MES. This process aims at contextualizing the various contextual dimensions and creates a unique situation at a moment *t*. Another process introduced in this paper gains knowledge over time and then improves reliability of the manager.

2 Business Context Information Manager

2.1 Definitions

According to the interactional view of Dourish [2], the context influences activities and similarly different activities give rise to different contexts. Some relevant work underlines the fact that the context is relative to something in particular: the context of an action, background interactions, etc. [1]. In respect of the definition of context given by Dey [3], we define a situation as:

Definition. *A situation is a stable interpretation (snapshot) of the context of an object at a specific time t.*

Every situation is characterized by a set of information (cf. Dey definition) which is organized in *contextual dimensions* to describe the various complex elements (i.e. user, system, task, environment...) implied in the context. So, we define a contextual dimension as:

Definition. *A contextual dimension composing the context of an object describes an external element that may have an impact on this object.*

The contextual dimensions are not predefined a priori by the system. With regards to the user applications, the contextual dimensions and their contextual elements are selected in each situation.

In this paper we particularly focus on the dynamics of the interactions related to the context as underlined by Dourish [3]. Indeed, interactions exist between various contextual dimensions. For example, consider the following context for a specific information system composed of two contextual dimensions: user and task. The task dimension may have an interaction with the user dimension because this latter becomes stressed when he is performing it. That is to say, we cannot consider contextual dimensions independently within a situation. This makes reference to the **stability** property in the situation definition. Consequently before any situation generation we have to manage all the interactions between contextual elements of various contextual dimensions.

2.2 Concepts of Our Approach

The BCIM has to be generic as well as the generic definition of context given in the previous section. In other words, it must take into account various contextual dimensions. In the following, we illustrate the various concepts underlying our approach:

General Context = {Contextual Dimension}
Contextual Dimension = {Contextual Element}
Contextual Element = {Contextual Element} | {Name, Value, Constant, Belief}

A contextual dimension corresponds to a tree structure. Leaf nodes are characterized by their name, their value, a Boolean that indicates if the element can evolve (i.e. for the contextual dimension "User", an element "name" could be considered as constant unlike to an element "tiredness" that can evolve through situations). The belief value (real number) allows the context manager to gradually measure the accuracy of the value. Indeed, some changes can be done due to the interactions between contextual dimensions. So it is important to give to the information system the belief value relatively to the contextual element values.

Situation_t = {{Contextual Dimension_t}, Validity, {Actions}}

A situation at a moment *t* is a stable snapshot of the context. The validity (a Boolean) indicates if a situation is valid or not according to specific rules (called legal business rules). The set of actions contains those that have been realized by the user during this situation. To get a stable set of contextual dimensions at time t, a process is applied (described in next section: MES process): every contextual dimension is adapted according to the interactions it has with the other contextual dimensions in the General context. Such adaptation is repeated while interactions between contextual dimensions exist.

In our approach, the proposed BCIM relies on a set of rules related to these interactions between contextual dimensions. To extract this knowledge and reuse it in an effective way, we decided to use ***association rules***.

2.3 Overall Architecture of BCIM

In this section we introduce the overall architecture of our context manager with particular regard on MES and the extracting rules process. As illustrated by (Fig 1), BCIM takes into account all that can be qualified as contextual.

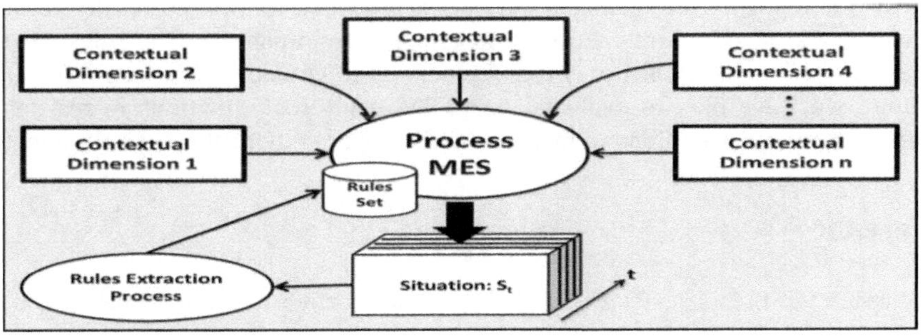

Fig. 1. The overall architecture of the context manager

The BCIM has four main purposes related to context management that are important for context-aware IS. First, the BCIM Checks the situations validity using a specific kind of rules (legal business rules). It also addresses the lack of information in the situations and anticipates actions. Finally, it provides the contextual elements to IS.

MES Process
For the effectiveness of any IS based on our context manager, it is essential for all contextual dimensions to be adapted and confronted to each other. The goal is to get the best possible situation. To achieve the adaptation of one dimension, depending on the others, the MES process uses the rules to describe the various transformations to be applied. MES initiates an adaptation cycle that respects our context definition and its originality. Indeed, the situation stability gives rise to the dynamic interaction between contextual elements we wanted to reach. Every dimension is adapted by the use of all other dimensions. We therefore emphasize that the construction of a situation is a recursive process. Indeed, we cannot consider each dimension of a context separately. Thus, these rules are applied successively on the dimensions until a stability point of the context at a moment *t* is found; that is what we call situation. A stable situation can arise from large number of iterations (the stability process).

Rules Extraction Process
The BCIM must be able to evolve over time. In other words, the set of rules used by the MES process should grow to enhance contextual information accuracy. For this purpose, we propose rules extraction process based on past situations because they contain information about what happens in practice. For the BCIM, the rules extraction process is based on the classical association rules extraction methods. It is important to notice that this process concentrates only on valid situations.

3 Conclusion

In this paper, we first introduced a novel interpretation of the context that considers any modelled and valuated contextual dimension. This interpretation is original because it focuses on the dynamics between all these contextual dimensions rather than how information is represented. We defined a BCIM based on this interpretation of context, i.e. the manager takes into account these contextual dimensions and the dynamics of the relations between them. In this work, we mainly present the two processes composing the manager. The MES process exploits the BCIM knowledge to manage the possible interactions and creates the situations. The rules extraction process, improves the BCIM over time by making it gain new knowledge. As a matter of future work we plan to evaluate the BCIM using real situations in real business context. Moreover, we intend to integrate and compare other rules extraction methods.

References

1. Bazire, M., Brézillon, P.: Understanding context before using it. Modeling and Using Context, 29–40 (2005)
2. Dourish, P.: What we talk about when we talk about context. Personal Ubiquitous Comput. 8, 19–30 (2004)
3. Dey, A.K., Abowd, G.D., Salber, D.: A conceptual framework and a toolkit for supporting the rapid prototyping of context-aware applications. Human-Computer Interaction 16, 97–166 (2001)

Communicative Inferences and Context of Interests

Marco Cruciani

University of Trento, via Inama 5
38213 Trento, Italy
cruciani@disi.unitn.it

Abstract. The paper examines the determination of the explicit content of communication via inferential processes based on the speakers' situational interests. The paper's argument is based on the hypothesis that the meaning of natural language expressions depends on the situational extra-linguistic interests of speakers. It is maintained that interests affect the sentences of natural language when semantic conventions, semantic context, and pragmatic context are unable to determine a unique meaning for a sentence. In particular, the paper addresses the question of the determination of meaning via inference where the speaker's interest is a premise for communicative inferences. The notion of interest is viewed as (preference for) a state of affairs which implies the possibility conditions of the agent's goal. The context of interests is viewed as the set of states of affairs that make a sentence true and contemporaneously satisfy the situational interests of the speaker. The last part of the paper illustrates a real-life case of linguistic dispute.

Keywords: Semantic underdeterminacy, semantic context, pragmatic context, context of interests, meaning in use, goal, communicative inference, linguistic dispute.

1 Introduction

The paper examined the determination of the explicit content of communication via inferential processes based on the speakers' situational interests. Generally, the inferential processes involved in real communications integrate linguistic knowledge (syntax and semantics) and factual knowledge (contexts) to obtain a unique proposition. The premises of these processes consist of the linguistic form of an expression, semantic conventions applied to the linguistic form, and shared knowledge about the situation in which an expression is used. The conclusion consists of the proposition explicitly expressed by a speaker with a sentence.

Various kinds of processes are involved in communication: for instance, the saturation of indexical expressions, where semantic context fixes the values of some contextual parameters; the selection of structural and semantic ambiguity, where pre-semantic use of context selects a plausible interpretation; the free enrichment of truth-conditions, where pragmatic context adds a part of semantic content to obtain an evaluable proposition; bridging, where pragmatic context fixes the causal and temporal relations between propositions, etc. (see [1]).

M. Beigl et al. (Eds.): CONTEXT 2011, LNAI 6967, pp. 71–81, 2011.

In particular, the paper focuses on the semantic and pragmatic context. Semantic context is composed of some objective elements of the situation of utterance and is used to decode only some problematic kinds of expressions: indexical and demonstrative expressions such as "I", "here", "now" and "this", "that", etc. (see [2])[1]; pronouns such as "she", "he", etc. (e.g. anaphoric use); cases of structural and lexical ambiguity (see [5])[2]; and verbal tense.[3] In semantics, truth conditions lie at the level of the objective context of utterance and conventional meaning (obtained by linguistic rules and semantic conventions). Pragmatists do not agree, and they argue that we need supplementary contextual information in order to fix truth conditions. This information consists of shared knowledge (encyclopaedic and local), the discourse or sentence in which an expression is used, and elements of the physical surroundings.[4] A technical distinction between information on the semantic context and information on the pragmatic context is that the former is made accessible by, and constrained to, linguistic form of expression, while the latter is made accessible by the speaker's communicative intentions and is not constrained to linguistic form.

The paper introduces the notion of 'meaning in use' based on the truth-conditional notion of meaning taken from analytic philosophy: that is, the meaning of a sentence identifies with its conditions of truth, and the meaning of an expression identifies with its contribution to the truth conditions of the sentence in which the expression appears [9]. The central notion of interest is taken from cognitive social theory: the agent's interest is viewed as (preference for) a state of affairs which implies the possibility conditions of an agent's goal (see [10]). Hence, as we shall see, the notion of meaning in use is based on the notion of state of affairs: on the one hand, the state of affairs provides the truth conditions of a sentence; on the other, it provides the possibility conditions of a speaker's goal.

The context of interests is viewed as the set of states of affairs which make a sentence true and contemporaneously satisfy the situational interests of the speakers. The context of interests differs from semantic context because the context of interests concerns non-linguistic knowledge not constrained to linguistic form like the pragmatic context. But the context of interests also differs from the pragmatic context because the latter refers to current or past situations, whereas the context of interests refers to states of affairs not yet established.

I have argued elsewhere in detail that interests affect the sentences of natural language when semantic conventions, semantic context, and pragmatic context are unable to determine a unique meaning (see [11], [12], [13], [14]). Instead, this paper specifically addresses the question of meaning determination via inferential processes, where the premises of inferences consist of non-linguistic knowledge available from the states of affairs that correspond to the speaker's situational interests.

---

[1] Kaplan [2] inaugurated a formal approach to semantic context in particular regard to indexical expressions. However Kaplan [3], when introducing the "directing intention", admits a 'cognitive turn' for the reference of demonstrative pronouns (see [4]).

[2] Perry [5] maintains that the context of use can have pre-semantic and post-semantic uses. In the former case, it intervenes before the semantic context assigns an interpretation (e.g. ambiguity); in the latter case, it intervenes after an interpretation has been made to determine the "speaker's meaning" (cf. [6]).

[3] On possessive expressions see Clark [7].

[4] On background of meaning see Searle [8].

2 Semantic Underdeterminacy and Contextual Dependence

This section briefly illustrates the phenomenon of semantic underdeterminacy and points out the necessity to use context to determine meaning. That it is necessary to consider non-linguistic knowledge to determine the meaning of a sentence is due to the fact that the conventional meaning (via syntax and semantics) underdetermines the proposition explicitly expressed by a sentence used by a speaker in a specific situation; that is to say, it is not possible via conventional meaning to determine a unique proposition for a sentence – this is so also for sentences without syntactic and semantic ambiguity and indexical expressions (*latu senso*) (cf. [8], [15], [16], [17]).

Consider the following sentences:

(1) "Sonia cuts the pie";
(2) "Sonia cuts the paper";
(3) "Sonia cuts the grass".

The verb "to cut" is not ambiguous, but the meaning of "to cut" in the three sentences is different. It possible to determine the meaning for each sentence considering non-linguistic sorts of knowledge: for example, encyclopaedic knowledge, that is, the ways in which we generally cut pies, paper and grass; or local knowledge, that is, the ways in which Sonia generally cuts pies, paper and grass; and also in general considering the discourse in which an expression is used and information from the physical surroundings. Hence the meaning depends on different (combinations of) contexts. Put differently, if we change the contextual coordinates, we obtain different plausible meanings.

Essentially in accordance with the pragmatic view, semantic underdeterminacy is a phenomenon that pervades all natural language. Hence, the meanings of all expressions depend on non-linguistic knowledge. But the question is this: how do we select relevant information? As we shall see, relevant information is individuated by the interests and goals of agents.

3 Meaning in Use

This section illustrates the notion of meaning in use as conceived here.

The notion of meaning in use for declarative sentences is founded on the relation between the states of affairs that make a sentence true and the speaker's preferences ordering in regard to the states of affairs that make the sentence true. A sentence can be true with respect to different sets of truth conditions, which correspond to different states of affairs (more technically, they correspond to sets of states of affairs). The state of affairs preferred by a speaker because it implies his/her goal provides the truth conditions which determine the meaning in use in the specific situation. From this perspective, the determination of meaning in use is viewed as a selection of a state of affairs which makes a sentence true (via truth conditions) and satisfies the agent's interest in situation

The schema in figure 1 illustrates the notion of meaning in use. At the bottom of the schema there is a sentence which, given a context of use (here semantic and pragmatic context), has some plausible interpretations. Each interpretation refers to a

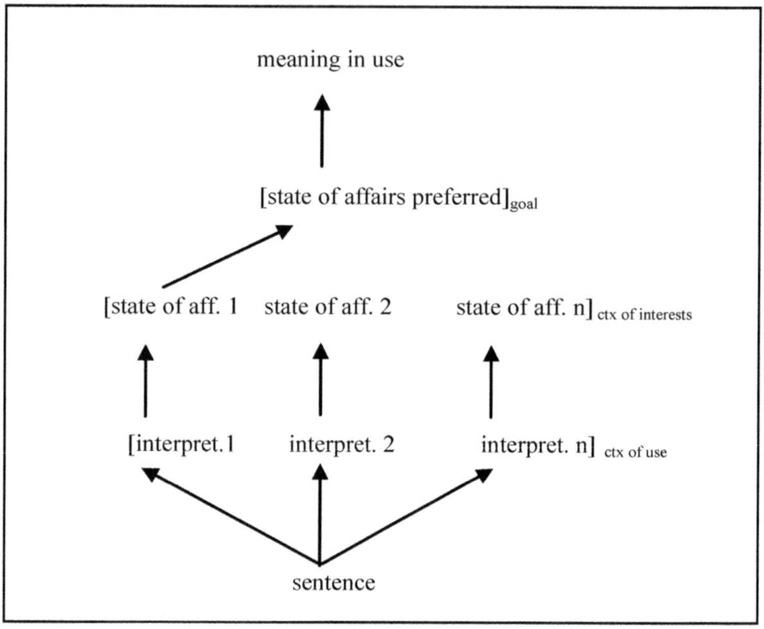

Fig. 1. Meaning in use

state of affairs which makes the sentence true: that is, it refers to specific truth conditions. The correspondence between the state of affairs preferred by a speaker and one of the states of affairs which make the sentence true determines the meaning in use. In other words, when the possibility conditions of the speaker's goal match the truth conditions of the sentence, we have meaning in use. I would stress that meaning in use concerns the explicit level of communication, that is, the truth-conditional level.

4 Explicit Communication

This section illustrates the relation between meaning and explicit content of communication and points out some pragmatic processes involved in communication.

The boundary of explicit communication and implicit communication – that is, "what is said" and "what is implicated" by a speaker with a sentence – is much debated. However, in the literature there is broad agreement on the implicit level of communication: generally, the speaker's meaning *à la* Grice is considered as "what is implicated" by a speaker (see [18]). Instead, there is no agreement on the explicit level of communication and the role of conventional meaning in fixing the proposition explicitly expressed by a sentence (see [19], [20], [21], [22], [23], [24], [25], [26], [27]).

At the explicit level of communication we have a complete proposition which is evaluable in truth-conditional terms. To determine the proposition explicitly expressed by a speaker (that is, a unique set of truth conditions), some inferential and associative processes are necessary (e.g. free enrichment, bridging, transfer, narrowing, broadening, etc.). When "what is said" (a unique proposition) is fixed with regard to the specific situation, conversational implicature and additional contextual information determine "what is implicated" by a speaker, determining another level of sense. This level of sense is not a truth-conditional level: that is, the implicit meaning of sentences does not depend on the truth conditions of those sentences. However, this paper is only concerned with the truth-conditional level of communication.

The following schema illustrates the relations among the levels of sense, pragmatic processes, and contexts in a 'standard' pragmatic view after Grice:

1. SENTENCE
   Semantic conventions and context
   - Saturation
   - Disambiguation
   - Verbal tense determination
2. CONVENTIONAL MEANING
   Pragmatic context
   - Free enrichment
   - Bridging
   - Transfer
3. EXPLICIT COMMUNICATION
   What is said, proposition, truth conditions
   - Implicature
4. IMPLICIT COMMUNICATION
   What is implicated

Not all pragmatists (relevant theorists, linguists and philosophers) agree on the logical and temporal sequence of these processes, on the relations between the explicit and implicit level, or on the role of context. For instance, relevant theory considers parallel processes (e.g. enrichment and implicature) and the explicit and implicit content of communication on the same temporal and logical planes (see [20]); linguistics considers a sequence of processes, and the explicit content is divided in two parts: minimal and maximal proposition. The minimal proposition is obtained via completion and depends on the semantic context; the maximal proposition is obtained via enrichment and depends on the pragmatic context; then the implicit content is eventually obtained via conversational implicature (see [24]); in philosophical contextualism, Recanati [22], [23] distinguishes primary (e.g. free enrichment) and secondary (e.g. implicature) processes: the former are considered associative processes and determine "what is said"; the latter are considered inferential processes and determine "what is implicated". However, this paper is concerned with the explicit level of communication ("what is said"), and I believe it plausible that the explicit content of communication has logical and temporal priority over the implicit content. I also maintain that it is obtained via inferential processes.

The following schema illustrates the relations and levels of sense, pragmatic processes and contexts as they are conceived here.

1. SENTENCE
   Semantic conventions and context

   - Saturation
   - Disambiguation
   - Determination verbal tense

2. CONVENTIONAL MEANING
   Context of interests

   - **Enrichment via interest**
   - Bridging
   - Transfer

3. EXPLICIT COMMUNICATION
   What is said, proposition, truth conditions

   - Implicature

4. IMPLICIT COMMUNICATION
   What is implicated

I would stress that the enrichment via interests is not free enrichment; rather, it is constrained to the states of affairs that satisfy the situational interests of the speakers. More precisely: the states of affairs that satisfy the interests of the speakers provide the conditions that make sentences true. These conditions are used in the premises of communicative inferences.

5 Communicative Inferences

This section illustrates the type of communicative inferences considered here: that is, non-demonstrative inferences – e.g. abduction (see [28]). They are structured as follows:

P_1: Form and semantic conventions
P_2: Contextual information

C: What is said

Consider the following sentence:

(4) "The bank is wet".

In (4) the meaning of the word "bank" is not determined; it can mean a financial institute or land alongside a river. In cases of this kind, non-linguistic context provides information with which to select a plausible interpretation. For example, on the one hand, if (4) is produced by a speaker close to an angler who is about to fish, then "bank" plausibly refers to the land alongside a river and (4) plausibly means that alongside the river there is high humidity; on the other hand, if the speaker is near to the doors of a financial institute, then the word "bank" plausibly refers to the institute and (4) plausibly means that the floor of the financial institute has just been washed. In both cases the non-linguistic information is directly perceived from physical surroundings (i.e. the angler and the financial institute). Hence, the meaning of (4) is obtained through an inference composed of two premises: sentence (4) (semantic conventions applied to the linguistic form) and the contextual information in which (4) is produced; the conclusion consists of a unique proposition. The two possible inferences are as follows:

P_1:"The bank is wet"
P_2: Direct perception of the financial institute

C:"The floor of the financial institute has just been washed".

P_1: "The bank is wet"
P_2: Direct perception of the fisherman

C: "There is high humidity alongside the river".

Consider (4) produced by a speaker close to angler about to fish: the word "wet" can refer to both high humidity and water on grass, rocks, etc. Here the form or the way in which water is on the bank is not determined. We need further information: for instance, yesterday it rained alongside the river (local knowledge); or generally there is high humidity alongside rivers (encyclopedic knowledge), to determine the ways in which there is water on the bank. The two possible inferences are as follows:

P_1: "The bank is wet"
P_2: Yesterday it rained alongside the river

C: "There is water on grass, etc. alongside the river".

P_1: "The bank is wet"
P_2: Generally there is high humidity alongside rivers

C: "There is high humidity alongside the river".

Consider the following sentence:

(5) "Frank is a graduate and works in a chemical laboratory".

(5) can be true both if Frank works in a laboratory because of his degree and if Frank works in a laboratory independently of his degree. If we consider only syntax and semantic conventions, we are not able to determine the truth-conditional level of (5). In cases of this kind, contextual information determines temporal and causal relations between propositions:

P_1: "Frank is a graduate and works in a chemical laboratory"
P_2: Frank's activities

C: "Frank works in a chemical laboratory because of his degree".

The inferential processes in (4) and (5) are respectively those of selection of ambiguity, enrichment of truth conditions, and bridging. In (4) we can infer an interpretation of the word "bank" on the basis of contextual information directly perceived from the physical surroundings, and consequently we can infer an interpretation of the word "wet" on the basis of local or encyclopedic knowledge. In (5) it is possible to determine a unique interpretation fixing the temporal or causal relation via local knowledge (i.e. Frank's activities): for instance, Frank took his degree in chemistry and six months ago was working in a shop. Here the information used is made available by the communicative intentions of the speaker and concerns shared local knowledge.

Finally, I would stress that the validity of inference does not depend on logical relations between premises; that is, it is not necessary for communication that the non-linguistic information used in the second premise be made available by, or constrained to, linguistic form of expression.[5]

6 A Real-Life Case

This section illustrates a case of a linguistic dispute which arose with regard to a contractual clause, and where semantic conventions and pragmatic context are unable to explain the determination of meaning. Consequently, the context of interests is taken into account. The clause runs as follows:

> In particular, it is understood that the employment relationship established with you will be resolved upon *cessation of the absence* of Miss Maria Rossi, and however not beyond 23 December 2005.[6]

The linguistic dispute arose with regard to the expression "cessation of the absence". This clause regulated the working conditions and hours of a recent graduate hired by an insurance company to substitute M.R. while she was on maternity leave. During the substitution period M.R. resigned and the employer terminated the graduate's employment on the grounds that the absence of M.R. had 'ceased', because M.R. no

---

[5] For instance, the saturation of indexical expressions requires a logical relation between premises: for example, the relation between "I" and the identity of the speaker in the sentence "I am here".

[6] In Italian the clause runs as follows: "In particolare resta inteso che il rapporto di lavoro con lei instaurato si risolverà alla *cessazione dell'assenza* della signora Maria Rossi e comunque non oltre il 23 dicembre 2005".

longer belonged to the company. The graduate argued that the clause referred to the absence of M.R. during maternity leave, not to her resignation.

We may use semantic conventions to determine the meaning of the expression. I have translated the definitions from Italian into English. The Italian De Mauro dictionary provides two possible interpretations for the word "cessation":

- a) termination;
- b) interruption, suspension.

It gives four possible interpretations for the word "absence":

- c) being away: *absence from work*;
- d) lack: *lack of air, lack of light, lack of gravity*;
- e) situation of uncertainty about a person's life subjected to a judicial decision: *declaration of absence*;
- f) temporary loss of consciousness: *in particular due to epilepsy, hysteria, intoxication.*[7]

We can interpret the expression "cessation of the absence" through different combinations (compositionality) of the various definitions of the single terms (e.g. the combinations *be* or *af*). But we are unable to determine a unique meaning for the expression because semantic items do not provide a criterion with which to choose one interpretation rather than another: they are on the same plane. How can we select which interpretation is plausible?

We can try to use the text of the clause to discern which interpretation is plausible, and in doing so we can coherently individuate the expression "interruption of absence from work" among the others because it is compatible with the situation under examination. But if we compare it with the interpretations of the two agents, we see that it is compatible with both of them. Here the pragmatic context does not sufficiently specify the truth-conditions with respect to the real situation.[8]

How is it possible to explain the linguistic behaviour of the company? It is possible by showing that the company's interest drove the determination of meaning: the company's interest before the controversy was effectively to hire the graduate; it is possible to state this because the company was not obligated to hire a substitute for M.R; it was obligated only to keep the job of M.R. after maternity leave. Hence the fact that the company wanted to dismiss the graduate when M.R. resigned shows that the company's interest changed because its goal changed. For instance the graduate's

---

[7] The Italian definitions are as follows: "Cessazione": a) il porre fine, l'aver termine; b) interruzione, sospensione. "Assenza": c) l'essere assente, lontano: *assenza dal lavoro; d)* mancanza: *assenza d'aria, di luce, di gravità; e)* situazione d'incertezza sull'esistenza in vita di una persona scomparsa da almeno due anni, sancita mediante sentenza del giudice: *dichiarazione d'assenza;* f) perdita momentanea della coscienza, spec. dovuta ad epilessia, ad isterismo, a forme d'intossicazione o ad eccessiva stanchezza.

[8] It is possible to refer to semantic and pragmatic context collapsed together in accordance with what Bouquet and Giunchiglia [29] called "context of work". A context of work is composed of the knowledge that an agent uses to resolve a problem (see [30], [31]). The question is this: which knowledge pertains to the context of work?

work was unsatisfactory and the director found somebody better than him. I point out the following question: if company's interest changes, then company's meaning will change. Hence knowing the variation of situational interests we can infer meaning in use in regard to the specific situation.

7 Conclusion

The aim of this paper has been to show the dependence of meaning on speakers' situational interests. The paper has proposed the notion of meaning in use based on the notions of truth conditions of sentences and possibility conditions of situational goals.

Meaning in use concerns the explicit level of communication: that is, it corresponds to the proposition explicitly expressed by a sentence (truth-conditional content) used by a speaker in a specific situation.

The pragmatic process of enrichment involved in explicit communication is considered an inferential process. In particular, the paper has proposed an inference where the first premise is a sentence and the second premise is the speaker's interest. The epistemological plausibility of the proposal is that the second premise is structured in terms of the possibility conditions of a goal, so that it is compatible with the notion of meaning as truth conditions. The cognitive plausibility of the proposal is that the inference does not depend on the logic of language, but on the psychology of individuals; that is, the inference is produced on the basis of shared knowledge between speaker and addressee which is not constrained to linguistic form.

Finally, I would stress that if we consider interests as premises, then the information used concerns future states of affairs not yet established and connected to the speaker's goals. In these terms, the determination of meaning in use in explicit communication is compatible with the view that the contextual variability of meaning is explained by the contextual variability of goals which agents intend to realize.

Acknowledgements. Special thanks to Sonia Guglielminetti for her valuable advice.

References

1. Bianchi, C.: Pragmatica cognitiva. I meccanismi della comunicazione, Laterza, Roma-Bari (2009)
2. Kaplan, D.: Demonstratives. An essay on semantics, logic, metaphysics, and epistemology of demonstratives and other indexicals. In: Almong, J., Perry, J., Wettstein, H. (eds.) Themes from Kaplan. Oxford University Press, Oxford (1977/1989)
3. Kaplan, D.: Afterthoughts. In: Almong, J., Perry, J., Wettstein, H. (eds.) Themes from Kaplan. Oxford University Press, Oxford (1989)
4. Bianchi, C.: Nobody loves me: quantification in context. Philosophical Studies 130(2), 377–397 (2006)
5. Perry, J.: Indexical and demonstratives. In: Hale, R., Wright, C. (eds.) Companion to the Philosophy of Language. Blackwell, Oxford (1997)
6. Bianchi, C.: Pragmatica del linguaggio, Laterza, Bari-Roma (2003)
7. Clark, H.H.: Arena's of Language. The University of Chicago Press, Chicago (1992)

8. Searle, J.: The Background of meaning. In: Searle, J., Kiefer, F., Bierwisch, M. (eds.) Speech Act Theory and Pragmatics. Reidel, Dordrecht (1980)
9. Tarski, A.: The semantic conception of truth and the foundation of semantics. Philosophical and Phenomenological Research 4, 341–356 (1944)
10. Conte, R., Castelfranchi, C.: Cognitive and Social Action. University College London, London (1995)
11. Cruciani, M.: On the notion of intended meaning. In: Ohlsson, S., Catrambone, R. (eds.) Proceedings of the 32th Annual Conference of the Cognitive Science Society, pp. 1028–1033. Cognitive Science Society, Austin (2010)
12. Cruciani, M.: Significato inteso, stati di cose e livello esplicito della comunicazione. Sistemi Intelligenti XXII 3, 505–513 (2010)
13. Cruciani, M.: Intended meaning and situational interest. In: Taatgen, N., van Rijn, H. (eds.) Proceedings of the 31th Annual Conference of the Cognitive Science Society, pp. 2747–2752. Cognitive Science Society, Austin (2009)
14. Cruciani, M.: Cono del linguaggio, negoziazione degli interessi e significato inteso di clausole contrattuali ambigue. Sistemi Intelligenti XXI 3, 473–488 (2009)
15. Travis, C.: Saying and Understanding. Blackwell, Oxford (1975)
16. Travis, C.: The True and False: The Domain of Pragmatics. Benjamins, Amsterdam (1981)
17. Searle, J.: Expression and Meaning. University Press Cambridge, Cambridge (1979)
18. Grice, P.: Studies The Way of Words. Cambridge University Press, Cambridge (1989)
19. Sperber, D., Wilson, D.: Relevance Theory: Communication and Cognition. Blackwell, Oxford (1986)
20. Carston, R.: Implicature, explicature and truth-theoretic semantics. In: Kempson, R. (ed.) Mental Representations. Interface Between Language and Reality. Cambridge University Press, Cambridge (1988)
21. Carston, R.: Linguistic meaning, communicated meaning and cognitive pragmatics. Mind and Language 17(1-2), 127–148 (2002)
22. Recanati, F.: The pragmatics of what is said. Mind Language 4(4), 207–232 (1989)
23. Recanati, F.: Direct Reference: From Language to Thought. Blackwell, Oxford (1993)
24. Bach, K.: Conversational impliciture. Mind Language 9(2), 124–162 (1994)
25. Travis, C.: Pragmatics. In: Hale, R., Wright, C. (eds.) A Companion to the Philosophy of Language. Blackwell, Oxford (1997)
26. Levinson, S.: Presumptive meanings. The theory of generalized conversational implicature. MIT Press, Cambridge (2000)
27. Bianchi, C.: Semantics and pragmatics: distinction reloaded. In: Bianchi, C. (ed.) The Semantics/pragmatics Distinction. Stanford, Csli (2004)
28. Hobbs, J.R.: Abduction in Natural Language Understanding. In: Horn, L., Ward, G. (eds.) The Handbook of Pragmatics. Blackwell, Oxford (2004)
29. Bouquet, P., Giunchiglia, F.: Reasoning about theory adequacy. A new solution to the qualification problem. Fundamenta Informaticae 23, 247–262 (1995)
30. Giunchiglia, F.: Contextual reasoning. Epistemologia 16, 345–364 (1993)
31. Bouquet, P.: Contesti e ragionamento contestuale. Il ruolo del contesto in una teoria della rappresentazione della conoscenza. Genova, Pantograf (1998)

Enabling Privacy-Preserving Semantic Presence in Instant Messaging Systems

Anca Dumitrache[1,4], Alessandra Mileo[2], Antoine Zimmermann[3], Axel Polleres[2], Philipp Obermeier[2], and Owen Friel[4]

[1] DERI, NUIG, Galway, Ireland
{alessandra.mileo,axel.polleres,philipp.obermeier}@deri.org
[2] INSA-Lyon, LIRIS, France
Antoine.Zimmermann@insa-lyon.fr
[3] Cisco Systems, Galway, Ireland
ofriel@cisco.com
[4] Jacobs University, Bremen, Germany
a.dumitrache@jacobs-university.de

Abstract. In pervasive environments, presence-based application development via Presence Management Systems (PMSs) is a key factor to optimise the management of communication channels, driving productivity increase. Solutions for presence management should satisfy the interoperability requirements, in turn providing context-centric presence analysis and privacy management. In order to push PMSs towards flexible, open and context-aware presence management, we propose some adaptation of two extensions to standard XML-based XMPP for message exchange in online communication systems. The contribution allows for more complex specification and management of nested group and privacy lists, where semantic technologies are used to map all messages into RDF vocabularies and pave the way for a broader semantic integration of heterogeneous and distributed presence information sources in the standard PMSs framework.

Keywords: Presence Management Systems, XMPP, XML, Nested Groups, Privacy List, Context-awareness, Rule-based Policies.

1 Motivations

Presence, also known as "presence information", conveys the ability and willingness of a user to communicate across a set of devices [4]. Presence has become an essential building block for many applications, both on the Web and in enterprise information systems, where being able to communicate efficiently with colleagues, customers, partners, suppliers and peers is essential. The concept of *presence* is a key ingredient for efficient communication, but it should take users' privacy into account, and the presence status of partners and resources should be provided to the other users according to such privacy settings.

When it comes to privacy-preserving Presence Management Systems (PMSs), the context in which users and resources may or may not be seen as available plays an important role as well, both in terms of physical context (e.g., location, ongoing meetings, booked resources), and virtual presence in online communication channels (e.g., IP telephony, video conferences or Instant Messaging (IM)).

M. Beigl et al. (Eds.): CONTEXT 2011, LNAI 6967, pp. 82–96, 2011.

The contextual accessibility of presence information optimises communication time and hence time to resolution, in turn driving productivity increase, customer satisfaction and business revenues.

Despite the importance of delivering presence-based services to applications in both corporate and home environments, current PMSs still fail in providing a context- and privacy- aware presence management for users, which is in turn open and flexible enough to support easy integration of arbitrary sources of presence information through the use of open standards. In terms of interoperability, available standards for presence and presence-related information systems define an abstract model of presence, a data model, several data formats, and protocols that have been recently extended to provide additional flexibility, as detailed in Sect. 2.2. Unfortunately, the current standards and their extensions are still unsupported by the majority of IM tools, and they are not flexible enough to enhance interoperability, context-awareness and personalised privacy.

In order to push the existing PMSs towards a more flexible, open and context-aware concept of presence (later defined in this paper as *semantic presence*), we consider two existing extensions of the standard Extensible Messaging and Presence Protocol (XMPP) as detailed in Sect.2: the first extension enables to structure contacts of an IM client into (possibly nested) sub-groups (XEP-0083), while the second allows to define access to presence information via declarative rules, grouped into *privacy lists* (XEP-0016), for users to personalise the way they enable or disable communication with other entities or clients.

The main outcome of this work is the elaboration of these two extensions through the definition and implementation of i) mechanisms to deal with more complex users' taxonomies (including multiple inheritence for user groups) and ii) context-dependent privacy rules for accessing and sharing presence information. As part of our contribution, we address interoperability issues, by providing a mapping of both nested groups and privacy lists into semantic data structures based on RDF. This paves the way for the integration of PMS privacy settings with dynamic information that can be extracted from web sources (e.g. Facebook, Linkedin, etc.), email filters, google calendars and alike, as well as sensor information.

In order to make the reader familiar with the state-of-the-art in PMS standards and terminology, a basic overview is provided in Sect.2. Sect.3 provides a characterisation of the semantic presence framework, and Sect.4 shows how we modified the XMPP extensions for nested groups and privacy lists towards a context- and privacy- aware access to presence information that takes interoperability issues into account. A preliminary evaluation is presented in Sect.5 based on a prototype of the extended presence framework run on an XMPP presence server, and several open issues and next steps are summarised in Sect.6.

2 Overview and Concepts

2.1 Privacy and Access Control Policies

Policies are becoming the emerging paradigm for configuring complex systems and controlling the interaction between distributed entities, in that they represent an abstract way to define the changing behaviour of a system without changing the implementation. Privacy and Access control policies are the best known and well explored example of the use of policies in complex systems. They are concerned with the (declarative) specification of *who* is allowed to access *which* information according to some *conditions*.

Traditional role-based policies [14] cannot be applied when the role of the various actors is not known in advance (e.g. in open environments) or when it cannot be accessed by some applications. In this setting, attribute-based access control models turn out to help [5]. Context-centric approaches can provide a valid support to dynamic attribute-based access control, but given the heterogeneous nature of contextual information, some abstraction is needed to enhance interoperability.

Several solutions have been proposed, to semantically describe the conditions (or the *context*) in which policies are to be applied to enhance appropriate security [8,12]. Some of these solutions support mainly context-awareness [1] and semantic interoperability for policy integration and reuse [16,7,17,18]. In the *Proteus* policy model [15], a set of semantically annotated attributes trigger the appropriate context-related policy which returns permitted/forbidden actions for that specific context [16]. Conflict resolution between possible incompatible contexts are defined at design-time by specific constraints aimed at selecting which context should be active in case of conflict: this makes the approach not flexible enough to be adapted to different domains. Security issues have also been considered in *XACML* [11] though little support is provided for interoperability and flexibility to integrate new domain-related knowledge. The semantic policy language *REI* [7] provides a strong support to interoperability and flexibility in both integration and definition of policy for distributed security control, in particular in the definition and evaluation of actions, based on deontic logic, and in the conflict resolution mechanism, based on priorities and precedences.

The top-down approach that is generally adopted by the policy frameworks mentioned earlier provides a solid basis for research in this area, but it is sometimes too general to capture specific issues that are present in real environments, and target them appropriately. In this paper we adopt a bottom-up approach to allow for personalised privacy settings, rather than dealing with general security issues. We consider a context as a special view on presence information, which goes beyond the possibility of allowing or forbidding access to it: users can contextually adapt and transform the presence information by making a given rule list active, while semantic mappings enhance integration and interoperability.

Ideally, the general top-down and the specific bottom-up approaches will converge to a point where policy frameworks can benefit from generality principles but without losing the specificity needed to solve a given problem in a more effective and efficient way.

2.2 Presence Management System: Models and Protocols

A presence management system is described by connections between objects that expose their presence state (called *presentities*) and objects expressing standing interest in presence information related to a set of presentities (called *watchers*).

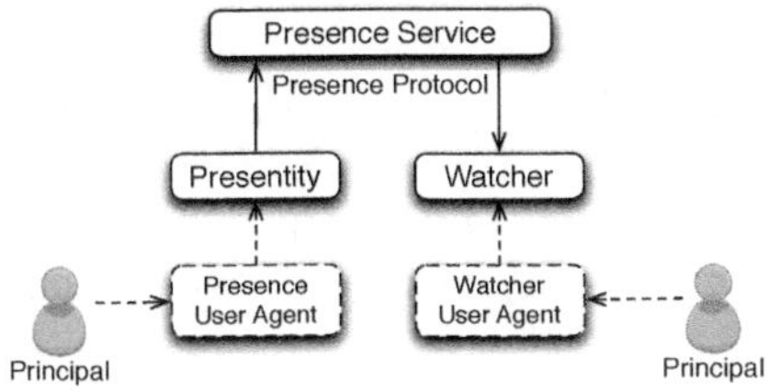

Fig. 1. Simple model of a presence service

The IETF working group SIMPLE[1] published a set of standards for presence information systems. These are identified as RFCs followed by an identification number, and they define an abstract model of presence, a data model, several data formats and protocols for message exchange. In *RFC 3856*, **presence** is described as as *the ability, willingness, or desire to communicate across a set of devices*. In the abstract presence model introduced in *RFC 2778* [2], both presentities and watchers interact with the presence system via User Agents (UA), which manipulates presence information for them.

The flow of information from a presentity towards a watcher is ensured by a presence service as illustrated in Fig.1, where the *Principals* are the people, groups, and/or software outside the presence system, which use the system as a mean of coordination and communication.

In order to enable the near-real-time exchange of structured yet extensible data in form of messages between watchers and presentities of a PMS, the IEFT also defined the Extensible Messaging and Presence Protocol (XMPP)[2], a set of open technologies for instant messaging, presence, multi-party chat, voice and video calls, collaboration, lightweight middleware, content syndication, and generalised routing of XML data. All messages exchanged in a PMS under XMPP are referred to as *stanzas*, while a user's *roster* consists of groups of contacts where each group is identified by a label.

The XMPP Standards Foundation (XSF) develops extensions to XMPP through a standard process centred around XMPP Extension Protocols (XEPs). Many extensions to XMPP have been proposed to enable representation and sharing of various context elements, e.g., current location and user activities. Among these extensions, we focus on those that mainly affect contextual and privacy-preserving presence management:

XEP-0083 on *Nested Roster Groups*, which allows the client's roster to store nested subgroups without breaking existing clients;

XEP-0016 on *Privacy Lists*, which defines a flexible method for communication blocking.

In the specific scenario of online PMS based on XMPP, dynamic and modular context-awareness for privacy setting is not properly addressed. In fact:

[1] SIP, `http://www.ietf.org/dyn/wg/charter/simple-charter.html`

[2] `http://xmpp.org`

- it's not possible to define presence at different levels in accordance with some watcher's properties, nor to dynamically change presence information according to the context (activity, position, current agenda);
- there is a lack of support for appropriate policy mechanisms and a uniform semantic model of context for both the presentities and the watchers;
- policies are all-or-nothing: one can decide who to show presence to but it's not possible to share different presence statuses to different watchers;
- properties of watcher are strictly hierarchical: groups can be defined and nested, but they cannot incorporate multiple subgroups or be defined implicitly in terms of static properties;
- overlapping groups and distributed policies can create conflicts in presence results, and conflict resolution mechanisms should take contextual aspects into account in order to dynamically adapt to presentities' and watchers' contexts.

In this paper, we address these limitations by extending XEP-0083 and XEP-0016.

2.3 RDF, SPARQL and OWL

The *Resource Description Framework* (*RDF*) [10] is a data modelling language to describe resources on the Web identified by a URI. Resources are typically Web sites or services, but can also refer to physical or immaterial entities which are not directly obtainable through the Web. A RDF document is essentially a set of triples, whose components, in ascending order, are distinguished as *subject*, *property* and *object*. Each RDF triple (s, p, o), intuitively, specifies an instance of a distinct property p which puts a subject s and an object o into relation. Moreover, a RDF document can be interpreted as a graph containing nodes and arcs to represent resources (or literal values) and their relationships.

Similar to schemata for relational databases, the semantics of RDF data can be further enriched by ontological background information. Ontological languages can be encoded in RDF and support the definition of classes (of resources and literals) and properties, as well as the definition of inclusions of classes and properties. The W3C recommends the *Web Ontology Language* (*OWL*) [9], which is strongly influenced by Description Logics, a carefully analysed set of formal logics for concept descriptions with extensively studied fragments that are tractable or decidable with highly optimised algorithms and efficient implementations

Additionally, W3C recommends *SPARQL* [13], the standard language for querying RDF. SPARQL is well supported and widely deployed with a respectable number of query engines implemented and integrated in various RDF stores (Jena ARQ, Sesame 2, OpenLink Virtuoso, AllegroGraph, 4store, etc)[3].

3 The Semantic Presence Framework

Semantic Presence. Disclosed information in corporate environments should be controlled by personal policies as well as corporate level policies, such that

[3] A comprehensive list of SPARQL implementations is available at `http://www.w3.org/wiki/SparqlImplementations`.

only those watchers who conform to a certain profile can access specific presence information of a presentity, at a given time, in a certain (dynamic) context. Therefore, beyond the dynamic nature of heterogeneous presence information, users' privacy profiles should also play a role in the presence model. We therefore generalise the definition of presence to that of *semantic presence* as follows:

Definition 1. ***Semantic presence*** *[6] is defined as the* contextualised *availability of a person or a resource, where both the presentity's and the watcher's contexts are taken into account. The context-related aspects that contribute to the identification of semantic presence can be determined and influenced by:*

- *Presentities'/Watchers' physical/virtual presence;*
- *Presentities'/Watchers' profiles, including group membership and preferences;*
- *Presentities' privacy policies;*
- *Governing (Corporate) policies.*

In this work we specifically focus on profiles and privacy policies, and illustrate the interoperability of our approach via RDF mapping.

Scenario. We consider a user, Buster, and his communication with other user accounts connected via IM clients, in a real-work situation.

The group taxonomy for Buster is represented in Fig.2, and it constitutes an important source of contextual information for the semantic presence framework.

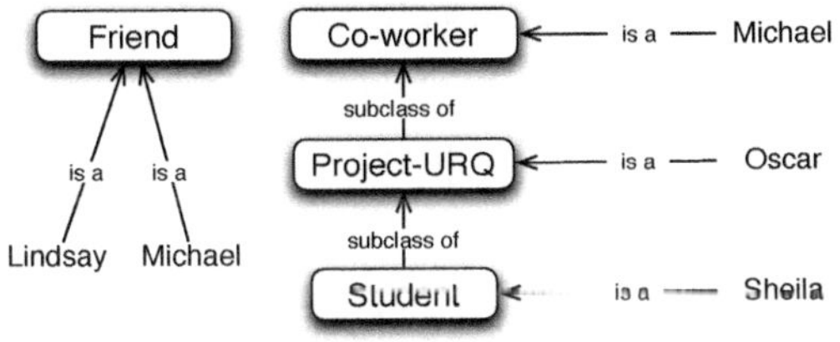

Fig. 2. Buster's taxonomy of groups

The active privacy settings for Buster are represented by a list of privacy rules, which are applied whenever Buster changes his status to "in a meeting":

1. show status as "available" to all co-workers;
2. show status as "unavailable" to students;
3. block all messages from contacts which are not part of the *co-workers* group.

When Buster joins a meeting with his co-workers on Project-URQ, he selects the status "in a meeting" (or it is selected automatically according to his calendar). As soon as the status changes, Buster receives a notification of a conflict, since two inconsistent rules with the same priority are applicable for Sheila: she is a student and so she should see Buster as "unavailable", but she is also a co-worker, thus she is allowed to still see Buster as "available". Buster is asked to solve this conflict by assigning priorities to the conflicting privacy rules, and these priorities will be applied by the semantic presence system in any future conflict related to that specific privacy list.

Requirements. A similar messaging system needs to deal with a more flexible and modular knowledge management mechanism for groups, contacts and their relations and properties. Desirable features of the systems are also its capacity of inferring implicit knowledge from explicit representations and dealing with a more fine-grained policy control. As a result, the user's status and the message content can be adapted to different classes of users via specific policies that are concerned with privacy issues and contextual settings. Presence information as well as the classification of users into groups should be dynamically updated, based on properties of the recipients and of the message. In this respect, semantic technologies can be useful to gather this dynamic knowledge and adapt policy evaluation accordingly. The general idea presented in this paper is that of enabling the XMPP-based Instant Messaging framework to:

- intercept and rewrite messages (or XMPP *stanzas*) based on high-level policies specified in a rule-like fashion and dynamically evaluated according to context- and user- related settings.
- map XMPP stanzas, groups and privacy rules into RDF (Resource Description Framework), a standard model for data interchange on the Web which facilitates data merging even if the underlying schemas differ, and specifically supports the evolution of data schemas over time without requiring all the data consumers to be changed.

All information passed through XMPP stanzas is stored on the server side, but since access to this information is restricted to a single authentified user, this sharing of information between client and server does not constitute a serious threat on privacy.

4 Implementation

The framework described in Sect.3 can be obtained by introducing two main extensions to XMPP: the first is related to the organisation of contacts of the IM client into a hierarchical taxonomy, and the second is related to the introduction of policy rules that determine how messages need to be managed according to how the sender and/or the receiver are related in this taxonomy. In the next subsections we detail how these two aspects have been implemented as extensions to XMPP.

4.1 Nested Groups

According to XMPP [3], a user's roster consists of a list of contacts, where contacts may have group labels attached to them, but there is no notion of "group" as a separate entity, a limitation in term of group management that our extension addresses. To improve this, we introduce the notion of *nested groups*, such that groups in rosters can be handled separately and related by a binary relation *subGroup*, where A subGroup B means that group A contains a subset of the users from group B.

Users are connected to an XMPP server via a Jabber client. Each user on this server is logged in by a personal user account and communication between server and client takes place by an exchange of XMPP stanzas. In order to implement the concept of Semantic Presence, the Jabber software client has to support the regular roster management extended by methods for nested groups. Moreover, for each user account, all roster information including group taxonomy, is persistently stored at the XMPP server, in RDF.

The following operations need to be supported:

- adding subgroup relations, including multiple supergroups: in this case, the server should enforce that group members are also members of all the supergroups of the group they belong to;
- removing a subgroup relation: in this case, all the group membership that were the consequence of the nesting should not exist anymore.
- visualisation: a user is able to get a convenient hierarchical visualisation of the group nesting in his/her roster.

A user should be able to manipulate a contact or an entire group in his roster by adding, renaming or deleting groups as well as by defining *virtual groups* on the basis of (set) intersection or union of existing groups. Based on this rich classification of contacts into groups, privacy rules can be applied over intersection, union of groups, and any combination of these operations.

All information about a user's roster and groups are stored on the server side but since access to this information is restricted to a single authentified user, this sharing of information between client and server does not constitute a serious threat on privacy.

Group Management. In order to allow for more complex group taxonomies to be created, we define new stanzas, such that it is possible to create/update/delete and relate groups independently of the roster items.

Example 1. Group creation:

```
<iq from='juliet@example.com/balcony' type='set' id='group_1'>
  <query xmlns='jabber:iq:group'>
    <group name='Servants'/>
    <group name='Friends'/>
  </query></iq>
```

The stanza in Ex.1 is creating two groups, 'Servants' and 'Friends'. The server must update the group information in persistent storage, and also push the change out to all of the user's available resources that have requested the roster. Stanza types are *presence*, *message*, *iq*. The roster push consists of an *iq* stanza of type *set* from the server to the client and enables all available resources to remain in sync with the server-based roster information. The server pushes the updated roster information to all available resources that have requested the roster and then replies with an *iq* result to the sending resource. As required by the semantics of the *iq* stanza kind, each resource that received the roster push must reply with an *iq* stanza of type *result* (see Ex.3) or *error*.

Example 2. Add subgroup relations:

```
<iq from='juliet@example.com/balcony' type='set' id='group_2'>
  <query xmlns='jabber:iq:group'>
    <group name='LocalFriends'>
      <subgroupof>Friends</subgroupof>
      <subgroupof>Nearby</subgroupof>
    </group></query></iq>
```

The stanza in Ex.2 defines 'LocalFriends' as a subgroup of two groups, 'Friends' and 'Nearby'.

Example 3. Client requests/receives current roster from server:

```
<iq from='juliet@example.com/balcony' type='get' id='group_1'>
  <query xmlns='jabber:iq:group'/>
</iq>

<iq to='juliet@example.com/balcony' type='result' id='group_1'>
  <query xmlns='jabber:iq:group'>
    <group name='Friends'/>
    <group name='Servants'/>
    <group name='Nearby'/>
    <group name='LocalFriends'>
      <subgroupof>Friends</subgroupof>
      <subgroupof>Nearby</subgroupof>
    </group></query></iq>
```

The stanza in Ex.3 shows both the request and the answer from the server which contains the list of all groups and their subgroup relations.

Example 4. Delete a group:

```
<iq from='juliet@example.com/balcony' type='set' id='group_4'>
  <query xmlns='jabber:iq:group'>
    <group name='Nearby' remove='true' />
  </query></iq>
```

As with adding a group, when deleting a group the server updates the group information in persistent storage, initiate a group push to all of the user's available resources that have requested the group hierarchy (with the 'remove' attribute set to a value of *true*), and send an *iq* result to the initiating resource. The server should return an error when trying to remove a non empty group, or a group having subgroups.

We now illustrates how privacy rules can be used to enable Semantic Presence.

4.2 Privacy Lists

The same mechanism used for group management, is also applied for creating privacy lists composed by privacy rules: the roster pushes an *iq stanza* for the creation of both the privacy list and the policy rule. Directions are either *inbound* or *outbound*, meaning that the rule apply to incoming and outgoing stanzas. Subscription types restrict the application of the rule depending on mutual subscription (or lack thereof) of the sender and receiver. The values can be *to*, *from*, *both* or *none*. When all criteria for a rule are match, the *action* is performed, as explain below. Ex.5 illustrates a privacy list stanza with one rule.

Example 5. Create a privacy list and add rules to the list:

```
<iq from='juliet@example.com/balcony' type='set'
  <query xmlns='jabber:iq:privacy'>
    <list name='MyList' />
  </query></iq>

<iq from='juliet@example.com/balcony' type='set'
  <query xmlns='jabber:iq:privacy'>
    <list name='MyList' />
      <item type='jid'
            value='Juliet@example.com/balcony'
            action='allow'
            order='4'>
        <presence-in/>
      </item></list></query></iq>
```

Analogous to roster and group information, a users's privacy list is stored on the server side and can only be accessed via authentication.

Syntax of Policy Rules. Formally, we define a (policy) rule as an expression

$$Action \leftarrow Condition$$

where Action stands for either *allow*, *block* or *transform(e)* with a POSIX extended regular expression e; Condition is an expression defined over a set of fixed predicate symbols *Preds* and a set of constant symbols *Cons*. Specifically, a Condition can be an expression of the form

1. $p(c)$ where $p \in Preds$ and $c \in Cons$;
2. $expr_1 \wedge expr_2$ where $expr_1, expr_2 \in Cons$;
3. $expr_1 \vee expr_2$ where $expr_1, expr_2 \in Cons$;
4. $\neg exp$ where $exp \in Cons$.

Furthermore, *Cons* exclusively comprises the constants *payload*, *presence*, *message*, *iq*, *to*, *from*, *both*, *none*, *inbound*, *outbound*, all possible group names and all POSIX regular expressions, while *Preds* is a fixed set which exclusively contains the symbols *stanzaType*, *direction*, *subscriptionType*, *affects*, *owner* and *regexMatch*.[4]

Semantics of Policy Rules. The evaluation of a policy rule p is always tied to an XMPP session of a Jabber user and a current send or receive action of a stanza by the user. We formally integrate these diverse information as a contextual session $cs = (cs_{jid}, cs_{groups}, cs_{presence}, cs_{stanza})$ which holds the user's Jabber ID (cs_{jid}), the roster groups (cs_{groups}), given as a set of JIDs, the user's presence status ($cs_{presence}$) and the stanza which is currently processed (cs_{stanza})., i.e. sent or received by the user.

The evaluation of the rule itself is conducted in two major steps. First the truth value of the condition has to be determined. Second, if the Condition is true the Action has to be applied. A function *atomicTv* maps each condition $c \in Cons$ to true or false as follows:

[4] Note that future extensions may generalise rules to include other n-ary predicates.

$atomicTv(stanzaType(c))$	is true iff c is the stanza type of cs_{stanza}
$atomicTv(direction(c))$	is true iff c is the direction of cs_{stanza}
$atomicTv(subscripitonType(c))$	is true iff c is the subscription type of cs_{stanza}
$atomicTv(affect(c))$	is true iff c is the 'from' or is in a group that contain the 'from' (for an inbound stanza) or c is the 'to' or is a group that contains the 'to' (for an outbound stanza) of cs_{stanza}
$atomicTv(owner(c))$	is true iff c is cs_{jid}
$atomicTv(regexMatch(c))$	is true iff the payload of cs_{stanza} matches the regular expression c

If the condition of the policy rule is true, the corresponding action is applied to cs_stanza, and the message can be i) blocked, ii) allowed or iii) transformed by a sed (Unix stream editor) rewriting command e and afterwards forwarded to the receiver.

An example of rule could be

$$\begin{aligned} block \leftarrow\ & stanzaType(message) \\ & \wedge regexMatch(/.*\texttt{Cisco}.*/) \\ & \wedge \neg affects(Cisco-Staff) \\ & \wedge subscriptionType(to) \end{aligned}$$

which says that each message containing the word 'Cisco' is blocked when sent to a user who is not in group 'Cisco-Staff'.

Processing Privacy Rules. The processing of the privacy rules is made in two steps. The first step consists in retrieving the potentially applicable privacy rules from the RDF store with a SPARQL query, based on the type of the stanza, the sender, the recipient and the subscription type assigned to the contact affected by the rule. This may involve some reasoning over the RDF data, especially to accurately determine implicit group membership from the group nesting. An optimised implementation would store user specific information (roster and privacy list) in memory so that this step can be performed very fast.

Rules that are retrieved this way may still not apply to the stanza in question, because there can be additional conditions that cannot be directly represented in RDF, such as a time frame, a location an expression of the possible payloads affected by the rules (cf. *regexMatch* in our simple policy rule syntax). To decide this, a dedicated policy engine interprets the condition (which must be in a language understandable by such an engine) and evaluates it as explained above. Rules are processed in order of priority and whenever a rule is applicable, the engine stops processing the rest of the rules fir that privacy list. Software clients should inform users when two rules with equal priority apply to a given stanza.

Enabling Interoperability. In order to make our proposal easily extensible, we provide a mapping of XMPP stanzas into RDF, for both nested groups and privacy rules. This also allows roster groups to be interconnected with existing enterprise level staff member management. For instance, an RDF version of Active Directory could be integrated in the roster management system to facilitate categorisation of contacts. The mapping is illustrated in Fig.3b and Fig.4b and

```
<iq type='set'>
  <query xmlns='jabber:iq:groups'>
    <group name='URQ'>
      <subgroupof>
        Coworkers
      </subgroupof>
      <subgroupof>
        Semantic Search Stream
      </subgroupof>
    </group>
  </query>
</iq>
```

(a)

```
group:urq
  rdf:type sioc:UserGroup ,
           owl:Class ;
  rdfs:label "URQ" ;
  rdfs:subClassOf
           group:coworkers ,
           group:semSearchStream .
```

(b)

Fig. 3. Translation of roster group 'URQ' given by stanza (a) into an OWL class (b)

```
<iq type='set'
    from='michael@corp.com'>
  <query xmlns='jabber:iq:privacy'>
    <list name='MyList'>
      <item type='group'
            value='Coworkers'
            action='transform'
            ed='available'
            order='3'>
        <presence-out/>
      </item>
      <item action='allow'
            order='68'/>
    </list>
  </query>
</iq>
```

(a)

```
:Michael
  rdf:type privacy:UserAccount ;
  privacy:has_privacy_list
           list:myList .
list:myList
  rdfs:label "MyList" ;
  privacy:has_privacy_rule
           rule:myRule .
rule:myRule
  privacy:affects group:Coworkers ;
  privacy:applies_to
           privacy:presence ;
  privacy:has_action
           transform:available ;
  privacy:priority "3" ;
  privacy:direction
           privacy:outbound .
transform:available
  privacy:transformation
           "available" .
```

(b)

Fig. 4. Translation of a privacy list (a) into OWL (b)

it paves the way for integrating heterogeneous sources of contextual knowledge (provided that the same semantic mapping is given for this knowledge), such as sensors and corporate policies.

5 Preliminary Experiments

We conducted a set of preliminary experiments based on the runtime of the application in various extreme cases, for the purpose of assessing how our component will scale in a real-world situation (i.e. having a large group hierarchy of up to 30 nested groups, as defined in the Psi[5] XMPP IM client). More intensive testing will be done in future experiments, when the conflict resolution mechanism will be made more expressive and some of the issues mentioned in Sect.6 will be tackled.

As seen in Fig.5, the reaction time grows proportionately with the increase of the number of users and the hierarchy depth, the likely reason being that the

[5] http://psi-im.org/

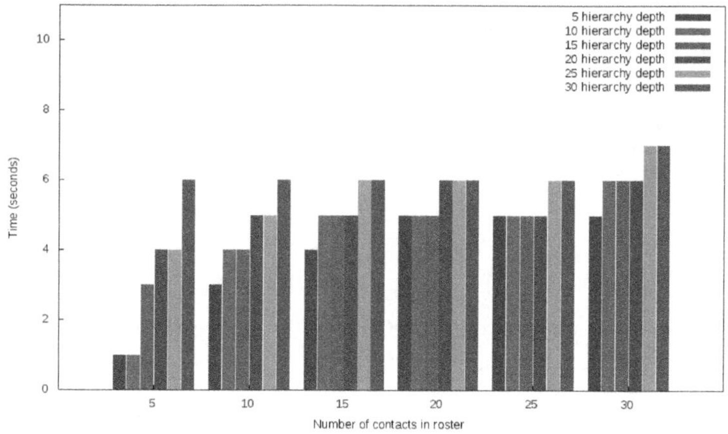

Fig. 5. Approximate runtime (in seconds) when applying privacy XMPP stanza

implementation is currently non-optimised w.r.t. the number of queries against the triple store. However, when discussing a real-world scenario, it should be taken into account that, even in a corporate environment, roster groups are usually declared and maintained by users, and therefore the complexity of their hierarchy is limited by the fact that groups need to stay human-readable. In this context, hierarchy depths of more than 10 become very unlikely. As demonstrated by our evaluation, in cases with small group depth, the runtime measurements showed a negligible delay. We conclude that, even if the runtime of the component increases with group depth, this would have little impact in a real-world scenario, and therefore our component can be deemed scalable.

6 Future Work and Conclusion

In this paper we present a bottom-up approach to specify and evaluate privacy settings in XMPP-based PMSs on the basis of contextutal group information. The proposed implementation takes advantage of semantic technologies for flexible and interoperable solutions to Semantic Presence and it paves the way for numerous challenging issues we already started to tackle, including the following:

Temporal-/location- based validity of rules refers to advanced privacy rules to change the granularity of the location attached to presence information: for instance, colleagues may know the exact room in which the person is, while external collaborators are only notified with the city in which the user is.

Federated policies consider that presence should reconcile general company policies with users' privacy settings. Interruptions are counterproductive in the workplace and adequate handling of (corporate) policies to avoid these could be of potentially high impact. Some companies that ban the use of social networks for those reasons, so active support by presence systems might be desirable.

Physical presence is also a key aspect in context-aware pervasive environments, thus the extention of XMPP to take into account sensor data, aggregated at the right level of granularity is of interest, where the management and processing of a large amount of dynamic sensor data can be a challenge.

Conflict analysis requires to deal with efficient conflict resolution strategies, taking presence information, groups structure and roles into account.

These aspects are all relevant for advanced semantic presence management and we believe semantic technologies and abstract policy specification and enforcement introduced in this paper can help addressing these challenges.

References

1. Acharya, A., Banerjee, N., Chakraborty, D., Dasgupta, K., Misra, A., Sharma, S., Wang, X., Wright, C.: Programmable presence virtualization for next-generation context-based applications. In: PerCom, pp. 1–10 (2009)
2. Jabber Software Foundation: A model for presence and instant messaging (2000)
3. Jabber Software Foundation: Extensible messaging and presence protocol (xmpp): Instant messaging and presence (2004)
4. Jabber Software Foundation: A presence event package for the session initiation protocol (sip) (2004)
5. Frikken, K., Atallah, M., Li, J.: Attribute-based access control with hidden policies and hidden credentials. IEEE Transactions on Computers 55, 1259–1270 (2006)
6. Hauswirth, M., Euzenat, J., Friel, O., Griffin, K., Hession, P., Jennings, B., Groza, T., Handschuh, S., Zarko, I.P., Polleres, A., Zimmermann, A.: Towards Consolidated Presence. Collaborate Com. (2010)
7. Kagal, L., Finin, T.W., Joshi, A.: A policy based approach to security for the semantic web. In: Fensel, D., Sycara, K., Mylopoulos, J. (eds.) ISWC 2003. LNCS, vol. 2870, pp. 402–418. Springer, Heidelberg (2003)
8. Ko, H., Won, D., Shin, D., Choo, H., Kim, U.: A semantic context-aware access control in pervasive environments. In: Gavrilova, M.L., Gervasi, O., Kumar, V., Tan, C.J.K., Taniar, D., Laganá, A., Mun, Y., Choo, H. (eds.) ICCSA 2006. LNCS, vol. 3981, pp. 165–174. Springer, Heidelberg (2006)
9. McGuinness, D.L., van Harmelen, F.: OWL web ontology language overview. W3C recommendation, W3C (February 2004)
10. Miller, E., Manola, F.: RDF primer. W3C recommendation, W3C (February 2004), `http://www.w3.org/TR/2004/REC-rdf-primer-20040210/`
11. Moses, T.: eXtensible Access Control Markup Language (XACML) Version 1.0. (February 2003)
12. Priebe, T., Dobmeier, W., Kamprath, N.: Supporting attribute-based access control with ontologies. In: Int'l Conf. on Availability, Reliability and Security, pp. 465–472 (2006)
13. Prud'hommeaux, E., Seaborne, A.: SPARQL query language for RDF. W3C recommendation, W3C (January 2008), `http://www.w3.org/TR/2008/REC-rdf-sparql-query-20080115/`
14. Sandhu, R., Coyne, E., Feinstein, H., Youman, C.: Role-based access control models. Computer 29(2), 38–47 (1996)

15. Toninelli, A., Montanari, R., Kagal, L., Lassila, O.: A semantic context-aware access control framework for secure collaborations in pervasive computing environments. In: Cruz, I., Decker, S., Allemang, D., Preist, C., Schwabe, D., Mika, P., Uschold, M., Aroyo, L.M. (eds.) ISWC 2006. LNCS, vol. 4273, pp. 473–486. Springer, Heidelberg (2006)
16. Toninelli, A., Montanari, R., Kagal, L., Lassila, O.: Proteus: A semantic context-aware adaptive policy model. In: POLICY, pp. 129–140 (2007)
17. Uszok, A., Bradshaw, J.M., Johnson, M., Jeffers, R., Tate, A., Dalton, J., Aitken, S.: Kaos policy management for semantic web services. IEEE Intelligent Systems 19, 32–41 (2004)
18. Uszok, A., Bradshaw, J.M., Lott, J., Breedy, M.R., Bunch, L., Feltovich, P.J., Johnson, M., Jung, H.: New developments in ontology-based policy management: Increasing the practicality and comprehensiveness of kaos. In: POLICY, pp. 145–152 (2008)

Towards Context-Based Explanations for Teacher Support

Anneli Edman, Jenny Eriksson Lundström, and Narin Akrawi

Dept. of Informatics and Media, Uppsala University, Sweden
{anneli.edman,jenny.eriksson,narin.akrawi}@im.uu.se

Abstract. To enable deep learning from a system is not a trivial matter. By including domain context in the construction of the explanations the user is able to reflect on the effects of the knowledge, and not solely on the knowledge in isolation. In addition, in our approach the contextualized knowledge is to be viewed in the context of a particular goal or objective and how any reasoning result is reached in relation to this objective. In this paper we outline context-based explanations and their composition for a sample explanation supporting teachers in developing their own didactical skills.

1 Introduction

According to [5] "context is the key factor of intelligent assistant systems. Making context explicit allows us to use knowledge in its context of use, to capture variants in the reasoning, to generate relevant explanation." Hence, using context for the generation as well as the content of these explanations may enhance deep learning, provided that the explanations present the context of the domain in an appropriate way. Unfortunately, regardless of the system or application used for these systems, the reasoning and explanations of intelligent assistant systems, such as e.g. knowledge management systems, are in general solely based on and generated from the formalized part of the domain context.

Mentor [13] is a knowledge management system constructed to support teachers' reflection over their own didactic skills. Mentor gives individualized feedback based on answers to questions that the teacher has given regarding the design of courses. The questions are derived by [16] based on [3]. The feedback is based on Bloom's revised taxonomy, which is used for a classification of different objectives and skills that teachers need to reflect upon to support students' deep learning [2]. The revised taxonomy incorporates both the kind of knowledge to be learned (knowledge dimension) and the process used to learn (cognitive process dimension). Both dimensions can be used to help write clear, focused educational objectives. As part of the design of Mentor, the questions were re-evaluated by two focus groups of pedagogues from Uppsala University to further establish the relation between the didactical instructions and the pedagogical objectives of Bloom's revised taxonomy [1]. In Mentor canned text explanations based on informal domain knowledge are presented to the teacher in order to

M. Beigl et al. (Eds.): CONTEXT 2011, LNAI 6967, pp. 97–103, 2011.

provide feedback on their tutoring activities. However, storing syntactical strings that express informal knowledge in a system only means that these strings are made available for syntactical manipulation. As a result the explanations are not well fitted to the individual teacher's needs.

In this paper, the focus is on context-based explanations for Mentor [13] and an outline of their composition. Consequently, the methods for formalization and dynamical generation of the context-based explanations, and the user system interaction is only briefly touched upon.

The paper is outlined as follows: In Section 2 some aspects on learning from knowledge management systems are presented. In Section 3 a sample presentation of context for a teacher support tool is given. In Section 4 we present context-based explanations and a sample composition of relevant knowledge as discussed in the literature. In Section 5, we conclude and outline further work.

2 Learning from Explanations in Knowledge Management Systems

To enable learning from a system is not a trivial matter. In order to provide for a deep learning cf. e.g. [12] it is necessary to provide the teacher with comprehension of the feedback and how the results of the self-diagnostic test relate to the domain. Comprehensive understanding requires the realization of both top-down and bottom-up procedures cf. Figure 1 and e.g. [17][9][14]. It means that the teacher needs to be introduced to domain knowledge at a level of increasingly more detail (top-down). In addition, the teacher needs opportunities for reflecting on the effect of the introduced knowledge for the overall domain (bottom-up).

To enable appropriate explanations on which the users' are to reflect and learn, it seems necessary to complement the formalized knowledge by informally reproducing relevant parts of the domain. This allows the user to reflect on the effects of the particular knowledge in the context of the domain.

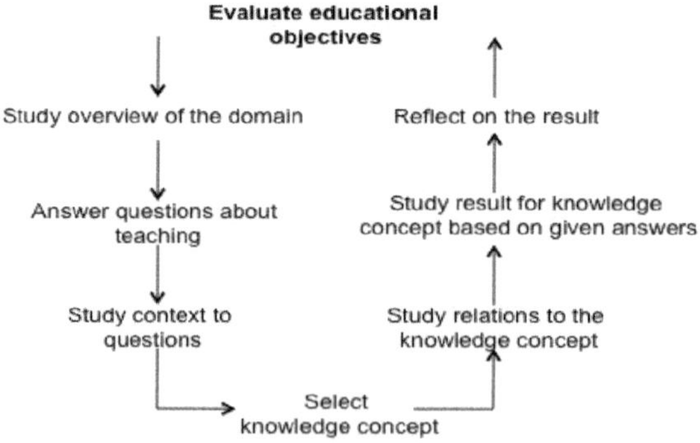

Fig. 1. Procedures of learning

In knowledge management systems by which the user is to learn or to develop the own knowledge or reasoning skills, explanations may be as important as the conclusions themselves [6]. Explanations facilitate the user's confidence in the system's conclusions and could aid and facilitate the user's participation in the system's reasoning, e.g. by enabling the user to provide the input needed. As stated above our objectives are the design, modeling and generation of explanations for intelligent assistant systems that are to support expert's development of their own knowledge and accompanying skills. It means that we set out to model the domain context to enable the generation of context-based explanations, i.e. explanations that allow for a dynamic aggregated view of the reasoning carried out for a particular session.

3 A Sample Presentation of Context for a Teacher Support Tool

The revised Bloom's taxonomy is a basis in the reasoning of Mentor. The knowledge dimensions comprises four types of knowledge; factual, conceptual, procedural and meta-cognitive. The cognitive process dimension refers to remembering, understanding, applying, analyzing, evaluating and creating. This taxonomy is chosen of two main reasons: on the first hand to map teachers' answers to the taxonomy and on the other hand to give the teachers different kind of feedback based on the educational objectives in the taxonomy.

Through the taxonomy Mentor needs to highlight where in the taxonomy the teacher's strategies are placed. The knowledge descriptions may be classified according to the type of object. The informal knowledge is structured as objects in a context tree cf. Figure 2. Learning within a domain implies understanding the domain context in depth as well as width. Through the context tree both the depth and the width are shown on a high abstraction level. A rough distinction can be made between the objects according to their participation in

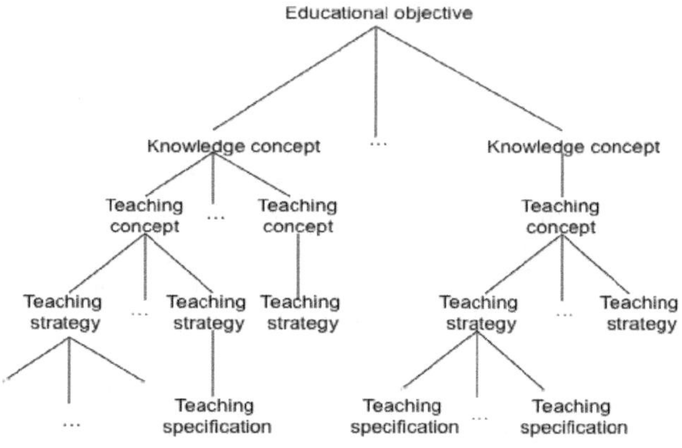

Fig. 2. Objects related to Mentor as a context tree

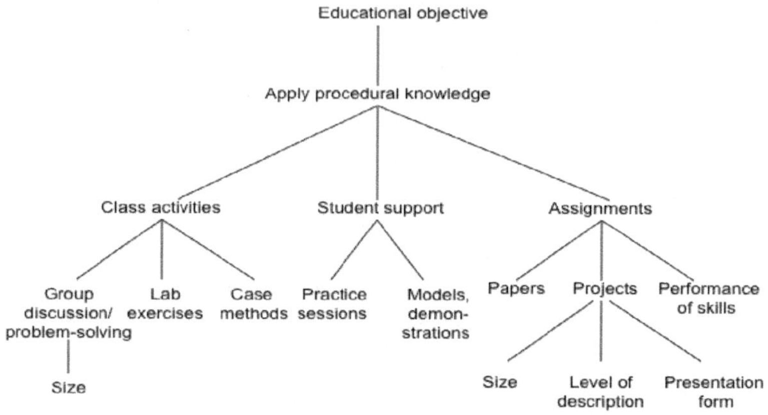

Fig. 3. A context tree for explanations regarding the knowledge concept *apply procedural knowledge*

different phases of the problem solving. The educational objective is the goal object, which the system will try to conclude a value for. Related to the educational objective are knowledge concepts and these can be found in the revised Bloom's taxonomy. The knowledge concepts are related to teaching concepts and these objects in turn are related to teaching strategies and teaching specifications. During a session the user provides values for the teaching specifications. All objects between the educational objective and the teaching specifications are subgoals in the reasoning. Note that every teaching strategy has at least one teaching specification. In Figure 3 the context tree is instantiated with the knowledge concept *apply procedural knowledge*, the teaching concepts *class activities*, *student support*, and *assignments*. The teaching strategy is exemplified by *lab exercises*, *papers*, and *projects*. An example of a teaching specification for the example *projects* is e.g. size.

4 Context-Based Explanations

As stated above, domain context in a system can be viewed as a combination of formal and informal knowledge. The formal knowledge can be formalized but this formalization is only partial with respect to the domain (cf. e.g.[11]. The informal knowledge consists of knowledge that cannot be formally captured. The reason, of course, is that the various forms of knowledge communicated by human beings are richer than formal representations. The informal knowledge relates to and complement the formalization. Parts of the informal knowledge can be captured in a system but also be provided by a user.

If both formal and informal knowledge is captured in the system it is possible to generate dynamic explanations utilizing both knowledge types, which is in line with the research presented in [6]. The general idea of [6] is that the more explicitly the knowledge underlying a system's design is represented the better explanations the system can give. More of the domain knowledge can be captured if different reproduction forms are used. Hence, a combination of informal and formal domain knowledge may mirror the context of a domain. The explanations based on this combination of domain knowledge can therefore be seen as context-based.

Context-based explanations may be more flexible and easier to tailor to a particular user. Explanations should be tailored to the user's needs and they should simplify complex information to the user accurately, guide both the research and the focus of attention, teach the user, develop a model of the current user, etc., as exemplified by [4].

Some of the advantages with context-based explanations are at the same time the challenges. Since more knowledge has to be included in the system the knowledge acquisition phase will be protracted. The required knowledge may be difficult to attain and, moreover, it may be difficult to reproduce it in the system. Furthermore, the architecture has to be quite advanced to be able to deal with this kind of explanations.

Many investigations regarding demands on explanations have been described cf. e.g. [8][15][7]. [10] classified the information needed in context-based explanations. The following four categories of information were discerned:

(I) Problem solving strategy: A description of the system's reasoning, e.g., the order by which the subgoals will be investigated

(II) Justification of the system's domain knowledge: Contextual knowledge that can justify that both the system's knowledge and problem solving are reliable within the current domain

(III) Local problem solving: A description of how the system's problem solving will be carried out for a sub goal

(IV) Term description: An explanation or description of a concept that takes part in the problem solving, could, e.g., be related to input or to goals.

The first explanation type, problem solving strategy, describes what [8] refers to as strategy, [15] calls methods the program employs, and [7] see as control strategy. Justification of the system's knowledge is a demand that [7] has on explanations and can be compared to the support knowledge of [8] and the justification of the actions of the program of [15]. Local problem solving can include structural knowledge cf. [8], which consists of abstractions that are used to index the domain knowledge. This explanation type can also be referred to how well data match local goals, described by [7]. The last type of explanation, term description, matches the demand presented in [15] that questions involving confusion about the meaning of terms should be answered.

5 Conclusion

To enable deep learning from a system is not a trivial matter. It is necessary to provide the teacher with comprehension of the feedback and how the results of the self-diagnostic test relate to the domain. In addition, comprehensive understanding requires the realization of both top-down and bottom-up procedures. To enable this setting, the teacher needs to be introduced to domain knowledge at a level of increasingly more detail (top-down). Moreover, the teacher needs opportunities for reflecting on the effect of the introduced knowledge for the overall domain (bottom-up).

We address this challenge by context-based explanations. It is well established that explanations facilitate the user's confidence in the system's conclusions and aids the user's participation in the system's reasoning, e.g. giving correct input. Using explanations to support the teacher's own learning process enhances the process if the explanations present the context of the teaching methods in an appropriate way. By means of the context-based explanations the user is able to reflect on the effects of the teaching methods in the context of a particular educational objective and how the result is reached in relation to a knowledge concept. We go forth with the modeling, formalization and implementation of context-based explanations.

References

1. Akrawi, N.: Enhanced teaching strategies: Elicitation of requirements for a support system for teachers. In: Proceedings of International Conference on Computer Supported Education (2010)
2. Anderson, L., Krathwohl, D.: A Taxonomy for Learning, Teaching, and Assessing: A Revision of Bloom's Taxonomy of Educational Objectives. Longman, New York (2001)
3. Brinko, K.: Visioning your course: Question to ask as you design your course. The Teaching Professor (February 1991)
4. Brézillon, P.: Context needs in cooperative building of explanations. In: Proceedings of the First European Conference on Cognitive Science in Industry (1994)
5. Brézillon, P.: From expert systems to context-based intelligent assistant systems: a testimony. Knowledge Engineering Review 26(1), 19–24 (2011)
6. Chandrasekaran, B., Swartout, W.: Explanations in knowledge systems, the role of explicit representation of design knowledge. IEEE expert, 47–49 (June 1991)
7. Chandrasekaran, B., Tanner, M.C., Josephson, J.R.: Explanation: The role of control strategies and deep models. In: Expert Systems: The user interface, pp. 219–246. Ablex Publishing Corporation, New Jersey (1988)
8. Clancey, W.: Extensions to rules for explanation and tutoring. Artificial Intelligence 20, 215–251 (1983)
9. Clancey, W., Letsinger, R.: Neomycin: Reconfiguring a rule-based expert system for application to teaching. In: Proceedings of IJCAI 1981 (1981)
10. Edman, A.: Generating context-based explanations. In: Proceedings of ES 2002, The Twenty-second SGAI International Conference on Knowledge-Based Systems and Applied Artificial Intelligence, Cambridge, England (2002)
11. Edman, A., Hamfelt, A.: A system architecture for knowledge based hypermedia. International Journal of Human-Computer Studies 51, 1007–1036 (1999)
12. Marton, F., Hounsell, D., Entwistle, N.: Hur vi lär (The Experience of Learning). Rabén Prisma, Stockholm (1996)

13. Mayiwar, N., Edman, A.: Mentor: a knowledge management system supporting teachers in their leadership. In: Proceedings of Network-Based Education 2007, The Power of Media in Education (2007)
14. Stanton, N., Stammers, R.: Learning styles in a non-linear training environment. In: Proceedings of Hypertext II, University of York, England (1989)
15. Swartout, W.: Explaining and justifying expert consulting programs. In: Proceedings of the Seventh International Joint Conference of Artificial Intelligence, Vancouver, B.C. Canada, pp. 815–823 (1981)
16. UCIrvine Instructional Resources Center, Univ. of California Irvine. Teaching resources guide (2006), http://www.irc.uci.edu/TRG/Preparing_To_Teach/Planning/designing_questions.htm
17. Wærn, Y.: Cognitive Aspects of Computer Supported Tasks. John Wiley, Chichester (1989)

An Experiment in Hierarchical Recognition of Group Activities Using Wearable Sensors

Dawud Gordon[1], Jan-Hendrik Hanne[2], Martin Berchtold[2], Takashi Miyaki[1], and Michael Beigl[1]

[1] Karlsruhe Institute of Technology, Karlsruhe, Germany
firstname.lastname@kit.edu
[2] Technische Universität Braunschweig, Brunswick, Germany
{j-h.hanne,m.berchtold}@tu-bs.de

Abstract. Pervasive computing envisions implicit interaction between people and their intelligent environments instead of individual devices, inevitably leading to groups of individuals interacting with the same intelligent environment. These environments must therefore be aware not only of user contexts and activities, but the contexts and activities of groups of users as well. This poster will demonstrate an experiment conducted towards understanding hierarchical multi-user group activity recognition using wearable sensors. The experiment will explore different data abstraction levels in terms of recognition rates, power consumption and wireless communication volumes for the devices involved.

Keywords: Group activity recognition, context recognition, distributed systems, multi-user, wearable.

1 Introduction

Context and activity recognition provide intelligent devices in the environment with the ability to act proactively in the interest of users. Implicit pro-active interaction based on situational awareness becomes more important in order to prevent us from entering a state of permanent distraction and informational overload due to constantly having to administrate and respond to the myriad of intelligent devices in our immediate environment. As intelligent devices pervade our everyday environment, devices will interact with multiple users at once, meaning that these devices will need to be aware not only of the activities and contexts of individual users, but also of groups of users as well.

The group activity is not necessarily the same as the sum of the activities of the individuals in it [4]. This implies that the activity or context of a group is a function of the activity or context of each individual in the group, in the same way that the context or activity of a single user is a function of sensor measurements. Since carryable or wearable technology is steadily on the rise, leveraging these devices for sensing seems to be a logical approach. Using wearable technology (badges, mobile phones, coffee cups, etc.) for group activity or

M. Beigl et al. (Eds.): CONTEXT 2011, LNAI 6967, pp. 104–107, 2011.

context recognition is inherently a hierarchical problem, where data from wearable sensors on multiple users must be aggregated in order to infer the group context. As with other areas of research, such as context prediction [5], group activity recognition (GAR) can be conducted on data at different levels of context abstraction. The lower the abstraction level (e.g. sensor measurements), the more information is contained in the data, but the more energy is required for transmitting this data. Conversely, the higher the data is abstracted towards context labels (e.g. "walking"), the less it costs to communicate, but it contains less information [5].

In this work we present an experiment which will research the accuracy/power-consumption trade-off in GAR based on the context abstraction level using a distributed wearable sensing system. The study is done in an office setting using intelligent coffee cups along the lines of the MediaCup [1] and mobile phones. Using the system, recognition of office group activities such as meetings, presentations and coffee breaks is examined by monitoring individual colleagues.

2 System Design

The system used was made up of a wireless sensor network and a mobile phone. Wireless sensor nodes equipped with 3D acceleration sensors were attached to coffee mugs (Smart Mugs) in a university/office setting. One node was connected to a smart-phone using a USB adapter and acted as a bridge between the WSN and the smart-phone. The nodes sampled activity and context data at the mugs, processed this data to the desired local abstraction level, and forwarded this data to the smart-phone for further processing to classify the group activity.

The wireless sensor nodes used in this experiment were jenParts from the open-source Jennisense Project[1] which uses a combination of the ConTiki operating system [3] and the JENNIC JN5139 wireless microprocessor and includes open source sensor and bridge board designs. The nodes where equipped with a battery and an analog 3D acceleration sensor and were attached to coffee mugs, which we will refer to as Smart Mugs (see Fig. 1).

The nodes sample the sensors at a rate of 33 Hz and can be configured to process this data to different context abstraction levels. The preprocessing operations are dependent on the mode: in raw sensor data mode, the sensors are sampled but no further preprocessing operations are performed (low context abstraction level [5]). In feature mode, the features average and variance are calculated over the window (medium abstraction). In classification mode, these features are classified to local activities using a previously trained local classifier (either kNN or DT, high abstraction), the result of which indicates which activity is being performed by the user holding the mug. This locally generated information is finally forwarded to the smart-phone which tries to identify the global group activity based on this local information.

[1] The Jennisense project: `http://www.jennisense.teco.edu`

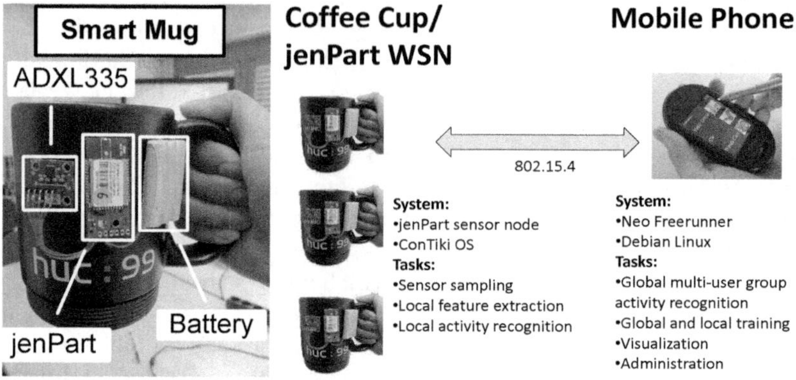

Fig. 1. Left: The Smart Mug **Right:** Network Topology of the Experiment

The smart-phone used is the Neo Freerunner (Neo) from the Openmoko Project[2] running a distribution of Debian Linux. It serves as a processing platform for classifying the global context or activity based on the data aggregated from all nodes in the WSN, either raw sensor data, locally extracted features, or locally classified activities depending on the mode. The Neo also serves as a context classifier training platform for the jenParts in the WSN. Following the approach presented by Berchtold et al. [2], after being set in training mode by the Neo, each jenPart gathers data and forwards it to the Neo along with a local annotation indicated by labeling activities using the button on the jenParts. Once this process is complete, the Neo trains the selected classifier, segments the trained classifier into packet-sized chunks, and sends these chunks sequentially to the nodes in a JSON format.

3 Experiment

In order to research the energy consumption and quality of recognition based on the context abstraction level in a distributed scenario, a multi-user experiment was conducted. In the first phase, activities were performed to train the local classifiers on the Smart Mugs. In the second phase, the three subjects conducted other activities as a group in order to train and test the global group classifier. The power consumption of each node as well as the consumption of the mobile phone was also monitored. During the course of this experiment, 3 subjects performed 7 different activities, 3 of which were group activities and 4 of which were individual activities involving the Smart Mugs. In total, over 45 minutes of data were collected, consisting of over 22,700 sample windows, approximately evenly distributed between group and individual activities.

In the first phase of the experiment, the Smart Mugs were evaluated in terms of power consumption and accuracy for different levels of abstraction. Each user

[2] `http://www.openmoko.com/`

performed a set of activities, each one for a duration from approx 2 - 15 minutes. The local activities were as follows: the subject has placed the mug on the **table** (or other surface), the subject is holding the mug in their **hand**, the subject is **drinking** from the mug, and the subject is **gesticulating**.

In the second phase the global classification rates for all modes were evaluated. The subjects conducted the following activities for 4 - 5 minutes a piece using the Smart Mugs trained in the previous phase: **Meeting**, **Presentation** and **Coffee break**. Offline, the first half of the data was used to train 6 different classifiers and the second half to evaluate their performance. For each of the 3 abstraction levels which are transmitted to the Neo, both a kNN and a DT classifier were trained for global GAR for comparison, and the second half of the data was used to evaluate the performance of the 6 different classifiers.

4 Conclusion

This paper described an experiment in the field of multi-user group activity recognition using wearable sensors. A hierarchical approach to recognizing these activities was examined, where nodes forward information about the subject's activities to a central device which attempts to recognize the activity that the group is currently performing. In this experiment, different context abstraction levels where conducted at the mugs and the entire network was monitored in terms of power consumption and activity recognition rates. The results have not yet been evaluated, but they are expected to provide insight into the effects of the context abstraction level on group activity recognition using wearable sensors.

The authors would like to acknowledge funding by the European Commission for the ICT project "CHOSeN" (Project number 224327, FP7-ICT-2007-2).

References

1. Beigl, M., Gellersen, H.-W., Schmidt, A.: Mediacups: experience with design and use of computer-augmented everyday artefacts. Comput. Netw. 35, 401–409 (2001)
2. Berchtold, M., Budde, M., Gordon, D., Schmidtke, H., Beigl, M.: ActiServ: Activity recognition service for mobile phones. In: ISWC 2010: Proceedings of the Fourteenth International Symposium on Wearable Computers, pp. 83–90. IEEE Computer Society, Seoul (2010)
3. Dunkels, A., Grönvall, B., Voigt, T.: Contiki - a lightweight and flexible operating system for tiny networked sensors. In: Proceedings of the First IEEE Workshop on Embedded Networked Sensors, Tampa, Florida, USA (November 2004)
4. Gu, T., Wu, Z., Wang, L., Tao, X., Lu, J.: Mining emerging patterns for recognizing activities of multiple users in pervasive computing. In: 6th Annual International on Mobile and Ubiquitous Systems: Networking Services, MobiQuitous 2009, pp. 1–10 (July 2009)
5. Sigg, S., Gordon, D., von Zengen, G., Beigl, M., Haseloff, S., David, K.: Investigation of context prediction accuracy for different context abstraction levels. IEEE Transactions on Mobile Computing, 2011 (to appear)

Global Peer-to-Peer Classification in Mobile Ad-Hoc Networks: A Requirements Analysis

Dawud Gordon, Markus Scholz, Yong Ding, and Michael Beigl

Karlsruhe Institute of Technology, TecO, Karlsruhe, Germany
firstname.lastname@kit.edu
http://www.teco.kit.edu/

Abstract. This paper examines global context classification in peer-to-peer ad-hoc mobile wireless networks (P2P-MANETs). To begin, circumstances are presented in which such systems would be required to classify a global context. These circumstances are expounded upon by presenting concrete scenarios from which a set of requirements are derived. Using these requirements, related work is evaluated for applicability, indicating no adequate solutions. Algorithmic approaches are proposed, and analysis results in a benchmark as well as bounds for distribution of processing load, memory consumption and message passing in P2P-MANETs.

Keywords: Distributed Classification, Context Recognition, Peer-to-Peer, MANET, WSN, Requirements Analysis.

1 Introduction

One of the advantages of pure P2P-MANETS[9] over structured client-server network architectures is their ability to adapt to new situations and account for mobility without drastically increasing complexity. The concepts of situational, context and activity recognition have been expanded to include ad-hoc mobile networks, such as wireless sensor nodes and cellular phones. In the ad-hoc network and embedded systems fields, these approaches have been focused on devices which are capable of recognizing their local situations and using this information for local decision making or communicating it to a centralized back-end system with various degrees of preprocessing, compression and data fusion.

These paradigms, while very useful for many applications, stand in contrast to the concept of P2P-MANETs. In embedded systems, local recognition by a device of its own situation can be very useful in local decision making processes. In distributed sensing systems, transmission of local situational information to a central location allows the system to recognize global situations and reduces the volume of communication when compared to forwarding unprocessed data.

For fully distributed ad-hoc wireless systems such as P2P-MANETs however, there is no theoretical, algorithmic or practical support available for global context recognition in related work. This paper will begin by identifying environments and example scenarios for global recognition in P2P-MANETs in Section 2, and extracting a list of requirements based on those scenarios in Section 3. In

M. Beigl et al. (Eds.): CONTEXT 2011, LNAI 6967, pp. 108–114, 2011.

Section 4, related work will be examined for applicable approaches, followed by a discussion in Section 5 and the conclusion in Section 6.

2 Application Scenario

Local situations refer to a situation occurring in the immediate environment of a network node, or subset of nodes, and can be sensed and recognized by that node or nodes. Global situations on the other hand, occur over the domain of the entire MANET and are not directly measurable at any one position, but are rather deduceable only when confronted with distributed measurements from multiple nodes within the network. The necessity to recognize global situations arise under the following circumstances:

The network has sporadic access to a data sink, network bridge or other communication module. A typical application for this kind of setting is provided by the landmarke ad-hoc firefighter support network[11]. This network is deployed in an environment with unstable communication channel characteristics[12]. However, despite a connection loss to the central uplink, the individual firefighter should still be informed about the situation of the entire team.

The network has access but at an exorbitant price in terms of energy consumption, bandwidth, delay, etc. An exemplary use case for this setting could be free-range monitoring of livestock where only an expensive uplink is available to inform the care taker. While activities of individual animals are important, situations affecting the whole herd (e.g. herd fragmentation, being harried by a wolf, etc.) call for a global classifier (Fig. 1).

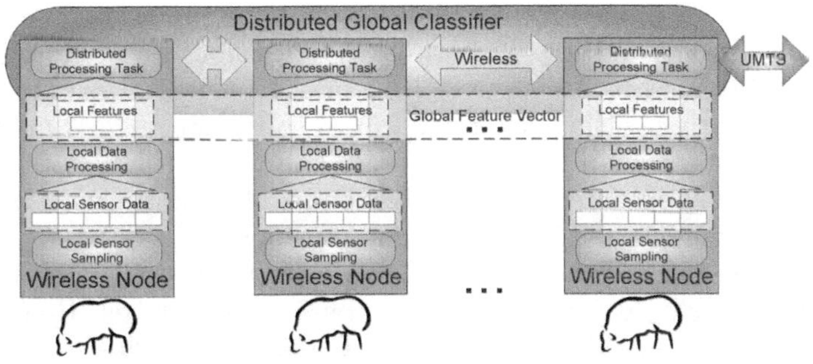

Fig. 1. Distributed Classifier Architecture in a P2P-MANET for Livestock Monitoring

The network without uplink must be situationally aware and act locally. Deploying P2P-MANETs in real life settings usually leads to incorrect function of the network due to unforeseen permutations of environmental features. For instance, in the case of a distributed, autonomous sensor-actor system for monitoring and controlling a pump station, the observation of local network parameters could be the input to a distributed algorithm which could identify different types of failure situations and initiate preventative measures.

3 Requirements Analysis

Based on the application scenarios, it is possible to highlight the requirements which a distributed classification algorithm must fulfill:

Requirement 1. *Survival of Node Failures.* In all three scenarios it is clear that nodes may drop out of the network without warning due to connectivity issues or node failures. The global classifier algorithm must be able to continue functioning, even if in an impaired fashion, implying that any single point of failure within the network would break with this requirement.

Requirement 2. *Recovery from Node Failures.* Not only must the algorithm be able to survive failures, it is also crucial that it can recover from these failures, meaning that successive node replacements do not lead to long term degradation of the algorithm. In the livestock monitoring example, imagine a situation where there is a certain animal throughput, meaning animals are constantly being added to and removed from the herd. Without this capability the performance of the classification algorithm would slowly degrade over time as each animal which leaves the herd causes the irreparable loss of a certain amount of functionality.

Requirement 3. *Ability to Approximate the Mapping Function.* Each of the three scenarios represents a different mapping function from the input signals to the contextual ground truth. Moreover, in each scenario, the exact context which the system recognizes is only vaguely fixed and may be arbitrarily complex. As a result of this, an algorithm which would be able to accomplish these tasks must be able to learn the solution, no matter how complex the mapping function is.

4 Related Work

In parallel computing multiple nodes work simultaneously to reduce processing time compared to a sequential approach. A brief review of algorithms from this field showed that these either rely on a central coordinator [2], [10] or are managed by dedicated scheduling instances [7], failing to fulfill Req. 1 (survive node failures) or building on different conditions and cost models than MANETs.

Collaborative models and in-network data fusion are one of the most straightforward methods for P2P based classification. Therein each node contributes to a global consensus based on locally recognized situations. However, while approaches [14,6] from this field employ different strategies to reach a global consensus, they are limited in the complexity of the mapping from local input to the global decision. These approaches observe the state of each of the nodes, and make a decision about the global situation based on these states, but without observing the identity or functionality of each node (voting). The global context algorithm is then only a function quantities of local contexts, in violation of Req. 3 as it can only map a subset of classification functions (see sec. 5 for a discussion). Recently [13] and [5] presented novel methods of processing context data within the nodes of a wireless network. However, there the classification is carried out by a single node, violating Req. 1 and 2. Finally, [8] presents a framework for distributed inference based on Bayesian networks and belief propagation. While this approach meets all requirements, "convergence may take a long time, or it may never happen" if the variables or the network are dynamic [8], making it inappropriate for situational recognition.

In Organic Computing, approaches such as swarm intelligence are distributed paradigms for solving optimization problems inspired by the biological processes of swarming, flocking and herding. Various authors from this field, e.g. [3], [1] present algorithms for the distributed detection and global classification of situations. However, these algorithms conduct this in a collaborative fashion which does not support Req. 3, or use a central unit to perform recognition over a feature map generated in a distributed fashion which is not reconcilable with Req. 1. In short, distributed classification approaches from the area of Organic Computing cannot be directly applied to global situational recognition in P2P-MANETs.

5 Analysis and Discussion

Social Role. In the machine monitoring example, all objects will have been present at classifier training time. This means that if a machine component is separated from the network and then later returns, the classifier will correctly map the data generated by that object to the output function of the classifier, as specified by Req. 1. The implication is that when the object is reconnected, whatever power was lost with respect to recognition at disconnect is regained.

In the case of livestock monitoring, animals may leave the herd and be replaced by other unique individuals. This presents the problem of how to include the new animals in classification. Simply substituting the data from the new animal in the global vector (see Figure 1) can also be problematic, as there is no reason to believe that the new animal plays the same role in the herd dynamics. Eventually, constant animal throughput would cause complete randomization of local vector locations in the global vector, leading to degradation of algorithmic performance, and situational inferences based on the previous data would no longer necessarily remain valid, violating Req. 2. This leads to the following:

Lemma 1. *A system in which new data is appended to the global vector at a position which is not role-dependent can be modeled by randomly re-locating the data from each node in the global vector at each classification phase.*

A possible way to combat this effect would be to train the classifier using random positions for each partial vector (the data generated by each node) from each object in the total feature vector. This assumes de facto homogeneity among the objects (e.g. livestock animals) as the information gathered from a certain animal can be input at any location on the feature vector without affecting the output of the classifier. Since no single object can assume a specific role, the only functions which can be mapped by the classifier at learning time are quantity-based functions (e.g. if the majority is sleeping then the herd is sleeping), rather than inferences based on the roles of certain individuals as to the situation of the whole (e.g. inferences based on the dominant roles of certain individuals). This yields the following:

Lemma 2. *A classifier trained on a global vector in which features from each object are appended to the global vector at random positions can only learn mappings based on quantities or counts of nodes.*

Unfortunately, functions over the quantities of objects reduces the system to majority and voting-based collaborative systems such as [14]. Standard classifiers implicitly learn object roles in the learning process as feature (vector) positions in the input vector are constant over time. A system in which these positions are not constant must therefore explicitly account for these fluctuations.

Theorem 1. *A global classifier which does not observe the individuality or role of each of the objects being monitored is only capable of classifying global contexts which can be reduced to functions over quantities and counts of node states.*

Brute Force Method. The simplest solution to the global classifier problem in terms of complexity is the brute force approach, in which each node transmits all locally generated data required for global context classification to every other node in the network, and then each node locally classifies the global situation. Theoretically, if the classifier is identical on each node, and the data vector is also identical, each node should locally classify the identical global situation.

The disadvantages include the amount of memory required by each node to store the entire classifier, the number of transmissions required to transmit all data generated to every other node, as well as energy consumption due to the redundancy. On the other hand, the network is extremely stable as failed nodes do not adversely affect the classification of the rest of the network, as long as the classifier used can accommodate the variable feature vector length (see [4]). Also, new nodes which are added to the network must only receive the parameters for the classifier and be added to the global list of data publishers and subscribers in order to become functioning members of the new system.

Other Solutions. One approach would be to select a classification algorithm which easily lends itself to distributed execution and apply this to the entire network. Such algorithms are often referred to as connectionistic methods, (e.g. neural network, multi-agent system, spatial reasoning, etc.) which involve processors (neurons) and connections between these processors. This would reduce processor load and memory required when compared to the brute force approach, though it is initially unclear what affect this would have on communication between nodes. Such a method requires time synchronization which is indeed costly in ad-hoc P2P networks, though it would overcome the convergence issues of [8], and increased communication could possibly be combated by P2P self-organization.

Another approach would be to distribute the data instead of the execution. This could be accomplished by adapting instance-based learning methods such as k-Nearest-Neighbors or Self Organizing Maps to be distributed over multiple nodes along the principle that vectors which are close to each other are also close to each other in terms of hops. Once again, self-organization could be employed to account for varying network structure and mobility, but the amount of communication incurred and the advantages over brute force must be studied.

Resource Consumption Analysis. Assuming N peer-to-peer nodes and objects in the network, and a distributable global classification algorithm with memory consumption M and processing load P. The brute force approach incurs the full memory consumption of M and processing load P locally at each node, as the classifier is redundantly stored and executed. The number of messages which have to be passed between nodes is $N - 1$, as each node needs to communicate local features to every other node in order to build the global feature vector, or $N(N - 1)$ messages in total. The memory consumption is thereby increased to $(M + S_g)$, where S_g is the size (length) of the global feature vector.

For a distributed connectionist reasoning approach, assuming each node is an input, output and hidden processor (e.g. neuron), then each node will have to pass 2 messages. Each processor requires input and generates output, where the input for the input processors is generated locally, and the output processor is output locally. In other words, per classification phase $2N$ messages must be passed by the system. Local memory consumption is now that incurred by 3 of $3N$ processors, where $3N$ processors can be held in M memory, or $\frac{M}{N}$, plus the length of the local feature vector, giving $\frac{M}{N} + S_l$. Each node must execute 3 of $3N$ processors, where the total processing load is P, yielding a load of $\frac{P}{N}$ per node. This indicates that this approach would reduce memory consumption by $\frac{M(N-1)}{N} + (S_g - S_l)$, processing load by $\frac{P(N-1)}{N}$ and the number of messages passed by $N(N - 3)$.

Taking this one step further, we can hypothesize about the lower bounds for resource consumption in P2P-MANETs. In an optimal situation, each node sends local information to the exact logical location where it is needed (1 hop), and the system has no redundancy, indicating that each node transmits 1 message per classification phase, for a total of N messages. Also, optimally the system would distribute the memory consumption M and processor load incurred P equally across all nodes, yielding $\frac{M}{N}$ and $\frac{P}{N}$ respectively. This indicates that while being optimal in terms of memory and processor requirements, the connectionist reasoning approach would still be sub-optimal in terms of message passing by a factor of 2.

6 Conclusion

This work began by identifying the need for peer-to-peer classification of global situations in MANETs. This is based on three different circumstances which occur in a subset of standard deployments, where either there is no communication with the outside world, that communication is very expensive, or a link is only available from time to time. These situations were elaborated on by presenting three example scenarios, safety monitoring in firefighter teams, monitoring and alerts in livestock management, and industrial monitoring and controlling. These scenarios were then analyzed in order to extract requirements for a peer-to-peer classification algorithm in wireless ad-hoc networks. This analysis indicated a further requirement of respecting heterogeneity of the different objects being monitored. Hypothetical upper and lower bounds for processing load, memory usage and communication volumes were elaborated, and a brute force (upper bound) and neural network (close to lower bound) approach were examined.

The authors acknowledge joint funding by the DFG under the project "Sense-Cast", the EC under "CHOSeN" and the BMBF under "Koordinator".

References

1. Brueckner, S.A., Van Dyke Parunak, H.: Swarming distributed pattern detection and classification. In: Weyns, D., Van Dyke Parunak, H., Michel, F. (eds.) E4MAS 2004. LNCS (LNAI), vol. 3374, pp. 232–245. Springer, Heidelberg (2005)
2. Caragea, D., Silvescu, A., Honavar, V.: A framework for learning from distributed data using sufficient statistics and its application to learning decision trees. Int. J. Hybrid Intell. Syst. 1, 80–89 (2004)
3. Dasgupta, P.: A multiagent swarming system for distributed automatic target recognition using unmanned aerial vehicles. IEEE Transactions on Systems, Man and Cybernetics, Part A: Systems and Humans 38(3), 549–563 (2008)
4. Gordon, D., Sigg, S., Ding, Y., Beigl, M.: Using prediction to conserve energy in recognition on mobile devices. In: 9th International Conference on Pervasive Computing and Communications, PERCOM Workshops (2011)
5. Lu, G., Xue, W.: Adaptive weighted fusion algorithm for monitoring system of forest fire based on wireless sensor networks. In: International Conference on Computer Modeling and Simulation, vol. 4, pp. 414–417 (2010)
6. Luo, P., Xiong, H., Lü, K., Shi, Z.: Distributed classification in peer-to-peer networks. In: Proceedings of the 13th ACM SIGKDD International Conference on Knowledge Discovery and Data Mining, KDD 2007, pp. 968–976. ACM, New York (2007)
7. Natarajan, R., Sion, R., Phan, T.: A grid-based approach for enterprise-scale data mining. Future Gener. Comput. Syst. 23, 48–54 (2007)
8. Paskin, M.A., Guestrin, C.E.: Robust probabilistic inference in distributed systems. In: Proceedings of the 20th Conference on Uncertainty in Artificial Intelligence, UAI 2004, pp. 436–445. AUAI Press, Arlington (2004)
9. Schollmeier, R.: A definition of peer-to-peer networking for the classification of peer-to-peer architectures and applications. In: Proceedings. First International Conference on Peer-to-Peer Computing, pp. 101–102 (August 2001)
10. Scholz, M., Flehmig, G., Schmidtke, H.R., Scholz, G.H.: Powering smart home intelligence using existing entertainment systems. In: the 7th International Conference on Intelligent Environments, IE 2011 (2011)
11. Scholz, M., Riedel, T., Decker, C.: A flexible architecture for a robust indoor navigation support device for firefighters. In: Proceedings of the 7th International Conference on Networked Sensing Systems (2010)
12. Schubert, E., Scholz, M.: Evaluation of wireless sensor technologies in a firefighting environment. In: Proceedings of the 7th International Conference on Networked Sensing Systems (2010)
13. Sigg, S., Beigl, M.: Expectation aware in-network context processing. In: Proceedings of the 4th ACM International Workshop on Context-Awareness for Self-Managing Systems, CASEMANS 2010. ACM, New York (2010)
14. Wittenburg, G., Dziengel, N., Wartenburger, C., Schiller, J.: A system for distributed event detection in wireless sensor networks. In: IPSN 2010: Proceedings of the 9th ACM/IEEE International Conference on Information Processing in Sensor Networks. ACM, New York (2010)

Towards a Multi-perspectival Approach of Describing Context

Thomas Grill and Manfred Tscheligi

ICT&S Center, University of Salzburg, Salzburg, Austria

Abstract. Describing context for using it within a research and development process is an ambitious task. Different people with different background knowledge, goals, and thus aspects on context are participating in such a process and require context information for different purposes. In this paper we address this issue by defining a structural description model where we regard factors relevant to the different participants and thus perspectives of such a process. The proposed model is based on context models existing in the literature and current ways of using context in the areas of software engineering and human computer interaction.

Keywords: Context, Context Model, Human Computer Interaction.

1 Introduction

Context plays a major role in any research and development process. The main actors within such a process require an elucidation of contextual situations and factors during their work. Tasks that include contextual descriptions range from the design of new products and the evaluation and analysis of existing products to a broad range of research areas. This paper depicts a meta-model of context describing a structural approach of analyzing and describing contextual information relevant for an interactive system.

2 Towards "Perspectives on Context"

Within the recent years numerous models of context have been defined as e.g. by Schmidt [3] and Tarasewich [4]. The meta model elaborated in this work combines the aspect of designing contextual interfaces, i.e. the design of user interfaces residing within a specific context and using contextual information for specific purposes, and a user perspective with respect to an interactive system.

By doing this we address the link between a user's perspective and the effect of an interaction on a user. This combines a user experience perspective with a designer and developer perspective when focusing on an interactive system.

The different perspectives on context are based on the entities participating in such an interactive system. The identified entities are the user, the world he is interacting in, the social context he resides in, the user interface used for an interaction, as well as the system or application providing the interactive functionality.

M. Beigl et al. (Eds.): CONTEXT 2011, LNAI 6967, pp. 115–118, 2011.

2.1 User - System Interaction

The general goal of an interactive system is to provide functionality to a user. The functionality is provided to the user via one distinct or multiple user interfaces having a bridging function between the two participants of an interactive system, which are a user and the system (see Figure 1).

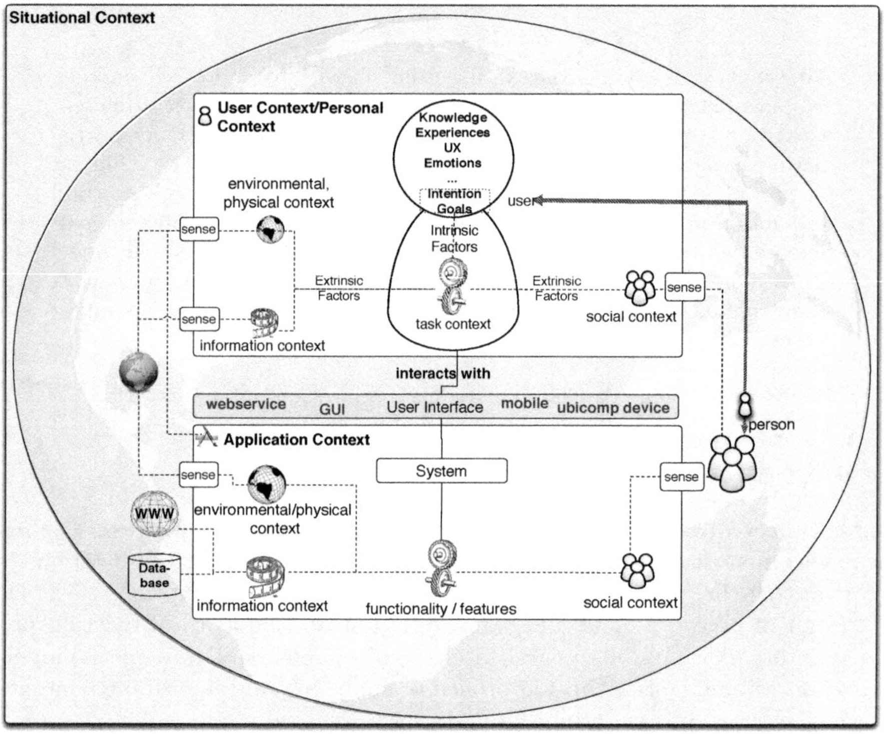

Fig. 1. Context Description Model

This situation along with the entities interacting within such a system is described and characterized by interaction parameters and context factors.

The User Context or personal context contains the sum of all parameters or factors (intrinsic or extrinsic) relevant for a distinct user to interact with a system via a user interface. Intrinsic factors can be defined as e.g. knowledge and memories that reside within the user while extrinsic factors describe any information the user may perceive and which are relevant to a specific interaction.

The Application Context contains all parameters relevant to implement a system providing a certain functionality while focusing on a data centric description approach. The user interface as part of the system builds the bridge between the system and the real world.

2.2 Context in a User-System Interaction Model

In the interaction model elaborated in Section 2.1 we were able to identify two different participating entities, each having its own perspective on context. Both stakeholders of the interaction process intrinsic to the model are shown by the particular relevant sub-contexts, being the user and the application context.

The User Context. In order to interact with a system the user needs to be part of the interactive system and the interaction process based on an interaction model as defined by e.g. [2]. The different perspectives on context relevant to the user context can thus be described by the following sub-contexts.

The Task Context. The task context represents according to Bradley and Dunlop [1] the functional relationship of the user with other people, objects, and the benefits (e.g. resources available) or constraints (e.g. time pressure) this relationship places on the user's achievement of his or her goal. According to this definition the execution of a task depends on the factors intrinsic and extrinsic to the user. Such factors provide input to a cognitive process resulting in the potential execution of a dedicated task situated within the task context.

The Environmental Context. The environmental or physical context represents environmental context factors such as noise, light, temperature, etc. The information itself is sensed and interpreted by a human.

Social Context. The social context is represented through the people involved in a specific interaction. Parameters like the amount of people, the type of people, the interest of people, being part of a group of people, etc. influence and shape the user's perspective on social context. The user himself is always part of the social context he interacts in and has a distinct relationship to the people being part of such a context. Such a social context may be influenced through the physical or virtual presence of people relevant to the interaction.

Information Context. The information context consists of any external knowledge that is accessible to the user and which may influence his decisions. Such information may be information stored in databases, in the internet, but also knowledge acquired through past experiences of the user.

The Application Context. An application or system implements the functionality and features of an application as well as a user interface that bridges the gap between the functional parts of the system and the user.

The functional requirements contain every available information that is required to design and develop a certain functionality to be provided by a system. The factors of the application context thus refer to data that can be obtained either through sensors providing information about the environmental, physical or social sub-context. Such data can be used and interpreted directly by the application or by a context interpretation framework which reasons about data.

The Interaction Environment. The user-system interaction as described in Section 2.1 represents an interaction between a human and an interactive system occurring in an environment the user as well as the system resides in. Figure 1 introduces this environment in the form of a globe surrounding such an interactive system. Both main actors in the interactive system, i.e. the user and the application may sense and use information located in the real world. The sensed information builds the basis for identifying and defining contextual information with the intention to use this information to design an interactive system.

The Situational Context represents a snapshot of a distinct context situation that relates to a specific interaction scenario. Such a specific interaction scenario is based on the information contained in the User Context as well as in the Application Context (see Figure 1).

The Temporal Context completes the Context Description Model. The temporal context bases on the viewpoint of the situational context which provides a snapshot of interaction with a focus on all interaction relevant information from the user's point of view as well as from the application's point of view. Based on this snapshot a context history is developed, which allows to analyze the contextual information's evolution from a timelines' perspective. The establishment of such a context history provides insights into the effects of the relevant contextual parameters over time.

3 Conclusion and Future Work

In this paper we elaborate a model that allows to describe and use contextual information within a research and development process. We are currently evaluating the proposed model and could already show the validity of the model in interaction contexts describing different application areas. Future work will include the development of a tool that integrates the description of the different perspectives on context for use within different steps of such a process.

References

1. Bradley, N.A., Dunlop, M.D.: Towards a multidisciplinary model of context to support context-aware computing. Journal of Human-Computer Interaction 20(4), 403–446 (2005)
2. Grill, T., Ibrahim, I.K., Kotsis, G.: Agent interaction in ambient intelligent environments. In: Proceedings of DPSWS, November 30 - December 2, vol. 19. IPSJ (2005)
3. Schmidt, A., Beigl, M., Gellersen, H.-W.: There is more to context than location. Computers and Graphics 23(6), 893–901 (1999)
4. Tarasewich, P.: Towards a comprehensive model of context for mobile and wireless computing. In: Proc. of AMCIS 2003, pp. 114–124 (2003)

The Emotion Ontology: Enabling Interdisciplinary Research in the Affective Sciences

Janna Hastings[1,2,*], Werner Ceusters[3], Barry Smith[4], and Kevin Mulligan[1]

[1] Department of Philosophy and Swiss Centre for Affective Sciences, University of Geneva, Geneva, Switzerland
hastings@ebi.ac.uk

[2] Chemoinformatics and Metabolism, European Bioinformatics Institute, Hinxton, UK

[3] Department of Psychiatry and Ontology Research Group, New York State Center of Excellence in Bioinformatics & Life Sciences, University at Buffalo, NY, USA

[4] Department of Philosophy and National Center for Ontological Research, New York State Center of Excellence in Bioinformatics & Life Sciences, University at Buffalo, NY, USA

Abstract. Affective science conducts interdisciplinary research into the emotions and other affective phenomena. Currently, such research is hampered by the lack of common definitions of terms used to describe, categorise and report both individual emotional experiences and the results of scientific investigations of such experiences. High quality ontologies provide formal definitions for types of entities in reality and for the relationships between such entities, definitions which can be used to disambiguate and unify data across different disciplines. Heretofore, there has been little effort directed towards such formal representation for affective phenomena, in part because of widespread debates within the affective science community on matters of definition and categorization. To address this requirement, we are developing an Emotion Ontology (EMO). The full ontology and generated OWLDoc documentation are available for download from https://emotion-ontology.googlecode.com/svn/trunk/ under the Creative Commons – Attribution license (CC BY 3.0).

Introduction

High quality ontologies in the biomedical sciences enhance the potential for integration of the exploding quantities of experimental and clinical data that have become available on-line. When appropriately designed, ontologies allow annotations of data to be unified through disambiguation of the terms employed in a way that allows complex statistical and other analyses to be performed which lead to the computational discovery of novel insights [8].

* Corresponding author

M. Beigl et al. (Eds.): CONTEXT 2011, LNAI 6967, pp. 119–123, 2011.

Affective science is the study of emotions and of affective phenomena such as moods, affects and bodily feelings. It combines the perspectives of many disciplines, such as neuroscience, psychology and philosophy [2]. Emotions have a deep and profound influence on all aspects of human functioning, and altered or dysfunctional emotional responses are implicated in both the etiology and the symptomology of many pathological conditions. Depression, for example, which is characterised by abnormally low affect and generally flattened emotional reactions, is one of the fastest-growing public health problems in many countries, corresponding to massive growth in sales of pharmaceuticals (and other substances) which target human affect [6].

Research in affective science faces the need to integrate results obtained on the basis of subjective reports and those obtained by neuroscientific or other methodologies, and to compare results across disciplines, requiring a shared, disambiguated and clear reference terminology for the domain [3,9]. To address this, we are developing an Emotion Ontology (EMO).

1 Ontology Overview

An overview of the organising upper levels of EMO, aligned with the Basic Formal Ontology (BFO) [12,4] and the Ontology of Mental Disease (OMD) [1] is illustrated in Figure 1.

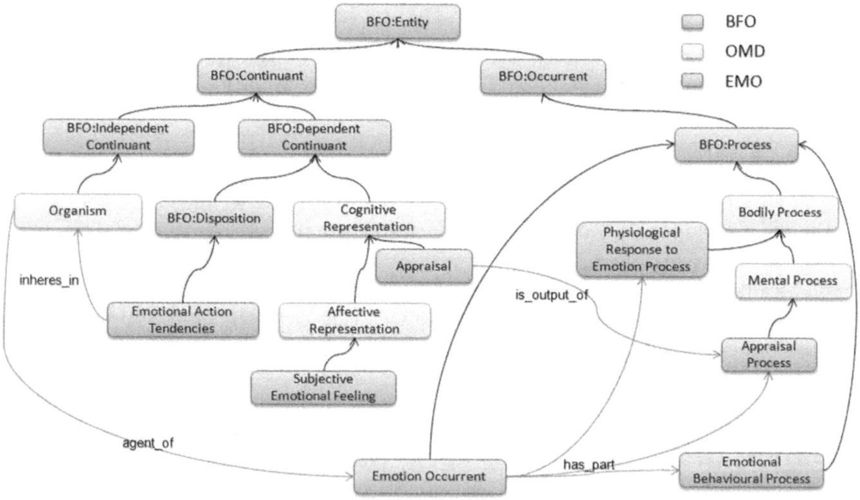

Fig. 1. An overview of the Emotion Ontology. Unlabelled arrows represent 'is a' relations.

Each aspect of the ontology from this upper level is then developed further with specific subtypes annotated and defined beneath them. Figure 2 gives an illustration of some of the entities in the ontology.

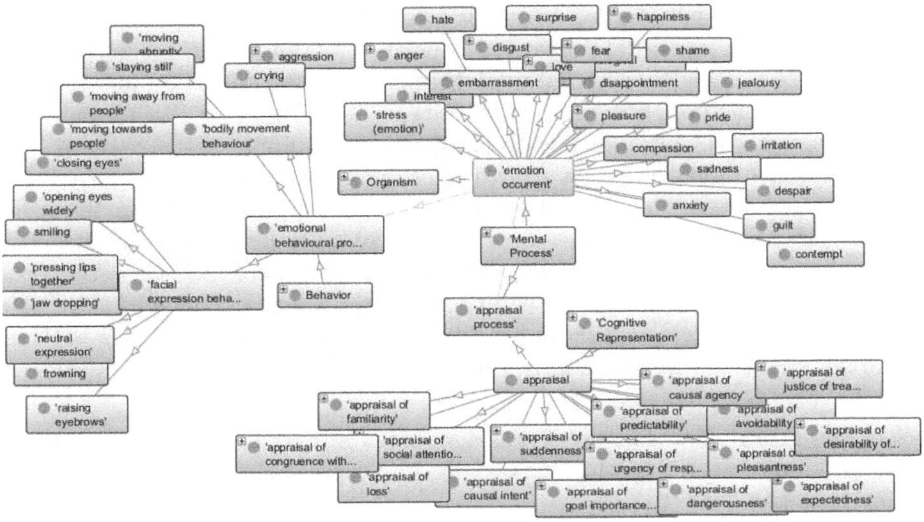

Fig. 2. Example expanded subtypes of upper level entities

2 Requirements and Future Work

The proper formal characterisation and standardisation of descriptions of mental processes in ontologies is increasingly being recognised as essential to advance many research agendas in the brain and mind sciences [7]. Recognising the need for clear categorical distinctions in support of research design, the accumulation of research findings, and linking affective science to the biomedical science of affective disorders, emotion researchers have long been proposing typologies and lists of emotions and affective phenomena [3]. Thus far, a broad shared agreement on definitions for emotion terms has not been achieved, although there is agreement on many of the relevant constituent elements [3].

Requirements in computing and artificial intelligence have led to the development of ontology-like resources for emotions. *Affective computing* aims to integrate emotional responses into computer interfaces in order to produce more realistic systems which are able to respond to the emotional communication of their users. To facilitate affective computing, Lopez *et al.* propose a slim ontology schema for describing emotions in *human-computer interfaces* [5]. Also motivated by affective computing requirements, the W3C's emotion markup language (EML)[1] is an XML-based standard for markup of emotions in text or databases. Another computing application which has led to developments in this domain is natural language processing, for which Valitutti and Stock developed an emotion lexicon [14] and Triezenberg has developed an emotion terminology which categorises emotion types and related behaviour [13].

[1] http://www.w3.org/TR/emotionml/

Effectively marking up references to emotions relies on an unambiguous shared understanding of what emotion terms denote. All of the ontology-like resources that have thus far been developed make use of emotion terms assumed to be defined elsewhere. The formal and unambiguous scientific definition for terms in this domain is therefore still an open requirement, and it is to fill this gap that the power of shared community-wide ontologies is required.

Our approach, following best practices promoted by the OBO Foundry [10] and the principles of Ontological Realism [11], will be to engage each of the different sub-communities, both scientific and computational, at every stage in the development of EMO in order to address and reconcile, rather than ignore, fundamental terminological and definitional disagreements. This will allow the application of the developed ontology to multiple application scenarios both in support of scientific research and in support of intelligent computing.

Acknowledgements. This work was supported in part by the Swiss National Science Foundation, and by the US National Institutes of Health under Roadmap Grant 1 U 54 HG004028.

References

1. Ceusters, W., Smith, B.: Foundations for a realist ontology of mental disease. Journal of Biomedical Semantics 1(1), 10 (2010)
2. Davidson, R.J., Scherer, K.R., Goldsmith, H.H.: Handbook of Affective Sciences. Series in Affective Sciences. Oxford University Press, Oxford (2003)
3. Frijda, N.H., Scherer, K.R.: Emotion definitions (psychological perspectives). Oxford University Press, New York (2009)
4. Grenon, P., Smith, B., Goldberg, L.: Biodynamic ontology: Applying BFO in the biomedical domain. In: Stud. Health Technol. Inform., pp. 20–38. IOS Press, Amsterdam (2004)
5. López, J.M., Gil, R., García, R., Cearreta, I., Garay, N.: Towards an ontology for describing emotions. In: Lytras, M.D., Damiani, E., Tennyson, R.D. (eds.) WSKS 2008. LNCS (LNAI), vol. 5288, pp. 96–104. Springer, Heidelberg (2008)
6. Patel, V., Flisher, A.J., Hetrick, S., McGorry, P.: Mental health of young people: a global public-health challenge. The Lancet. 369(9569), 1302–1313 (2007)
7. Poldrack, R.A.: Mapping mental function to brain structure: How can cognitive neuroimaging succeed? Perspectives on Psychological Science 5(6), 753–761 (2010)
8. Rubin, D.L., Shah, N.H., Noy, N.F.: Biomedical ontologies: a functional perspective. Briefings in Bioinformatics 9(1), 75–90 (2008)
9. Scherer, K.R.: What are emotions? and how can they be measured? Social Science Information 44, 695–729 (2005)
10. Smith, B., Ashburner, M., Rosse, C., Bard, J., Bug, W., Ceusters, W., Goldberg, L.J., Eilbeck, K., Ireland, A., Mungall, C.J., Leontis, N., Rocca-Serra, P., Ruttenberg, A., Sansone, S.A., Scheuermann, R.H., Shah, N., Whetzel, P.L., Lewis, S.: The OBO Foundry: coordinated evolution of ontologies to support biomedical data integration. Nat Biotechnol. 25(11), 1251–1255 (2007)

11. Smith, B., Ceusters, W.: Ontological realism as a methodology for coordinated evolution of scientific ontologies. Applied Ontology 5, 139–188 (2010)
12. Smith, B., Grenon, P.: The cornucopia of formal ontological relations. Dialectica 58, 279–296 (2004)
13. Triezenberg, K.: The Ontology of Emotion. Ph.D. thesis, College of Liberal Arts (09 (2005)
14. Valitutti, R., Stock, O.: Developing affective lexical resources. PsychNology Journal, 61–83 (2004)

Autodoxastic Conditional Reasoning: The Monotonic Case

Haythem O. Ismail and Aya S. Mahfouz

German University in Cairo
Department of Computer Science
{haythem.ismail,aya.mahfouz}@guc.edu.eg

Abstract. Ramsey's test for conditionals seems to be in conflict with the so-called Thomason conditionals. A Thomason conditional is a conditional in which either the antecedent or the consequent is a statement about the reasoning agent's own beliefs. Several authors have pointed out that resolving the apparent conflict is to be sought by abandoning the belief revision interpretation of the Ramsey test in favor of a suppositional interpretation. We formalize an AGM-style notion of supposition, showing that it is identical to revision for agents who are not autodoxastic—agents who do not reason about their beliefs. We present particular realizations of supposition in terms of revision and identify the relations between the conditionals supposition and revision give rise to.

1 Ramsey, Thomason, and Moore

In this paper, we attempt to consolidate two issues that, apparently, are in tension: the Ramsey test for conditionals and the so-called Thomason conditionals. The Ramsey test grounds the plausibility of conditionals (roughly, sentences of the form "If P then Q") in a process of belief change. In an often quoted excerpt from [1], Robert Stalnaker gives a procedural interpretation of the Ramsey test:

> First, add the antecedent (hypothetically) to your stock of beliefs; second, make whatever adjustments are required to maintain consistency (without modifying the hypothetical belief in the antecedent); finally, consider whether or not the consequent is then true.

Researchers in artificial intelligence (AI) and philosophical logic will immediately recognize the process Stalnaker is referring to as one of belief revision [2]. This is certainly a welcome interpretation of the Ramsey test, since belief revision has been thoroughly investigated both in AI (for example [3,4]) and philosophy. Unfortunately, interpreting the Ramsey test as implying a process of belief revision has been dealt at least two blows.

First, Peter Gärdenfors [5] proved that the belief revision interpretation of the Ramsey test is inconsistent with a minimal set of harmless demands on a logical theory. We do not address this problem here; but see [6]. Second, a number of authors, since 1980 [7] till the turn of the decade [8,9,10,11], have pointed out

M. Beigl et al. (Eds.): CONTEXT 2011, LNAI 6967, pp. 124–137, 2011.

that the Ramsey test, *à* la Stalnaker, provides counter-intuitive judgments of some conditionals—the so-called Thomason conditionals [7].

Thomason conditionals are conditionals in which either the antecedent or the consequent are statements about the reasoning agent's own beliefs. In particular, they come in four main forms:[1]

TC1. If ϕ, then I believe ϕ.
TC2. If I believe ϕ, then ϕ.
TC3. If ϕ, then I do not believe ϕ.
TC4. If I do not believe ϕ, then ϕ.

Given the Stalnaker (belief-revision) interpretation of the Ramsey test, one should accept **TC1** and **TC2**, and reject **TC3** and **TC4**; otherwise, one would succumb to accepting a Moore-paradoxical sentence:

M1. ϕ and I do not believe ϕ.
M2. Not ϕ and I believe ϕ.

But these judgments are not always correct, as several examples attest.

(1) ? If Sally is a spy, then I believe that Sally is a spy.

(2) ? If I believe that Sally is a spy, then Sally is a spy.

(3) If Sally were deceiving me, I would believe that she was not deceiving me (because she is so clever).[2]

(4) Even if I were not to believe that Sally is a spy, she would be a spy (my misconceptions do not change the facts).

A number of authors have attempted to reconcile the Ramsey test with such data [8,9,10,11]. The main idea is that Stalnaker's interpretation of the Ramsey test is not exactly faithful to Ramsey's real proposal. However, except for Willer [10] who presents a theory within the framework of update semantics, these proposals are largely informal. In this short report, we propose to stay as close as possible to the AGM belief revision tradition [2]. We introduce an AGM-style belief change operator—supposition—that, we claim, adequately accounts for Thomason conditionals if taken to be the belief change operator implicit in Ramsey's test. Unlike [10], however, we retain the common epistemic reading of the Ramsey test side by side with the suppositional one. Hence, we distinguish two classes of conditionals, based on these two readings.

[1] Strictly speaking, the agent's own beliefs need not explicitly appear in a conditional to make the same "Thomason-effect", but even in such cases, beliefs of the agents are assumed to establish the relevance of the antecedent to the consequent.

[2] This is a classical example attributed to Richmond Thomason (hence, "Thomason conditionals"), but appears in print in [7].

2 Autodoxastic Agents

We call an agent that can reason about its beliefs an autodoxastic agent. Why is it paradoxical for an autodoxastic agent to hold beliefs such as **M1** and **M2**? Intuitively, in normal situations (which we assume throughout), an agent cannot hold that ϕ is true and simultaneously fail to believe it; or hold that ϕ is not true and, nevertheless, believe it. But things are not that simple, or otherwise how would one reply to Chalmers and Hájek's remarks [8] about the oddity of unconditionally accepting **TC1** and **TC2**?

The two pairs $(\mathbf{M1}, \mathbf{M2})$ and $(\mathbf{TC1}, \mathbf{TC2})$ both make sense in some contexts of reasoning, and make no sense in others. In some contexts of reasoning—*regular* contexts—the contexts within which the agent normally and usually reasons, what the agent takes to be true is identical to what it believes. In such contexts, **TC1** and **TC2** are totally acceptable, while **M1** and **M2** are impossible. In *non-regular* contexts, the opposite is true: **M1** and **M2** are possible while **TC1** and **TC2** are usually not acceptable.

What are these non-regular contexts? These are hypothetical contexts of reasoning, in which the agent entertains what the world would be like under one or more suppositions. But once the agent is endowed with the capacity for hypothetical reasoning, it may suppose anything about the world, even things about its own beliefs and their incompatibility with how the (hypothetical) world is. Certainly, the agent may entertain worlds in which ϕ is true, but it does not believe it. Hence, in non-regular contexts **M1** and **M2** are not paradoxical at all. In addition, **TC1** and **TC2** are clearly irrational, in general. Thus, unlike in **TC1** and **TC2**, the "if" in **TC3** and **T4** does not mean "if I accommodate ϕ (respectively, $\neg\phi$) in my regular context" (the belief revision, epistemic reading); rather, it means "if I suppose ϕ (respectively, $\neg\phi$) in a non-regular context" (the suppositional reading).

This being said, our task then is to formalize the distinctions between (i) regular and non-regular contexts, (ii) revision and supposition, and (iii) epistemic and suppositional conditionals.[3]

3 Truth is in the "I" of the "B" Holder

Suppose we have a logical language with an operator **B** for belief and a constant **I** that denotes the reasoning agent; the agent whose beliefs are represented by sentences of the language. What characterizes a regular context of reasoning? According to our discussion so far, regular contexts of reasoning should admit **TC1** and **TC2**. Thus, we may label a context "regular" if it admits the following **B**-schema (after Tarski's T-schema).

[3] We use "autodoxastic" rather than "autoepistemic" not just to be different from Moore [12]. In Moore's autoepistemic logic, only what correspond to our regular contexts are considered. Thus, for an autoepistemic agent, knowledge and belief are equivalent. In our case, since we consider non-regular contexts of reasoning, using the term "autoepistemic" is at least misleading; we stand by "autodoxastic" then.

$$\phi \equiv \mathbf{B}(\mathbf{I}, \phi)$$

But on closer examination, this formula is too strong. For example, the following line of reasoning is possible.

$$\neg\mathbf{B}(\mathbf{I}, \phi) \Longrightarrow \neg\phi \Longrightarrow \mathbf{B}(\mathbf{I}, \neg\phi)$$

Hence, the following would be derivable:

$$\neg\mathbf{B}(\mathbf{I}, \phi) \supset \mathbf{B}(\mathbf{I}, \neg\phi)$$

The agent, thus, holds an opinion about every proposition. Now, we may try to avoid this by abandoning the **B**-schema and sticking to Moore's notion of autoepistemic models [12], in which regularity is enforced through non-monotonic rules of inference. This, however, will not be our favorite route in this paper. First, we believe that (a variant of) the **B**-schema would still be derivable. Second, we will be forced to adopt a non-monotonic logic. In this first report on autodoxastic conditional reasoning, we would like to focus on properties of revision and supposition in the monotonic case, without getting entangled into the complications that a non-monotonic treatment is bound to get us into.

Hence, we shall adopt a weakened version of **B**-schema. In particular, the problematic direction (viz $\phi \supset \mathbf{B}(\mathbf{I}, \phi)$) will be replaced by the weaker formula

$$\phi \supset \overrightarrow{\mathbf{B}}(\mathbf{I}, \phi)$$

where $\overrightarrow{\mathbf{B}}(\mathbf{I}, \phi)$ is $\mathbf{B}(\mathbf{I}, \phi)$ with **B** pushed inside till the outermost positive disjunction or existential quantifier.[4] To make this notion precise, we need to introduce a particular language for reasoning about belief.

4 *Log*$_A$B

The language we use in the representation of and reasoning about belief is *Log*$_A$**B** [14,15], an algebraic logic of belief, consisting only of sorted terms and no formulas. Instead, a special sort of terms is taken to denote propositions. Semantically, the domain of propositions is a complete, non-degenerate, Boolean algebra [16]. Thus reifying propositions provides us with high expressivity compared to standard modal approaches to belief ([17,18], for instance), while avoiding the complications and susceptibility to self-reference paradoxes that plague syntactical approaches [19,13].

For example, the sentence "John believes that Sally is a spy" may be represented in *Log*$_A$**B** by the term

$$\mathbf{B}(J, Spy(S))$$

[4] A similar manoeuver was made by Perlis [13] with the T-schema in order to avoid paradoxes of self-reference.

where $Spy(M)$ is a functional term denoting the proposition that Mary is a spy, while $\mathbf{B}(J, Spy(M))$ is a functional term denoting the proposition that John believes that Mary is a spy. Thus, the belief operator is neither a modal operator nor a predicate symbol, but a function symbol **B** denoting a function from pairs of agents and propositions to propositions. The sentence "John believes everything that Sally believes" may be easily expressed in $Log_A\mathbf{B}$:

$$\forall x[\mathbf{B}(S, x) \supset \mathbf{B}(J, x)]$$

For limitations of space, we only give a brief presentation of $Log_A\mathbf{B}$ syntax; for more details about the syntax and semantics, see [14,15]. A $Log_A\mathbf{B}$ language is a set of terms partitioned into two base syntactic sorts, σ_P and σ_I. Intuitively, σ_P is the set of terms denoting propositions and σ_I is the set of terms denoting anything else. A distinguished subset σ_A of σ_I comprises agent-denoting terms. Standard propositional connectives in B are function symbols on σ_P; quantifiers are treated as punctuation symbols that, together with variables and σ_P terms, construct σ_P terms. The belief operator **B** is a dyadic function symbol that forms a σ_P term when combined with, respectively, a σ_A and a σ_P term.

For the purpose of this paper, we introduce to $Log_A\mathbf{B}$ a function symbol $\overrightarrow{\mathbf{B}}$, akin to **B**, and is interpreted in such a way that it forms terms which are logically equivalent to σ_P terms with occurrences of **B** distributed and pushed inwards to the outermost occurrences of positive disjunctive terms. More precisely, if $[\![\cdot]\!]$ is the semantic interpretation function, then the following restrictions on the interpretation of $\overrightarrow{\mathbf{B}}$ apply; $\alpha \in \sigma_A$, $\{\phi, \psi\} \subseteq \sigma_P$, and π is an atomic σ_P term.

- $[\![\overrightarrow{\mathbf{B}}(\alpha, \pi)]\!] = [\![\mathbf{B}(\alpha, \pi)]\!]$
- $[\![\overrightarrow{\mathbf{B}}(\alpha, \neg\phi)]\!] = [\![\neg\overrightarrow{\mathbf{B}}(\alpha, \phi)]\!]$
- $[\![\overrightarrow{\mathbf{B}}(\alpha, \phi \vee \psi)]\!] = [\![\mathbf{B}(\alpha, \phi \vee \psi)]\!]$
- $[\![\overrightarrow{\mathbf{B}}(\alpha, \exists x[\phi])]\!] = [\![\mathbf{B}(\alpha, \exists x[\phi])]\!]$

$\wedge, \supset, \equiv$, and $\forall$ are defined in the usual way in terms of $\neg$, $\vee$, and $\exists$.

In the rest of the paper, we assume a $Log_A\mathbf{B}$ language $\mathcal{L}_0$. If $\mathcal{L} \subseteq \mathcal{L}_0$, then $\mathcal{L}^\tau$ denotes the set of terms of sort τ in $\mathcal{L}$. Such a set $\mathcal{L}$ is propositionally closed if it is the closure of some subset of $\mathcal{L}_0$ under Boolean connectives and quantification.

5 Revision

For the purpose of this paper, we assume contexts to be sets of $\mathcal{L}^P$ terms, where $\mathcal{L}$ is a propositionally-closed subset of $\mathcal{L}_0$. An $\mathcal{L}$ context system is a set $\mathbb{C}$ of $\mathcal{L}$-contexts satisfying certain closure properties; for example, deductive closure. However, nothing much hangs on what these properties exactly are; some of them will be pointed out as we proceed with the discussion.

For an $\mathcal{L}$ context system $\mathbb{C}$, revision is a mapping $\circledast : \mathbb{C} \times \mathcal{L}^P \longrightarrow \mathbb{C}$. The six basic AGM postulates for revising a context $\mathcal{K}$ with a $\mathcal{L}^P$ term ϕ, denoted $\mathcal{K} \circledast \phi$, are [2]:

($A^{\circledast}1$) Closure: $\mathcal{K} \circledast \phi \in \mathbb{C}$.[5]
($A^{\circledast}2$) Success: $\phi \in \mathcal{K} \circledast \phi$.
($A^{\circledast}3$) Consistency: If $\text{Cn}(\mathcal{K} \circledast \phi) = \mathcal{L}^P$ then $\text{Cn}(\{\phi\}) = \mathcal{L}^P$.
($A^{\circledast}4$) Expansion 1: $\text{Cn}(\mathcal{K} \circledast \phi) \subseteq \text{Cn}(\mathcal{K} \cup \{\phi\})$.
($A^{\circledast}5$) Expansion 2: If $\neg\phi \notin \text{Cn}(\mathcal{K})$, then $\text{Cn}(\mathcal{K} \cup \{\phi\}) \subseteq \text{Cn}(\mathcal{K} \circledast \phi)$.
($A^{\circledast}6$) Extensionality: If $\phi \equiv \psi \in \text{Cn}(\varnothing)$, then $\text{Cn}(\mathcal{K} \circledast \phi) = \text{Cn}(\mathcal{K} \circledast \psi)$.

In the above postulates, where $\Gamma \subseteq \mathcal{L}^P$, $\text{Cn}(\Gamma)$ is the set of consequences of Γ—the closure of Γ under a set of $Log_A\mathbf{B}$ rules of inference. In particular, we envision a set of natural deduction rules as in [6]. Throughout the discussion, Cn is taken to be monotonic.

In the rest of the current section, unless otherwise stated, we consider only the case when $\mathcal{L} = \mathcal{L}_0$. The fundamental distinction we make in autodoxastic context systems is that between regular and non-regular contexts.

Definition 1. *For every $\alpha \in \sigma_A$, a context $\mathcal{K} \in \mathbb{C}$ is α-regular if the following reflection principles are in* $\text{Cn}(\mathcal{K})$.

($\mathbf{R}\uparrow$) $\forall p\, [p \supset \overrightarrow{\mathbf{B}}(\alpha, p)]$ *and*
($\mathbf{R}\downarrow$) $\forall p\, [\mathbf{B}(\alpha, p) \supset p]$

The ability to quantify over propositions allows us to succinctly represent the reflection principles. Otherwise, in a modal setting for instance, each of ($\mathbf{R}\uparrow$) and ($\mathbf{R}\downarrow$) would correspond to an infinite conjunction of instances. In particular, within $Log_A\mathbf{B}$, we can revise with $[(\mathbf{R}\uparrow) \wedge (\mathbf{R}\downarrow)]$, whereas a modal approach will require an infinitary logical treatment.

The following results immediately follow.[6]

Observation 1. *Let $\mathcal{K}$ be an α-regular context.*

1. *$\mathcal{K}$ is α-consistent:* $\forall p\, [\mathbf{B}(\alpha, \neg p) \supset \neg\mathbf{B}(\alpha, p)] \in \text{Cn}(\mathcal{K})$
2. *$\mathcal{K}$ is α-positively-faithful:* $\forall p\, [\mathbf{B}(\alpha, \mathbf{B}(\alpha, p)) \supset \mathbf{B}(\alpha, p)] \in \text{Cn}(\mathcal{K})$
3. *For all $n \in \mathbb{N}$, $\phi \supset \overrightarrow{\mathbf{B}}^n(\alpha, \phi) \in \text{Cn}(\mathcal{K})$, where $\overrightarrow{\mathbf{B}}^1(\alpha, \phi) = \overrightarrow{\mathbf{B}}(\alpha, \phi)$ and $\overrightarrow{\mathbf{B}}^i(\alpha, \phi) = \mathbf{B}(\alpha, \overrightarrow{\mathbf{B}}^{i-1}(\alpha, \phi))$, for $i > 1$.*

Thus, regularity entails consistency, faithfulness, and a kind of positive introspection with respect to $\overrightarrow{\mathbf{B}}$. Most importantly, however, such a context has the property that ϕ and $\mathbf{B}(\alpha, \phi)$ are almost synonymous. This is the essence of subjective belief as discussed in Section 2.

It should be noted that some anomalous inferences are not possible. For example, $\forall p\, [\neg\mathbf{B}(\alpha, p) \supset \mathbf{B}(\alpha, \neg p)]$ is generally not derivable in an α-regular context, whereas it would have been had we decided to replace $\overrightarrow{\mathbf{B}}$ in ($\mathbf{R}\uparrow$) with $\mathbf{B}$. (See the discussion of Section 2.)

---

5 Thus, $\mathbb{C}$ is closed under revision with terms in $\mathcal{L}^P$.

6 All proofs are mostly straightforward, and are deferred, for completeness, to an appendix. For limitations of space, proofs of observations are omitted.

In addition to the standard AGM postulates, the following postulate constrains the effect of revision on the regularity of the revised context. In essence, it requires the adopted revision strategies to protect $(\mathbf{R} \uparrow)$ and $(\mathbf{R} \downarrow)$ as much as possible.

$(A^{\circledast}7)$ Regularity: If $\mathcal{K}$ is α-regular and $\mathcal{K} \circledast \phi$ is not α-regular, then $[\neg(\mathbf{R}\uparrow) \vee \neg(\mathbf{R}\downarrow)] \in \mathrm{Cn}(\{\phi\})$.

From $(A^{\circledast}2)$, $(A^{\circledast}3)$, $(A^{\circledast}7)$, and monotonicity of Cn, $(T^{\circledast}1)$ immediately follows:

$(T^{\circledast}1)$ Regularity preservation: If $\mathcal{K}$ is α-regular, then $\mathcal{K} \circledast \phi$ is not α-regular if and only if $[\neg(\mathbf{R} \uparrow) \vee \neg(\mathbf{R} \downarrow)] \in \mathrm{Cn}(\{\phi\})$.

Example 1. Let $\mathcal{K}$ be an α-regular context. Clearly, $\mathcal{K} \circledast [p \wedge \neg\mathbf{B}(\alpha, p)]$ is not regular. Intuitively, if one is to revise their beliefs with an atomic proposition and the fact that they do not believe that very proposition, then one is implicitly abandoning $(\mathbf{R} \uparrow)$. Similarly, $\mathcal{K} \circledast [\neg p \wedge \mathbf{B}(\alpha, p)]$ is not regular. But, this time, the new information is in direct contradiction with $(\mathbf{R} \downarrow)$. □

6 Supposition

Corresponding to the basic revision postulates, the following is a set of postulates for idealized supposition. There is one supposition operator $\oplus_\alpha : \mathbb{C} \times \mathcal{L}^P \longrightarrow \mathbb{C}$ for every $\alpha \in \mathcal{L}^A$, where $\mathbb{C}$ is an $\mathcal{L}$ context system.

$(A^{\oplus_\alpha}1)$ Closure: $\mathcal{K} \oplus_\alpha \phi \in \mathbb{C}$.
$(A^{\oplus_\alpha}2)$ Success: $\phi \in \mathcal{K} \oplus_\alpha \phi$.
$(A^{\oplus_\alpha}3)$ Consistency: If $\mathrm{Cn}(\mathcal{K} \oplus_\alpha \phi) = \mathcal{L}^P$, then $\mathrm{Cn}(\{\phi\}) = \mathcal{L}^P$.
$(A^{\oplus_\alpha}4)$ Extensionality: If $\phi \equiv \psi \in \mathrm{Cn}(\varnothing)$, then $\mathrm{Cn}(\mathcal{K} \oplus_\alpha \phi) = \mathrm{Cn}(\mathcal{K} \oplus_\alpha \psi)$.

The above postulates are identical to their revision counterparts. Only the expansion postulate are missing. In general, supposition causes more damage to a context than revision; it may add more than the supposed proposition to the context and, even when the supposed proposition is consistent with the context, preservation of the old information is not guaranteed.

In case $\mathcal{L} = \mathcal{L}_0$, the following regularity-related postulates constrain the behavior of $\oplus_\alpha$.

$(A^{\oplus_\alpha}5)$ Expansion 1: If $\mathcal{K} \cup \{\phi\}$ is not α-regular, then $\mathrm{Cn}(\mathcal{K} \oplus_\alpha \phi) \subseteq \mathrm{Cn}(\mathcal{K} \cup \{\phi\})$.
$(A^{\oplus_\alpha}6)$ Expansion 2: If $\neg\phi \notin \mathrm{Cn}(\mathcal{K})$ and $\mathcal{K} \cup \{\phi\}$ is not α-regular, then $\mathrm{Cn}(\mathcal{K} \cup \{\phi\}) \subseteq \mathrm{Cn}(\mathcal{K} \oplus_\alpha \phi)$.
$(A^{\oplus_\alpha}7)$ Regularity: If $\mathcal{K} \oplus_\alpha \phi$ is α-regular, then $[(\mathbf{R} \uparrow) \wedge (\mathbf{R} \downarrow)] \in \mathrm{Cn}(\{\phi\})$.

From $(A^{\oplus_\alpha}2)$ and $(A^{\oplus_\alpha}7)$, the following immediately follows.

$(T^{\oplus_\alpha}1)$ $\mathcal{K} \oplus_\alpha \phi$ is α-regular if and only if $[(\mathbf{R} \uparrow) \wedge (\mathbf{R} \downarrow)] \in \mathrm{Cn}(\{\phi\})$.

The intuition behind ($A^{\oplus_\alpha}6$) is that consistent supposition in a non-regular context should adhere as much as possible to the revision postulates. ($A^{\oplus_\alpha}7$) guarantees that, unless forced, supposition always yields a non-regular context. In fact, we can prove the following.

Observation 2. *If $\mathbb{C}$ is an $\mathcal{L}$ context system, such that every $\mathcal{K} \in \mathbb{C}$ is not α-regular, an operator $\odot : \mathbb{C} \times \sigma_P \longrightarrow \mathbb{C}$ is a revision operator if and only if it is an α-supposition operator.*

Example 2. The condition requiring all contexts in $\mathbb{C}$ to be not α-regular is satisfiable by placing restrictions on the underlying language $\mathcal{L}$. Following are examples of such restrictions.

1. $\mathcal{L} = \{\phi | \phi$ does not contain the symbol $\mathbf{B}\}$: In this case, we restrict reasoning to objective sentences only. Neither ($\mathbf{R} \uparrow$) nor ($\mathbf{R} \downarrow$) can be in any context.
2. $\mathcal{L} = \{\phi | \phi$ does not contain the symbol $\overrightarrow{\mathbf{B}}\}$: Here, the function symbol $\overrightarrow{\mathbf{B}}$ is not part of the language. Thus, ($\mathbf{R} \uparrow$) cannot be in any context.
3. $\mathcal{L} = \{\phi | \phi$ does not contain $\mathbf{B}(\alpha, \psi)$ as a sub-term for any term $\psi\}$: Since $\mathbf{B}(\alpha, \psi)$ is not mentionable in the language, then so are ($\mathbf{R} \uparrow$) and ($\mathbf{R} \downarrow$).

□

Thus, for an autodoxastic agent α, the above example shows that revision and α-supposition are indistinguishable under at least the following conditions: (i) α cannot reason about belief, (ii) α can reason about belief but not about introspection, and (iii) α can reason about beliefs and introspection but not about its own beliefs.

7 Varieties of Supposition

The postulates of supposition are general enough to admit a number of different supposition operators, each with a different intuitive flavor. Before defining these operators, however, one notion is needed.

Definition 2. *For a context $\mathcal{K}$ and an $\mathcal{L}^P$ term ϕ, the set of α-deregulation subsets of $\mathcal{K}$ with respect to ϕ, is the set*

$$\Delta_\alpha(\mathcal{K}, \phi) = \{\mathcal{K}' | \mathcal{K}' \subseteq \mathcal{K} \text{ and } \mathcal{K}' \cup \{\phi\} \text{ is not } \alpha\text{-regular}\}$$

The set of α-deregulation closures of $\mathcal{K}$ with respect to ϕ is the set

$$\delta_\alpha(\phi, \mathcal{K}) = \{\mathcal{K}' \in \Delta_\alpha(\mathcal{K}, \phi) | \text{ there is no } \mathcal{K}'' \in \Delta_\alpha(\mathcal{K}, \phi) \text{ such that } \mathcal{K}' \subset \mathcal{K}''\}$$

The following observations about deregulation subsets immediately follow.

Observation 3. *Let $\mathcal{K}$ be an $\mathcal{L}$ context, $\phi \in \mathcal{L}^P$, and $\alpha \in \mathcal{L}^A$.*

1. *If $\mathcal{K}' \in \Delta_\alpha(\mathcal{K}, \phi)$, then $\mathcal{K}'$ is not α-regular.*
2. *If $\mathcal{K} \in \Delta_\alpha(\mathcal{K}, \phi)$, then $\delta_\alpha(\phi, \mathcal{K}) = \{\mathcal{K}\}$.*

3. $\Delta_\alpha(\phi, \mathcal{K}) = \varnothing$ *if and only if* $[(\mathbf{R}\uparrow) \wedge (\mathbf{R}\downarrow)] \in \mathrm{Cn}(\{\phi\})$.
4. If $\phi \in \mathcal{K}$, *then* $\mathrm{Cn}(\mathcal{K}' \circledast \phi) = \mathrm{Cn}(\mathcal{K}' \cup \{\phi\}) = \mathrm{Cn}(\mathcal{K}')$, *for every* $\mathcal{K}' \in \delta_\alpha(\phi, \mathcal{K})$.

Using the notion of deregulation closures, we may now define particular supposition operators. Two of these are especially interesting, we call them conservative post-deregulation and conservative pre-deregulation operators. These operators are conservative in the sense that they preserve as much of the original context as possible.

Definition 3. *Let* $\odot_\alpha : \mathbb{C} \times \mathcal{L}^P \longrightarrow \mathbb{C}$.

1. $\odot_\alpha$ *is a conservative post-deregulation operator if*

$$\mathcal{K} \odot_\alpha \phi = \begin{cases} \mathcal{K} \circledast \phi & \text{if } \delta_\alpha(\phi, \mathcal{K}) = \varnothing \\ \mathcal{K}' \circledast \phi & \text{otherwise, for some } \mathcal{K}' \in \delta_\alpha(\phi, \mathcal{K}) \end{cases}$$

2. $\odot_\alpha$ *is a conservative pre-deregulation operator if*

$$\mathcal{K} \odot_\alpha \phi = \begin{cases} \mathcal{K} \circledast \phi & \text{if } \delta_\alpha(\phi, \mathcal{K}) = \varnothing \\ \mathcal{K}' \circledast \phi & \text{otherwise, for some } \mathcal{K}' \in \delta_\alpha(\phi, \mathcal{K} \circledast \phi) \end{cases}$$

In what follows, a conservative deregulation operator is either a conservative post-deregulation or a conservative pre-deregulation operator.

Theorem 1. *A conservative deregulation operator is a supposition operator.*

A corresponding pair of deregulation operators are more aggressive than the conservative ones in the method they employ for deregulation.

Definition 4. *Let* $\odot_\alpha : \mathbb{C} \times \mathcal{L}^P \longrightarrow \mathbb{C}$.

1. $\odot_\alpha$ *is an aggressive post-deregulation operator if*

$$\mathcal{K} \odot_\alpha \phi = \begin{cases} \mathcal{K} \circledast \phi & \text{if } \delta_\alpha(\phi, \mathcal{K}) = \varnothing \text{ or } \delta_\alpha(\phi, \mathcal{K}) = \{\mathcal{K}\} \\ \mathcal{K}' \circledast \phi & \text{otherwise, for some } \mathcal{K}' \in \delta_\alpha(\phi, \mathcal{K} \circledast \neg[(\mathbf{R}\uparrow) \wedge (\mathbf{R}\downarrow)]) \end{cases}$$

2. $\odot_\alpha$ *is an aggressive pre-deregulation operator if*

$$\mathcal{K} \odot_\alpha \phi = \begin{cases} \mathcal{K} \circledast \phi & \text{if } \delta_\alpha(\phi, \mathcal{K}) = \varnothing \text{ or } \delta_\alpha(\phi, \mathcal{K}) = \{\mathcal{K}\} \\ \mathcal{K}' \circledast \phi & \text{otherwise, for some } \mathcal{K}' \in \delta_\alpha(\phi, (\mathcal{K} \circledast \phi) \circledast \neg[(\mathbf{R}\uparrow) \wedge (\mathbf{R}\downarrow)]) \end{cases}$$

In what follows, an aggressive deregulation operator is either an aggressive post-deregulation or an aggressive pre-deregulation operator.

Theorem 2. *An aggressive deregulation operator is a supposition operator.*

The four supposition operators presented above are deregulation operators varying along two orthogonal dimensions. Conservative deregulation eliminates α-regularity with as minimal perturbation to the context as possible (where minimality is determined by $\circledast$). Thus, by conservatively supposing ϕ, an agent assumes ϕ to be true, but makes no assumption about the completeness or fallibility of its beliefs. As far as such an agent is concerned, the suppositional context admits the possibility of omniscience and infallibility. By aggressive supposition, on the other hand, the agent consciously adopts that it is either ignorant or fallible.

The second factor distinguishing deregulation operators is whether the first revision precedes or follows the deregulation step. The difference is the following: in post-deregulation, the agent supposes only the truth of ϕ, but not that it believes ϕ; pre-deregulation supposes both that ϕ is true and the agent believes it.

8 Conditionals

With a number of belief change operators at our disposal, we now introduce a class of conditional connectives. Let $\mathcal{L}_1$ be the closure of $\mathcal{L}_0$ under the set of binary P-operators $\{\circledast\!\!\rightarrow\} \cup \{\oplus\!\!\rightarrow_\alpha\}_{\alpha \in \mathcal{L}_0^A}$. For every operator $\odot\!\!\rightarrow$ in this set, we add the following two rules to our inference cannon.

$$(\odot\!\!\rightarrow E)\frac{\phi \odot\!\!\rightarrow \psi}{\psi \in \mathrm{Cn}(\mathcal{K} \odot \phi)}$$

$$(\odot\!\!\rightarrow I)\frac{\psi \in \mathrm{Cn}(\mathcal{K} \odot \phi)}{\phi \odot\!\!\rightarrow \psi}$$

$(\odot\!\!\rightarrow E)$ and $(\odot\!\!\rightarrow I)$ are bridge rules [20] constituting the two directions of the Ramsey test, where the underlying operation of belief change is interpreted as $\odot$.

The following is a simple corollary of Observation 2.

Observation 4. *If $\mathbb{C}$ is an $\mathcal{L}$ context system, such that every $\mathcal{K} \in \mathbb{C}$ is not α-regular, then there is an α-supposition operator, $\oplus_\alpha$, such that, for every $\phi, \psi \in \mathcal{L}^P$, $[\phi \circledast\!\!\rightarrow \psi \equiv \phi \oplus\!\!\rightarrow_\alpha \psi] \in \mathrm{Cn}(\mathcal{K})$, for every $\mathcal{K} \in \mathbb{C}$.*

Of course, the particular α-supposition operator referred to is nothing but $\circledast$ itself. Hence, the equivalence of $\circledast\!\!\rightarrow$ and $\oplus\!\!\rightarrow_\alpha$.

Strong connections between $\circledast\!\!\rightarrow$ and $\oplus\!\!\rightarrow_\alpha$ may be established, if we consider only deregulation operators. First of all, it might be tempting to declare that $\circledast\!\!\rightarrow$ and $\oplus\!\!\rightarrow_\alpha$ are equivalent in contexts which are not α-regular. This, however, is not true; our first result is a negative result.

Non-Theorem 1. *Let $\oplus_\alpha$ be a deregulation operator on an $\mathcal{L}$ context system $\mathbb{C}$. For every $\phi, \psi \in \mathcal{L}^P$ and $\mathcal{K} \in \mathbb{C}$, if $\mathcal{K}$ is not α-regular, then $[\phi \circledast\!\!\rightarrow \psi \equiv \phi \oplus\!\!\rightarrow_\alpha \psi] \in \mathrm{Cn}(\mathcal{K})$.*

Counterexample 1. Let $\mathcal{K} = \{(\mathbf{R}\!\uparrow), p\}$. Clearly, $\mathcal{K}$ is not α-regular. Also, clearly, $(p \supset (\mathbf{R}\!\downarrow)) \circledast\!\!\rightarrow [(\mathbf{R}\!\uparrow) \wedge (\mathbf{R}\!\downarrow)] \in \mathrm{Cn}(\mathcal{K})$. Nevertheless, whatever the deregulation operator we assume, $(p \supset (\mathbf{R}\!\downarrow)) \oplus\!\!\rightarrow_\alpha [(\mathbf{R}\!\uparrow) \wedge (\mathbf{R}\!\downarrow)] \notin \mathrm{Cn}(\mathcal{K})$, since $\mathcal{K} \oplus_\alpha (p \supset (\mathbf{R}\!\downarrow))$ is not α-regular, given $(T^{\oplus_\alpha}1)$. ◻

On the background of Observation 4, the above non-theorem shows that, once a language is expressive enough to represent regularity, supposition and revision are not generally equivalent in non-regular contexts. We may, however, achieve positive results by strengthening the conditions of non-regularity.

Theorem 3. *Let* $\oplus_\alpha$ *be a deregulation operator on an* $\mathcal{L}$ *context system* $\mathbb{C}$. *For every* $\phi, \psi \in \mathcal{L}^P$ *and* $\mathcal{K} \in \mathbb{C}$, *if* $\mathcal{K} \cup \{\phi\}$ *is not* α*-regular, then* $[(\phi \circledast\!\!\rightarrow \psi) \equiv (\phi \oplus\!\!\rightarrow_\alpha \psi)] \in \mathrm{Cn}(\mathcal{K})$.

In other words, deregulation and revision with ϕ are equivalent whenever the mere expansion with ϕ will not result in α-regularity. Here, we rely on a strengthening of the conditions of non-regularity. On the other hand, by weakening the relation between $\circledast\!\!\rightarrow$ and $\oplus\!\!\rightarrow_\alpha$ we get a strong positive result for conservative pre-deregulation.

Theorem 4. *Let* $\oplus_\alpha$ *be a conservative pre-deregulation operator on an* $\mathcal{L}$ *context system* $\mathbb{C}$. *For every* $\phi, \psi \in \mathcal{L}^P$ *and* $\mathcal{K} \in \mathbb{C}$, $[(\phi \oplus\!\!\rightarrow_\alpha \psi) \supset (\phi \circledast\!\!\rightarrow \psi)] \in \mathrm{Cn}(\mathcal{K})$.

A similar pervasive result cannot be derived, however, for conservative post-deregulation.

Non-Theorem 2. *Let* $\oplus_\alpha$ *be a conservative post-deregulation operator on an* $\mathcal{L}$ *context system* $\mathbb{C}$. *For every* $\phi, \psi \in \mathcal{L}^P$ *and* $\mathcal{K} \in \mathbb{C}$, $[(\phi \oplus\!\!\rightarrow_\alpha \psi) \supset (\phi \circledast\!\!\rightarrow \psi)] \in \mathrm{Cn}(\mathcal{K})$.

Counterexample 2. Let $\mathcal{K} = \{(\mathbf{R}\uparrow), (\mathbf{R}\downarrow), \neg\mathbf{B}(\alpha, p)\}$. From $(A^{\circledast}7)$, it follows that $\mathrm{Cn}(\mathcal{K} \circledast p) = \mathrm{Cn}(\{(\mathbf{R}\uparrow), (\mathbf{R}\downarrow), p\})$. On the other hand, $\mathrm{Cn}(\mathcal{K} \oplus_\alpha p) = \mathrm{Cn}(\{p, \neg\mathbf{B}(\alpha, p)\})$. □

Similar to conservative post-deregulation, no assumption weaker than the non-regularity of $\mathcal{K} \cup \{\phi\}$ may guarantee any implications between $\circledast\!\!\rightarrow$ and aggressive $\oplus\!\!\rightarrow$. Basically, since aggressive supposition involves an initial revision with $\neg[(\mathbf{R}\uparrow) \wedge (\mathbf{R}\downarrow)]$, $\mathrm{Cn}(\mathcal{K} \oplus_\alpha \phi) \subseteq \mathrm{Cn}(\mathcal{K} \circledast \phi)$ is, in general, not true. On the other hand, since $\mathcal{K} \circledast \phi$ may be α-regular while $\mathcal{K} \oplus_\alpha \phi$ is usually not, $\mathrm{Cn}(\mathcal{K} \circledast \phi) \subseteq \mathrm{Cn}(\mathcal{K} \oplus_\alpha \phi)$ is not guaranteed either.

9 Conclusions

Despite the apparent tension between the Ramsey test and Thomason conditionals, a suppositional interpretation of the Ramsey test resolves the conflict. We have presented two classes of conditionals, the epistemic conditionals based on belief revision, and the suppositional conditionals based on supposition. Four supposition operators where defined in terms of revision. These operators give rise to different classes of suppositional conditionals, each with its own features. Relations between these conditionals and the corresponding epistemic conditional, we believe, conform with our intuitions. In particular, we have shown that, in the absence of regular contexts, revision and supposition are identical. This explains the elusiveness of the distinction between the epistemic and the suppositional readings of the Ramsey test, which is only revealed in autodoxastic contexts where non-regular contexts are admitted.

The work presented here is in no way complete: formal semantics for $Log_A\mathbf{B}$ expanded with conditionals is yet to be elucidated; the relation between revision, supposition, and update [21] awaits investigation; and a non-monotonic treatment of autodoxastic logic seems to be the next natural step.

References

1. Stalnaker, R.: A theory of conditionals. In: Rescher, N. (ed.) Studies in Logical Theory. American Philosophical Quarterly, Monograph Series, vol. 2, pp. 98–112. Basil Blackwell Publishers, Oxford (1968)
2. Alchourron, C.E., Gärdenfors, P., Makinson, D.: On the logic of theory change: Partial meet contraction and revision functions. The Journal of Symbolic Logic 50(2), 510–530 (1985)
3. Nebel, B.: A knowledge level analysis of belief revision. In: Brachman, R., Levesque, H., Reiter, R. (eds.) Principles of Knowledge Representation and Reasoning: Proceedings of the First International Conference (KR 1989), pp. 301–311. Morgan Kaufmann, Toronto (1989)
4. Williams, M.A.: Transmutations of knowledge systems. In: Doyle, J., Sandewall, E., Torasso, P. (eds.) Principles of Knowledge Representation and Reasoning: Proceedings of the Fourth International Conference (KR 1994), pp. 619–629. Morgan Kaufmann, San Francisco (1994)
5. Gärdenfors, P.: Belief revisions and the Ramsey test for conditionals. The Philosophical Review 95(1), 81–93 (1986)
6. Ismail, H.O.: A reason maintenance perspective on relevant Ramsey conditionals. Logic Journal of the IGPL 18(4), 508–529 (2010)
7. van Fraassen, B.: Review of Brian Ellis, Relational belief systems. Canadian Journal of Philosophy 10(3), 497–511 (1980)
8. Chalmers, D., Hájek, A.: Ramsey + Moore = God. Analysis 67, 170–172 (2007)
9. Barnett, D.: Ramsey + Moore ≠ God. Analysis 68, 168–174 (2008)
10. Willer, M.: New surprises for the Ramsey test. Synthese 176, 291–309 (2010)
11. Hannes, L.: God – Moore = Ramsey (a reply to Chalmers and Hájek). Topoi 30(1), 47–51 (2011)
12. Moore, R.C.: Semantical considerations on nonmonotonic logic. Artificial Intelligence 25, 75–94 (1985)
13. Perlis, D.: Languages with self-refernce I: Foundations. Artificial Intelligence 25, 301–322 (1985)
14. Ismail, H.O.: $Log_A\mathbf{B}$: An algebraic logic of belief. In: Beierle, C., Kern-Isberner, G. (eds.) Proceedings of the Workshop on Relational Approaches to Knowledge Representation and Learning: Workshop of the 32nd German Conference on Artificial Intelligence, pp. 2–18 (2009)
15. Ismail, H.O.: $Log_A\mathbf{B}$: A first-order, non-paradoxical, algebraic logic of belief. Logic Journal of the IGPL (in Press)
16. Burris, S., Sankappanavar, H.P.: A Course in Universal Algebra. Springer, Heidelberg (1982)
17. Hintikka, J.: Knowledge and Belief: An Introduction to the Logic of the Two Notions. Cornell University Press, Ithaca (1962)

18. Fagin, R., Halpern, J., Moses, Y., Vardi, M.: Reasoning about Knowledge. The MIT Press, Cambridge (1995)
19. Kaplan, D.: Quantifying in. Synthese 19, 178–214 (1968)
20. Giunchiglia, F., Serafini, L.: Multilanguage hierarchial logics (or: How we can do without modal logics). Artficial Intelligence 65, 29–70 (1994)
21. Katsuno, H., Mendelzon, A.: On the difference between updating a knowledge base and revising it. In: Principles of Knowledge Representation and Reasoning: Proceedings of the second International Conference (KR 1991), pp. 387–394 (1991)

A Proofs

A.1 Proof of Theorem 1

Let $\odot_\alpha$ be a conservative post-deregulation operator. Since $\mathcal{K} \odot_\alpha \phi$ is basically the result of revising some context with ϕ, then $\odot_\alpha$ satisfies $(A^{\oplus_\alpha}1)$ through $(A^{\oplus_\alpha}4)$.

($\mathbf{A}^{\oplus_\alpha}$5). If $\mathcal{K} \cup \{\phi\}$ is not α-regular, then by the second clause of Observation 3, $\delta_\alpha(\mathcal{K}, \phi) = \mathcal{K}$. Hence, $\mathcal{K} \odot_\alpha \phi = \mathcal{K} \circledast \phi$. Thus, by $(A^{\circledast}4)$, $\odot_\alpha$ satisfies $(A^{\oplus_\alpha}5)$.

($\mathbf{A}^{\oplus_\alpha}$6). If $\delta_\alpha(\mathcal{K}, \phi) = \varnothing$, then $\mathcal{K} \cup \{\phi\}$ is α-regular, and $(A^{\oplus_\alpha}6)$ is trivially true of $\odot_\alpha$. Otherwise, let $\mathcal{K}' \in \delta_\alpha(\mathcal{K}, \phi)$. If $\mathcal{K} \cup \{\phi\}$ is not α-regular, then $\mathcal{K}' \in \delta_\alpha(\mathcal{K}, \phi)$, and, by the second clause of Observation 3, $\mathcal{K}' = \mathcal{K}$. Hence, $\mathcal{K} \odot_\alpha \phi = \mathcal{K} \circledast \phi$ and, by $(A^{\circledast}4)$, $\text{Cn}(\mathcal{K} \cup \{\phi\} \subseteq \text{Cn}(\mathcal{K} \odot_\alpha \phi))$.

($\mathbf{A}^{\oplus_\alpha}$7). If $\delta_\alpha(\mathcal{K}, \phi) = \varnothing$, then $\mathcal{K} \odot_\alpha \phi = \mathcal{K} \circledast \phi$. Moreover, $\Delta_\alpha(\mathcal{K}, \phi) = \varnothing$ and, by the third clause of Observation 3, $[(\mathbf{R}\uparrow) \wedge (\mathbf{R}\downarrow)] \in \text{Cn}(\{\phi\})$. Hence, $(A^{\oplus_\alpha}7)$. On the other hand, if $\delta_\alpha(\mathcal{K}, \phi) \neq \varnothing$, then $\mathcal{K} \odot_\alpha \phi = \mathcal{K}' \circledast \phi$, for some $\mathcal{K}' \in \delta_\alpha(\mathcal{K}, \phi)$. Since $\mathcal{K}' \cup \{\phi\}$ is not α-regular, then, by $(A^{\circledast}4)$ and the monotonicity of Cn, it follows that $\mathcal{K} \odot_\alpha \phi = \mathcal{K}' \circledast \phi$ is not α-regular either. Thus, $(A^{\oplus_\alpha}7)$ trivially follows.

Now, let $\odot_\alpha$ be a conservative post-deregulation operator. Similar to the post-regulation case, $\odot_\alpha$ satisfies $(A^{\oplus_\alpha}1)$ through $(A^{\oplus_\alpha}4)$.

($\mathbf{A}^{\oplus_\alpha}$5). If $\delta_\alpha(\mathcal{K}, \phi) = \varnothing$, then $\mathcal{K} \odot_\alpha \phi = \mathcal{K} \circledast \phi$, which, by $(A^{\circledast}4)$, satisfies $(A^{\oplus_\alpha}5)$. Otherwise, $\mathcal{K} \odot_\alpha \phi = \mathcal{K}' \circledast \phi$, for some $\mathcal{K}' \in \delta_\alpha(\mathcal{K} \circledast \phi, \phi)$. Since $\phi \in \mathcal{K} \circledast \phi$ (by $(A^{\circledast}2)$), then, from the fourth clause of Observation 3, it follows that $\text{Cn}(\mathcal{K} \odot_\alpha \phi) = \text{Cn}(\mathcal{K}' \circledast \phi) = \text{Cn}(\mathcal{K}' \cup \{\phi\})$. But by $(A^{\circledast}2)$, $(A^{\circledast}4)$, and monotonicity of Cn, $\text{Cn}(\mathcal{K}' \cup \{\phi\}) \subseteq \text{Cn}((\mathcal{K} \circledast \phi) \cup \{\phi\}) = \text{Cn}(\mathcal{K} \circledast \phi) \subseteq \text{Cn}(\mathcal{K} \cup \{\phi\})$. Hence, $(A^{\oplus_\alpha}5)$.[7]

($\mathbf{A}^{\oplus_\alpha}$6). If $\delta_\alpha(\mathcal{K}, \phi) = \varnothing$, then $\mathcal{K} \cup \{\phi\}$ is α-regular, and $(A^{\oplus_\alpha}6)$ is trivially true of $\odot_\alpha$. Otherwise, let $\mathcal{K}' \in \delta_\alpha(\mathcal{K} \circledast \phi, \phi)$. If $\mathcal{K} \cup \{\phi\}$ is not α-regular, then, by $(A^{\circledast}4)$ and monotonicity of Cn, so is $\mathcal{K} \circledast \phi$. But by $(A^{\circledast}2)$, $\mathcal{K} \circledast \phi = (\mathcal{K} \circledast \phi) \cup \{\phi\}$. Thus, $\mathcal{K} \circledast \phi \in \delta_\alpha(\mathcal{K} \circledast \phi, \phi)$, and, by the second clause of

[7] In this proof, we did not make use of the assumption that $\mathcal{K} \cup \{\alpha\}$ is not α-regular. An alternative proof goes along the lines of the corresponding proof for conservative post-deregulation.

Observation 3, $\mathcal{K}' = \mathcal{K} \circledast \phi$. Hence, $\mathcal{K} \odot_\alpha \phi = (\mathcal{K} \circledast \phi) \circledast \phi$ and, by $(A^{\circledast}2)$ through $(A^{\circledast}5)$, $\text{Cn}(\mathcal{K} \odot_\alpha \phi) = \text{Cn}((\mathcal{K} \circledast \phi) \circledast \phi) = \text{Cn}(\mathcal{K} \circledast \phi)$. Thus, by $(A^{\circledast}5)$, $(A^{\oplus_\alpha}6)$ follows.

$(\mathbf{A}^{\oplus_\alpha}\mathbf{7})$. The proof is similar, *mutatis mutandis*, to the proof in the case of a conservative post-deregulation operator. □

A.2 Proof of Theorem 2

For limitations of space, we only prove the case of aggressive post-deregulation operators. $(A^{\oplus_\alpha}1)$ through $(A^{\oplus_\alpha}6)$ are obviously satisfied.

To prove $(A^{\oplus_\alpha}7)$, consider three cases. First, if $\delta_\alpha(\mathcal{K}, \phi) = \varnothing$, then, by the third clause of Observation 3, $[(\mathbf{R}\uparrow) \wedge (\mathbf{R}\downarrow)] \in \text{Cn}(\phi)$, which implies $(A^{\oplus_\alpha}7)$. Second, if $\delta_\alpha(\mathcal{K}, \phi) = \{\mathcal{K}\}$, then $\mathcal{K} \cup \{\phi\}$ is not α-regular. By the monotonicity of Cn, $\mathcal{K} \odot_\alpha \phi = \mathcal{K} \circledast \phi$ is also not α-regular. Thus, $(A^{\oplus_\alpha}7)$ is trivially true. Third, $\mathcal{K} \odot_\alpha \phi = \mathcal{K}' \circledast \phi$ for some $\mathcal{K}' \in \delta_\alpha(\phi, \mathcal{K} \circledast \neg[(\mathbf{R}\uparrow) \wedge (\mathbf{R}\downarrow)])$. But, by definition of δ, $\mathcal{K}' \cup \{\phi\}$ is not α-regular. Thus, by monotonicity of Cn, so is $\mathcal{K}' \circledast \phi$, from which $(A^{\oplus_\alpha}7)$ trivially follows.

A.3 Proof of Theorem 3

The proof is straightforward for the two cases of aggressive deregulation operators, since the α-non-regularity of $\mathcal{K} \cup \{\phi\}$ implies that $\delta_\alpha(\mathcal{K}, \phi) = \{\mathcal{K}\}$, which in turn implies that $\mathcal{K} \oplus_\alpha \phi = \mathcal{K} \circledast \phi$.

The case of a conservative post-deregulation operator is also straightforward: If $\mathcal{K} \cup \{\alpha\}$ is not α-regular, then $\delta_\alpha(\mathcal{K}, \phi) = \{\mathcal{K}\}$, which implies that $\mathcal{K} \oplus_\alpha \phi = \mathcal{K} \circledast \phi$. For a conservative pre-deregulation operator, note that $\mathcal{K} \cup \{\alpha\}$ being not α-regular implies, by monotonicity of Cn, that $\mathcal{K} \circledast \phi$ is also not α-regular. But, given $(A^{\circledast}2)$, $(\mathcal{K} \circledast \phi) \cup \{\alpha\} = \mathcal{K} \circledast \phi$. Thus, $\delta_\alpha(\phi, \mathcal{K} \circledast \phi) = \{\mathcal{K} \circledast \phi\}$. Hence, $\mathcal{K} \oplus_\alpha \phi = (\mathcal{K} \circledast \phi) \circledast \phi = \mathcal{K} \circledast \phi$, by $(A^{\circledast}2)$ through $(A^{\circledast}5)$.

In all cases, given $(\circledast\!\!\rightarrow E)$, $(\circledast\!\!\rightarrow I)$, $(\oplus\!\!\rightarrow_\alpha E)$, and $(\oplus\!\!\rightarrow_\alpha I)$, it follows that $[(\phi \circledast\!\!\rightarrow \psi) \equiv (\phi \oplus\!\!\rightarrow_\alpha \psi)] \in \text{Cn}(\mathcal{K})$.

A.4 Proof of Theorem 4

If $\delta_\alpha(\mathcal{K}, \phi) = \varnothing$, then $\mathcal{K} \oplus_\alpha \phi = \mathcal{K} \circledast \phi$. Otherwise, by the third clause of Observation 3, $[(\mathbf{R}\uparrow) \wedge (\mathbf{R}\downarrow)] \notin \text{Cn}(\{\phi\})$. Thus, there is a $\mathcal{K}' \in \delta_\alpha(\phi, \mathcal{K} \circledast \phi)$ such that $\mathcal{K} \oplus_\alpha \phi = \mathcal{K}' \circledast \phi$. By the fourth clause of Observation 3, $\text{Cn}(\mathcal{K} \oplus_\alpha \phi) = \text{Cn}(\mathcal{K}' \circledast \phi) = \text{Cn}(\mathcal{K}') \subseteq \text{Cn}(\mathcal{K} \circledast \phi)$. Thus, given $(\circledast\!\!\rightarrow E)$, $(\circledast\!\!\rightarrow I)$, $(\oplus\!\!\rightarrow_\alpha E)$, and $(\oplus\!\!\rightarrow_\alpha I)$, it follows that $[(\phi \oplus\!\!\rightarrow_\alpha \psi) \equiv (\phi \circledast\!\!\rightarrow \psi)] \in \text{Cn}(\mathcal{K})$.

Delayed Synapses: An LSM Model for Studying Aspects of Temporal Context in Memory

Predrag Jakimovski and Hedda R. Schmidtke

Pervasive Computing Systems, TecO,
Vincenz-Prießnitz-Strasse 3, 76131 Karlsruhe, Germany
{predrag.jakimovski,hedda.schmidtke}@kit.edu
http://www.teco.edu

Abstract. Spiking neural networks are promising candidates for representing aspects of cognitive context in human memory. We extended the liquid state machine model with time-delayed connections from liquid neurons to the readout unit to better capture context phenomena. We performed experiments in the area of spoken language recognition for studying two aspects of context dependency: influence of memory and temporal context. For the experiments, we derived a test data set from the well-known Brody-Hopfield test set to which we added varying degrees of Gaussian noise. We studied the influence of temporal context with a further specially designed test set. We found that the temporal context encoded in the pattern to be recognized was recognized better with our delayed synapses than without. Our experiments shed light on how context serves to integrate information and to increase robustness in human signal processing.

Keywords: Spiking neural networks (SNN), liquid state machine (LSM), context-dependency, memory acquirements, fading memory (FM).

1 Introduction

Artificial neural networks (ANN) have been proposed as a means to model the human ability to successfully adapt to, and react in a complex environment. However, ANNs have the disadvantage of not modeling the information encoded temporally in the signal. A further class of neural networks are spiking neural networks (SNN), which mimic the behavior of biological neural networks. A liquid state machine consists of a SNN with a readout unit implemented by perceptrons. The readout unit of the LSM proposed by [12] interprets only the current snapshot of the liquid states. In this paper, the concept of an LSM is extended, so that not only the current liquid state can be taken into account but also past liquid states. The extension of the approach is realized using time-delayed connections from liquid neurons to the readout unit.

The structure of the article is as follows. We first introduce the classical model and our extension for modeling memory (Sect. 2). We then present our experimental setup and the test-bed we implemented, and discuss the results (Sect. 3).

M. Beigl et al. (Eds.): CONTEXT 2011, LNAI 6967, pp. 138–144, 2011.

2 Liquid State Machine Model

The human brain processes information from the environment in real-time and immediately delivers a "meaningful" response. The liquid state machine (LSM) was developed as a model to simulate properties of a biological brain and to mimic its behavior for real-time processing [10]. A liquid state machine consists of a spiking neural network (SNN) with a readout unit implemented by sigmoid neural networks. The approach is based on the idea that a recurrent neural network that is sufficiently dynamically complex and becomes excited by a continuous stream of information $u(\cdot)$, such as a stream of auditory input, retains this information for a longer duration while processing it. The complex network becomes an information *medium*. The spatio-temporal stream is transformed into a high-dimensional spatial pattern $x(t)$, also called the *liquid state*, from which information can be retrieved. The metaphor refers to water into which stones are thrown. As the stones hit the water splashes and ripples on the surface are created, from which an observer can infer the location where the stone where thrown. The role of the observer is played by a readout unit, which can be implemented by a simple machine learning mechanism, such as a neural network [3].

Formally an LSM M is a filter L^M. Mathematically, L^M is an operator, which when applied to a function u, yields an intermediate result x: $x(t) = (L^M u)(t)$. The output $x(t)$ depends on $u(t)$ and, in a non-linear manner, on the previous inputs $u(s)$. A readout function f^M transforms the output $x(t)$ into a target output $y(t)$ so that $y(t) = f(x(t))$. The classical architecture of the LSM model is shown in figure 1.

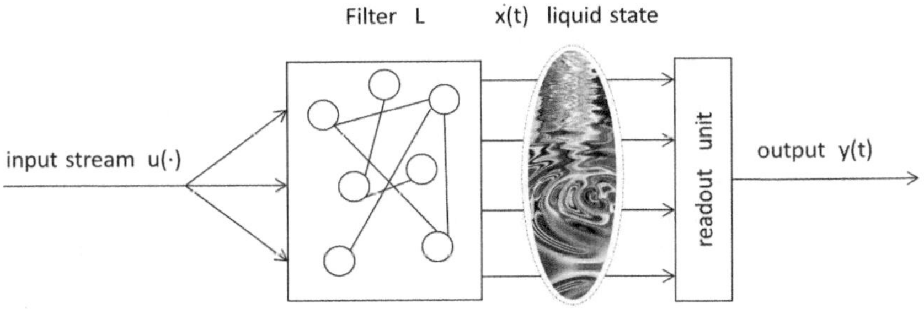

Fig. 1. The flow-graph shows the principal processing of a conventional LSM: A low-dimensional input stream $u(t)$ excites filter L, consisting of a recurrent neural network (RNN); A readout unit is interpreting immediately the liquid state $x(t)$ generated by L. Inside of the dotted ellipse indicates water circles and represents the current liquid state.

In general the readout unit f is memoryless, i. e. the former liquid states $x(s)$, $s < t$, are not considered at t. Therefore, the chosen type of liquid filter L must have the ability to retain the past information into the liquid state $x(t)$. In this way the readout unit f is enabled to generate adequate correct output $y(t)$.

This will be only possible if the liquid filter L fulfills the *separation property* (SP) [10]: For any input stream u, v the liquid filter L is reacting sufficiently different, i. e. the liquid filter L is producing different liquid states $x(t)$ by $u(\cdot) \neq v(\cdot)$.

A liquid filter L which exhibits the SP, features also the property of *fading memory (FM)* [2]. That means that the liquid filter L is retaining information of an input stream u over a fixed time span. In the modeling of information processing, the fading memory property is essential because novel incoming information can only be processed as novel information if previous information fades.

In the realization of the LSM, the liquid state $x(t)$ is modeled by a n-dimensional vector. The dimension of the vector is fixed by the number of neurons used in the liquid filter. For the neuron-type, the classical Leaky-Integrate-and-Fire-neuron (cf. [10] for an introduction) is chosen, which fires a spike at a fixed time point t_i and produces a discrete time series of spikes called spike train. The spike activity of every single neuron in a time window determines after a low-pass filtering the n components of the liquid vector. The n-dimensional vector is called a *snapshot* of the liquid state $x(t_i)$. In practice, a time window of length with $30ms$ up to $150ms$ is chosen based on experimental data acquired from human behavior experiments [4].

In comparison to its simple neural network readout unit, the LSM achieves better classification results. The advantage of the LSM is its specific way of integrating temporal context: everything within a certain time window is retained, but everything outside is removed as the fading memory property requires. The question then is how memories, as they are retained for a longer duration, i.e. on a coarser temporal granularity, can be integrated with the model. While we cannot offer an answer to this question on the neurobiological side, we propose the idea of *delayed synapses* to model integration on a coarser level of temporal granularity, i.e. for time windows of a longer duration [13].

The challenge is to integrate memory functionality into the model, in order to acquire context. To realize this we employ so-called delayed synapses, which set back the emitting spikes of a neuron N_i by using different time delays. In particular all delayed synapses belonging to a neuron N_i are leading to the readout unit directly. In this way past information that occurred before the current time window of the LSM is provided to the readout unit. When the readout unit captures the current liquid state $x(t)$, it captures also the past simultaneously. In Figure 2, an operating LSM with delayed synapses is shown.

3 Experiments

To give proof to our approach we initially deployed the Brody-Hopfield benchmark to show the capabilities of the LSM. The benchmark itself originates in speech recognition and was used to test SNN models by Brody and Hopfield [5,6] for the first time. The speech benchmark consists of 500 audio files, recorded by five female speakers speaking the digits “zero” to “nine”. The task here is to recognize the spoken digits successfully. For testing our approach we transformed

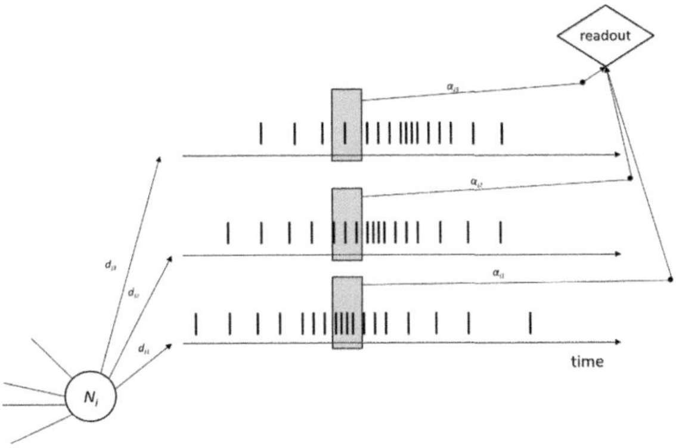

Fig. 2. Illustration of the readout event. The three readout synapses delay the spike emitted by the liquid-neuron N_i by d_{i_1}, d_{i_2} and d_{i_3} respectively, so that the readout unit can evaluate liquid-states with regard to the time. During training phase of the readout unit the weights α_{i_1}, α_{i_2} and α_{i_3} will be adjusted by means of the p-delta learning rule.

the audio files into spatio-temporal spike patterns by using auditory models of the human ear. It is assumed that the inner hair cells of the ear transmit the electromagnetic pulses called spikes onto the auditory nerve directly.

To build up the evaluation platform a generator based on work in [11] for creating SNN was implemented. SNN with 135 neurons and 40 input neurons were created and for the readout unit of the LSM an one-layer ANN was deployed, called parallel perceptron which was developed by Auer [1].

3.1 Test with Noisy Brody-Hopfield Digits

So far, the whole framework of the LSM were integrated and tested by the Brody-Hopfield benchmark. Here, the digits "one" and "four" were used to train and test the LSM and white noise was added to increase recognition difficulty. The new data set consists of 500 samples partitioned into randomly chosen 300 samples for training and 200 samples for the test set. During the training phase 10-fold cross-validation was applied. The evaluation was performed by two randomly generated LSMs, i. e. *lsm_0adv2.net* and *lsm_0adv8.net* were chosen. The readout interval for the parallel perceptron was set to $[150, 180]$ms.

The tests yield success rates of 85.5% and 71.0%, respectively. Training the readout unit without any liquid filter resulted in 62.5% success. The evaluation results of our model extension are listed in table 1. The setting for each trial is fixed by the number of delayed synapses and the delay. For example, the setup with 3 delayed synapses and 10ms delay means three links from each liquid neuron to the readout unit delays the emitting liquid neuron in 10ms, 20ms and 30ms, respectively. In this way context information from the past can be captured by the readout unit.

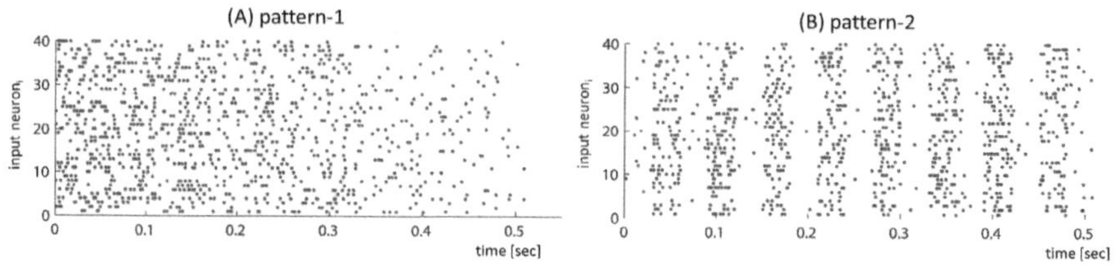

Fig. 3. Two patterns in the ArtBM-Benchmark

Table 1. Performance results of trails with different number of applied delayed synapses

number of synapses	*lsm_0adv2.net* 5ms	10ms	15ms	20ms	30ms	50ms	*lsm_0adv8.net* 5ms	10ms	15ms	20ms	30ms	50ms
1 del. syn.	84.5	87.0	87.0	86.0	86.5	86.0	72.0	73.0	73.0	74.0	76.5	73.5
2 del. syn.	86.0	87.0	88.5	88.5	87.5	86.5	72.0	74.0	77.5	74.0	77.0	83.0
3 del. syn.	87.0	87.5	88.5	88.0	85.5	87.0	71.5	77.0	75.0	75.5	80.5	88.0
5 del. syn.	87.5	89.0	87.5	86.0	89.5	–	74.5	74.0	76.0	81.5	91.5	–
7 del. syn.	88.0	88.0	86.0	87.5	–	–	76.5	76.0	81.5	93.0	–	–
10 del. syn.	89.5	86.0	89.0	–	–	–	74.0	81.0	92.0	–	–	–
$\frac{1}{n}\sum_{i=1}^{n} R_i$	87.08	87.42	87.75	87.2	87.25	86.5	73.42	75.83	79.17	79.60	81.38	81.5

The evaluation described previously revealed a conventional LSM provides in general better performance than a trained parallel perceptron without a preceding liquid filter. As table 1 shows, the model extension using time delayed synapses provides better performance than the classical LSM. However, through the evaluation new issues came up: Why is there a large performance difference between the investigated LSMs? Why does the performance not rise steadily by increasing the number of delayed synapses? Further on, why does the performance vary of the chosen LSMs differently strong? In the following this issues are discussed.

3.2 Further Investigation Results

Investigating the separation property (SP) of the engaged LSMs by using constructed input streams with known distances to each other which are calculated by l^2-norm, the output trajectories indicate the separability during time (not depicted here). These explained the strong different performance of the LSMs, but did not show the proof of real improvement. In order to do this, we designed an artificial benchmark for binary classification called ArtBM. Here, the samples consisting of spatio-temporally spike patterns were constructed in the manner that spatial information in the signal is suppressed and temporal encoded. The spatial and temporal structure of the samples is best explained by Fig 3. The entire benchmark consist of 1500 samples divided into 1000 randomly chosen samples for training and 500 test samples. For the evaluation setting the readout interval was fixed to [510, 540]ms. The evaluation of the classical approach resulted in 59.6% and 81.4% for the two chosen LSMs, respectively. The results of the model extension are listed in table 2. Here, the model extension yielded almost better performance by choosing different evaluation settings. The best result with 99.8% success was achieved by choosing 5 delayed synapses and a time delay of 20ms. In this trial only 1 of 500 test samples was classified false.

Table 2. Evaluation results of our LSM model extension

lsm_0adv2.net	1 delayed synapse	2 delayed synapses	3 delayed synapses	4 delayed synapses	5 delayed synapses
10ms	64.6	72.6	83.0	92.0	94.8
20ms	76.2	93.0	93.8	93.8	96.2
30ms	86.8	89.8	93.6	93.8	91.6
60ms	85.4	92.8	90.2	86.6	85.8
90ms	79.8	82.2	83.0	88.2	90.4
180ms	78.2	90.4	90.4	–	–
lsm_0adv8.net	1 delayed synapse	2 delayed synapses	3 delayed synapses	4 delayed synapses	5 delayed synapses
10ms	81.4	83.4	89.8	97.2	99.2
20ms	84.0	98.4	98.6	98.6	99.8
30ms	91.8	98.6	98.6	99.2	98.8
60ms	94.8	98.0	98.4	99.2	99.0
90ms	82.4	89.8	91.6	82.8	94.4
180ms	84.6	71.8	71.8	–	–

4 Conclusion

Spiking neural networks are promising candidates for studying aspects of temporal context in human memory. In this paper, we extended the liquid state machine model with time-delayed connections from liquid neurons to the read out unit to capture and study the influence of temporal contexts of different durations. We performed two types of experiments in the area of spoken language recognition. For the first experiments, we derived a test data set from the well-known Brody-Hopfield test set to which we added varying degrees of Gaussian noise. We studied the influence of temporal context with a specially designed test set. We found that the temporal context encoded in the pattern was recognized better with our delayed synapses than without. Our experiments shed light on how context serves to integrate information and to increase robustness in human signal processing.

LSM are just one possible approach in which it is possible to model context-dependency. In future works we plan to generalize our approach to context-dependency to generalize it to alternative approaches, such as the "echo state" approach [7,8]. In particular, we hope to find an implementation for our context-dependent pattern recognition that is similarly powerful as LSMs and also applicable as a tool for real-time pattern recognition.

Acknowledgments. This research is supported by the project Polytos, in the BMBF-funded excellence cluster "Printed Organic Circuits and Chips"[1].

References

1. Auer, P., Burgsteiner, H.M., Maass, W.: The p-delta learning rule for parallel perceptrons. Science (2002)
2. Boyd, S., Chua, L.O.: Fading memory and the problem of approximating nonlinear operators with voltera series. IEEE Trans. on Circuits and Systems 32, 1150–1161 (1985)
3. Feldbusch, F., Kaiser, F.: Simulation of spiking neural nets with INspiRE. In: IEEE Conference on Systems, Man and Cybernetics, SMC (2005)
4. Gerstner, W., Kistler, W.: Spiking Neuron Models. Cambridge University Press, Cambridge (2002)
5. Hopfield, J.J., Brody, C.D.: What is a moment? cortical sensory integration over a brief interval. Proc. Natl. Acad. Sci. USA 97(25), 13919–13924 (2000)
6. Hopfield, J.J., Brody, C.D.: What is a moment? transient synchrony as a collective mechanism for spatiotemporal integration. Proc. Nat. Acad. Sci. USA 98(3), 1282–1287 (2001)
7. Jaeger, H.: Adaptive nonlinear system identification with echo state networks. Advances in Neural Information Processing Systems 15, 593–600 (2003)
8. Jaeger, H., Haas, H.: Harnessing nonlinearity: Predicting chaotic systems and saving energy in wireless communication. Science 304, 78–80 (2004)
9. Maass, W., Joshi, P., Sontag, E.: Computational aspects of feedback in neural circuits. PLOS Computational Biology (2006)
10. Maass, W.: Liquid state machines: Motivation, theory and applications. World Scientific Review 189 (2010)
11. Maass, W., Markram, H.: On the computational power of recurrent circuits of spiking neurons. In: Electronic Colloquium on Computational Complexity, vol. 22 (2001)
12. Maass, W., Natschläger, T., Markram, H.: Real-time computing without stable states: A new framework for neural computation based on perturbations. Neural Computation 14(11), 2531–2560 (2002)
13. Schmidtke, H.R.: Granularity as a parameter of context. In: Dey, A.K., Kokinov, B., Leake, D.B., Turner, R. (eds.) CONTEXT 2005. LNCS (LNAI), vol. 3554, pp. 450–463. Springer, Heidelberg (2005)

[1] `http://www.innovationlab.de/en/research/excellence-cluster-forum-organic-electronics/research-projects/printed-organic-circuits-and-chips-polytos/`

Modelling with Problem Frames: Explanations and Context in Ambient Intelligent Systems

Anders Kofod-Petersen[1] and Jörg Cassens[2]

[1] Department of Computer and Information Science,
Norwegian University of Science and Technology,
7491 Trondheim, Norway
anderpe@idi.ntnu.no

[2] Institute for Multimedia and Interactive Systems (IMIS),
University of Lübeck,
23562 Lübeck, Germany
cassens@imis.uni-luebeck.de

Abstract. When designing and implementing real world ambient intelligent systems we are in need of applicable information systems engineering methods. The tools we find in the intelligent systems area focus on the knowledge engineering parts, whereas traditional software engineering techniques are usually not designed with the peculiarities of intelligent systems design in mind. This holds in particular for explanation-aware intelligent systems. This work looks at problem frames for explanations and investigates how problem frames can be used to elicit, analyse, and specify these specific requirements. The point of departure is an existing ambient intelligent information system for the hospital ward domain. The work presented here analyses how such a system can be redesigned with a focus on explanation-awareness.

1 Introduction

Ambient intelligence describes environments where human beings are surrounded by intelligent artefacts supported by computing and network technology. Such environments augment everyday objects such as furniture and clothes. In addition, an ambient intelligent environment should be aware of the presence of a person, perceive the needs of this person, and respond to them in an unobtrusive and intelligent manner [1]. Ambient intelligence is laying in the intersection of pervasive computing, ubiquitous computing, and artificial intelligence.

The ability to explain itself, its reasoning and actions, has been identified as one core capability of any intelligent entity [2]. The question of what is considered to be a good explanation is context dependent [3], leading to the necessity to design the explanatory capabilities of an ambient intelligent system together with the modelling of the different situations the system is likely to encounter.

The work presented in this paper targets the requirements elicitation, analysis, and specification processes. We make use of the notion of problem frames [4], which appears to be a promising method both in helping to elicit requirements

M. Beigl et al. (Eds.): CONTEXT 2011, LNAI 6967, pp. 145–158, 2011.

and in later transformation of design documents into actual systems. We have previously suggested additional problem frames that target explanatory capabilities explicitly [5], and we will here demonstrate how problem frames can be put to use in revealing limitations of an existing ambient intelligent systems design and can help to take needs into account arising from explanatory capabilities when (re-) designing such a system.

The rest of the paper is organised as follows: Section 2 gives an overview of related work; Section 3 give a short introduction to problem frames; Section 4 details the use of problem frames specific to ambient intelligent systems; Section 5 briefly describes the existing ambient intelligent information system for hospital wards and how *context awareness* and *context sensitivity* is applied; Section 6 describes how the requirements for a redesign of the existing application can be analysed and specified by applying problem frames. The papers ends with a conclusion and outlook on future work.

2 Related Work

The use of patterns [6] is common for different software engineering approaches. Patterns can be used in different software development phases and they can have different foci. We can also identify knowledge engineering approaches making use of patterns for the development of intelligent systems. This includes efforts to provide reusable architectures by describing the abilities of (a library of) generic problem solving methods. An example for a component model is the Unified Problem-Solving Method Development Language UPML, cf. [7].

There are several methods and languages that use patterns and focus explicitly on the knowledge aspects of system design. For example, the goal of the INRECA [8] methodology is to support the development of (industrial) case-based reasoning (CBR) applications. Software process models from existing CBR applications are stored in an experience base that is structured at three levels. The *common generic level* is a collection of very generic processes, products, and methods for CBR applications. At the *cookbook level*, we find software models for particular classes of applications (so called recipes). At the *specific project level*, experiences from particular projects are stored. We can identify the recipes at the cookbook level as patterns.

Another well-known approach is the CommonKADS methodology [9]. It is based on two different views on the development process of knowledge based systems: the *result perspective* encompasses a set of models of different aspects of the knowledge based system and its environment, and the *project management perspective* starts from a spiral life-cycle model that can be adapted to the particular project. The CommonKADS template knowledge model provides a way of (partially) reusing knowledge models in new applications and can be understood as patterns in a software engineering sense.

When we look towards the software engineering world, we can see that patterns are used in different phases of the design process.

On the software architecture level, we find *architecture patterns* [10]. At this level, we encounter concepts like 'Blackboards', 'Model-View-Controller', or

'Pipes and Filters'. For finer grained software development close to the actual implementation, one can make use of design patterns that look inside towards the computer and its software [11]. Design patterns deal with concepts like 'Factories', 'Facade', and 'Decorater'.

Early on in the requirements engineering process, Jackson's *problem frames* [4] are at the core of a method to classify software development problems. Problem frames look out into the world and attempt to describe the problem and its solution in the real world. Problem frames introduce concepts like 'Information Display' and 'Commanded Behaviour'. Jackson's set of basic problem frames can be extended to be better able to model domain specific aspects. For example, Hatebur et al. [12] introduce new problem frames for security problems.

Phalp and Cox demonstrate that people are capable of selecting the right problem frames [13]. This study suggests that problem frames are indeed a suitable method for correctly assigning formal models to a given problem description and therefore a helpful tool in the requirements engineering process.

Hall and Rapanotti [14] have introduced extensions to the basic problem frames that will better facilitate socio-technical systems. They introduce a 'user interaction frame', and employ the model-view-controller perspective to ease decomposition. We will build on this results in our own work on ambient intelligent systems as a special class of socio-technical systems where user interaction is not only achieved via explicit communication, but also through the behaviour of both system and user.

3 Problem Frames

The main purpose of any problem frame [4] is to propose a machine that improves the combined performance of itself and its environment by describing the machine's behaviour in a specification. Jackson originally described five different basic frames. In general, a problem frame assumes a user driven perspective. Most basic frames assume that the user is in control and dictates the behaviour of the machine. Since intelligent systems (ideally) take a much more pro-active approach and mixed initiative issues become relevant, new problem frames addressing these topics have to be developed. For the course of this paper, we will focus on frames targeting explanatory aspects and will not discuss other types.

Problem frames can be described by problem frame diagrams. These diagrams consist basically of dashed ovals, representing the requirements, plain rectangles, denoting application domains, and a rectangle with a double vertical stripe, standing for the machine (or software machine) domain to be developed. These entities become the nodes of the frame diagram. They are connected by edges, representing shared phenomena and denoting an interface. Dashed edges refer to requirement references. Dashed arrows designate constraining requirement references.

The domains are of different types, indicated by a letter in the lower right corner. A 'C' stands for a *causal* domain whose properties include predictable causal relationships among its phenomena. A 'B' denotes a *biddable* domain that lacks positive predictable internal behaviour. Biddable domains are usually associated with user actions. An 'X' marks a *lexical* domain. Such a domain is a physical representation of data and combines causal and symbolic phenomena.

4 Problem Frames and Ambient Intelligence

Following the definition of ambient intelligence [1], in general an ambient intelligent system can be fitted into a *Required Behaviour* problem frame. Figure 1 illustrates this. `AmI!C1` is the phenomena shared between the machine and the environment, and controlled by the systems; that is the actuators. The `E!C2` is the phenomena shared between the machine and the environment, which is not controlled by the machine; that is the sensors. Finally, `C3` refers to the behaviour that the machine is to exhibit.

Fig. 1. Ambient Intelligent Systems as a Controlled Behaviour Frame

Even though required behaviour frames are generally and by definition suitable for ambient intelligent systems, some special cases exist where explicit user interaction is required other than through *behavioural interfaces*. It has been argued that any adaptive system in general, and an ambient intelligent system in particular, must be able to change its interaction style and exhibit the ability to explain its behaviour [15]. This ability requires that the system can communicate with the user through suitable interfaces, such as displays. In addition, the user should have the option to explicitly request an explanation of the system's behaviour. Thus, a suitable problem frame is required to capture this.

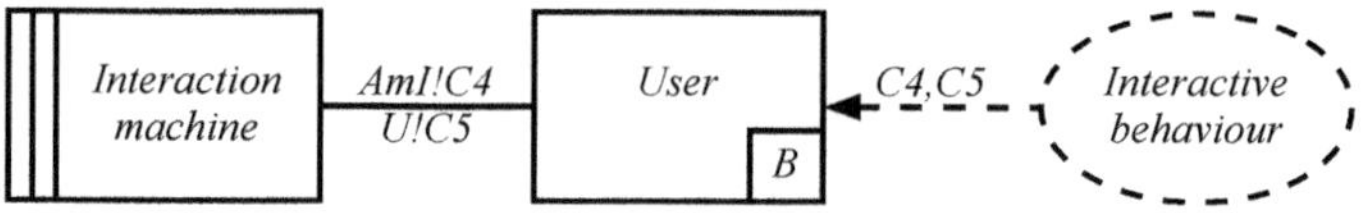

Fig. 2. User Interaction Frame (adopted from [14])

Following the argumentation of Hall and Rapanotti [14], we employ the *User Interaction Frame*, depicted in Figure 2. `AmI!C4` is the symbolic phenomena shared between the machine and the user, where the machine can display information to the user. `U!C5` is the causal shared phenomena between the machine

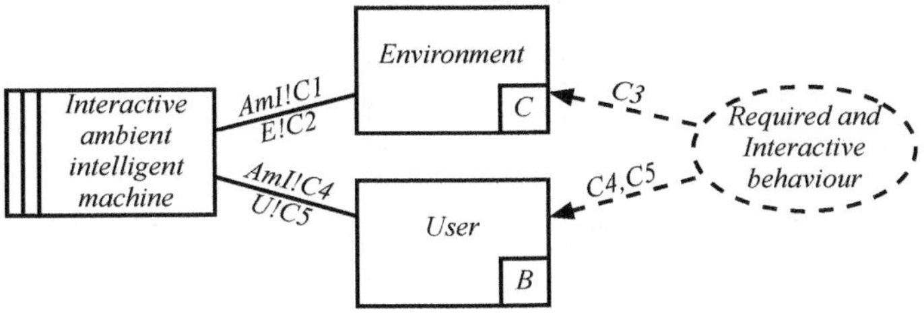

Fig. 3. Interactive Ambient Intelligence Frame

and the user, where the user initiates commands. Finally, `C4,C5` are the rules of conduct between the machine and the user.

Again following Hall and Rapanotti, we can combine these two frames into an *Interactive Ambient Intelligence Frame*, as depicted in Figure 3. Here, interactive, explanatory capabilities are combined with the environment controlling aspects of ambient intelligent systems. This aggregation differs significantly from the original *required behaviour frame* [4]. The behaviour of the ambient intelligent system is not mainly guided by explicit input from the user, but is a result of the pro-activeness of the system and implicit interaction (for example the location of the user). But it opens up for direct interaction, for example by the user requesting an explanation. This will, however, not command the whole behaviour of the system directly, but only a small part of it. In that sense it further on differs from the *user commanded frame* in [14] as the system can take actions that are not triggered through commands explicitly issued by the user.

4.1 Explanation Problem Frames

Taking a closer look at Figure 3, we will see that the upper part captures the behaviour of the ambient intelligent system, whereas the lower part represents the interactive properties of the system. We will use this part of the general frame to model the explanation abilities. To this end, however, we have to decompose the lower part in order to model different types of explanation.

The list of explanation requirements can be described as a list of the explanation goals that a system must be able to satisfy. Sørmo et al. identify five different explanations goals that a system might have to handle [2]. This work has been further expanded in [15], where the explanation goals have been combined with the ambient intelligence paradigm. Our own work focuses on the four goals that are not related to applications as an educational tool: The goal of *transparency* is concerned with the system's ability to explain how an answer was reached. *Justification* deals with the ability to explain why the answer is good. When dealing with the importance of a question asked, *relevance* is the goal that must be satisfied. Finally, *conceptualisation* is the goal that handles the meaning of concepts.

Following these four goals of explanations, we have previously constructed four problem frames that each captures one kind of explanation [5]. The *transparency*

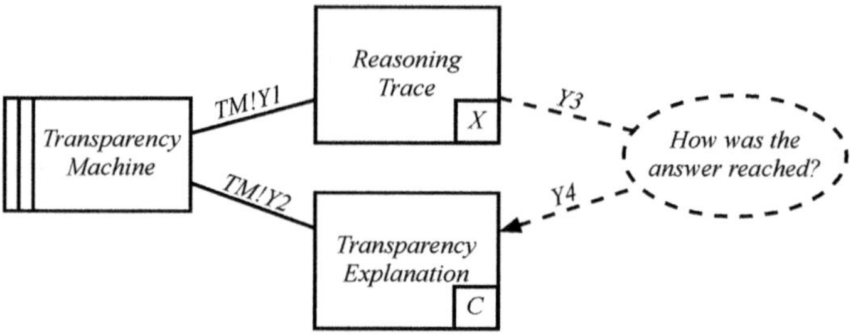

Fig. 4. Transparency Explanation

goal is concerned with how the system finds a solution to a given problem. This allows the user to inspect the reasoning process to identify the cause of any abnormal behaviour. The transparency explanation frame is depicted in Figure 4. Here the `Reasoning Trace` is a lexical domain, which allows the `Transparency Machine` to read the reasoning trace trough the shared phenomena `TM!Y1`. The `Transparency Explanation` is the causal domain, which the machine can control through the shared phenomena `TM!Y2`. In short, the `Transparency Machine` has to inspect the reasoning trace and present the relevant information to its user.

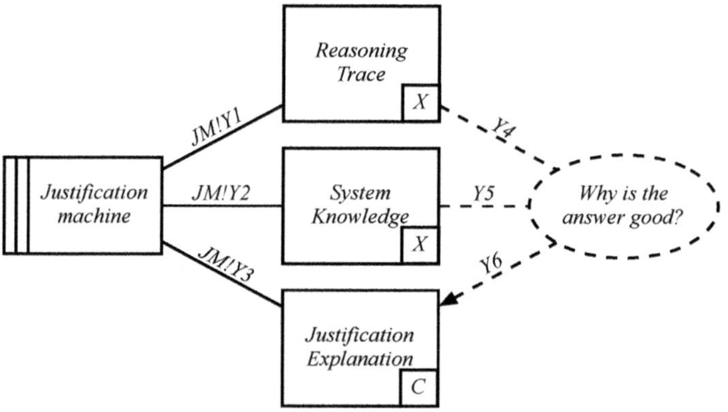

Fig. 5. Justification Explanation

The *justification goal* is closely related to the *transparency goal.* Justification can be seen as a simplification of the reasoning process that the system actually goes through. The main purpose of this explanation goal is to convince the user that the reasoning is sound. In general, whereas transparency explanations are for experts that are interested in the exact details of the reasoning, justification explanations are for novice users that are interested in being persuaded of the system's reasoning. Figure 5 displays the problem frame of a justification explanation goal. This frame resembles the one for transparency explanations, with the addition of the lexical domain `System Knowledge`. This domain facilitates the expansion of a transparency explanation by allowing the `Justification Machine` to inspect the system's knowledge through the shared phenomena `JM!Y2`.

5 Hospital Ward System

The application in question is an ambient intelligent information system for supporting medical personnel at a hospital ward. The persons involved deal with different activities, like ward rounds, pre-ward round meetings, and different forms of examination. The staff has to access a large variety of different information systems. The main goal is to have a system that makes the information sources needed in different situations (such as specific journals, test results, and treatment plans) available pro-actively. To this end, the system must first identify the activity the system's user is involved in, identify his role, and then query the information sources that are likely to be accessed.

Following the definition of ambient intelligence in [1], the system *perceives* its environment, becomes *aware* of ongoing situations, and is *sensitive* to the idiosyncrasies of the particular situations.

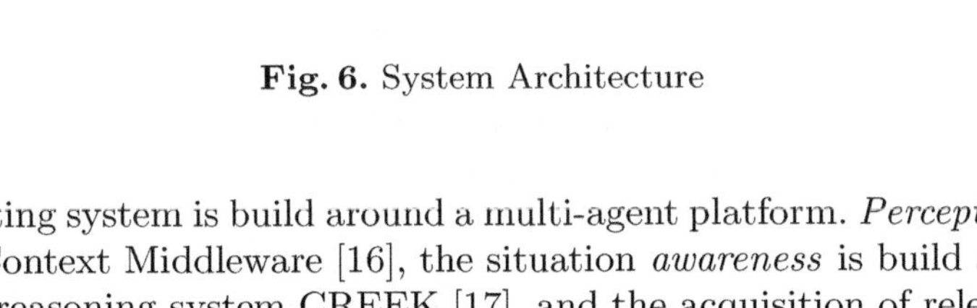

Fig. 6. System Architecture

The existing system is build around a multi-agent platform. *Perception* is handled by a Context Middleware [16], the situation *awareness* is build around the case-based reasoning system CREEK [17], and the acquisition of relevant information (*sensitivity*) is facilitated by dynamic task decomposition [18]. Situations were identified and the knowledge model populated through an ethnographical study conducted at the cardiology ward [19]. The whole system was implemented using the Jade [20] agent framework.

In our system, we use explanations in two distinct ways: first, enhancing and promoting the reasoning process; called the *system centric* view. Second, delivering some knowledge about the reasoning process, its results, or implication to the user; called the *user centric* view. Table 1 shows how these two different

Table 1. Context and Explanations

	Context Awareness	**Context Sensitivity**
System Centric	Explanations to **recognise** the situation	**Identify** the desired system behaviour
User Centric	**Elucidate** why a situation was identified	**Explicate** why a certain behaviour was chosen

usages of explanations relate to the *awareness* and *sensitivity* aspects of our system. For the purpose of this paper we will disregard the perception layer of the architecture as the perception layer demonstrates no reasoning capabilities, and only structures perceived data syntactically.

In the setting of our general frame for interactive ambient intelligent systems depicted in Figure 3, the *system centric* explanations relate the upper part, whereas the *user centric* explanations relate to the lower part. The explanation problem frames for user goals can be put to use in the lower part or *user centric* view, but modified versions reflecting the system's intentions are important for the upper part or *system centric* view as well. For the remainder of this paper, we describe how to make use of explanation problem frames for the explication aspect, describing the user centric and context sensitive use of explanations.

5.1 Example

To clarify the functionality of this system, we will present a small example. It sketches an execution taken from a simulated system run, using the real data set gathered at the cardiology ward. In this case we are dealing with a *pre-ward round* situation. A pre-ward round is a particular type of meeting that occurs every morning. Usually, the physician in charge and the nurse in charge are present. They discuss each of their patients, including their current condition, any changes, and the treatment plan.

The Context Middleware monitors the different sensors in the environment, and discovers a change, which provokes a change in the current context [16]. This change in the context is transferred to the CBR sub-system, which retrieves the best matching case based on the sensor values.

In this example, the CREEK component retrieves a case describing another pre-ward round. Having identified the ongoing situation as a pre-ward round, the CBR engine now extracts the goal of this type of situation. In this case, the goal is to gather the relevant information. This goal is sent to the sensitivity part to be solved [21].

The Sensitivity part of this system receives the goal and matches it to a general decomposition tree that contains the tasks required to satisfy the goal. In this example the task tree that matches a pre-ward round goal is as follows:

1. Acquire name of patient.
2. Acquire changes in patient's conditions since yesterday.

3. Acquire any new results from tests.
4. Examine, and possible change, medication scheme.
5. Note changes in treatment.

Each solvable task is matched to an action performed by an available, willing and able agent. The system currently offers 19 different agents, each representing one information system at the hospital ward. Together these 19 agents offers 21 different information services.

The initial problem of finding the patients name can be facilitated by the *Patient List Agent.* The 'Acquire Information' task is decomposed into one task that acquires changes which are supplied by the *Electronic Patient Record*, the *WiseW* application and the *Patient Chart*, and another task that acquires results which can be delivered by the *Patient Chart* and the *WiseW* application.

This plan is now executed and the information acquired through the different agents is returned to the user; thus ending an execution cycle of this system. Figure 7 depicts the decomposition tree constructed for this example, including the matching agents and their services.

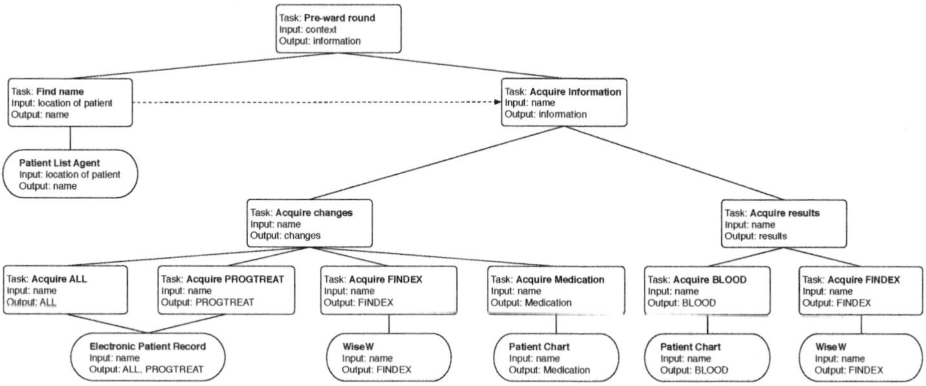

Fig. 7. Pre-ward Round Plan

6 Redesigning the Existing Application

As stated in the previous section, we have performed an ethnographical study to elicit the requirements for an ambient intelligent hospital ward information system. The results of the study were used to model the different situations the system could encounter. Further on, the analysis of artifacts used during the different situations was incorporated into the task decomposer so that suitable information source could be queried in different contexts.

In the first incarnation, explanatory capabilities were not explicitly included in the design specifications. However, the socio-technical theory used in the study design and application allows us to elicit the possible explanation goals users of the system might have [15]. Therefore, a re-design on the grounds of the data already gathered is feasible.

6.1 Example

Revisiting the example of the previous section, we have the instance where the system correctly classifies an ongoing situation as a pre-ward round. If we focus on the context sensitive part of the system, its main purpose is to examine the artifacts, represented by agents, in the environment and find those that can supply relevant information. So far this application only supplies information without any explanation of its behaviour.

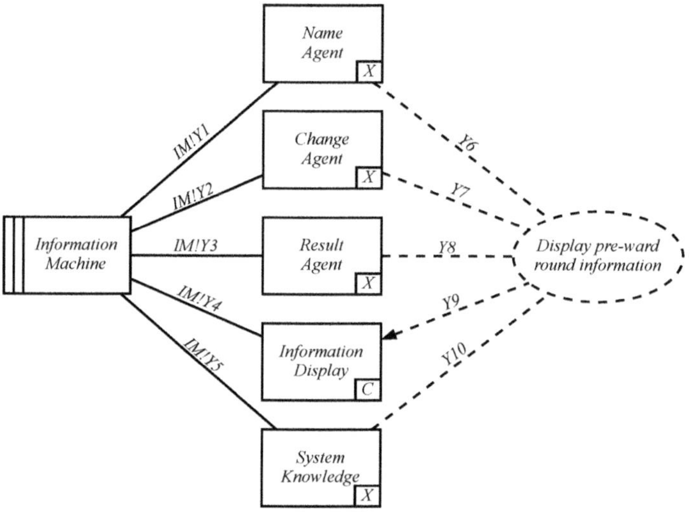

Fig. 8. Ambient Information Display

In order to demonstrate how the explanation goal problem frames can be used to model explanatory needs in the problem domain, we will start with a simplified problem diagram for our application (Figure 8). This is essentially modelling the behaviour of the system without direct user interaction and reflecting the capabilities the existing system was designed to have. This part is a decomposition of the upper part of the *Interactive Ambient Intelligence Frame* from Figure 3. We have modified Jackson's *information display* problem frame and used it as a starting point for the diagram. You can see three domains representing (groups of) the agents mentioned above.

Additionally, you see the `Display` domain which stands for the information display of the system and `System Knowledge` for deciding which data sources to use. For the sake of clarity and simplicity, we have abstracted away the sensor parts of as well as the context aware parts of our example application and focus solely on the information gathering and display parts. Let us now assume that the results displayed by the system are of such a nature that the physician using the system requires an explanation. Let us for the sake of simplicity of the example further focus on a subset of the identified explanation goals.

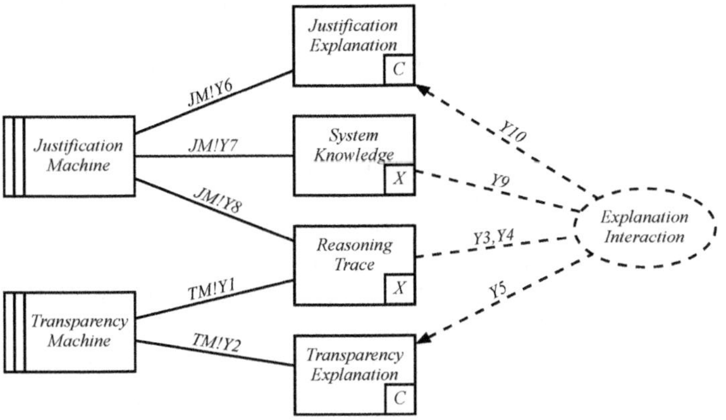

Fig. 9. Transparency and Justification Explanation

We want to integrate the explanation sub problems described by the two problem frame diagrams for the *Transparency* and the *Justification* goal to model the explanatory capabilities of the system. This combination is covered in the frame depicted in Figure 9. This model is a decomposition of the lower part of the *Interactive Ambient Intelligence Frame* from Figure 3. In the work presented here, we decide upon which of the two explanations to present as a function of the user's level of competence. That is, expert users are subject to transparency explanations and novice users to justification explanations [22].

By integrating Figure 8 modelling the ambient intelligence capabilities without explicit user interaction and Figure 9 capturing direct user involvement exemplified for explanations, we have a model (albeit simplified) of our explanation-aware ambient intelligent system. We can now re-visit the example problem described above. The expert user physician wishes to know how the combination of information displayed was reached. According to the transparency explanation problem frame, this can be achieved by displaying the reasoning trace. This can for example be done by showing that the top task 'Pre-ward round' was selected as a function of the classification, by displaying how the decomposition tree looks like, and by supplying information about the agents selected.

For the justification explanation, the novice user physician would like to know why this combination of information is any good. This can be achieved by relating the reasoning trace to the domain model of the system. For example, according to the domain model, the 'Acquire Medication' task could be satisfied not only by the *Patient Chart* but also by the *Electronic Patient Record*. However, as the *Electronic Patient Record* agent was busy serving other requests only the *Patient Chart* could respond to this request.

6.2 Analysing the Existing Application

The results of our ethnographical study are pointing towards the necessity to support four of the five different user goals introduced by Sørmo et al. [2], namely *transparency*, *justification*, *relevance*, and *conceptualisation*. This can be expressed in design specification documents which explicitly include the explanatory needs. When we look at the existing application, we can see that it does support the *transparency*, *conceptualisation*, and *justification* goals, where the latter is even only supported partially.

The fact that the system lacks certain explanatory capabilities is hardly surprising since they were not the main focus of the earlier implementation. However, the use of problem frames in general and explanation problem frames in particular helps us in identifying the deficiencies of the existing design, understanding and communicating explanatory needs, as well as exploring possible solutions to overcome these deficiencies.

Since we have started with data from an existing workplace analysis, we have not tested the hypothesis that (explanation) problem frames can be put to use in communicating with prospective users during the requirements elicitation phase. But we assume problems frames can enhance the cooperation between the requirements engineers and these users, as indicated by Phalp and Cox [13].

In the requirements analysis, introducing explanation frames facilitates the explication and formalisation of the findings of our ethnographical study and thereby deepens our understanding of the problem domain.

The use of problem frames as a method during requirement specification aids us in checking the completeness of the specification and helps us to incorporate explanatory needs which could otherwise be overlooked. This should also lead to a design which encompasses more features. If we had done the original system specification with the help of (explanation) problem frames, the missing support for the *relevance* goal would have been uncovered.

An explanation aware requirements specification is also fruitful in the transition from design to implementation. Earlier work by Roth-Berghofer and others has coupled explanation goals with the knowledge containers of case-based reasoning systems [23]. Having an explicit representation of explanation goals helps in identifying requirements for the knowledge containers, easing the way from a specification document to the structure and content of the knowledge containers.

7 Conclusion and Future Work

We have suggested the use of problem frames for analysing and specifying requirements for explanation-aware ambient intelligent systems. By introducing explanation patterns we have enhanced the toolbox for designing ambient intelligent systems.

We have shown how the use of explanation specific problem frames can help in recognising and explicating design requirements resulting from the necessity of intelligent systems to be able to explain their own reasoning and behaviour.

There are several issues that we have not addressed in this paper and which are left for further work. First and foremost, we have to explore further the relation between the design documents and the actual implementation. Our results show that problem frames help us to identify which explanatory knowledge and mechanism should be provided, but the methods for the next step in identifying the missing "knowledge containers" and suggesting remedies have to be extended over the existing work on the relation between explanation goals, explanation kinds, and knowledge containers.

References

1. Ducatel, K., Bogdanowicz, M., Scapolo, F., Leijten, J., Burgelman, J.C.: ISTAG scenarios for ambient intelligence in 2010. Technical report, IST Advisory Group (2001)
2. Sørmo, F., Cassens, J., Aamodt, A.: Explanation in case-based reasoning – perspectives and goals. Artificial Intelligence Review 24, 109–143 (2005)
3. Leake, D.: Goal-based explanation evaluation. In: Goal-Driven Learning, pp. 251–285. MIT Press, Cambridge (1995)
4. Jackson, M.: Problem Frames – Analysing and Structuring Software Development Problems. Addison-Wesley, Boston (2001)
5. Cassens, J., Kofod-Petersen, A.: Designing explanation aware systems: The quest for explanation patterns. In: Roth-Berghofer, T.R., Schulz, S., Leake, D. (eds.) Explanation-Aware Computing – Papers from the 2007 AAAI Workshop. Number WS-07-06 in Technical Report, pp. 20–27. AAAI Press, Vancouver (2007)
6. Alexander, C., Ishikawa, S., Silverstein, M., Jacobson, M., Fiksdahl-King, I., Angel, S.: A Pattern Language. Oxford University Press, New York (1977)
7. Fensel, D., Benjamins, R., Decker, S., Gaspari, M., Groenboom, R., Grosso, W., Musen, M., Motta, E., Plaza, E., Schreiber, G., Studer, R., Wielinga, B.: The component model of upml in a nutshell. In: WWW Proceedings WICSA1, 1st Working IFIP Conference on Software Architectures, San Antonio, Texas (1999)
8. Bergmann, R., Althoff, K.D., Breen, S., Göker, M., Manago, M., Traphöner, R., Wess, S.: Developing Industrial Case-Based Reasoning Applications, 2nd edn. LNCS, vol. 1612. Springer, Berlin (2003)
9. Schreiber, G., Akkermans, H., Anjewierden, A., de Hoog, R., Shadbolt, N., de Velde, W.V., Wielinga, B.: Knowledge Engineering and Management – The Common KADS Methodology. MIT Press, Cambridge (2000)
10. Avgeriou, P., Zdun, U.: Architectural patterns revisited – a pattern language. In: Proceedings of the tenth European Conference on Pattern Languages of Programs (EuroPlop 2005), Irsee, pp. 1–39 (2005)
11. Gamma, E., Helm, R., Johnson, R., Vlissides, J.: Design Patterns: Elements of Reusable Object-Oriented Software. Addison-Wesley, Boston (1995)
12. Hatebur, D., Heisel, M.: Problem frames and architectures for security problems. In: Winther, R., Gran, B.A., Dahll, G. (eds.) SAFECOMP 2005. LNCS, vol. 3688, pp. 390–404. Springer, Heidelberg (2005)
13. Phalp, K., Cox, K.: Picking the right problem fram – an empirical study. Empirical Software Engineering 5, 215–228 (2000)
14. Hall, J., Rapanotti, L.: Problem frames for sociotechnical systems. In: Mate, J.L., Silva, A. (eds.) Requirements Engineering for Sociotechnical Systems, pp. 318–339. Idea Group Publishing, USA (2005)
15. Kofod-Petersen, A., Cassens, J.: Explanations and Context in Ambient Intelligent Systems. In: Kokinov, B., Richardson, D.C., Roth-Berghofer, T.R., Vieu, L. (eds.) CONTEXT 2007. LNCS (LNAI), vol. 4635, pp. 303–316. Springer, Heidelberg (2007)

16. Kofod-Petersen, A., Mikalsen, M.: Context: Representation and reasoning – representing and reasoning about context in a mobile environment. Revue d'Intelligence Artificielle 19, 479–498 (2005)
17. Aamodt, A.: Knowledge-intensive case-based reasoning in CREEK. In: Funk, P., González Calero, P.A. (eds.) ECCBR 2004. LNCS (LNAI), vol. 3155, pp. 1–15. Springer, Heidelberg (2004)
18. Gundersen, O.E., Kofod-Petersen, A.: Multiagent based problem-solving in a mobile environment. In: Coward, E. (ed.) Norsk Informatikkonferance 2005, NIK 2005, pp. 7–18. Institutt for Informatikk Universitetet i Bergen (2005)
19. Cassens, J., Kofod-Petersen, A.: Using activity theory to model context awareness: a qualitative case study. In: Sutcliffe, G.C.J., Goebel, R.G. (eds.) Proceedings of the 19th International Florida Artificial Intelligence Research Society Conference, pp. 619–624. AAAI Press, Melbourne (2006)
20. Bellifemine, F., Caire, G., Poggi, A., Rimassa, G.: Jade – a white paper. TILAB EXP "in search of innovation" 3, 6–19 (2003)
21. Kofod-Petersen, A., Aamodt, A.: Contextualised Ambient Intelligence Through Case-Based Reasoning. In: Roth-Berghofer, T.R., Göker, M.H., Güvenir, H.A. (eds.) ECCBR 2006. LNCS (LNAI), vol. 4106, pp. 211–225. Springer, Heidelberg (2006)
22. Mao, J.Y., Benbasat, I.: The use of explanations in knowledge-based systems: Cognitive perspectives and a process-tracing analysis. Journal of Managment Information Systems 17, 153–179 (2000)
23. Roth-Berghofer, T.R., Cassens, J.: Mapping Goals and Kinds of Explanations to the Knowledge Containers of Case-Based Reasoning Systems. In: Muñoz-Ávila, H., Ricci, F. (eds.) ICCBR 2005. LNCS (LNAI), vol. 3620, pp. 451–464. Springer, Heidelberg (2005)

Enhancing Alignment Based Context Prediction by Using Multiple Context Sources: Experiment and Analysis

Immanuel König, Christian Voigtmann, Bernd Niklas Klein, and Klaus David

Chair for Communication Technology (ComTec), University of Kassel,
D-34121 Kassel, Germany
comtec@uni-kassel.de

Abstract. Context aware applications are reactive, they adapt to an entity's context when the context has changed. In order to become proactive and act before the context actually has changed future contexts have to be predicted. This will enable functionalities like preloading of content or detection of future conflicts. For example if an application can predict where a user is heading to it can also check for train delays on the user's way. So far research concentrates on context prediction algorithms that only use a history of one context to predict the future context. In this paper we propose a novel multidimensional context prediction algorithm and we show that the use of multidimensional context histories increases the prediction accuracy. We compare two multidimensional prediction algorithms, one of which is a new approach; the other was not yet experimentally tested. In theory, simulation and a real world experiment we verify the feasibility of both algorithms and show that our new approach has at least equal or better reasoning accuracy.

Keywords: context, context prediction, multidimensional context prediction alignment.

1 Introduction

The ubiquity of sensors today, and in the future even more so, can be exploited to get a very accurate picture of a user, what he is doing and the condition of his surroundings, in short the user's context. Important examples for ubiquitous sensors are smart phones, which are equipped with ever more sensors, like GPS, accelerometers and gyroscopes. Context aware applications are reactive, they adapt to a user's context when the context has changed. For example they can adjust the heating and lighting when a user arrives in his home.

In the future more and more applications will be context enabled [1]. A next step will then be to even use future contexts. Such a forecast of upcoming context is called context prediction. The prediction of context enables proactive applications that not only react when a context has changed, but can act beforehand. In the example described above the context aware home of the user could know in advance of his homecoming. This could be used by the heating system to already have reached the desired temperature in the user's home when he arrives.

M. Beigl et al. (Eds.): CONTEXT 2011, LNAI 6967, pp. 159–172, 2011.

Context prediction can be done using different algorithms like ARMA [2], neural networks [3] or alignment [4] and using different contexts, such as position, temperature, or light intensity. The research so far is concentrating on methods that predict a single context based on the history of this single context. But as the task of a prediction algorithm is to predict the future as accurate as possible based on the past, thus we should not unnecessarily reduce the knowledge of the past by just considering one single context and its history. A prediction based on multiple context sources is called multidimensional context prediction. In this paper we show that the use of multidimensional context histories increases the prediction accuracy. We compare two multidimensional prediction algorithms, which we call M1 (method 1) and M2, respectively. In theory, simulation and a real world experiment we verify the feasibility of both algorithms and show that our new approach M2 has at least equal or better reasoning accuracy.

The document is organised as follows: Section 2 gives an overview of different approaches of multidimensional context prediction. Also an introduction to our new approach M2 is given. In Section 3 an analytical comparison of an existing and our new approach is given. Section 4 presents the results of our experimental measurements of the two context prediction algorithms M1 and M2. In Section 5 a simulation concerning the influence of more context source to the two algorithms is presented. In Section 6 the conclusions are given.

2 Related Work

A comprehensive overview of context prediction is given by Mayrhofer in [5] and [2]. In his work he uses ARMA [2] for a prediction algorithm developed for application domains such as finance predictions. In his framework, the usage of more than one context source is proposed.

The use of an alignment based algorithm was proposed by Sigg in [4]. He proposed the use of a system which is storing occurred contexts of the past in a history. To predict the next context he monitors the last few occurred contexts and tries to find them in the context history. The search is done with an alignment [8] based search algorithm. The alignment algorithm is searching for the best matching part in the history. Once the best matching part in history is found, the following symbol in the history is assumed to be the next context.

The alignment algorithm is used in bioinformatics to find a DNA matching. Its strengths are finding subsequences in a sequence with gaps or with mismatches and it can handle non numerical symbols. Therefore, alignment is especially useful in the area of context processing because context can be nominal. Also the sensing of context in a real environment can include gaps in case that a sensor is not reachable or includes faulty data when the sensor is irritated.

For the use of multiple context sources Sigg proposes an algorithm [7] which we call method1 (M1) in the following. Since the alignment can only handle one-dimensional histories, the multidimensional history needs to be merged into a new one-dimensional one by mapping context. Therefore he is dividing the history in timeslots. Then he is mapping the different symbols, one from each context source, at a certain timeslot and labels them with a new symbol. The mapping itself is done by combining a unique set of symbols, one of each time series, into a new unique symbol. It does not matter which symbol is chosen for the new time series as long as the mapping is unique, so the mapping can be done forwards and backwards. The same mapping is done with the last few observed contexts from the different context sources. The whole mapping has to be done with one mapping table. This ensures that one mapping of symbols in the history is mapped to the same new symbol each time it occurs. The mapping is illustrated in Fig. 1. The blue, green and red rows $k_1 \ldots k_3$ are the different context patterns in the history. The light blue row k_4 consists of the mapped new built unique sy

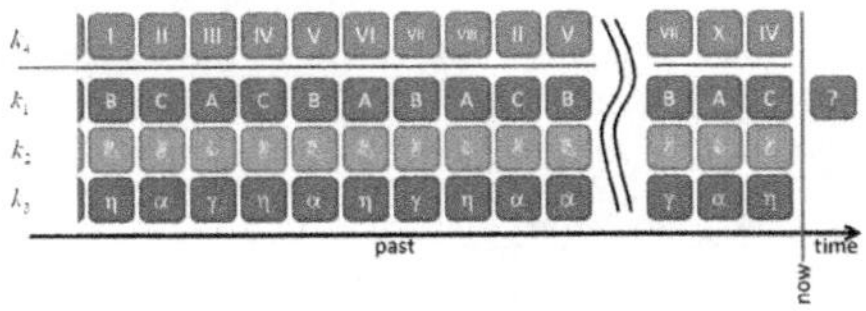

Fig. 1. The mapping of M1. The light blue time series k_4 is generated with the mapping. The mapping is done with the whole history including the last occurred symbols.

The next step is to perform a search using the above described alignment matching algorithm and the new pattern in the new build history k_4. The predicted symbol will be the follower of the point of discovery. This step is illustrated in Fig. 2 where the orange field is the point of discovery and the purple field marks the predicted symbol.

Fig. 2. The alignment search in k_4. The orange box is the point of discovery of the alignment algorithm. The purple box is the predicted symbol.

The predicted symbol in k_4 needs to be mapped backwards in the end to get the predicted symbols in the original context patterns.

This enhancement from the one-dimensional approach to the multi-dimensional approach seems to be a simple step if the one-dimensional prediction system is already implemented. From our point of view this approach can be improved with some enhancements. In the process of mapping all errors of the used context sources are preserved. The errors are preserved as they result in a new mapped context containing all errors which were previously dissipated over all context sources. The alignment algorithm could handle some errors as it can find the searched subsequence even with some mismatches. But if there are too many errors, especially in the last observed symbols, the prediction accuracy decreases. To avoid this problem while using the strength of the alignment algorithm in context prediction we propose a new multidimensional alignment based context prediction algorithm, which we call method 2 (M2).

New Prediction Approach: M2

Our approach is based on a multi-dimensional context history and an alignment based search algorithm. The first step is to use the alignment algorithm to find a place in the history where the last few occurred contexts have already been appeared. We do this for every context source *separately*. The second step is to take the following symbol in the history as prediction. This is illustrated in Fig. 3 where an example of a history is shown. The search is done three times, once in each part of the history $k_1 \ldots k_3$. The orange fields are the points of discovery and the purple fields are the predicted values.

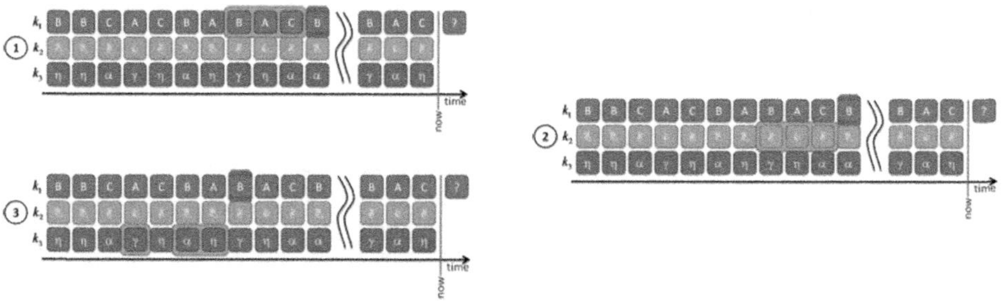

Fig. 3. The alignment search in each time series. The search is done three times, once in each part of the history $k_1 \ldots k_3$. The orange box is each time the point of discovery of each search. The purple box is the prediction. The predicted symbol is always taken from the k_1 history as the context k_1 has to be predicted.

The difference to the M1 approach is that we take the next symbol from the context row that should be predicted, which is in Fig. 3 k_1. The following symbol is *always* taken from the context history related to the context which has to be predicted. This is done even if the search has been done in a different context history. To clarify it we will use the context sources 'position' and 'temperature'. The goal is to predict the context 'position'. In the first step we try to find with alignment a matching pattern in the history of the 'positions' and the search pattern is the last occurred pattern of 'positions'. Next we take the following entry in the history of 'positions' as a prediction. Now we repeat this with the 'temperature'. We try to find the 'temperature' pattern in the 'temperature' history. But in the end we do not take the 'temperature' from the 'temperature' history as we want to predict the 'position'. Instead we take the 'position' *at that time* in the history where we found the matching 'temperature' pattern. This means we are predicting the 'position' with the information out of the 'temperature' history. In the last step we rate the two predictions to get one prediction. In our first approach we use a simple majority voting system for this rating.

Taking a context from a certain history based on a search in another history can only be useful if the two context histories are correlated. And this is only the case if the context sources of the two histories are correlated. This is pointing to the changes which had to be made on M1 where all context sources are assumed to be totally correlated by mapping them all together. To find a certain mapped symbol exactly the same mapping has to appear in the history. If a gap or a potential wrong symbol has been recorded in the history due to inaccuracies or other issues with the sensor the same mistake has to occur again to use the mapped context. In our approach gaps and mismatches can occur at a certain time in different context sources without generating new symbols and thus disabling other symbols from being found by the alignment algorithm.

Definitions
For the following investigation several definitions are necessary:

Definition of Time Series: Let $i \in N$ and t_i describe any interval i in time. A context time series *k* is a non-empty, time-ordered set of context elements *k(i)* each with a timestamp t_i attached. [7]

Any time series can be generated by different context sources or due to different context interpreters relying on the same physical sensors. An example of four time series is shown in Fig. 1. In this example the context element $k_1(4)$ is an "A".

Format of Context
In our discussion we only consider context sources which change time synchronously. If two or more context sources change asynchronously an interpolation can be done, shown in [7 S73]. The contexts can be non ordinal which extends our algorithm to handle non numerical values as many real world contexts are only symbolic.

Probability of Correctness
We also assume for each context symbol a probability of being correct. This does not need to be known in order to use a context prediction system but for an analytical view we will still use it. Such a value could for example be based on the context acquisition step, an interpretation step or just the loss of information in a context database.

Definition of Probability of Correctness: For every $k(i) \in$ k we define $P_k(i)$ as the probability that context element *k(i)* is without an error. P_k describes the probability that the time series *k* is without an error. An error is a difference between the value of *k(i)* and the according value in the real world.

Prediction Accuracy
A prediction is accurate if the predicted symbol matches the really occurring symbol, otherwise it is inaccurate.

Context History
A context history is a context time series containing the past context elements of a context source. A multidimensional context history is a set of multiple context histories based on multiple context sources.

Correlated Context Sources
For our approach we assume a correlation between the different context sources. For example a person could carry a mobile device with a temperature sensor and a sensor for location. If the person is changing its location it will probably also change the temperature. And the location and temperature will change in a recognizable pattern as some places may have certain temperatures.

Alignment for Context Prediction
In this paper we use an alignment based algorithm for context prediction. A detailed description can be found in [4]. The main idea is to use an alignment algorithm to search in the context history. Once a matching is found the following symbol of the point of discovery will be predicted as the next occurring symbol.

In the following part the mathematical analysis discusses both approaches in detail.

3 Analytical Proof

In this section we will analytically prove that M2 as a multidimensional context prediction algorithm with a multiple alignment search is better (or equal) in terms of prediction accuracy than M1, which uses a mapping and a single alignment search.

Idea of the Proof
The concept of the analytical proof is to show how M1 and M2 depend on the correctness of their used histories. Afterwards they can be compared based on the history elements they use and their probability of being correct. For this we need a mathematical model and the variables that are shown in the table below.

Table 1. Used variables

Variable	Definition
i, j, o	Control variables
m	Number of context time series
n	Number of elements in a context time series
k_j	Context time series j
$k_j(i)$	Element i of context time series j
$k_j(n+1)$	Predicted element for context time series j
$k_{j,o}(n+1)$	Predicted element for context time series j, based on time series o
P_{pre}	Probability prediction is right
$P_{pre\ j,o}$	Probability prediction for time series j based on time series o is right
P_{k_j}	Probability time series j is without an error
$P_{k_j}(i)$	Probability element i of time series j is without an error
P_{M1}	Probability multidimensional prediction algorithm M1 is without an error
P_{M2}	Probability multidimensional prediction algorithm M2 is without an error

Without loss of generality we assume that the probability that no error has occurred in the prediction step P_{pre} and $P_{pre\ j,o}$ is equal for each prediction step. As we will see the amount of errors in the used history for prediction by P_{pre} is higher than the amount of errors used in each single prediction $P_{pre\ j,o}$. Each prediction is based on the data it uses and so also based on the errors in the used data. Considering this we can consequently follow $P_{pre\ j,o}$ will always be better than P_{pre}. But as we need to compare M1 and M2 we will set

$$P_{pre} = P_{pre\ j,o}. \tag{1}$$

Analytical View on M1

First we have a closer look on the algorithm M1. The probability the prediction of M1 is correct P_{M1} can be calculated as

$$P_{M1} = P_{pre} * P_{k_{m+1}}. \tag{2}$$

P_{km+1} represents the probability that the used history k_4 is correct. This is also used in a similar way in [7]. Of course the prediction algorithm depends on numerous values and may also depend on the used context history. Therefore we can describe (2) as a simple model but as an erroneous history can only decrease P_{pre} and we use (2) in both surveys we do not lose generality.

Now we need a way to get the probability P_{km+1}. We calculate this by multiplying the probabilities of correctness of each element in k_4

$$P_{k_{m+1}} = \prod_{i=1}^{n} P_{k_{m+1}}(i). \tag{3}$$

Each newly created symbol $k_4(i)$ has a probability of correctness depending on the probability of correctness of the symbols $P_{kj}(i)$ which were mapped to get $k_4(i)$. This can be described as

$$P_{k_{m+1}}(i) = \prod_{j=1}^{m} P_{k_j}(i). \tag{4}$$

It means a symbol in k_4 cannot be correct if a single symbol used for a certain mapping is wrong. Of course a wrong symbol would be created by M1 if any element in the history is wrong. This would end either in a complete new symbol or in a wrong use of an existing symbol of k_4.

As we are using products of probabilities with usual values from zero to one we can also say:

$$P_{k_{m+1}}(i) \leq \min\left(P_{k_1}(i), P_{k_2}(i), P_{k_3}(i), \ldots, P_{k_m}(i)\right) \tag{5}$$

This is a logical consequence of M1 as we are just using a simple mapping. Each newly created symbol cannot be more correct than the most incorrect single symbol used to build the mapping. No new knowledge is generated in the mapping. This leads us with (3) to

$$P_{k_{m+1}} \leq \min\left(P_{k_1}, P_{k_2}, P_{k_3}, \ldots, P_{k_m}\right). \tag{6}$$

One can get this with putting (3) into (5) and rearranging the arguments of the min() function. If we multiply this by P_{pre} we get the expression

$$P_{M1} \leq \min\left(P_{pre} * P_{k_1}, P_{pre} * P_{k_2}, P_{pre} * P_{k_3}, \ldots, P_{pre} * P_{k_m}\right). \tag{7}$$

The left is changed to P_{M1} with (2). The right side describes a very interesting aspect: Each single search and prediction would lead to a better (or equal) result than the prediction with M1. Keeping in mind that we are using alignment for the single prediction we could come to the conclusion that working with some wrong symbols is one of the strength of alignment. But as k_4 is collecting all wrong symbols the task is getting very difficult.

Taking (7) into account we could finish the proof here as M2 is just performing a single search and prediction. M2 also takes the probably best prediction by choosing the majority but even if it would take the prediction with the lowest probability of being correct it would at least make an equal or more accurate prediction than M1. To get a closed mathematical proof we continue showing also the dependencies of M2 and compare it to M1.

Analytical View on M2

The probability that M2 is errorless is an average of the probabilities of correctness from the single predicted symbols as they are chosen by M2. This needs to be done because M2 is taking an average of all predicted symbols as long as they are part of the majority. In a mathematical expression this would mean:

$$P_{M2} = \frac{1}{\text{elements in maj.}} \sum_{o=1}^{m} P_{pre\ j,o} \Big|_{k_1(n+1)=maj.} \tag{8}$$

$P_{pre\ j,o}$ is the probability of being correct for a single prediction. Like in (2) it can be calculated by a multiplication of the probabilities of being correct of the used history and the probability of the prediction being correct.

$$P_{pre\ j,o} = P_{pre} * P_{k_o} \tag{9}$$

The average value of any series is always between (or equal) the smallest and the largest single value. Combining (8) and (9) and using the average value we can write:

$$\begin{aligned}
&\min\left(\left[P_{pre\ j,1} * P_{k_1}\right]_{k_1(n+1)=maj.}, \ldots, \left[P_{pre\ j,m} * P_{k_m}\right]_{k_j(n+1)=maj.}\right) \\
&\leq P_{M2} \leq \\
&\max\left(\left[P_{pre\ j,1} * P_{k_1}\right]_{k_1(n+1)=maj.}, \ldots, \left[P_{pre\ j,m} * P_{k_m}\right]_{k_j(n+1)=maj.}\right)
\end{aligned} \tag{10}$$

The expression shows only some predictions are used in the calculation. To compare M1 and M2 we need to get rid of the conditions. To achieve this we should have a closer look on two cases.

Case One

A not used single prediction has a lower probability of being correct than all used predictions

$$\left[P_{pre\ j,\xi} * P_{k_\xi}\right]_{k_\xi(n+1)\neq maj.} \leq \min\left(\left[P_{pre\ j,1} * P_{k_1}\right]_{k_1(n+1)=maj.},\dots,\left[P_{pre\ j,m} * P_{k_m}\right]_{k_j(n+1)=maj.}\right). \tag{11}$$

In this case and with (10) and (11) we could also write

$$\left[P_{pre\ j,\xi} * P_{k_\xi}\right]_{k_\xi(n+1)\neq maj.} \leq \min\left(\left[P_{pre\ j,1} * P_{k_1}\right]_{k_1(n+1)=maj.},\dots,\left[P_{pre\ j,m} * P_{k_m}\right]_{k_j(n+1)=maj.}\right) \leq P_{M2}. \tag{12}$$

By adding the omitted probability into the min() function we still can say

$$\min\left(P_{pre\ j,1} * P_{k_1}, P_{pre\ j,2} * P_{k_2}, P_{pre\ j,3} * P_{k_3},\dots, P_{pre\ j,m} * P_{k_m}\right) \leq P_{M2}. \tag{13}$$

Case Two

A not used single prediction has a higher probability of being correct than the one with the minimal probability of the used predictions

$$\left[P_{pre\ j,\xi} * P_{k_\xi}\right]_{k_\xi(n+1)\neq maj.} \geq \min\left(\left[P_{pre\ j,1} * P_{k_1}\right]_{k_1(n+1)=maj.},\dots,\left[P_{pre\ j,m} * P_{k_m}\right]_{k_j(n+1)=maj.}\right). \tag{14}$$

If we add the omitted probabilities into the min() function it still returns one of the probabilities which have already been in there as it has a lower value. In this case we can also say

$$\min\left(P_{pre\ j,1} * P_{k_1}, P_{pre\ j,2} * P_{k_2}, P_{pre\ j,3} * P_{k_3},\dots, P_{pre\ j,m} * P_{k_m}\right) \leq P_{M2}. \tag{15}$$

Both cases end in the same result. No we can go on to the next step: comparing P_{M1} and P_{M2}.

Comparing P_{M1} and P_{M2}

First we need to apply (1) to (13) so we get

$$\min\left(P_{pre} * P_{k_1}, P_{pre} * P_{k_2}, P_{pre} * P_{k_3}, \ldots, P_{pre} * P_{k_m}\right) \leq P_{M2}. \tag{16}$$

Comparing it to (7)

$$P_{M1} \leq \min\left(P_{pre} * P_{k_1}, P_{pre} * P_{k_2}, P_{pre} * P_{k_3}, \ldots, P_{pre} * P_{k_m}\right) \tag{17}$$

we can also write

$$P_{M1} \leq \min\left(P_{pre} * P_{k_1}, P_{pre} * P_{k_2}, P_{pre} * P_{k_3}, \ldots, P_{pre} * P_{k_m}\right) \leq P_{M2} \tag{18}$$

and

$$P_{M1} \leq P_{M2}. \tag{19}$$

Discussion of the Results

There are two main statements we can derive from this analysis:

1. M1 is not getting any better by adding additional context sources.
2. M2 is at least as good as M1, if we add additional context sources it is probably getting better.

This means our single context search algorithm M2 is less depended on errors that occurred in the history. If no errors are present in the history M1 and M2 are performing in the same way. But if we assume a non perfect context history one should use M2 for a multidimensional context prediction.

4 Real World Experiment

To support the findings of the mathematical analysis given in Chapter III, we made a real world experiment. For this experiment we logged the position and the temperature of a user. Therefore two data logging devices were carried by a person during daily life for over eight days. We decided to use the position and the surrounding temperature of a user as they are usually correlated. If a person is at home for example, the temperature will be the home temperature. If the same person is outside on the way to work the temperature will be the outside temperature.

Collecting the Position

To collect the position we used a Motorola Milestone, an Android based smart phone. This device was logging the position using Google Latitude. This data was downloaded and clustered into places and afterwards labeled using labels like ‘home’, ‘work’ and so on. Additionally the transitions between the places got a label like ‘way_work_home’ or ‘way_home_work’. This data stream of timestamps and labels was used as our first context source.

Collecting the Temperature

Since a measurement of the surrounding temperature is not possible with a Motorola Milestone we decided to use a SunSpot. A SunSpot is a sensor device form Sun with memory, a processor, an accumulator, communication possibilities and a sensor board which also contains a temperature sensor. The SunSpot was carried in parallel to the smart phone with the temperature sensor pointing away from the person to avoid any influence of the body temperature. We collected the temperature on the SunSpot once a second. The data was downloaded from the device each evening and the device was charged during the nighttime. After the whole dataset was collected we post processed the temperature values to get the three contexts: 'outside', 'inside' and 'unknown'.

Results of the Experiment

After both datasets were post processed we combined them to a table with three columns: the timestamp, the location and the inside/outside context. A short sample of the history table is given in Table 2. This table was split into a history and a test part. The history and a subpart of the test part were processed by the two algorithms M1 and M2. The algorithms were used to predict the next location of the user. The prediction was compared to the symbol which occurred in the test part right after the taken subpart. This testing routine was repeated with the whole test set more than 30 times. A matching prediction was rated as a correct prediction and a non matching prediction as a wrong prediction. Afterwards the average of the prediction accuracy was calculated.

Table 2. A short sample from the measured history

Unix time	Position	Temperature
1302281986159	way home training	unknown
1302282152990	way home training	inside
1302282163604	training	inside
1302286202056	restaurant	inside

The test was done two times. The first time only one context source, the location, was used. In the case of using only one context both algorithms are working in the same way. This behavior can be seen in Figure 4 where both algorithms perform equal with only one context source. This test was done to see what performance the algorithm can achieve with only the knowledge of one context. The second test was done with the use of both context sources, the location and the inside/outside context. These results are visualized in Figure 4. It can clearly be seen that the prediction accuracy increases by adding a second context and using M2. The prediction accuracy does not increase when using M1 and adding more context sources.

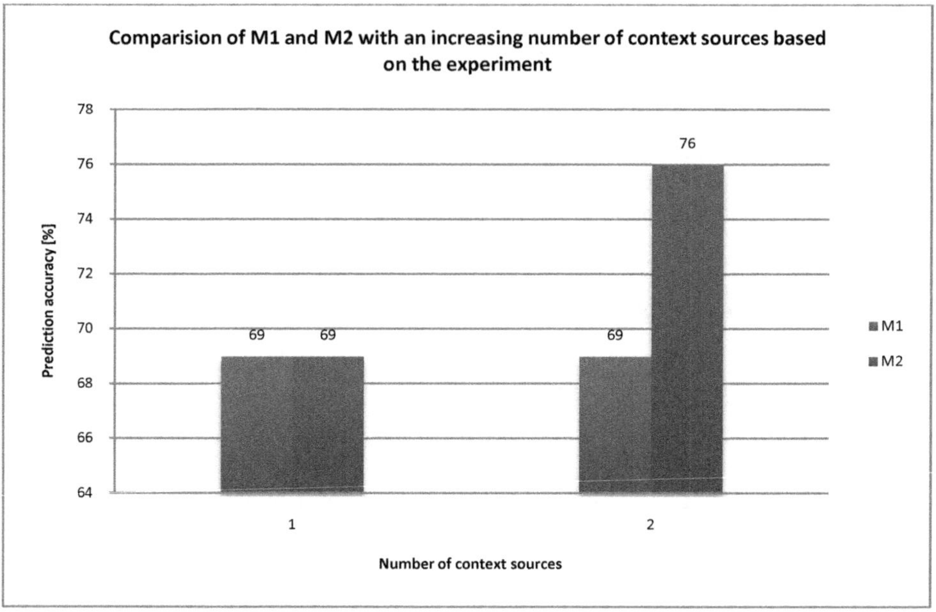

Fig. 4. The result of the experiment in a bar chart. The gain of prediction accuracy can clearly be seen by the increasing red bar on the right side.

Discussion of the Results

The result shows two main points:

1. The prediction results of M1 does not get any better by adding additional context sources.
2. The prediction accuracy of M2 can be increased by using the information of correlated context sources.

The first point was already shown in the mathematical analysis of the problem. It is not advised to add additional context source to the first algorithm as this can only decrease the prediction accuracy. The second point was intuitively clear but is now shown by experiment. The prediction accuracy of M2 is getting better when choosing matching context sources to enhance the prediction.

5 Simulation

In addition to the real word experiment described above we made a simulation to get different context sources for an entity. The main advantages of using the simulation are we get several contexts and can adjust the simulation environment easily. We also have control over the sensing errors as all sensors are software sensors.

We decided to use Siafu, an open source context simulator [9]. We loaded the office simulation delivered with the program and decided to use two different context sources: activity and noise level. We chose a simulation time of one week and observed 14 different staff members of the simulated office. The resulting history table was split into a history and a test set and then tested with M1 and M2. This was repeated 80 times with each subpart of the test set, similar to the real world experiment. Afterwards the averages of the results were taken.

Results of the Experiment

These results are shown in Figure 5. It can be seen that the prediction accuracy increases by adding a second context when using M2. The prediction accuracy decreases when using M1 and adding a second context.

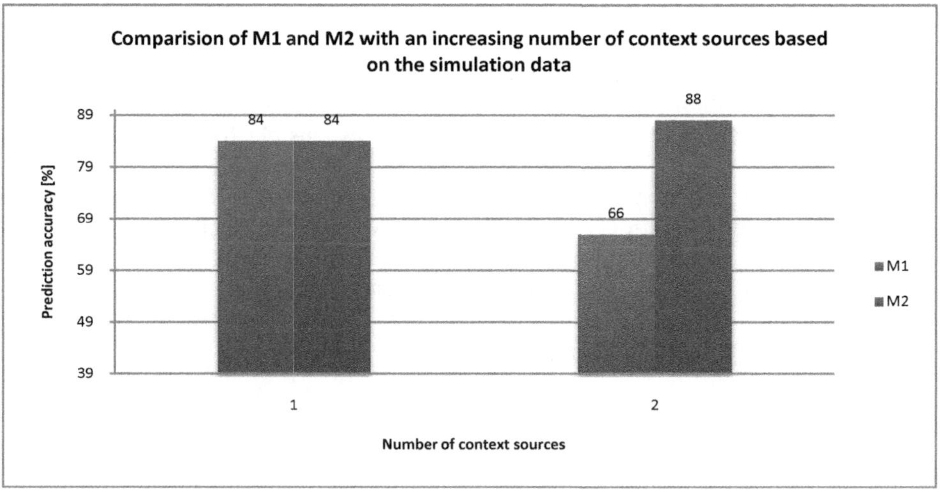

Fig. 5. The result of the simulation in a bar chart. The prediction accuracy of M1 is decreasing while the accuracy of M2 is increasing when an additional context sources is added.

Discussion of the Results

The result supports the two main points we have already seen in the real world experiment:

1. The prediction results of M1 do not improve by adding additional context sources. They got even worse.
2. The prediction accuracy of M2 can be increased by using the information of correlated context sources.

The results of the simulation are similar to the real world experiment.

6 Conclusion

In this paper we analyzed the influence of using correlated context sources on the accuracy of context prediction. So far research concentrates on prediction of a single context using only the history data of this context. We used two context prediction algorithms suited for multidimensional context history data. Both are based on the alignment prediction algorithm. The first algorithm M1 uses a mapping of context to generate one-dimensional histories out of multidimensional ones and was proposed in the literature before but was never examined in detail. The second approach M2 is not relying on mapping and is a new approach proposed by us.

We have mathematically proven that the M1 is not improving its prediction accuracy by adding additional context sources and that M2 is at least as good or better as M2. When additional context sources are added M2 is getting better by utilizing knowledge of correlated sources. As expected, in a real world experiment with two correlated context source, namely location and temperature, we got results that support the mathematical proof. By suing M2 the prediction accuracy could be improved from 69% (M1) to 76%.

Acknowledgement. The authors would like to acknowledge the German Federal Ministry of Education and Research (BMBF) for funding the project MATRIX (Förderkennzeichen 01BS0802). The authors are responsible for the content of the publication.

VENUS is a research cluster at the interdisciplinary Research Center for Information System Design (ITeG) at Kassel University. We thank Hesse's Ministry of Higher Education, Research, and the Arts for funding the project as part of the research funding program "LOEWE – Landes-Offensive zur Entwicklung Wissenschaftlich-ökonomischer Exzellenz". For further information, please visit: http://www.iteg.uni-kassel.de/venus.

References

1. Weiser, M.: The computer for the 21st century. Scientific American 3 (1991)
2. Mayrhofer, R.M.: An Architecture for Context Prediction. PhD thesis, Johannes Kepeler University of Linz, Linz, Austria (2004)
3. Petzold, J., Pietzowski, A., Bagci, F., Trumler, W., Ungerer, T.: Prediction of indoor movements using bayesian networks. In: Strang, T., Linnhoff-Popien, C. (eds.) LoCA 2005. LNCS, vol. 3479, pp. 211–222. Springer, Heidelberg (2005)
4. Sigg, S., Haseloff, S., David, K.: A novel approach to context prediction in Ubicomp environments. In: PIMRC 2006, Helsinki, Finland (2006)
5. Mayrhofer, R.: Context prediction based on context histories: Expected benets, issues and current state-of-the-art. In: Proceedings of the 1st International Workshop on Exploiting Context Histories in Smart Environments (ECHISE) at the 3rd Int. Conference on Pervasive Computing (2005)
6. Chen, G., Kotz, D.: A survey of context-aware mobile computing research. Tech. Report TR2000-381, Dept. of Computer Science, Dartmouth College (2000)
7. Sigg, S.: Development of a novel context prediction algorithm and analysis of context prediction schemes. PhD thesis, University of Kassel, Germany (2007)
8. Altschul, S.F., Gish, W., Miller, W., Myers, E.W., Lipman, D.J.: Basic local alignment search tool. Journal of Molecular Biology 215(3) (October 1990)
9. Siafu - An Open Source Context Simulator (May 2011), `http://siafusimulator.sourceforge.net`

Buy, Sell, or Hold? Information Extraction from Stock Analyst Reports

Yeong Su Lee and Michaela Geierhos

CIS, University of Munich, Germany

Abstract. This paper presents a novel linguistic information extraction approach exploiting analysts' stock ratings for statistical decision making. Over a period of one year, we gathered German stock analyst reports in order to determine market trends. Our goal is to provide business statistics over time to illustrate market trends for a user-selected company. We therefore recognize named entities within the very short stock analyst reports such as organization names (e.g. BASF, BMW, Ericsson), analyst houses (e.g. Gartner, Citigroup, Goldman Sachs), ratings (e.g. buy, sell, hold, underperform, recommended list) and price estimations by using lexicalized finite-state graphs, so-called local grammars. Then, company names and their acronyms respectively have to be cross-checked against data the analysts provide. Finally, all extracted values are compared and presented into charts with different views depending on the evaluation criteria (e.g. by time line). Thanks to this approach it will be easier and even more comfortable in the future to pay attention to analysts' buy/sell signals without reading all their reports.

1 Introduction

Buy, sell, or hold? It is a subtle question. Fortunately, there are many stock analysts keeping track of latest business developments and activities in this fast growing market, determining a company's value, and making recommendations. By analyzing stock analyst reports using linguistic and statistical approaches, we only show the recommendation tendency and identify the share price estimate.[1] For this purpose, we gathered about 21,000 unique short analyst reports from different websites that usually host analyst reports provided by dpa-AFX. These short texts were analyzed during a period of twelve months passed from demo launch (March, 2010 – February, 2011)[2]. In general, the positive recommendations exceed the negative ones. It might be caused by the fact that "first, some brokers might have a tendency to issue buy recommendations when a hold or sell is deserved (as has been alleged by some), while other brokers would be more

[1] Please note: We do not intend to recommend any action based on our analysis!

[2] For demonstration purposes, our prototype is available online at `http://www.cis.uni-muenchen.de/~yeong/FINANZEN/test_analyse.html`. Analysis provided by this web interface is based on six months of data only (March, 2010 – September, 2010).

M. Beigl et al. (Eds.): CONTEXT 2011, LNAI 6967, pp. 173–184, 2011.

forthcoming in their ratings. Second (and more innocuously), the definitions of buy, hold, and sell may differ across brokers" [1, p. 90]. Although it would also be reasonable to take the computational approaches to subjectivity and sentiment analysis as well as pragmatic analysis into account [2], we firmly stick to the linguistic and statistical analysis of stock recommendations. We therefore extract information about the analyzed share, analyst house, rating, price target and date of recommendation.

1.1 The Nature of Stock Analyst Reports

German stock analyst reports are succinct statements of approximately 25–75 words (150–600 characters) each.

> **WestLB** *belässt* **Vodafone** *auf* 'Reduce' – *Ziel* **145 Pence**
> *Die* **WestLB** *hat* **Vodafone** vor einem Zwischenbericht zum dritten Geschäftsquartal *auf* "Reduce" *mit einem Kursziel von* **145,00 Pence** *belassen.* Der Fokus dürfte auf dem Service-Umsatz liegen, der auf 10,99 Milliarden Pfund gestiegen sein sollte, *schrieb Analyst* **Wolfgang Sprecht** *in einer Studie vom Dienstag.*

These text sources contain many abbreviations and acronyms of analyst houses (e.g. WestLB) as well as company names (e.g. Vodafone). Therefore, a **named entity recognition** based on a rather limited context analysis is required. Moreover, there are only a few *German words* per sentence expressing the recommendation or the price target (e.g. Ziel). All other words in the above mentioned example are English terms (e.g. Reduce).

1.2 Limited Context Analysis and Local Grammars

The construction of grammars has always been a search for a complete generalization of how language works.

> "(...) grammarians and theoreticians have always attempted to describe the general features of sentences. (...) But beyond these generalities lies an extremely rigid set of dependencies between individual words, which is huge in size; it has been accumulated over the millenia by language users, piece by piece, in micro areas such as those we began to analyze here." [3, p. 325]

The goal of a local grammar is not to cover all sentences of a language at a formal level in strictly combinatorial terms. Local grammars instead enable the **description of a local context** and restrict the occurrence of certain lexical or morpho-syntactical features to a window of predefined size.

> "(...) the global nature of language results from the interaction of a multiplicity of local finite state schemes." [3, p. 330]

Thus, they avoid or reduce ambiguities that can happen for a simple keyword search. In this regard, they perfectly fit into the later detailed extraction process of named entities performed on our corpus of stock analyst reports (cf. Section 3) and enable us to restrict our analysis to the forecasted market trends.

1.3 Objectives of the Paper

We aim at providing business statistics over time to illustrate market trends for a certain company by extracting specific information from stock analyst reports. Finally, all extracted values are displayed in charts by time line and price target per analyst house.

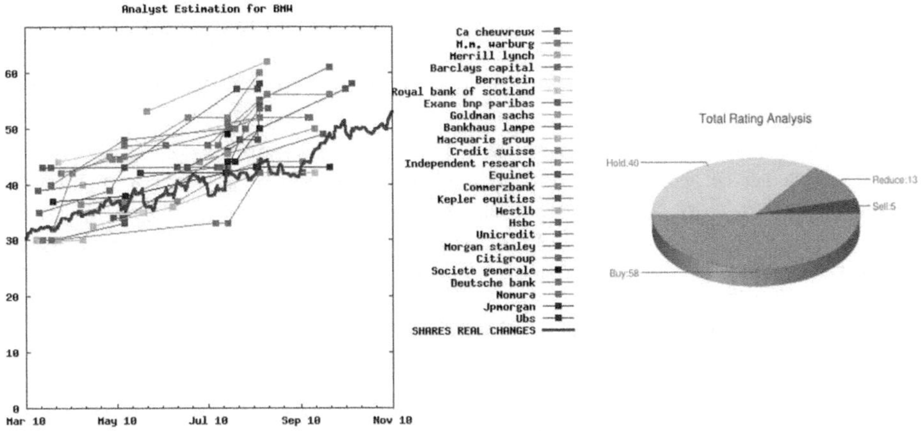

Fig. 1. Share price development and total rating statistics of BMW

In order to illustrate the share price development and compile the rating statistics it does not suffice to recognize the proper names (e.g. analyst house and shares); we have to establish a relationship between them, the price target and the corresponding rating recommendation. The extracted shares must be resolved across the documents because the very same shares are used in multiple variants by the analyst houses or cause ambiguity problems with other shares of the same written form.

Here we present a novel linguistic information extraction approach using so-called local grammars (cf. Section 3), not least because other implementations based on linguistic information and statistical methods [4] can only reach an F_1 score of 60–80% (cf. Section 2). By contrast, our named entity recognition (NER) approach performs much better on the short analyst reports in terms of precision and recall than the later mentioned systems do (cf. Section 2 and Table 2). In Section 4 we discuss the data postprocessing process in order to provide the statistics for share price development based on all rating recommendations (cf. Section 4.1), the analyst house (cf. Section 4.2) and the price target per share (cf. Section 4.3) over time. As expected our experiments (cf. Section 5) show the predicted correlation between the rating recommendation and the real price development.

2 Previous Related Work

There is related work that focuses on information extraction systems for business intelligence. Whereas the LIXTO system [5] concentrates on restructuring of raw HTML pages for information extraction purposes, the GATE-based systems [6,7] use an ontology for text mining and information extraction.

Others extract named entities from calls for tenders and perform cross-document name resolution [8]. However, they do not regard the specific analyst recommendation on which we concentrate. Other named entity recognition (NER) systems [9,10] exploit n-gram statistics which cannot be successfully applied on stock analyst reports due to the limitation of corpus size and the length of text respectively.

Furthermore, there are also some context- and grammar-based NER systems. It is the concept of identifying named entities triggered by keywords in context or within specific phrases that seem to be the very characteristics of context-aware systems. MacDonald [11] therefore introduced the notion of internal and external evidences for named entity recognition.

> "Internal evidence is derived from within the sequence of words that comprise the name. (...) By contrast, external evidence is the classificatory criteria provided by the context in which a name appears" [11].

Mikheev et al. [12] came to the conclusion that the size of dictionary does not considerably increase the recognition rate. However, their method has shortcomings concerning the entity recognition on texts providing little internal evidence; that is very common in stock analyst reports.

Surdeane et al. [4] presents an information extraction system exploiting predicate-argument structures. Their system uses the lexical and syntactic information provided by PropBank/TreeBank and benefits from the named entity information povided by the open-domain named entity recognizer demonstrated at MUC-6. It is based on several observations on predicate-argument features such as "most of the predicate arguments are prepositional attatchments (PP) or relative clauses (SBAR)" [4, p. 10]. Despite the application of linguistic information and its statistical implementation using the C5 decision tree, its performance is not very promissing (F_1-score of 60–80%).

Others [13,14] propose pattern-based NER. They construct some general linguistic-motivated patterns such as *cities like A, B, etc.* in order to identify a list of city names. But they do not investigate whole sentences and the relationships that have to be considered in stock analyst reports.

Giuliano et al. [15] exploit both global and local contexts for relation extraction from biomedical documents. They regard the relation extraction process as a kind of classification problem. On the one hand, they generate sample sentences out of text and then apply some kernel function on shallow linguistic information. But on the other hand, they use a protein and gene lexicon for the recognition of sentences where the type of entity is unknown. Their main interest is relation extraction only between entities; they do not concentrate on sentences with only one entity.

3 Applying Local Grammars for Entity Recognition

Local grammars are used for constraint-based – i.e. context-based – text analysis.

> "Short range constraints between words in sentences are crudely accounted for by Markobian models (...) It turns out that the long range constraints are taken care of automatically, so to say, by the interaction of the automata within the complete structured schema" [3, pp. 330–331].

This special feature of local grammars can be useful in different linguistic extraction tasks. Especially, local grammar-based named entitiy extraction has become an essential area of computational linguistics in recent years. These systems [16,17] had high values of precision. Nevertheless, the effort needed for the manual acquisition of local grammars of proper nouns made the development of an automatic method for their construction absolutely essential [18].

Formally, local grammars are recursive transition networks [19]. The construction and manipulation of those are facilitated by the free software tool Unitex[3] [20]. This platform provides all linguistic tools necessary for the processing of large corpora and enables the efficient handling of electronic lexica. Additionally, local grammars are represented by graph structures (cf. Figure 2). They are not intended to describe the entire grammar of a language, but they can be successfully used to describe the syntax and vocabulary of linguistic phenomena related to a specialized domain (here: stock analyst reports). In this regard, they perfectly fit into the extraction process and enable us to restrict our analysis to the relevant facts: NER on rating recommendations.

The starting point for a local grammar are the patterns. It is a corpus-driven approach that tries to construct a grammar which accounts for all occurrences, especially with regards to the analyzed sentence types. Therefore, the principal component of a local grammar is the sentence structure and locality[4].

3.1 Preprocessing

In order to apply these local grammars on our corpus of German stock analyst reports, it must be firstly preprocessed by Unitex (normalization, sentence end detection, tokenization, POS tagging). Since analyst recommendations are very

[3] `http://www-igm.univ-mlv.fr/~unitex`

[4] Locality in this context refers to the proximity of words within linguistic structure.

short text messages, Unitex performs a lexical analysis by comparing tokens to lexical entries and assigns each word to its possible grammatical categories[5]. Unitex therefore provides linguistic resources containing morphological, syntactic, and semantic information for about more than 300,000 German word forms.

3.2 Construction of Local Grammars for Entity Recognition

There is a limited number of verbs and sentence types occurring in analyst recommendations. Due to these repetitive structures we can use a rule-based approach and build local grammars for the sentences containing rating verbs.

The analysts usually observe the company activity and market performance before determining the share price estimate. Then, they can add them to their recommendation list, upgrade or downgrade their ratings, and finally remove them from their list. Figure 2 shows one local grammar which recognizes entities like analyst house, recommended shares, and analyst recommendations introduced by the verb *"aufnehmen (to take in)"*.

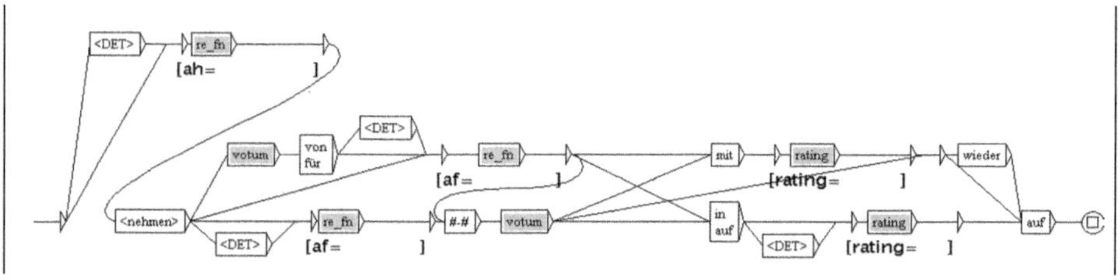

Fig. 2. A local grammar for entity recognition in the context of a rating expression

For the extraction of entities and rating values, we constructed a transducer (cf. finite-state graph in Figure 2) which labels the information searched for and produces the following sample output:

> [ah=Royal Bank of Scotland] nimmt [af= SAS] mit [rating= 'Hold'] wieder auf
> [ah=WestLB] nimmt [af= Klöckner & Co] in [rating= 'Small & Mid Cap Focus List']

The graph in Figure 2 consists of three sub-modules illustrated by shaded boxes. One sub-module named `rating` contains all commonly used rating expressions like those listed in Table 1.

The list can also include expressions such as *sustain focus list, european analyst focus list, credit suisse European focus list, building & construction most preferred list* so that it can be extended with both locality and branch expressions. We therefore constructed the sub-module `rating` generic enough in order to cover such expressions. It is displayed in Figure 3.

[5] Up to now there is no statistical tagging foreseen. Due to the shortness of analyst statements there is not enough training data in order to calculate reliable conditional probability values.

Table 1. Sample rating expressions (excerpt of German and English keywords)

kaufen	buy	outperform	overweight	selected list
akkumulieren	add	accumulate	buy/neutral	neutral/attractive
halten	hold	equal weight	market perform	market performance
reduzieren	reduce	hold/high risk	sell/attractive	short list
verkaufen	sell	underperform	underweight	least preferred

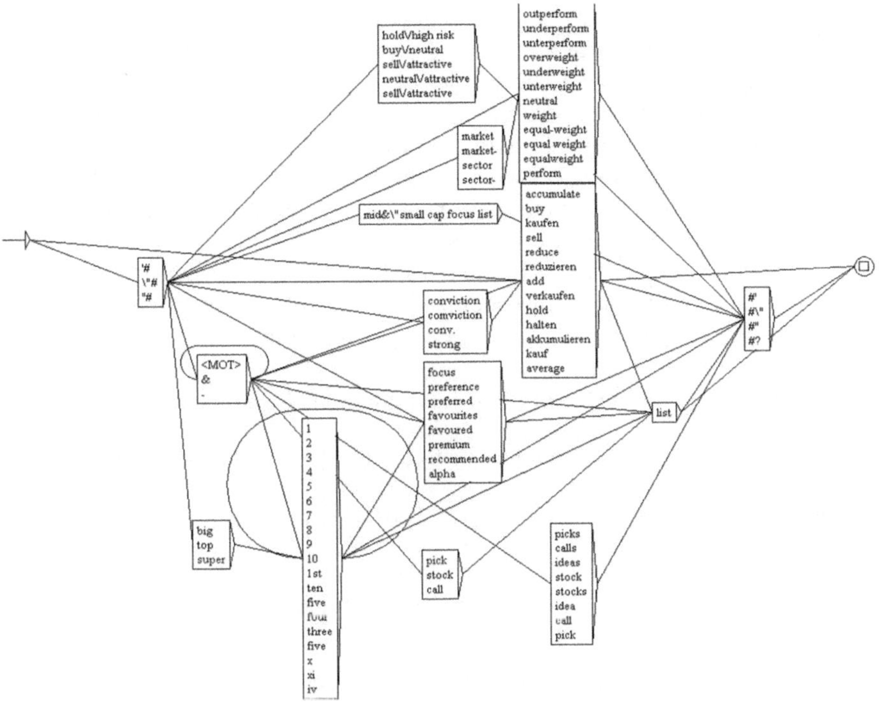

Fig. 3. Local Grammar for the recognition of rating expressions

Another sub-module `votum` treats words and phrases expressing analyst's judgment and opinion. And the third (`re_fn`) identifies the analyst house and shares applied together with the left and right contexts to the texts.

3.3 Evaluating a Local Grammar-Based NER System

As our goal is to recognize all possible entities in stock analyst reports, we test our local grammar-based NER approach on the whole corpus of 21,480 unique German stock analyst reports. The therefore developed local grammars are implemented as finite-state transducers being represented in about 50 graphs and covering different sentence structures. These are modeling the syntactic frame of about 70 verbs in the context of analyst houses, shares, rating and price target. We also consider local context types for price target, analyst name, and rating recognition.

Both shares and analyst houses are extracted from a sentence containing a rating verb so that they always correspond to each other. The rating and price target are extracted either from a sentence containing a rating verb in combination with shares and analyst houses or from different local contexts in other sentences. The analyst name is separately treated by using other local patterns.

Each recognized entity is checked according to its significance. There are 122 unique analyst houses, 1,345 unique shares, 76 unique rating expressions, 1,739 unique analyst names and 3,311 unique price targets. They are all validated: We may conclude that we have reached a perfect precision.

For each class of information item, it is proofed whether it is identified or not. If it is not recognized, then the whole text will be extracted for validation. So we have 228 texts with unrecognized shares and analyst houses respectively, 149 texts containing unrecognized rating expressions, 1,183 texts with unrecognized analyst names and 1,933 texts with an unrecognized price target. We examined if the searched entity really exists in the corresponding text labeled as "unrecognized". Regardless to say, all texts contain shares and analyst houses which we could not recognize. But other classes differ: Only 78 texts really contain an analyst name out of 1,183 unrecognized texts. 139 of 149 texts have a rating expression, and 290 of 1,933 texts have a price target.

Table 2. Evaluation results for local grammar-based entity recognition

	analyst house	shares	rating	analyst	price target
total nb. of occurrences	21,480	21,480	21,470	20,475	19,837
nb. of extracted units	21,252	21,252	21,331	20,397	19,547
nb. of correct matches	21,252	21,252	21,331	20,397	19,547
precision	100.0%	100.0%	100.0%	100.0%	100.0%
recall	98.9%	98.9%	99.3%	98.6%	98.5%

In Table 2, the excellent performance of our entity recognition system is shown. The precision is really perfect (100% per entity) and recall values also show that our local grammar-based method is feasible. The number of ratings shows that some sentences did not contain any rating expression. For example, in the case of *"steichen"* the shares are *deleted* from the recommendation list so that we could not assign any rating expression to the shares.

4 Postprocessing for Business Statistics

Before compiling the statistics for share price development based on all rating recommendations and the price target per share and analyst house over time, we have to do some further textual treatment.

For the former texts, the recognized rating recommendations are categorized into five pre-defined classes (buy, add, hold, reduce and sell) while the later texts are classified according to the *normalized* forms of shares, analyst houses, price target and date. Whereas the total rating statistics is calculated by counting the pre-defined classes corresponding to the normalized shares, the statistics of the share price development needs a more complex data structure. We therefore take a kind of hash table with the shares as keys and the analyst house, price target and issued date as values. In order to produce correct statistical estimations the recognized entities have to be normalized. This mainly concerns the three classes **analyst house**, **shares** and **rating**.

4.1 Rating Recommendation

During our studies, we collected 96 expressions for rating recommendations. They are classified into the five categories: *buy, add, hold, reduce, sell.* All rating expressions must be manually assigned to these classes because of their meaning properties.

Furthermore, there are three groups for rating expressions: One is for direct expressions like *buy, sell, hold*, the second group contains terms like *weight, perform* and the third one is about the listings (e.g. *selected list, preferred list*). Whereas the second group seems to be classified only according to three categories *overweight, underweight, equalweight* (without *add, reduce*), the last group must be classified according to other rating expressions appearing in the stock analyst reports.

However, the classification decision is not always clear. For example, if *neutral* is combined with the expression *most preferred list* in one sentence, we will not classify this statement as *"buy"* although it is the most common interpretation of *most preferred list.*

4.2 Analyst House

Our corpus contains 122 unique analyst houses. The normalization results in only 60. In addition to spelling errors and abbreviations like *Goldman* (instead of *Goldman Sachs*), there are also the acronyms like *MS* for *Morgan Stanley* or *IR* for *Independent Research.* During the postprocessing step we assigned all tokens to their corresponding normalized forms.

4.3 Shares

In comparison to the class *analyst house* we could recognize over 1,300 shares by means of local grammars. The identified shares must be normalized as well because of their numerous variations. In order to determine these forms we start with acronym resolution. We only accept sequences of capital letters as acronyms. Fortunately, the acronyms are often specified in parentheses with its preceded full name. If we find such a string, we assign the corresponding acronyms to those strings. That way, we can associate for example *VW* to *Volkswagen.* Otherwise, if we cannot find any acronym in parentheses, we apply the maximal forward matching [21,16,22] to the acronym. For reference we look up the names of the shares extracted from our corpus. If we have, for example, two candidates (*Vestas Wind Systems* and *vwd*) in our data for *VW*, the word *systems* will be deleted because it is a generic word. Then, we examine per candidate its average

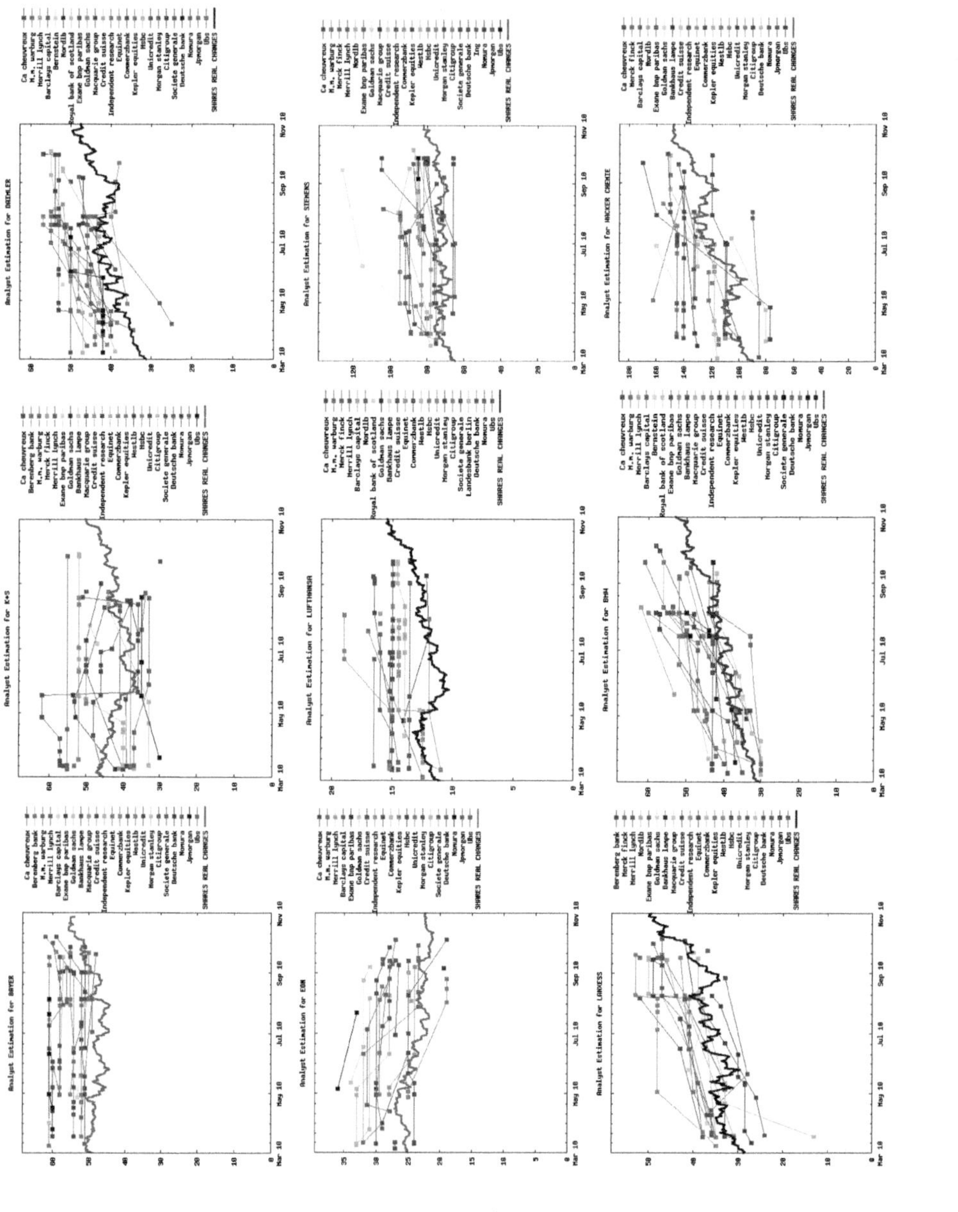

Fig. 4. Comparison of price estimates and real price development. From top to bottom and left to right: Shares of Bayer, K+S, Daimler, Eon, Lufthansa, Siemens, Lanxess, BMW and Wacker Chemie.

price currency and target given by the corresponding analyst house. The price currency for *Vestas Wind Systems* is given as *Krone* while the price currency for *VW* is given as *EUR*. We therefore can exclude it as candidate. Moreover, the average price target of *vwd* seems to be too low. For the abbreviated shares, we can apply the same process and get 887 unique shares.

5 Experiments

We evaluated the relevance between the rating recommendation and the real price development. For testing purposes, we sorted the shares by the recommendation frequency and tested the relevance for the 20 most frequent shares. The real price development was gathered from *Yahoo! Finance*.

The first nine examples are shown in Figure 4. The real price development is illustrated by the bold line. The graphics in Figure 4 show that if the price estimation tendency (either upwards or downwards) exeeds the others, then the real change seems to follow the recommendations (see charts no. 3,4,7,8,9 from top to bottom and left to right).

6 Concluding Remarks and Future Work

In this article, we could show that the local grammar-based entity recognition system is very promising in the restricted domain. Especially, its visualization tool Unitex can easily compile the sentence-level regular expressions. On the other hand, we can categorize the text according to shares, analyst houses, price estimation, rating recommendation, and issued date and produce the statistics. Hereby we normalized and disambiguated all the classes due to the fact that the very same shares can be written differently or the different shares can be written in the same way. The statistics showed some relevance between the recommendations and real changes.

Future work will be the integration of sentiment inference. Because the same rating recommendation expression can be used differently by the analyst houses and analysts, it is more likely to assess the overall recommendations, if the sentiment inference is integrated. The relation of shares to analyst houses with respect to the recommendation issuing will be another further task.

References

1. Barber, B.M., Lehaby, R., McNichols, M., Trueman, B.: Buys, holds, and sells: The distribution of investment banks' stock ratings and the implications for the profitability of analysts' recommendations. Journal of Accounting and Economics 41, 87–117 (2006)
2. Lin, L., Liotta, A., Hippisley, A.: A method for automating the extraction of specialized information from the web. CIS 1, 489–494 (2005)
3. Gross, M.: The Construction of Local Grammars. In: Roche, E., Schabés, Y. (eds.) Finite-State Language Processing. Language, Speech, and Communication, pp. 329–354. MIT Press, Cambridge (1997)

4. Surdeanu, M., Harabagiu, S., Williams, J., Aarseth, P.: Using Predicate-Argument Structures for Informaiton Extraction. In: Proceedings of the 41st Annual Meeting of the Association for Computational Linguistics, pp. 8–15 (2003)
5. Baumgartner, R., Frölich, O., Gottlob, G., Harz, P.: Web Data Extraction for Business Intelligence: the Lixto Approach. In: Proc. of BTW 2005 (2005)
6. Maynard, D., Saggion, H., Yankova, M., Bontcheva, K., Peters, W.: Natural Language Technology for Information Integration in Business Intelligence. In: 10th International Conference on Business Information Systems, Poland (2007)
7. Saggion, H., Funk, A., Maynard, D., Bontcheva, K.: Ontology-Based Information Extraction for Business Intelligence. In: Aberer, K., Choi, K.-S., Noy, N., Allemang, D., Lee, K.-I., Nixon, L.J.B., Golbeck, J., Mika, P., Maynard, D., Mizoguchi, R., Schreiber, G., Cudré-Mauroux, P. (eds.) ASWC 2007 and ISWC 2007. LNCS, vol. 4825, pp. 843–856. Springer, Heidelberg (2007)
8. Paradis, F., Nie, J.Y., Tajarobi, A.: Discovery of Business Opportunities on the Internet with Informaiton Extraction. In: IJCAI 2005, Edinburgh, pp. 47–54 (2005)
9. Silva, J., Kozareva, Z., Noncheva, V., Lopes, G.: Extracting Named Entities. A Statistical Approach. In: TALN 2004, Fez, Marroco, ATALA, pp. 347–351 (2004)
10. Downey, D., Broadhead, M., Etzioni, O.: Locating Complex Named Entities in web Text. In: Proc. of the Twentieth International Joint Conference on Artificial Intelligence (IJCAI 2007), Hyderabad, India (2007)
11. McDonald, D.: Internal and external evidence in the identification and semantic categorization of proper names. In: Boguraev, B., Pustejovsky, J. (eds.) Corpus Processing for Lexical Acquisition, pp. 21–39. MIT Press, Cambridge (1996)
12. Mikheev, A., Moens, M., Grover, C.: Named entity recognition without gazetteers. In: Proceedings of the Ninth Conference of the European Chapter of the Association for Computational Linguistics, pp. 1–8 (1999)
13. Etzioni, O., Cafarella, M., Downey, D., Popescu, A.M., Shaked, T., Soderland, S., Weld, D.S., Yates, A.: Unsupervised Named-Entity Extraction from the web: An Experimental Study. Artificial Intelligence 165(1), 134–191 (2005)
14. Banko, M., Cafarella, M.J., Soderland, S., Broadhead, M., Etzioni, O.: Open Information Extraction from the Web. In: Proceedings of IJCAI (2007)
15. Giuliano, C., Lavelli, A., Romano, L.: Exploiting shallow linguistic information for relation extraction from biomedical literature. In: Proc. EACL 2006 (2006)
16. Bsiri, S., Geierhos, M., Ringlstetter, C.: Structuring Job Search via Local Grammars. Advances in Natural Language Processing and Applications. Research in Computing Science (RCS) 33, 201–212 (2008)
17. Geierhos, M., Blanc, O.: BiographIE – Biographical Information Extraction from Business News. In: De Gioia, M. (ed.) Actes du 27e Colloque international sur le lexique et la grammaire, L'Aquila, September 10-13 (2008); Seconde partie. Lingue d'Europa e del Mediterraneo: Grammatica comparata. Aracne, Rome, Italy (2010)
18. Traboulsi, H.N.: Named Entity Recognition: A Local Grammar-based Approach. PhD thesis, University of Surrey (2006)
19. Woods, W.A.: Transition network grammars for natural language analysis. Commun. ACM 13(10), 591–606 (1970)
20. Paumier, S.: Unitex User Manual 2.1. (2010), http://igm.univ-mlv.fr/~unitex/UnitexManual2.1.pdf
21. Chi, C.H., Ding, C.: Word Segmentation and Recognition for Web Document Framework. In: Proceedings of Conference on Information and Knowledge Management, CIKM (1999)
22. Lee, Y.S.: Website-Klassifikation und Informationsextraktion aus Informationsseiten einer Firmenwebsite. PhD thesis, University of Munich, Germany (2008)

WPT: A Toolkit for Publishing a Web-Based Lifelog

Takuya Maekawa, Yasue Kishino, Yutaka Yanagisawa, and Yasushi Sakurai

NTT Communication Science Laboratories, 2-4 Hikaridai Seika-cho, Kyoto, Japan
surname.name@lab.ntt.co.jp

Abstract. This paper describes a toolkit for implementing lifelog applications that automatically generate web-based reports about daily lives from sensor data such as GPS data, acceleration data, and camera images that capture our daily activities. To design the toolkit, we collect example lifelog applications using a questionnaire survey where we ask participants what kinds of daily life data they want to record for later use and then clarify their characteristics. Based on the obtained information and our view, we realize an infrastructure that provides automatic report publishing and development support for generating reports from sensor data.

1 Introduction

The recent widespread availability of small inexpensive sensors and reductions in data storage costs have made it possible to realize V. Bush's Memex vision [2], in which everyday artifacts are stored for future access. Many researchers have been inspired by this vision and have implemented many lifelog applications. We can categorize lifelog applications into two groups according to the way in which the stored data is presented to users: (1) Some applications append metadata to stored sensor data by analyzing the data and/or sensor data obtained from other sensors to make it easy to retrieve the sensor data. For example, MyLifeBits [8] stores photos, videos, and sounds, and appends such metadata as captured dates and locations obtained from a GPS sensor. [5] supports the easy retrieval of video and audio that capture human activities by analyzing floor pressure sensor data in a home-like environment. (2) Other applications provide human readable reports converted from raw sensor data. Some of them achieve automatic report publishing. For example, eClass [1] captures college lectures and provides this material for later review. Forget-me-not [10] provides daily summaries based on user location data. As above, many kinds of lifelog applications have been developed. However, each application is designed according to its special settings and purpose. The above background indicates that there will be a great increase in demand for applications that record everyday lives. Therefore, toolkit support for developing such applications will be important. In this paper, we design and implement a Web-based lifelog Publishing Toolkit (WPT) that supports the developers of applications that automatically present a report generated from sensor data as an HTML document.

M. Beigl et al. (Eds.): CONTEXT 2011, LNAI 6967, pp. 185–199, 2011.

We explain application development on WPT. Developers construct an application simply by implementing components (context abstraction modules, report publishing modules, etc.) that run on our proposed infrastructure and building them into the infrastructure. For report publishing in WPT, the developers can leverage sensor data obtained from two types of sensors: *Physical sensors* – These are hardware sensors found in end-user environments such as thermometers and accelerometers. *Logical sensors* – These are software sensors that provide abstracted sensor data inferred from other physical and logical sensor outputs, e.g., recognize daily activities. Hereafter, we refer to data sensed by the two types of sensors collectively as *sensor data*. In our infrastructure, these sensors provide web services and the developers can easily retrieve their sensor data via these web services. This permits the developers to create web-based lifelogging applications by mashing up the web services provided by sensors and many kinds of existing web services on the Web such as calendar, web mail, e-commerce, weather information, and GIS services. To create rich lifelog reports, we can leverage the existing web services on the Web as a personal information directory, a knowledge base, rich visualization functions, and external sensors. In fact, the line graph in Fig. 1 is generated by employing Google Chart API, which allows the easy creation of chart images. In addition, the developers can implement lifelogging applications as they implement web applications because they can retrieve sensor data in the same way as they retrieve data from web services. An application implemented with WPT automatically publishes reports according to report publishing modules established by the developers. The developers implement the publishing modules based on our proposed event-driven model-view-controller (MVC) model where implementation of the modules is divided into three objects (model, view, and controller) according to their functions. This permits the developers to implement the objects independently, test and maintain each one, and reuse and replace them.

In section 2, we clarify the characteristics of report-based lifelog applications by examining many application examples to obtain a WPT design guideline. The application examples are obtained from a questionnaire survey where we asked the participants what kinds of daily life data they wanted to record for later use. Based on the findings obtained in section 2, we design WPT.

2 Questionnaire Survey

When designing WPT, we should know the characteristics of the applications to be implemented. To obtain application examples, we used a 90-minute free-form questionnaire to ask twelve participants (including 4 researchers) what kinds of data they wanted to store and how they wanted to reuse the data in their daily lives. Before giving the participants the questionnaire, we presented the state-of-the-art sensing and activity recognition technologies and asked them to assume a future environment where physical events and activities can be automatically detected. Then, we analyzed the characteristics of the applications. [17] investigated desired capture applications through questionnaires. However,

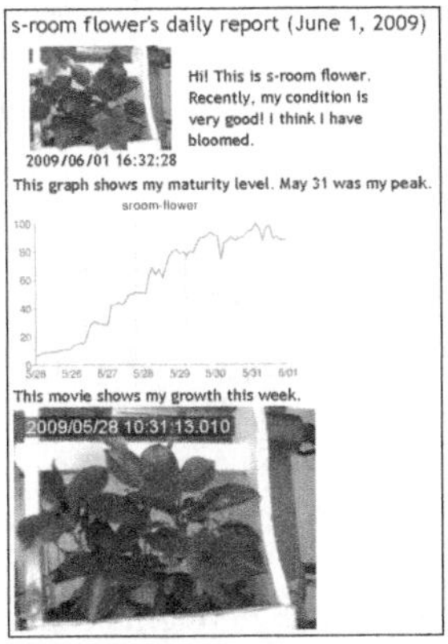

Fig. 1. Example report of flower maturity

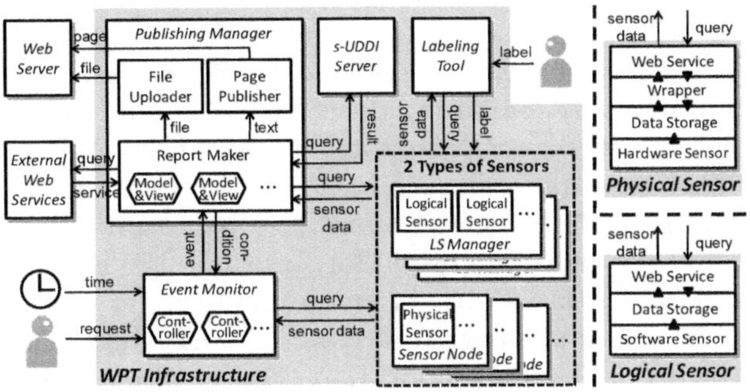

Fig. 2. Overview of WPT infrastructure

in their investigation, the participants proposed only about a dozen applications. [13] obtained application examples only for indoor environments by asking five participants the above questions. In this survey, we obtained 95 unique application examples for indoor and outdoor environments. We provide some examples. "**Example 1**: Record the amount of exercise taken throughout the day. This may promote exercise in daily life." "**Example 2**: Monitor CD players; we can know who likes what kind of music." "**Example 3**: If information about sightseeing spots and shops that I have visited is recorded, it can be used as my diary and will be useful for anyone visiting these spots in the future." We also obtained examples similar to famous lifelog applications shown in [1,10].

As with the above examples, the obtained application examples are abstract. We thus analyze the applications after concretizing them by examining how they are actually implemented in general settings. With Example 1, we assume an accelerometer attached to a shoe or a slipper. We can compute the amount of exercise from the amplitude of the acceleration data. Moreover, we may be able to present information in an easily understandable way by computing the change in the amount of exercise taken throughout a day and providing the results on a graph. This information can be presented to users at the end of each day or when they request it. In addition, we examine what kind of sensor data retrieval is performed to achieve this information presentation. We introduce findings obtained from the examples.

[Characteristics of Application Examples]: We can classify the participants' intended applications as daily life management (78.9%), memory aids (50.5%), and information sharing (22.1%). The daily life management applications are used for improving users' lives by exploiting stored data and by monitoring daily activities and environments. Most examples have more than one purpose. "**Example 4**: Record flower watering to control the amount of water provided because in an office with multiple persons there may be too much or too little watering" has both daily life management and information sharing purposes. Also, Examples 2 and 3 are used as memory aids as well as for information sharing. Because WPT is designed for publishing lifelogs on the web, we can easily achieve the information sharing purpose.

We found three cases where reports are produced. Most applications produce reports periodically (88.4%) and/or when a user requests them (82.1%). With Example 1, by computing the statistics in relation to the amount of exercise, we can issue exercise reports every day or at the user's request. Some applications publish reports when particular events occur (25.3%). One such application is "**Example 5**: Monitor an entrance because recordings of comings and goings at unusual times are useful for security." From the above results, WPT should support the three types of publishing medium.

The obtained applications are categorized into three groups according to entities to which the application relates: object-centric (63.2%), person-centric (29.5%), and place-centric (7.4%) applications. Object-centric applications relate to the states of a physical object, the use of a physical object, and object-related activities. Examples 2 and 4 are object-centric. Person-centric applications relate to a person's state and activity such as Examples 1 and 3. Place-centric applications relate to the states of a location, e.g., "**Example 6**: If the temperature in a room is recorded, I can know which part of the room is overcooled."

[Data Presentation]: We examined a sensor data presentation method that makes it easy for users to understand sensor data for each application example. As a result, we obtained five kinds of presentation methods. In 80.0% of applications, a graph is a useful way to represent sensor data changes. For example, a graph showing temporal changes in the amount of exercise is useful in Example 1. The following types of graphs were useful in the example applications; a line graph for plotting temporal changes in sensor data, a time-series graph for plotting duration information (start and end times) such as those related to sleeping and study, and bar and circular graphs for representing proportion information such as the ratio of genres of music to which a user listened. In 30.5% of applications such as Example 5, simply presenting stored multimedia sensor data, for example, presenting a movie recorded during dinner and when entertaining visitors, is useful. In 26.3% of applications, it is useful to show special events such as a hospital visit or house cleaning on a calendar. Presenting location-related sensor data such as an itinerary and the temperature at certain points in a room on a map is useful in 22.1% of applications. Furthermore, simply enumerating sensor data information with some conversion is useful in 35.8% of applications. In Example 3, we assume a logical sensor that outputs information about the locations a person visited during her travels by analyzing GPS data.

[Data Retrieval]: Here, we discuss how we specify a sensor from which sensor data are retrieved. As mentioned above, the application examples are classified into person-centric, object-centric, and place-centric applications. In each application, we want to access sensors related to an entity on which the application focuses. For instance, in Example 1, which reports the amount of exercise a person takes, we want to access an acceleration sensor attached to a shoe worn by that person, and a GPS sensor mounted on a cellphone carried by that person.

As above, we consider that it is intuitive for us to specify a sensor by tracing related entities from an entity on which the application focuses to the sensor, e.g., person→cellphone→GPS.

3 WPT Infrastructure

3.1 Core Components of WPT Infrastructure

The left portion of Fig. 2 shows the WPT infrastructure. The shaded region represents the modules that WPT supports. Here, we briefly introduce core components of the WPT infrastructure.

[Physical Sensor]: The upper right portion of Fig. 2 shows the structure of a physical sensor. The web service receives a query, decodes the query, retrieves the requested sensor data from the data storage, and returns the sensor data. The developers use SOAP to query the web service and receive sensor data. When the web service, which runs on a web server, retrieves sensor data from the data storage of physical sensors, the wrappers bridge the differences between sensor product types.

[Logical Sensor]: A logical sensor is virtually attached to an entity such as a person, an object, or a place. The lower right portion of Fig. 2 shows the structure of the logical sensor. A software sensor infers a high level context from low level sensor data retrieved from other sensors, and stores the result into the data storage. As shown in the left portion of Fig. 2, logical sensors run on their associated LS manager. LS managers are designed to run on their associated PCs. Recently, many systems infer (recognize) an abstracted context by using supervised machine learning [15,12,11], which is robust. Therefore, as shown in Fig. 2, WPT is equipped with a labeling tool that permits end-users to make labeled training data in their own environments.

[Publishing Manager and Event Monitor]: As shown in Fig. 2, the publishing manager publishes web pages and uploads multimedia files on a web server. The report maker in the manager automatically generates web pages from sensor data according to report publishing modules. For example, the report in Fig. 1 was generated by a report publishing module for flower monitoring. A report publishing module mainly consists of three objects; a model, a view, and a controller. The model retrieves the required data from sensors and external web services for report creation, and computes the data. The view creates HTML text by using data that the model retrieves and computes. The view also leverages external web services for data visualization. The controller decides when the report is created. When a certain condition is satisfied, the event monitor notifies the report maker, which executes the model and the view related to the condition. From our survey, we found that reports are generated periodically, when a user requests a report, or when a particular physical event occurs.

[s-UDDI Server]: When a model of a report publishing module retrieves sensor data from a sensor via a web service provided by the sensor, it must find the

URL of the web service. In the Web, a UDDI server provides a web service search service. On the other hand, the s-UDDI server (UDDI server for sensor environment) in the WPT infrastructure permits the developers to find desired web services provided by sensors in the real world.

3.2 Environment Model in WPT

WPT permits developers to implement applications (report publishing modules) that do not depend on end-user environments. WPT works according to information about an end-user environment input by the user. Before running an application implemented with WPT, the end-user inputs her environmental settings. We assume that there are entities in end-user environments and relationships between the entities. We also assume that physical and logical sensors sense these entities. The end-user inputs information about them as follows by using a special interface.

[Entities and Relationships between them]: We selected three types of entities in end-user environments: people, places, and physical objects. These entities are reportedly important for context-aware systems [6] and, in our survey in section 2, we found many applications related to these entities. The end-user registers people, places such as rooms, and physical objects such as furniture, and can input their attributes including their names and pictures. In addition, the end-user inputs the relationships between these entities, e.g., the place in which an object is installed, the location of an object in its place and the owner of an object. We defined the above relationships based on [3].

[Sensors]: The end-user then registers the sensor nodes in her environment by selecting sensor products (wrappers) and inputting required parameters such as the sensor node IDs used to retrieve sensor data, and then selects which person, place, or object to which each node is attached. The end-user can also register logical sensors from installed sensor types in the application as plug-ins, and then attach them to a person, place, or object.

[Report publishing modules]: Report publishing modules are also associated with a person, place, or object. Report publishing modules generate reports about their associated entities because, in our survey, we could classify the example applications as person, place, or object-centric applications. The report in Fig. 1 is generated by a module attached to a flower object in our environment.

In addition to the above information, the end-user inputs information for report publishing on the web, e.g., the IP address of a web server for report publishing. The inputting of environment-dependent information by end-users enables developers to implement environment-independent report publishing modules. This is because WPT works according to the end-user environment information.

4 Application Development with WPT

Developers construct an application simply by implementing the following three kinds of components: wrappers for sensor node products, logical sensors, and report publishing modules. One of the advantages of WPT is that most components are reusable. Wrapper implementations are not application-dependent. Also, logical sensors, e.g., those for recognizing ADLs and for temperature data abstraction, can be used for a wide variety of applications. Therefore, to facilitate their easy reuse, they are implemented as plug-ins. In addition, we separate a report publishing module into three objects; a model, a view, and a controller. As described below, this also permits the developers to reuse controllers (and part of the models). Namely, because most developers focus only on publishing module implementations, we explain them by using some examples after explaining our proposed event-driven MVC for publishing module implementations.

4.1 Event-Driven MVC

We divide a report publishing module into three objects (model, view, and controller). This is based on the MVC design pattern, which was originally proposed for implementing a GUI application with Smalltalk. Recently, to increase the reusability of the source code, the design pattern has been incorporated in web application frameworks such as Ruby on Rails. We describe a common MVC model used in web applications. The controller receives a user request and parses it. The controller then retrieves required data from the model according to the request. Finally, the controller sends the data to the view. The view creates HTML text from the received data. The model retrieves data from a database and processes them according to the request from the controller. The model then returns the result to the controller. Dividing an application into three objects enables the developers to reuse the source code. For example, by replacing the view, the developers can implement a new application with a different appearance. The MVC model is designed for an application that updates its screen (HTML) according to user's request. On the other hand, we want to create HTML text when a given condition is satisfied. Thus, in the event-driven MVC model, the controller monitors an occurrence of an event that satisfies the condition. When the condition is satisfied, the controller sends information about the event to the view. The view initializes the model by using the information and obtains required data from the model to create a report. In our model, the role of the controller is very simple. This reflects the findings of our survey described in section 2. Our survey revealed that the report publishing conditions are categorized into just three types: periodic (for example, every Wednesday at 12 midnight), when a specific physical event occurs, and when an end-user makes a request that triggers report generation. From these findings, we consider that controllers that monitor the first or second conditions are reusable in many report publishing modules. With the first type, if we implement a controller that can monitor an arbitrary time period specified by each module, the controller is reusable in any module. Thus, WPT includes controllers for the first and second types in the event monitor shown in Fig. 2. This enables report publishing modules to share the controller. However, with the third type, end-users may employ various request media including e-mail, a web form, and a special interface. Thus, the developers can implement controllers that monitor such inputs as plug-ins.

Based on the above idea, we define a report publishing module as including only a model, a view, and a condition of report publishing. A report publishing module consists of an XML file. The XML file mainly contains file paths to the model and the view, and the condition description. The model and view are binary executable files. An HTML template file for report creation is associated with the binary file of the view. Also, the condition of the publishing module that creates Fig. 1, for example, is described as `TimeController(23,59)` in the XML file. `TimeController` represents the type of controller that the module uses. The condition is specified in detail in `(23,59)`. In this case, the condition is satisfied every day at 23:59. By using the specification, the developers can specify various kinds of conditions. The condition information is sent to the event monitor when an application is started. When the condition is satisfied, the event monitor notifies the report maker. Then, an instance of the model related to the condition is created. After that, an HTML report is generated by embedding character strings output from methods of the model instance in the template.

4.2 Implementing Report Publishing Module

We introduce part of the source codes of a report publishing module that generates the flower report shown in Fig. 1. Figs. 3 and 4 show a pseudo source code of the model of the module and a template file of the view, respectively.

Sensor Data Retrieval and Processing. After the condition of report publishing is satisfied, the instance of the model is constructed. In the constructor of the model (between lines 7 and 25), the data required for creating the report are retrieved and processed. Here, the `flower` variable in line 8 represents the flower object with which the report publishing module is associated. Also, the `fireddate` variable in line 9 represents the time at which the condition of the module was satisfied. The `TriggeredEvent` class in line 7 contains event information sent from the event monitor shown in Fig. 2.

[Finding Web Service]: Between lines 10 and 15, a web service of the camera sensor that captures the flower is specified. To retrieve sensor data, the developers should find a web service (sensor) from which the data are retrieved. The developers search for web services using the s-UDDI server. The s-UDDI server permits the developers to intuitively form a query that specifies a desired sensor (web service) by using relationships between entities that exist in the real world. In our survey, we found that specifying a sensor by using real world entities is useful in the example applications. In this model, we want to specify a camera that monitors the flower. Line 10 creates a query for a web service search. Between lines 11 and 13, entities are enumerated to specify a camera from which sensor data are retrieved. Line 11 specifies a `PhysicalObject` entity whose id is identical to `flower.id`. Line 12 specifies a `SensorNode` that monitors the flower. Line 13 specifies a `MonitoringCamera` sensor mounted on the sensor node. As above, by enumerating entities, the developers can specify a sensor intuitively.

[Retrieving Sensor Data]: In line 14, the s-UDDI server finds sensors that satisfy the condition specified by `squery`, and then returns a set of interfaces

```
01: public class FlowerDiaryModel : ReportModel {
02:  private PhysicalObject flower;
03:  private DateTime fireddate;
04:  private List<RetrievedData> pictlist;
05:  private List<RetrievedData> filtered;
06:  private List<ProcessedDataTS> maturitylevel;
     /* Constructor of model */
07:  public FlowerDiaryModel(TriggeredEvent te,
      WPTEntity entity) {
08:   flower = (PhysicalObject)entity;
09:   fireddate = ((TimeEvent)te).fireDate;
      ...
      /* Web service search */
10:   sUddiQuery squery = new sUddiQuery();
11:   squery.AddEntity("PhysicalObject",
       "id='"+flower.id+"'");
12:   squery.AddEntity("SensorNode");
13:   squery.AddEntity("MonitoringCamera");
14:   Sensor [] sensors = suddi.FindSensor(squery);
15:   MonitoringCamera cam =
       (MonitoringCamera)sensors[0];
      /* Sensor data retrieval */
16:   MonitoringCamQuery query =
       new MonitoringCamQuery(start, end);
17:   pictlist = cam.GetData(query);
      /* Sensor data filtering and processing */
18:   BlackImageFilter filter
       = new BlackImageFilter();
19:   filter.setInput(pictlist);
20:   filtered = filter.Filtering();
21:   ColorOccpProc dataproc = new ColorOccpProc();
22:   dataproc.setInput(filtered);
23:   dataproc.setParams(GetFlowerColor(flower));
24:   maturitylevel = dataproc.Process();
      ...
25:  }
26:  public PhysicalObject GetFlower() {
27:   return flower;
28:  }
     ...
29: }
```

Fig. 3. Part of sample pseudo source code of model for generating the flower report in Fig. 1

```
<?xml version="1.0"?>
 <ReportTemplate>
  <title>
  $model.GetFlower().GetName()'s daily
   report ($model.GetTriggeredDate())
 </title>
 <description>
   ...
 </description>
 <more>
  <![CDATA[
  This graph shows my maturity level.
  $model.getPeakDate() was my peak.<br>
 <img src="http://chart.apis.google.com
  /chart?cht=lc&amp;chs=300x200&amp;
  chg=20,50,1,5&amp;chxt=x,y
  &amp;chtt=$model.GetFlower().GetName()
  &amp;chxl=$model.GetGraphLabel(10)
  &amp;chd=t:
  #foreach($d in $model.
                    GetGraphDataList())
  #if($velocityCount != 1),#end$d#end">
 This movie shows my growth this week.
 $model.GetMovieTag() ]]>
 </more>
</ReportTemplate>
```

Fig. 4. Part of sample template of view for generating the flower report in Fig. 1

that is used to access the search results (sensors). `MonitoringCamera` class in line 15 is an interface with monitoring cameras (web services). (`Sensor` is a base class of `MonitoringCamera`.) By using the interface, the developers retrieve data from the sensors. Line 16 formulates a query that specifies a time duration for the sensor data to be retrieved. The `MonitoringCamQuery` class is for querying a web service provided by a monitoring camera. Also, `start` and `end` represent the start and end times of the duration. In line 17, sensor data are actually retrieved from the camera. In the `GetData(*)` function, sensor data are retrieved from the web service by using SOAP. The `RetrievedData` class can contain a sequence of sensor data obtained from the web service.

[Processing Sensor Data]: Between lines 18 and 24 in Fig. 3, the temporal changes in the flower maturity level are computed from the retrieved sensor data (images). This is performed by simply counting the number of pixels in an image whose color is similar to that of the flower petal. WPT supports such sensor data processing based on the findings obtained in our survey in section

2. In WPT, the developers can process sensor data by building blocks of prepared filters and processors. The developers can also implement new filters and processors that are derived from their base classes, and incorporate them as plug-ins. Note that a processor is inherited from one of three types of base classes: `ProcessorTS` including an abstract method that outputs an array of time-series data, `ProcessorHG` including an abstract method that outputs an array of histogram data, or `ProcessorTI` including an abstract method that outputs an array of time interval data. We have prepared the three types of processor base classes because, in our survey, we found many applications that may use graphs generated from the above three types of data to present data in a way that is easy to understand. (Line, time interval, and circular graphs) Line 18 creates a filter that removes black images from the image sequences obtained from the camera to eliminate images captured during nighttime. The filter output is stored in `filtered` in line 20. Line 21 creates a processor `ColorOccpProc`. The temporal change in the maturity level is roughly calculated by using this processor. For each image in the image sequences, `ColorOccpProc` calculates the occupancy ratio of a specified color in the image and then outputs sequences of ratios. The processor input is set in line 22. In line 24, the preprocessor output is stored in `maturitylevel`. As above, the developers can process sensor data by building re-usable filters and processors.

Generating HTML Report. Fig. 4 shows a template file of the module that generated Fig. 1. In the template file, the developers can input the title, description, and detailed contents of the report in their corresponding tags ("title," "description," and "more" tags). The template includes a variable of the model (`$model`). By using the variable, return values of the variable's public methods are easily embedded in the template. For example, in line 4 in Fig. 4, we attempt to embed the flower's name in the title text. `GetFlower()` is a public method of the model variable shown in line 26 of Fig. 3. The method returns an instance of the flower. Also, `GetName()` is a method of the flower instance (`PhysicalObject` class) that returns the name of the physical object. Between lines 13 and 20, by using Google Chart API, a graph image is created that shows the temporal changes in the flower maturity level. In lines 19 and 20, the values of the maturity level, which are obtained by the `GetGraphDataList()` method of the model variable, are embedded for graph generation. The developers can use logic controls such as `#foreach` and `#if` provided by the template engine. As above, by using the template, the developers can create the contents of the lifelog report as they write an HTML document. This also makes it easy for the developers to incorporate existing web services into sensor-based lifelog applications.

4.3 Implementation of WPT

We implemented WPT on the Microsoft .NET Framework by using C# language. Table 1 tabulates our implemented library components. We have prepared several logical sensors. *Use detector* detects the use (movement) of its associated object by employing an accelerometer attached to the object. *Object-specific*

Table 1. Our implemented library components

Wrapper	- Our developed wireless sensor node - Mote [4] - GPS Logger installed on Android phone - Networked monitoring and still cameras
Logical sensor	- Use detector - Object-specific event detector - ADL detector - Travel abstractor
Sensor data visualize function	- Graph maker (line, bar, circular, and time-interval) - Movie maker (from an image sequence) - Superimposed map maker (superimposes sensor data on a map) - Calendar maker (superimposes sensor data on a calendar)

event detector detects physical events that are specific to about ten kinds of objects such as doors, cabinets, and drawers. It detects, for example, the opening and shutting of its associated object by using signals from accelerometers and direction sensors. *ADL detector* recognizes various kinds of ADLs such as make tea, cook pasta, cook rice, make juice, and brush teeth that occur in its associated place by employing the use of objects [15]. *Travel abstractor* finds locations that its associated person visited for a long time by using GPS data.

5 Three Example Applications

5.1 Travel Log

This application automatically generates a travel report for a person who has a GPS sensor and a still camera. Fig. 5 shows an example of report generated by a report publishing module attached to a person. This application plots the trajectory of a journey obtained from the GPS sensor on a map. The map is generated by using Google Maps API. This application also uses a logical sensor *Travel abstractor* that is attached to the person. By using abstracted sensor data obtained from the logical sensor, this application provides information about locations that the person visited. Location information includes the name of the nearest landmark and pictures taken by the person at the location. We use the GeoNames web services (www.geonames.org) to perform reverse geocoding. Furthermore, this application retrieves schedule information about the person from Google Calendar. As shown in the application, we must mash up existing web services and sensor data to build rich lifelog applications.

5.2 Flower Diary

This application automatically generates a daily report about the condition of a flower by using a camera installed to monitor the flower. Also, the application computes and presents the peak of the flower's maturity. Fig. 1 is an example report generated by a report publishing module attached to the flower. The source code of the module contains code for generating a graph and a movie as described in section 4.2.

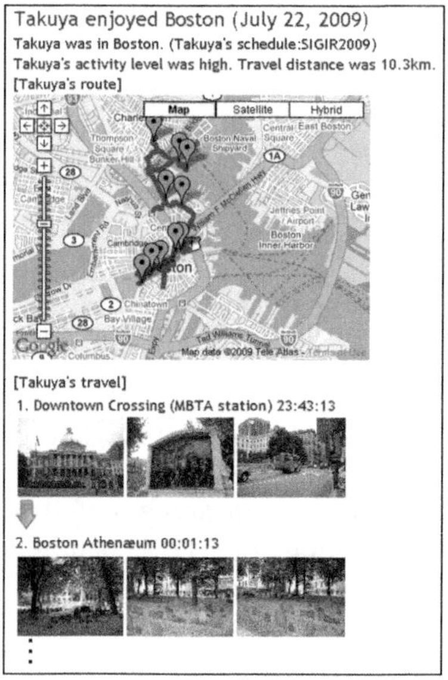

Fig. 5. Part of example travel report

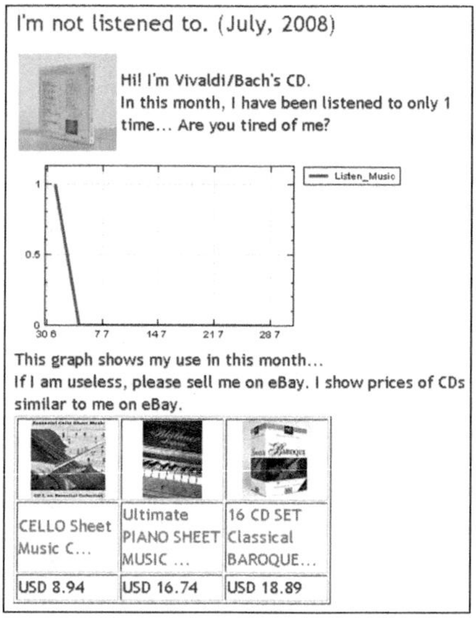

Fig. 6. Example CD report of Object-blog

5.3 Object-blog

By using WPT, we implement Object-blog in which anthropomorphic physical objects automatically post weblog entries to a weblog about sensor data obtained from sensors attached to the objects. We installed the Object-blog application in our home-like experimental environment equipped with various kinds of daily objects such as tables, chairs, cabinets, cooking utensils, a refrigerator, and a television. In this environment, we taped our implemented sensor nodes to 50 daily objects and installed eight monitoring cameras. Fig. 6 shows an example Object-blog report. The report is generated by a report publishing module that is attached to a CD. This application uses a logical sensor *ADL detector* to retrieve abstracted sensor data (ADLs) related to listening to music. The retrieved sensor data are used to construct a graph in the report. In addition, we use eBay web services to create a 'context-aware advertisement.'

6 Discussion

6.1 Implementation with WPT

To validate the effect of implementation support by WPT, we analyzed the source code of the models in the report publishing modules that generated the three report examples shown in section 5. We counted the number of lines required for retrieving sensor data, and for performing sensor data filtering and processing. As a result, on average, sensor data retrieval required 13.3 lines (5.7% of lines in model source code) and, filtering and preprocessing required 4.3 lines (1.9%). In the code, sensor data retrieval and processing (filtering and preprocessing) were conducted an average of 2.0 and 1.3 times. That is, on average, we could write a line of code for one instance of sensor data retrieval and one instance of sensor data processing in 6.7 and 3.3 lines, respectively. Thanks to WPT, we were able to retrieve and process sensor data in a small amount of code. Furthermore, we could implement these three example modules in less than two days. On the other hand, the source code of the model included many functions that return values to be embedded in templates, e.g., a function that returns an instance of the flower object shown in line 26 of Fig. 3. The average was 47.1 % of the lines. This is the cost incurred for ease of content creation with the templates and ease of code reuse (model reuse). If we construct a good model, we can construct various applications by replacing views.

6.2 Related Work

There are many toolkits and infrastructures designed to support the development of ubiquitous and pervasive computing applications. Context toolkit [6] and PTK [14] support the building of context-aware applications and peripheral display systems by context abstraction. [9] proposes an infrastructure that realizes ontology based context reasoning. Subtle [7] supports the implementation of context-aware applications on PCs by using supervised learning. INCA [16] is an infrastructure for generic capture and access applications such as capturing college lectures and meetings, and mainly supports data capture, storage, and access. On the other hand, WPT is specially designed for building report-based lifelog applications. We designed and implemented an event-driven report publishing architecture and sensor data retrieval and processing methods for the easy presentation of sensor data as web content. The design is based on knowledge obtained from our questionnaire survey, which collected many examples of report-based lifelog applications. Moreover, the design is based on our proposed event-driven MVC model to facilitate code reuse.

7 Conclusion

Artifacts used in our daily lives have been equipped with sensors, e.g., GPS sensors and cameras on cellphones. The trend will drive end-user demands for lifelog applications that provide human readable chronicles converted from raw sensor data. This paper developed WPT, which supports the development of lifelog applications that automatically produce human readable web-based reports about daily lives by using sensor data. To design WPT, we collected example lifelog applications by using a questionnaire survey, and then clarified the characteristics of the examples. Based on the obtained knowledge, we designed and realized WPT infrastructure and development support for generating reports from sensor data. In the infrastructure, the developers can easily reuse code because application development is divided into a number of components. With WPT, we implemented various example applications: outdoor location-based, vision-based, and indoor daily life related applications. We showed that WPT facilitated the implementation of the applications in terms of sensor data retrieval and processing, and mashing up external web services and sensor data.

References

1. Brotherton, J.A., Abowd, G.D.: Lessons learned from eClass: Assessing automated capture and access in the classroom. ACM Transactions on Computer-Human Interaction 11(2), 121–155 (2004)
2. Bush, V.: As we think. The Atlantic Monthly 176(1), 101–176 (1945)
3. Chen, H., Finin, T., Joshi, A.: An ontology for context-aware pervasive computing environments. In: IJCAI Workshop on Ontologies and Distributed Systems (2003)
4. Crossbow Technology, `http://www.xbow.com/`
5. De Silva, G.C., Yamasaki, T., Aizawa, K.: Evaluation of video summarization for a large number of cameras in ubiquitous home. In: ACM Multimedia 2005, pp. 820–828 (2005)
6. Dey, A.K., Abowd, G.D., Salber, D.: A conceptual framework and a toolkit for supporting the rapid prototyping of context-aware applications. Human–Computer Interaction 16(2), 97–166 (2001)
7. Fogarty, J., Hudson, S.E.: Toolkit support for developing and deploying sensor-based statistical models of human situations. In: CHI 2007, pp. 135–144 (2007)
8. Gemmell, J., Bell, G., Lueder, R., Drucker, S., Wong, C.: MyLifeBits: Fulfilling the Memex vision. In: ACM Multimedia 2002, pp. 235–238 (2002)
9. Gu, T., Pung, H.K., Zhang, D.Q.: Toward an OSGi-based infrastructure for context-aware applications. IEEE Pervasive Computing 3(4), 66–74 (2004)
10. Lamming, M., Flynn, M.: Forget-me-not: Intimate computing in support of human memory. In: FRIEND21: International Symposium on Next Generation Human Interface, pp. 125–128 (1994)
11. Maekawa, T., Kishino, Y., Sakurai, Y., Suyama, T.: Recognizing the use of portable electrical devices with hand-worn magnetic sensors. In: Lyons, K., Hightower, J., Huang, E.M. (eds.) Pervasive 2011. LNCS, vol. 6696, pp. 276–293. Springer, Heidelberg (2011)
12. Maekawa, T., Yanagisawa, Y., Kishino, Y., Ishiguro, K., Kamei, K., Sakurai, Y., Okadome, T.: Object-based activity recognition with heterogeneous sensors on wrist. In: Floréen, P., Krüger, A., Spasojevic, M. (eds.) Pervasive Computing. LNCS, vol. 6030, pp. 246–264. Springer, Heidelberg (2010)
13. Maekawa, T., Yanagisawa, Y., Kishino, Y., Kamei, K., Sakurai, Y., Okadome, T.: Object-blog system for environment-generated content. IEEE Pervasive Computing 7(4), 20–27 (2008)
14. Matthews, T., Dey, A.K., Mankoff, J., Carter, S., Rattenbury, T.: A toolkit for managing user attention in peripheral displays. In: UIST 2004, pp. 247–256 (2004)
15. Tapia, E.M., Intille, S.S., Larson, K.: Activity recognition in the home using simple and ubiquitous sensors. In: Ferscha, A., Mattern, F. (eds.) PERVASIVE 2004. LNCS, vol. 3001, pp. 158–175. Springer, Heidelberg (2004)

16. Truong, K.N., Abowd, G.D.: INCA: A software infrastructure to facilitate the construction and evolution of ubiquitous capture & access applications. In: Ferscha, A., Mattern, F. (eds.) PERVASIVE 2004. LNCS, vol. 3001, pp. 140–157. Springer, Heidelberg (2004)
17. Truong, K.N., Huang, E.M., Abowd, G.D.: CAMP: A magnetic poetry interface for end-user programming of capture applications for the home. In: Davies, N., Mynatt, E.D., Siio, I. (eds.) UbiComp 2004. LNCS, vol. 3205, pp. 143–160. Springer, Heidelberg (2004)

Smart Phone Sensing to Examine Effects of Social Interactions and Non-sedentary Work Time on Mood Changes

Aleksandar Matic, Venet Osmani, Andrei Popleteev, and Oscar Mayora-Ibarra

CREATE-NET,Via alla Cascata 56d/ 38123 Povo, Trento, Italy
name.surname@create-net.org

Abstract. The typical approach taken by clinical studies examining the factors that affect mood is to use questionnaires in order to record the activities that impact the mood. However, recording activities in this manner suffers from a number of issues including floor effect and difficulty in recalling past activities. Our work instead has focused on using unobtrusive monitoring technology to study mood changes during office hours and two associated factors that influence these changes, namely social activity and non-sedentary patterns. The pilot study ran over the course of 7 days of measurements with the participation of 9 knowledge workers. The results have shown that mood changes are highly correlated with both social interactions and non-sedentary work style. This study is the first to investigate the correlation between mood changes and non-sedentary behavior patterns, opening up a research avenue to explore psychological effects of increasing prevalence of sedentary behavior.

Keywords: Sedentary behavior, mood changes, accelerometers, sitting, social interactions, activity recognition, pervasive computing.

1 Introduction

As computational capabilities continuously improve and sensing devices shrink in size, the use of technology is enabling monitoring many aspects of individuals' life, from day to day activities up to various physiological parameters. The technology provides more objective and precise insight into domains that are difficult or even impossible to be monitored by a human observer. This affords acquiring new theoretical knowledge in various sciences such as medicine, sociology, psychology and psychiatry. A number of examples of using technology to measure new socio-medical phenomena can be found in the literature including Hasler et al. [26] that used automatic sound analysis to detect sinusoidal 24h rhythms in activities associated with positive affects. Using data from various sensors, Olguin et al. [39] measured and modeled organizational behavior at the individual and group levels. Fishbah et al. [40] employed the social badge, developed by MIT lab, to analyse informal social networks in companies aiming to increase employees' productivity. RFID-based indoor localization system enabled Kearns et al. [41] to correlate the moving patterns and the degree of cognitive impairment which is a foundation for the preventative system that can detect early stages of dementia.

M. Beigl et al. (Eds.): CONTEXT 2011, LNAI 6967, pp. 200–213, 2011.

Despite the research work and advancements in technology, clinical studies still rely mostly on self-reporting methods to describe past activities. These methods have a number of drawbacks, including floor effect and difficulties in recalling activities that have occurred in the past [42]. In particular, studies that capture mood changes and the associated factors typically suffer from subjectivity of perception regarding the factors that affected the mood and difficulty in recalling these factors. Mood changes during work time and the associated factors that affect the mood have not been studied in detail using advantages brought by context-aware applications.

In the current study, we attempt to automatically recognize behavioral parameters and investigate their influence on the mood of knowledge workers. Clearly, the potential number of factors that can affect the mood is high and some of these factors are difficult to be monitored directly. However, in our study we focused on external behaviour that can be directly measured using smart phone, namely sedentary patterns and social interactions, and how such behaviour affects the mood. In particular, for the purpose of this work we recognized a set of pleasant social interactions, namely interactions that occurred during coffee and snack breaks. The term coffee/snack break refers to the place where the interactions occurred during work time; therefore, for the rest of the paper we will refer to these as breaks. The survey, which will be presented later in the paper, shows that these short breaks are perceived as pleasant social interactions by participants in our experiments. In addition to social interactions the study was then extended to include sedentary patterns for two reasons: 1) sedentary behavior has been linked with insulin sensitivity [10], lipid metabolism [10] and sympathetic activity [44], which influence the mood, as shown through a number of clinical studies [44, 45, 46]; thus it was seen as a potential factor that may also affect the mood; 2) related to socialization patterns is also the behavior of workers' during workday, specifically number of overall breaks and their duration.

Study of mood changes and factors that influence these changes can provide a good estimation of the general wellbeing of the knowledge workers and avoid lost productive time. Mood changes affect work productivity and according to a study in [7], US workers with depressed mood reported much more Lost Productive Time (LPT) than those without depression (mean 5.6 hours/week versus 1.5 hours/week respectively), which costs employers an estimated $44 billion per year in LPT. More critically however, mood changes are associated with various disorders including bipolar disorder, clinical depression and mania.

The aim of this study was twofold: *i)* investigate correlation between measured social activity and self-reported mood changes; and *ii)* stemming from social activity, study of sedentary patterns and their influence on mood. Together, the results have shown an evident correlation between the reported mood changes and socialization activities and also between non-sedentary work style and mood changes. This study provides a basis to establish new health recommendations and create work place policies that minimize sedentary work style, so that the wellbeing of knowledge workers is further improved. Use of mobile phones will allow workers to get feedback on their mood changes scores and correlation with non-sedentary periods thus forming a part of persuasive feedback application that may be developed to encourage a healthier work style.

2 Related Work

This section reviews the current literature related to our work concerning mood variation studies, technological solutions applied for inferring social behaviour and research in sedentary lifestyle.

Robbins et al. [3] explored patterns of depressed mood periods in normal subjects with the goal of following diurnal variations as a function of time of the day. On the other hand, Volkers et al [9] argued that it is not possible to clearly infer how mood states are related to time of the day since conflicting findings were reported about the timing of mood highs and lows and the pattern of variations during the day. In addition, the authors claim that further analyses are needed to take into account the influences of work and leisure time activities. Stone et al [30] focused on activities and locations as determinants of daily mood variability while Vittengl and Holt [1] investigated correlations between social interactions and NA/PA (Negative affect/Positive affect). Positive correlations were found between PA and fun/active and necessary/informational types of social interaction and between NA and arguing/confronting and receiving help/support. No evidence was discovered between providing help/support and NA or PA. The above-mentioned studies applied methods of self-reporting for examining both psychological parameters and behavioral/environmental factors in order to uncover relations between the two. Concerning mood related research that exploits technological solutions, the goal was mostly to understand human affective behaviour and to recognize emotions, usually relying on video and audio sensors. Related work in this field is comprehensively covered in the survey carried out in [27]. However, yet not many studies have used technology to investigate determinants of psychological responses. One of those studies is elaborated by Hasler et al. [26] who examined daily variability in behaviour associated with PA and NA using Electronically Activated Recorder (EAR). By using that device to record ambient sounds, authors found that activities associated with PA (e.g. socializing, laughing and singing) varied according to a sinusoidal 24h rhythm centered around participants' average wake time, while that was not the case for activities usually associated with NA (e.g. arguing and sighing). In regards to investigating sociability at workplace, the study in [40] focuses on productivity and its relation to informal social networks at workplace.

Using accelerometers provided significant results in establishing the influence of sedentary behavior on various physiological aspects [10] including metabolism [15], vascular health [15] and bone mineral content [16]. Moreover, recent studies link sedentary lifestyle and obesity [17], cancer [18] and psychosocial health [19]. Sanchez-Villegas et al. [20] found that the risk of mental disorders was 31% higher for prolonged patterns of sitting in front of a computer or a TV, comparing subjects that spend more than 42h/week in front of a TV with those watching less than 10.5h/week.

However, there are no studies reported in the current literature that employ technological solutions to infer correlations between mood changes and socialization patterns. Furthermore, this work is the first to investigate the influence of sedentary behaviour on mood changes, which may provide the motivation for further investigation of psychological implications of increasing prevalence of sedentary work style.

3 Study of Mood Changes and Associated Factors

One's mood may depend on a number of different factors, such as circadian rhythms [13], type of environment [14], quality of sleep [9], state of health, private problems or some other factors incomprehensible not only through direct measurement but also difficult for an individual himself/herself to identify. Therefore, it may be impossible to consider all the factors that influence the mood and provide the ultimate conclusion about the exact cause of one's state of mood. For this reason, our approach is to follow relative changes of mood rather than focus on an absolute mood state, where we assume that interval between two mood assessments of a couple of hours (in our design) is not sufficient for a significant change in "background" factors. These factors, such as private problems for example, are likely to be constantly present during relatively longer periods of time while, the activities within that period have pre-dominant influence on relative changes of mood. The goal of our research is to capture patterns of these activities that, in most cases, provoke similar responses in individuals' mood.

In our study we chose to investigate how non-sedentary behavior and social contacts, perceived by the workers as pleasant, impact their mood. Typically, the study of mood changes is carried out through questionnaires in a clinical setting in which participants describe past activities. However, we have attempted to make this approach as unobtrusive as possible to minimize the impact on workers' routines, which may affect their mood and thus potentially decrease the chances of gathering representative results.

People cannot categorize past actions and their duration in an accurate manner as monitoring technology can (for instance, the exact duration of breaks or their mobility patterns). Moreover, people are prone to neglect certain parameters that influence their mood or overestimate the influence of other aspects (such as a very small effect of weather in individuals' day-to-day mood despite the commonly held conception that weather greatly affects the mood [8]). Large majority of the studies that addressed determinants of daily variations in psychological responses relied on self-administered questionnaires to record past activities, which presented difficulties in this research field. For example Clark and Watson [5, 6] argue that no such relation exists between NA and social activity, which is an opposing view to other studies [1, 3, 4], while Volkers at al. [9] claim that is not possible to clearly infer how mood states are related to the time of the day which was concluded by a number of other reports. In the paragraphs that follow we describe the two factors that were monitored during our study of mood changes, namely social activity and non-sedentary work style.

3.1 Social Activity

Empirical research has suggested that forms of social interactions and different mood states are interrelated [1]. It is widely accepted that social interaction and the way one feels are related [1]. Happy persons are more likely to involve themselves in social interactions than those who are feeling sad [2], and it is commonly held that talking to a friend about personal problems can make one feel better. In addition, several clinical studies (refer to Section 2) have found that social contacts exert influence on the state of mood in people.

Social interaction is typically an integral aspect of work, involving different types of conversations – from informal chats between colleagues to official meetings, negotiations or interviews. Therefore, social interaction can be perceived from workers' point of view both as a pleasant experience but also as a displeasing one (for example, an informal chat with colleagues versus an imposed meeting or an agreement from co-workers versus having an argument). This makes the workplace a source of stimulus both for positive and negative emotions.

In order to recognize a set of pleasant social interactions and investigate how they affect workers' mood, we based our approach on the location recognition, in particular focusing on break room and balconies. These are the locations where workers typically have breaks during working time and have the opportunity for a relaxed conversation with colleagues which was confirmed by the results of the survey (presented in Section 4.6). Our monitoring framework recognizes with a high certainty the location of the subjects, when they are in the break room, meeting room or on the balconies; therefore, as opposed to self-reporting methods, the monitoring system provides much more reliable and precise information about workers' behavior while not intruding in their routines. In this manner, it is possible to isolate, with a high probability, a part of pleasant social interactions and to assess their influence on the mood.

In addition to examining the effect of social interactions on workers' mood, we also analyse the duration of non-sedentary time in general and study the ratio between the time spent on breaks and sedentary periods during working time. According to our findings, sedentary patterns impact the mood and the section that follows describes this study.

3.2 Sedentary Work Style

Sedentary behavior (from the Latin "sedere" meaning "sitting") refers to the category of behaviors for which the energy expenditure is low, including prolonged sitting periods at work, home, in car, bus, and in leisure time [10]. Sedentary behavior, characterized by the SITT formula (Sedentary behavior frequency, Intensity, Time and Type), is often associated with deleterious health outcomes. These health outcomes are of different nature from causes attributed to a lack of moderate or intense physical activity outdoors [10]. Therefore, deleterious health outcomes still occur as a result of sedentary behavior, even if guidelines for physical activity are respected. Emerging studies suggest that independently and qualitatively different from a lack of moderate or intense physical activity, sedentary behavior has effects on human metabolism, physical function and health outcomes and therefore it should be considered as a separate and unique phenomenon [10]. Even if one meets physical activity guidelines, sitting for prolonged periods increases the risks for obesity, metabolic syndrome, type 2 diabetes and cardiovascular disease [10, 47].

4 Monitoring Setup

The goal of the reported work was to design a monitoring framework that can monitor when subjects have breaks and infer their sedentary patterns during working time. Our conceptual idea was to monitor primarily two behavioral aspects, namely subjects' location (such as break room, balcony, office or meeting room) and the amount of physical activity. Clearly, the monitoring technology should be as invisible as possible, while not imposing additional sensing devices that subjects would need to carry. Therefore, mobile phone, as widely accepted and commonly used by office workers, was an appropriate solution. Although the technology of smart sensing is moving towards further miniaturization, bringing a variety of embedded sensors, the challenge was to allow monitoring aforementioned parameters solely using a mobile phone. In the following sub-sections we detail our approach.

4.1 Non-sedentary Time

Accelerometers provide an important research tool able to reliably measure and classify a number of physical activities, including walking, jogging, sitting, standing [12], and more complex activities such as estimation of metabolic energy expenditure, sit-to stand transfers, and assessment of balance and intensity of physical activity [11]. In our study we focused on distinguishing between sedentary and non-sedentary time. Typical approach is recording accelerometer data in 1-min epochs and a threshold of <100 counts per minute (CPM) is chosen to classify sedentary time [10, 48]. Total sedentary time is calculated as a sum of all sedentary minutes, while each minute interval where number of accelerometer counts is above 100 is considered a non-sedentary break [48]. The current studies investigating sedentary behavior typically use dedicated devices such as ActiGraph, TriTrac, Caltrac, Actiwatch or Actical [48] that directly provide the number of counts.

In our study we opted for a mobile phone, not only because it does not require an additional sensing device to be carried, but also it does not impact the typical behavior routines of knowledge workers. In addition accelerometers are widely available in smart phones, due to their role in user interfaces [25]. Estimating physical activity using smart phones is usually based on the analysis of the raw accelerometer signal. In order to characterize activities, various features extracted from the signal are considered, including average acceleration, standard deviation, average absolute difference, average resultant acceleration, time between peaks and binned distribution [12]. In our study, distinguishing sedentary and non-sedentary time a simpler approach sufficed – we considered standard deviation (SD) of resultant accelerations over each one-minute interval - the square roots of the sum of the values of each axis (x, y and z) squared [11]. However, we compared the performance of the two approaches for inference of sedentary time in our experimental settings, namely SD analysis and CPM-based method.

Each time the measured acceleration value deviates from the normal gravitational acceleration g by more than a certain threshold it is considered a count [49]. Consistent with previous research, we summed counts in 1-min epochs and applied the widely accepted criteria for classifying sedentary time (<100 counts per minute). However, even off-the-shelf accelerometers differ in reported counts when evaluated together for the same activities over the same period, which may result in under- or overestimation of monitored activities [49]. Therefore, we found it necessary to calibrate the algorithm to calculate the counts in order to account for specific parameters of the used accelerometer. We performed a separate experiment with

different motions and activity levels, recording the accelerometer data and manually labeled the ground truth. From our experiment, the acceleration threshold of 0.75 g was found to provide the optimal sensitivity of counts to activity levels.
Within the same experiment, we compared the accuracy of SD analysis and counts per minute (CPM) to infer sedentary time and found the former to be more sensitive to low intensity motion.

Table 1. Accuracy of the approach based on SD/CPM Analysis

Activity	Sedentary Activity		Non Sedentary Activity	
	SD	CPM	SD	CPM
Sitting	92.5%	100%	7.5%	0%
Walking	0%	0%	100%	100%
Walking/ Standing	17%	29%	83%	71%

Considering the knowledge workers' routines the analyzed activities included: a) sitting (considering the phone placed on the desk and in the subject's pocket/case), b) walking (with different speed), c) alternately walking and d) standing. Table 1 shows confusion matrixes for both approaches. Being more sensitive to low intensity movements while subject is standing, SD approach correctly classified walking/standing as non-sedentary in higher number of cases than CPM method. The approach based on CPM was more accurate in inferring sedentary time due to its robustness on low intensity movements, typical for events when using the phone which resulted in false negatives for SD analysis. However, activities related to the phone use such as making phone calls, sending SMS or filling out the questionnaires were reported by a monitoring application during the experiments and the matching timestamps, when these activities occurred, were used to discard the associated accelerometer data. In this way, it was possible to correct false negatives in sitting activity detection in the case of SD analysis, which resulted in better overall performance of this method in comparison to CPM. Therefore, the recognition of sedentary/non-sedentary time was based on standard deviation analysis. Clearly, an issue with technological monitoring is that subjects may not always wear the device and this is an issue that we will address in the upcoming studies. However, the accelerometer logs have not shown periods of total inactivity, indicating that subjects kept the phone with themselves (such as in the pocket). The typical approach to deal with this issue, by using a 20-minute inactivity criterion to identify a non-wearing period was not applicable in our study as office workers may sit continuously for more than 20 minutes.

4.2 Location

We defined the following set of locations that were deemed important to monitor: break room, offices, meeting room, balconies and outside of the workplace. Within the scope of our study we aimed to recognize the duration of time in which subjects are in the break room or on the balconies. Since GPS is unusable indoors, another localization system that was accurate enough was needed, with the constraint of being available using solely a mobile phone. As an effective solution, we used our FM radio-based positioning system [21] that provides the median accuracy of around 1m, and it is convenient for installation in various environments. The mobile phone used in the tests was a Samsung i8000 with Windows Mobile 6.5 operating system, with MyExperience tool installed and with an embedded accelerometer and an FM receiver. Nonetheless, the positioning system is easily applicable for many smart phones with built-in FM radio receiver.

4.3 Measuring Mood Changes

Our method for assessing mood fluctuations during the day is based on EMA (Ecological Momentary Assessment) approach in order to compare retrospective and momentary mood data [50]. The EMA approach, which involves asking participants to report their psychological state multiple times a day, reduces the critical issue of retrospective recall of extended time intervals. The retrospective recall issue is related to cognitive and emotive limitations that bias the recall of autobiographical memory [50] influencing subject's report by most salient events during the recall interval. The questionnaire we used was derived from a well-established scale for mood study – the Profile of Mood States (POMS) scale that consists of 65 items in its standard version. However, long and repeated mood questionnaires become a burden on the subjects, therefore a short version of the POMS scale was used. In a similar way to the study conducted by Steptoe and Wardle [23], we derived 8 adjectives from the POMS scale (cheerful, sad, tensed, fatigued, energetic, relaxed, annoyed, friendly) used a 5-point scale and averaged the items related to positive and negative expression in order to generate a single scores. The difference of these scores (between two sequential questionnaires) was taken as measures of relative change of subject's mood. The questionnaires were administered three times a day, scheduled to best fit with the work routines, while also allowing the user to manually invoke the questionnaire. Typically, the questionnaires were answered in the morning, after lunch and at the end of working day.

4.4 Subjects

We recruited 9 participants from our research center (6 males, 3 females), not connected with this study, for 7 working days within a period of one month. The average age of participants was 28.4±2.8 years (11% were married) working 36.6±4.6 hours per week. The participants filled out the mood questionnaires in the beginning, in the middle and at the end of working day. There were no significant differences between men and women either in the relevant parameters (such as age, number of working hours or type of the job regarding sedentary routines) or in the measures (such as a number of reported positive/negative mood changes, average non sedentary time within one monitored interval or average number of breaks). None of the participants was a cigarette smoker nor reported health problems. The duration between two consecutive questionnaires was 187.4±47.5 and 161.3±48.5 minutes for morning and afternoon intervals respectively.

4.5 Data and Analysis

After discarding intervals due to non-completed reports, the data analyzed contained 112 monitored intervals, 54 and 58 intervals of positive and negative mood changes respectively. The overall duration of the recorded data was 339.8 hours, 181.2h in morning intervals (between first and second questionnaire) and 158.6h in afternoon intervals (between second and third questionnaire). Non-sedentary time in one interval was 35.4±18.2 minutes while the number of breaks was 1.6±0.7. The number of reported positive and negative mood changes was 5.3±1.7 and 5.7±2.1 respectively. The mean score for positive, negative and overall mood score was 2.89±0.65, 2.12±0.67 and 0.76±1.19 respectively. The mean within-subject correlation between positive and negative, positive and overall, negative and overall mood score was 0.147± 0,094, 0.734±0.102 and 0.511+0.211 respectively. Self-reported mood change, measured as a difference in scores between two consecutive questionnaires, was analyzed with respect to non-sedentary time and a number of breaks. Spearman correlations were calculated between non-sedentary time and mood scores and between a number of breaks and mood scores on a within-subject basis. Statistical analysis was performed using SPSS (SPSS, Inc. Chicago) while sedentary patterns and locations were inferred with R-2.13.

4.6 Background Measures

In order to investigate our assumption that social interactions during breaks are perceived in a positive way, we conducted two surveys, one that included participants of the study described in this paper and while the other one had 15 randomly chosen colleagues. We asked them to rate on a 5-point scale (from “not at all” to “very”) the statement: “Social interaction during breaks is mostly pleasant for me”. The mean score was 3.87 for participants of our study and 4.00 for a randomly chosen sample, varying in answers only from 3 to 5. Furthermore, both groups were asked to indicate the approximate percent of cases when they are going to a break with someone rather than alone. The possible answers were “<50%”, “50-60%”, “60-70%”, “70-80%”, “80-90%” and “90-100%”. The results show that breaks are centered on social interactions considering that one third of each sample reported 80-90%, while 5 participants out of 9 from the first sample and 7 out of 15 from the second sample are very likely (90-100% of cases) to socialize while taking a break Only one participant (belonging to the randomly chosen sample) reported that he usually takes a break alone.

5 Findings

5.1 Correlations between Non-sedentary Time and Mood Changes

Figure 1 shows the distributions of Spearman correlation between non-sedentary time and reported change in mood. The mean correlation between non-sedentary time and positive/negative/overall mood changes was 0.24±0.26 (*min*=-0.01, *max*=0.81), -0.26±0.36 (*min*=-0.91, *max*=0.33) and 0.38±0.32 (*min*=-0.02, *max*=0.86) respectively.

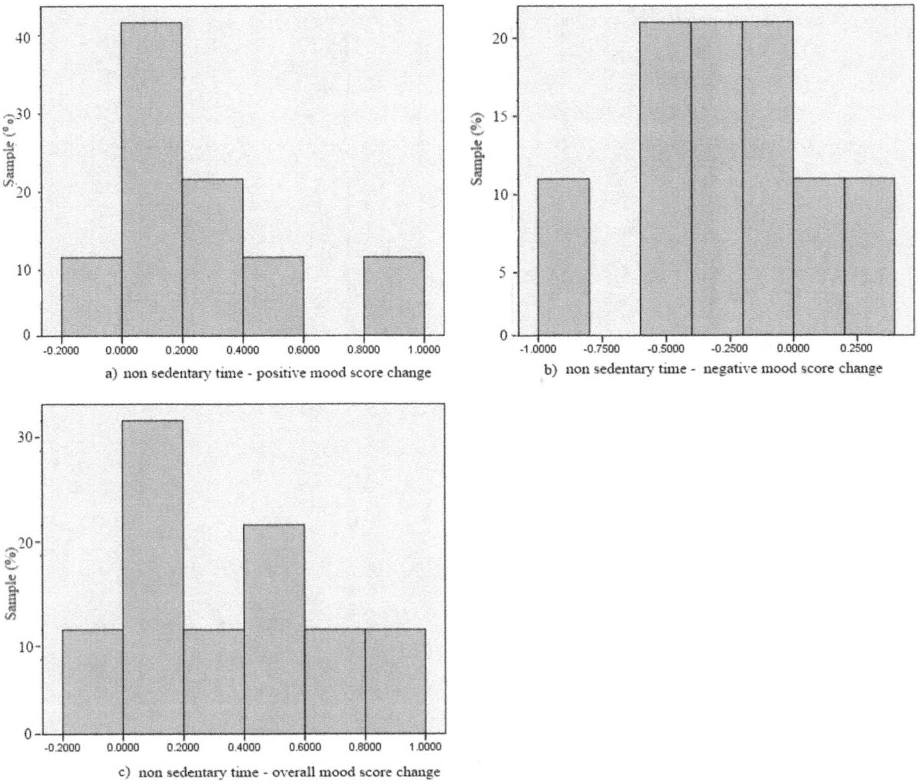

Fig. 1. Distributions of Spearman correlations between non-sedentary time and a) positive mood, b) negative mood and c) overall mood score change

The non-sedentary time/positive mood changes and non-sedentary-time/overall mood changes distributions were significantly greater than 0 (t=2.925, t=3.588 respectively, P<0.01) while non-sedentary time/negative mood changes distribution was significantly less than 0 (t=-2.392 P<0.025). None of the distributions was significantly skewed. The results suggest that the time spent in non-sedentary activities is positively correlated with changes in reported positive/overall mood and negatively correlated with changes in reported negative mood. On the other hand, the reported mood at the beginning of monitored intervals had moderately low impact on the non-sedentary behavior in the following interval (r=0.27, r=-0.18 and r=0.24 respectively for initial positive/negative/ overall mood score and non-sedentary time across subjects). This suggests that sedentary patterns were not influenced by subjects' mood.

5.2 Correlations between Breaks and Mood Changes

The distributions of Spearman correlations regarding number of breaks and reported mood score changes are shown on Figure 2.

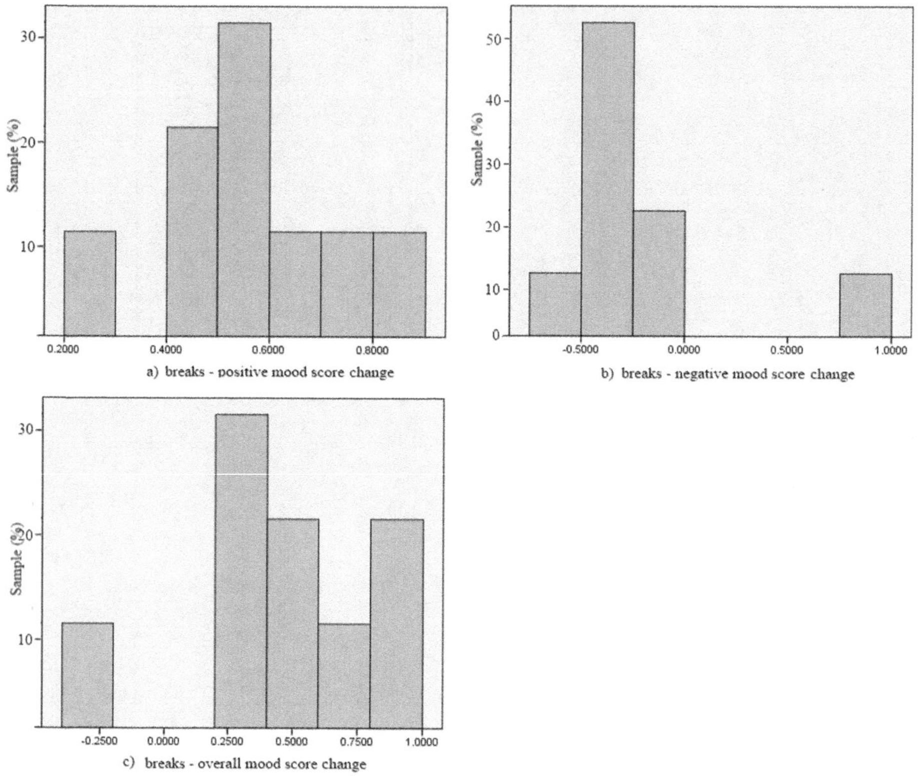

Fig. 2. Distributions of Spearman correlations between number of breaks and a) positive mood, b) negative mood and c) overall mood score change

The mean correlation between number of breaks and positive mood changes was 0.57±0.15 (*min*=0.29, *max*=0.83) Fig.2a; between number of breaks and negative mood changes was -0.21±0.43 (*min*=-0.66, *max*=0.86) Fig.2b; and between number of breaks and overall mood changes was 0.44±0.35 (*min*=-0.27, *max*=0.94) Fig.2c. The distribution of Spearman correlations between number of breaks and positive/overall mood changes were significantly greater than 0 (t=3.701 and t=8.293 respectively, $P<0.005$, $P<0.001$). However, the distribution of the Spearman correlation between number of breaks and reported mood change was not significantly different from 0 and it was significantly positively skewed. The results of this study indicate that the subjects were more likely to improve their mood when they had breaks, according to reported positive and overall mood scores. On the other hand, no associations have been found between number of breaks and negative mood score reports.

6 Conclusion

As evidenced from the results presented thus far, there is an evident correlation between breaks and positive and overall mood changes. Non-sedentary work style impacts changes of mood according to positive, negative and overall reported mood scores. Analyzing the psychological implications of prolonged sitting periods will form part of a persuasive feedback application that will be developed to encourage a healthy work style.

Additionally, controlled trials and higher number of participants are necessary to further confirm the findings from this pilot study. While preliminary, this is the first study to link sedentary patterns with mood changes, opening up a research avenue to explore psychological effects of increasing prevalence of sedentary habits.

References

[1] Vittengl, J.R., Holt, C.S.: A Time-Series Diary Study of Mood and Social Interaction. Motivation and Emotion 22(3), 255–275 (1998)

[2] Dardenne, B., Dumont, M., Gregoire, C., Sarlet, M.: Mood and positive testing in social interaction. European Journal of Social Psychology 41(1), 52–63 (2011)

[3] Robbins, P.R., Tanck, R.H.: A study of diurnal patterns of depressed mood. Motivation and Emotion 11(1), 37–49 (1987)

[4] Berry, D., Hansen, J.S.: Positive affect, negative affect, and Social Interaction. Journal of Personality and Social Psychology 71(4) (October 1996)

[5] Clark, L.A., Watson, D.: Mood and the mundane: Relations between daily life events and self-reported mood. Journal of Personality and Social Psychology 54(2), 296–308 (1988)

[6] Watson, D., Clark, L.A., McIntyre, C.W.: Affect, personality, and social activity. Journal of Personality and Social Psychology 63(3), 1011–1025 (1992)

[7] Stewart, W.F., Ricci, J.A., Chee, E., Hahn, S.R., Morganstein, D.: Cost of lost productive work time along US workers with depression. JAMA 289(23), 3135–3144 (2003)

[8] Denissen, J.J., Butalid, L., Penke, L., Van Aken, M.A.: The effects of weather on daily mood: A multilevel approach. Emotion 8(5), 662–667 (2008)

[9] Volkers, A.C., Tulen, J.H.M., Van Den Broek, W.W.: Relationships between sleep quality and diurnal variations in mood in healthy subjects, 1–5 (1998), http://www.nswo.nl/userfiles/files/publications/jaarboek-1998/volkers.pdf

[10] Tremblay, M.S., Colley, R.C., Saunders, T.J., Healy, G.N., Owen, N.: Psysiological and health implications of a sedentary lifestyle. Applied Physiology, Nutrition, and Metabolism 35(6), 725–740 (2010)

[11] Kwapisz, J., Weiss, G.M., Moore, S.A.: Activity recognition using cell phone accelerometers. Human Factors, 10–18 (2010), http://storm.cis.fordham.edu/~gweiss/papers/sensorKDD-2010.pdf

[12] Mathie, M.J., Coster, A.C.F., Lovell, B.H., Celler, B.G.: Accelerometry: providing an integrated, practical method for long-term, ambulatory monitoring of human movement. Journal of Physiological Measurement 25(2) (2004)

[13] Clark, L.A., Watson, D., Leeka, J.: Diurnal variation in the positive affect. Motivation and Emotion 13(3), 205–234 (1999)

[14] Adan, A., Guardia, J.: Circadian variation of selfreported activations: a multidimensional approach. Chronobiologia 20(3-4), 233–324 (1993)

[15] Hamburg, N.M., McMackin, C.J., Huang, A.L., Shenouda, S.M., Widlansky, M.E., Schulz, E., et al.: Physical inactivity rapidly induces insulin resistance and microvascular dysfunction in healthy volunteers. Arterioscler. Thromb. Vasc. Biol. 27(12), 2650–2656 (2007)

[16] Zwart, S.R., Hargens, A.R., Lee, S.M., Macias, B.R., Watenpaugh, D.E., Tse, K., Smith, S.M.: Lower body negative pressure treadmill exercise as a countermeasure for bed rest-induced bone loss in female identical twins. Bone 40(2), 529–537 (2007)
[17] Hu, F.B., Li, Y.T., Golditz, G.A., Willett, W.C., Manson, J.E.: Television watching and other sedentary behaviors in relation to risk of obesity and type 2 diabetes mellitus in women. JAMA 289(14), 1785–1791 (2003)
[18] Gierach, G.L., Chang, S.C., Brinton, L.A., Lacey, J.V., Hollenbeck, A.R., Schatzkin, A.R.A., Leitzmann, M.F.: Physical activity, sedentary behavior, and endometrial cancer risk in the NIH–AARP Diet and Health Study. Int. J. Cancer 124(9), 2139–2147 (2009)
[19] Martin, C.K., Church, T.S., Thompson, A.M., Earnest, C.P., Blair, S.N.: Exercise dose and quality of life: a randomized controlled trial. Arch. Intern. Med. 169(3), 269–278 (2009)
[20] Sanchez-Villegas, A., Ara, I., Guillén-Grima, F., Bes-Rastrollo, M., Varo-Cenarruzabeitia, J.J., Martínez-González, M.A.: Physical activity, sedentary index, and mental disorders in the SUN cohort study. Med. Sci. Sports Exerc. 40(5), 827–834 (2008)
[21] Matic, A., Popleteev, A., Osmani, V., Mayora, O.: FM radio for indoor localization with spontaneous recalibration. Journal of Pervasive and Mobile Computing 6(6), 642–656 (2010)
[22] Curran, S.L., Andykowski, M.A., Studts, J.L.: Short form of profile of mood states (POMS-SF):Psychometric information. Psychological Assessment 7(1), 80–83 (1995)
[23] Steptoe, A., Wardle, J.: Mood and drinking: a naturalistic diary study of alcohol, coffee and tea. Psychopharmacology 141, 315–321 (1999)
[24] Matic, A., Popleteev, A., Gabrielli, S., Osmani, V., Mayora, O.: Happy or Moody? Why so?: Monitoring daily routines at work and inferring their influence on mood. In: 5th Ubi-Health Workshop in conjunction with UBICOMP2010 Conference, Copenhagen, Denmark (2010)
[25] Mobile Dev&Design, `http://mobiledecdesign.com` (accessed: February 2011)
[26] Hasler, B.P., Mehl, M.R., Bootzin, R.R., Vazire, S.: Preliminary evidence of diurnal rhythms in everyday behaviors associated with positive affect. Journal of Research in Personality 42(6), 1537–1546 (2008)
[27] Zeng, Z., Pantic, M., Roisman, G.I., Huang, T.S.: A Survey of Affect Recognition Methods: Audio, Visual and Spontaneous Expressions. IEEE Transactions on Pattern Analysis and Machine Intelligence 31(1), 39–58 (2009)
[28] Thayer, R.E.: Problem perception, optimism, and related states as a function of time of day (diurnal rhythm) and moderate exercise: Two arousal systems in interaction. Motivation and Emotion 11(1), 19–36 (1987)
[29] Wood, C., Magnello, M.E.: Diurnal changes in perceptions of energy and mood. Journal of the Royal Society of Medicine 85(4), 191–194 (1992)
[30] Stone, A.A., Smyth, J.M., Pickering, T., Schwartz, J.: J. Daily mood variability: Form of diurnal patterns and determinants of diurnal patterns. Journal of Applied Social Psychology 26(14), 1286–1305 (2006)
[31] Hon, E.H., Lee, S.T.: Elecetronic Evaluation of the fetal heart rate patterns preceding fetal death, further observations. Am J Obstet Gynec col. 87, 814–826 (1965)
[32] Biocom Technologies – Heart Rate Variability basics, `http://www.biocomtech.com/hrv-science/heart-rate-variability-basics` (acessed: February 2011)
[33] Wu, W., Lee, J., Chen, H.: Estimation of heart rate variability changes during different visual stimulations using non-invasive real-time ECG monitoring system. In: International Joint Conference on Bioinformatics, System Biology and Intelligent Computing (2009)

[34] Malik, M.: For the Task Force of the ESC and NASPE, "Heart rate variability: standards of measurement, physiological interpretation and clinical use. Circulation 93(5), 1043–1065 (1996)
[35] Matsuanaga, M., Isowa, T., Miyakoshi, M., Kanayama, N., Mukarami, H., Fukuyama, S., et al.: Associations among positive mood, brain, and cardiovascular activities in an affectively positive situation. Brain Research 1263, 93–103 (2009)
[36] Geisler, F.C.M., Vennewald, N., Kubiak, T., Weber, H.: The impact of heart rate variability on subjective well-being is mediated by emotion regulation. Personality and Individual Differences 49(7), 723–728 (2010)
[37] Taelman, J., Vandeput, S., Spaepen, A., Van Huffel, S.: Influence of Mental Stress on Heart Rate and Heart Rate Variability. In: ECIFMBE 2008 IFMBE Proceedings 22, pp. 1366–1369 (2008)
[38] Shimmer – Wireless Sensing Solutions, http://www.shimmer-research.com (accessed: February 2011)
[39] Olguin, D.O., Gloor, P.A., Pentlandm, A.S.: Capturing Individual and Group Behavior with Wearable Sensors. In: AAAI Spring Symposium on Human Behavior Modeling (2009)
[40] Fishbach, K., Schoder, D., Gloor, P.A.: Analysis of Informal Communications Networks – A case study. Business & Information Systems Engineering 1(2), 140–149 (2009)
[41] RFID Journal, http://www.rfidjournal.com/article/view/4542/1 (accesed May 2011)
[42] Tudor-Locke, C.E., Myers, A.: Challenges and opportunities for measuring physical activity in sedentary adults. Sports Med. 31, 91–100 (2001)
[43] Jennings, G., Nelson, L., Nestel, P., Esler, M., Korner, P., Burton, D., Bazelmans, J.: The effects of changes in physical activity on major cardiovascular risk factors, hemodynamics, symphatetic function, and glucose utilization in man: a controlled study of four levels of activity. Circulation 73, 30–40 (1986)
[44] Reagan, L.: Insulin signaling effects on memory and mood. Current Opinion in Parmacology, Col. 7, 633–637 (2007)
[45] Wells, A., Read, N.W., Macdonald, A.: Effects of Carbohydrate and Lipid on Resting Energy Expenditure, Heart Rate, Sleepiness, and Mood. Physiological Behavior 63(4), 621–628 (1998)
[46] Gonder-Fredericl, L.A., Cox, D.J., Bobbitt, S.A., Pennebaker, J.: Mood changes associated with blood glucose fluctuations in insulin-dependend diabetes mellitus. Health Psychology 8(1), 45–59 (1989)
[47] Hamilton, M.T., Hamilton, D.G., Zderic, T.W.: Role of low energy expenditure and sitting in obesity, metabolic syndrome, type 2 diabetes, and cardiovascular disease. Diabetes 56(11), 2655–2667 (2007); 10.2337/db07-0882. PMID:17827399
[48] Trost, S.G., Mciver, K.L., Pate, R.R.: Conducting accelerometer-based activity assessments in field-based research. Medicine&Science in Sports&Exercise (2005), doi:10.1249/01.mss0000185657.86065.98
[49] Sivula, J., Lake, W.B., Betzold, R.A.: Method and apparatus for implementing activity sensing in a pulse generator, US Patent number 5.052.388 (1989)
[50] Smyth, J.M., Stone, A.A.: Ecological momentary assessment research in behavioral medicine. Journal of Happiness Studies 4, 35–52 (2003)
[51] Healy, G.N., Dunstan, D.W., Salmon, J., Cerin, E.: Breaks in sedentary time: Beneficial associations with metabolic risk. Diabetes care 31(4) (2008)

Monitoring for Digital Preservation of Processes

Martin Alexander Neumann[1], Till Riedel[1], Philip Taylor[2],
Hedda R. Schmidtke[1], and Michael Beigl[1]

[1] Karlsruhe Institute of Technology, Karlsruhe, Germany
{mneumann,riedel,schmidtke,beigl}@teco.edu
[2] SAP Research, Belfast, United Kingdom
philip.taylor@sap.com

Abstract. Digital Preservation is an important challenge for the information society. Reliable information and communication technology is crucial for most companies and software failure, is a considerable risk. Use of technologies such as Software as a Service (SaaS) and Internet of Services (IoS) means that business processes are increasingly supported by distributed, service oriented systems. We propose a concept and methods for capturing of contextual information, event causality and timing for Digital Preservation of distributed business processes and services. The architecture is derived from an architecture for monitoring sensing systems. We add a reasoner that can check whether processes adhere to explicit contracts and detect behavior anomalies, and we sketch how an inductive learner can be used to detect anomalies not covered by these contracts.

Keywords: Digital preservation, context monitoring, sensing systems.

1 Introduction

The main problem of digital storage, in contrast to traditional media such as paper or stone, is that specific computing technologies are needed to access it. Reading devices and formats change at a rapid speed that makes it difficult to restore information. The goal of Digital Preservation (DP) is the preservation of information that is stored digitally. DP of business processes and services is a novel and important challenge for the information society. Reliable information and communication technology is crucial for most companies, and software failure is a considerable risk. The presence of Software as a Service (SaaS) and Internet of Services (IoS) means business processes are increasingly supported by service oriented systems where numerous services provided by different providers located in different geographical locations are composed to form service systems which will continue evolving. Besides the advantages of SaaS and IoS, there is the danger of services and service providers disappearing (for various reasons) leaving partially complete business processes. DP of business processes and services therefore requires that the set of activities, processes and tools that ensure continued access to services and software necessary to produce the context within which information can be accessed, properly rendered, validated and transformed

M. Beigl et al. (Eds.): CONTEXT 2011, LNAI 6967, pp. 214–220, 2011.

into knowledge can be preserved. Means for DP are proposed for several layers of the network. *Software contracts and service contracts* protect the links between pieces of code with a formally verifiable interface [1]. *Conventional DP and digital archiving* ensure that data can be restored, even when the original storage technology is out of use [5]. *Virtualization* allows a nearly complete conservation of computing environments [4]. *Digital escrow services* ensure that software systems can survive their providers [7].

However, these methods do not yet take context into account. Often, it is not clear at a given time, which information would be required later to restore a system. What is a clear boundary of technical feasibility today can be a parameter to be represented in the future. Computing power is a straightforward example. Consider a time t_0 where we have a network connection whose speed is below the speed of a database lookup. Assume there is a race condition: our service internally sends a request to a remote server and concurrently looks up a required parameter in the database. As the database access is always faster than the network request, we obtain the parameter before the remote server response. If we later (time t_1) restore the digitally preserved system in a virtual environment, we might obtain a system in which the network is faster than the database leading to different results than with the original system. Capturing such constraints is therefore crucial. However, we often do not understand the parameters that make up these constraints. The context in which things happen is usually implicit, informal and natural to the actors at time t_0. It is something that they take as a constant, given information to which one does not need to pay attention. It becomes a relevant parameter that has to be modeled only for the actors at time t_1, to whom this information is no longer constant and given.

An important challenge is therefore to capture contextual information for preservation. Parameters of context that have to be preserved include timing constraints and causal links, i.e. parameters that are often at least partially constrained through Service Level Agreements (SLA) or service contracts, but also, e.g., the location of servers, which determine e.g. timezones and applicable law, as well as the involved natural or legal persons. Such parameters of context can be preserved if changes in these parameters can be detected: conventional debugging techniques can be used to monitor such changes for the formalized parts of the system. However, these tools cannot yet handle the full complexity of a system operating in an at least partially unpredictable environment. Advances on this challenge have been made in the area of debugging of sensing systems.

Debugging approaches based on analysis of a system's run time enable to monitor processes, as they have the ability to inspect the entire state of a system. Debugging approaches may either operate on a physical system or on a simulated one. Simulations differ in the degree of simulation accuracy and they offer high visibility into, and control on the run time state at high performance in contrast to physical systems. In addition, physical environments serve as the foundation for debugging techniques which for example offer entire system state inspection and step debugging [14]. They can for example be based on controlled testbed facilities which enhance the visibility into, and the control on networks and nodes. Tracing-based debugging techniques primarily refer to discrete event tracing, whereby events may, for example, be network messages [3] or events generated on sensor nodes [11]. Analysis on gathered traces may serve for fault detection only, or additionally offer isolation and identification of faults [12]. Program flow tracing is another type of tracing approach to address debugging [2]. Model-based approaches that continuously monitor systems to supervise formally-given knowledge on system behavior are closest to our approach. Models may for example be based on automata [6], Petri Nets (PNs) [13] or logic [8]. Our approach uses PN-based models which are given either explicitly or implicitly learned from informal knowledge.

We propose a concept and methods for capturing and monitoring such contextual information. Our architecture is based on an architecture for monitoring sensing systems (Sect. 2.1). We complement this with a deductive reasoner (Sect. 2.2) that can check whether processes adhere to explicit contracts to detect behavior anomalies, and we sketch how an inductive learner can be used to detect anomalies not covered by these contracts.

2 Monitoring of Processes in Context

Monitoring of process contexts provides the abilities to decide *when* to preserve *what* elements of a process (or the entire one) digitally, based on the supervision whether context behavior adheres to given contracts. Contracts on contexts can either be given *explicitly*, e.g. based on SLAs, or *implicitly*, based on learned normality behavior. Primarily, collected contexts are subject to be contracted on, i.e. the values that define contexts. Secondarily, the context behavior over time are contracted on based on their *causality* and *timing*.

We differentiate two types of processes: *legacy processes* which are not enabled for DP yet, and *DP-enabled processes* which have been explicitly designed for preservation. The difference between both types is that DP-enabled processes require defined process semantics, e.g. based on BPMN, and defined relevant process contexts – both of which may not available with legacy processes.

Legacy processes can be extended to learn the normality behavior of their relevant contexts and to supervise whether the contexts adhere to learned normality in future. This extension fosters anomaly detection in established processes and restored ones. Detected anomalies either reflect faults or deliberate process changes that indicate a new version of a process. Therefore, anomalies represent events to determine whether a new version of a process should be preserved, e.g. by the help of a DP engineer. The extension of legacy processes limits qualitative evaluation of anomalies (whether they reflect failure or deliberate change), because the extension lacks fine-grained association of anomalies to process elements with respect to process semantics. This association would provide qualitative evaluation of anomalies and DP at process element level.

This fundamental anomaly detection will also be available with future DP-enabled processes. In addition, DP-enabled processes will supersede this anomaly detection by offering fine-grained association of anomalies to process elements and qualitative evaluation of anomalies and DP at process elements scale. Contexts of DP-enabled processes will be well understood and defined at design time of processes. This enables explicit contracts consisting of rules on process contexts whose behaviors are well-defined with respect to process semantics, e.g. based on rules derived from the semantics.

2.1 Distributed State Inspection

The DSI concept offers to inspect sensor nodes in an entire (physical, simulated, mixed-mode) WSN and collect events sourced by the nodes, e.g. notifications of state changes. The concept is based on a 3-layer architecture shown in figure 1, of which the lower two provide state inspection and event tracing.

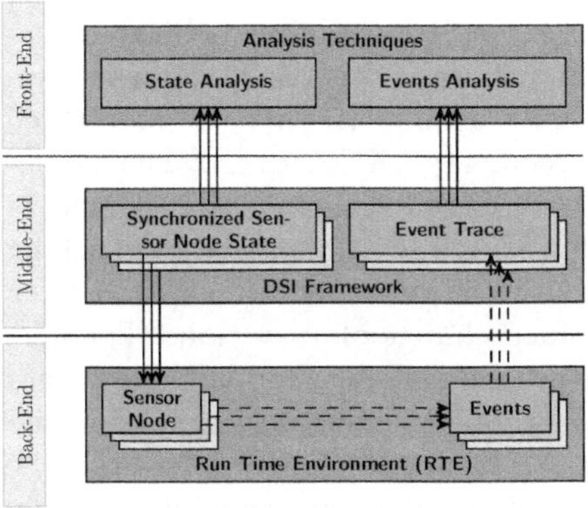

Fig. 1. DSI Architecture Overview

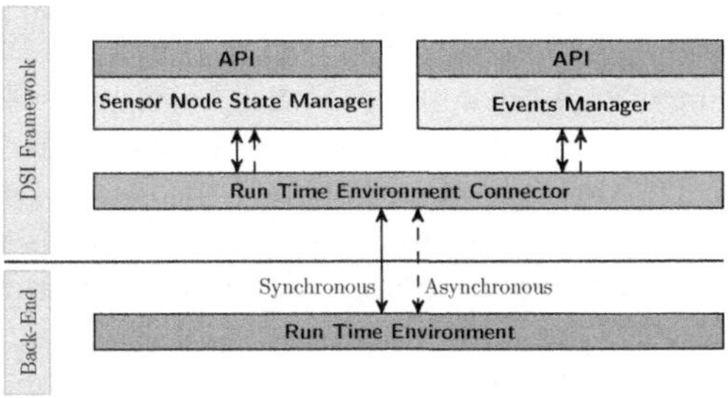

Fig. 2. Focus on DSI Framework

The *back-end* is formed by the Run Time Environment (RTE) for any programs on a WSN. The RTE provides the state of all running programs to clients. In addition, the RTE emits discrete events, e.g. in case a state on a sensor node changed. Events are emitted via an asynchronous interface to which clients can subscribe. The state inspection interface allows clients to connect to the RTE and perform state synchronization operations whose execution is performed synchronously between clients and the server. The *middle-end* is represented by a framework that encompasses the modules that enable sensor node state inspection and event tracing to *front-ends.* The framework asynchronously gathers events sourced by the RTE and continuously synchronizes the state of all sensor nodes in an asynchronous fashion after registering for relevant state changes on sensor nodes in the RTE.

The *DSI framework* is meant to be a foundation for analysis approaches (in the *front-end*) that analyze the distributed state of and discrete events from a WSN. From a client's perspective, the DSI framework offers a set of APIs to continuously synchronize a model of the RTE as illustrated in figure 2. The framework is founded on the *RTE Connector* which acts as a proxy to the shielded RTE, establishing a loose coupling (integrated but isolated) between the RTE and the other components of the framework.

Using events from the RTE, the *state manager* is notified of relevant state changes. Furthermore, the *events manager* organizes events from the RTE in general. Clients subscribe to event types in the events manager whereby the manager provisions the event gathering and notification of registered clients.

The DSI framework requires the RTE to offer the following features: (1) inspect the state of the programs in a WSN; (2) event generation; and (3) a notification mechanism for relevant state changes (clients register for notifications of relevant state changes via discrete events).

2.2 Context Engine

We extend the DSI concept by a *context engine* (depicted in figure 3), which is built on top of the DSI framework and provides the illustrated monitoring and anomaly detection capabilities. DP of software services requires dedicated reasoning systems, which, given a set of facts monitored with the monitoring system can determine: (1) *SLA compliance queries* asking whether the monitored set of facts is consisted with service level agreements (SLA); (2) *SLA preservation queries* asking whether the monitored set of facts fulfills the requirements of a DP case specified between the parties in an SLA; (3) *Anomaly queries* asking whether the monitored set of facts is consistent with previous behavior for detecting whether there might have been an unnotified change of operations. The idea is that the DSI framework enables monitoring contexts by mapping the values of contexts into the program state on the sensor nodes, effectively synchronizing a network-wide context representation of the RTE into the DSI framework. The context monitor translates the network-wide contextual information into a logical format to provide a logical representation of every monitored context change.

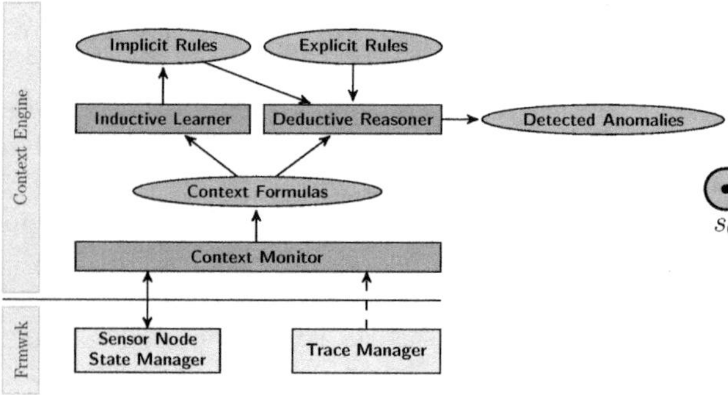

Fig. 3. Context Engine Architecture

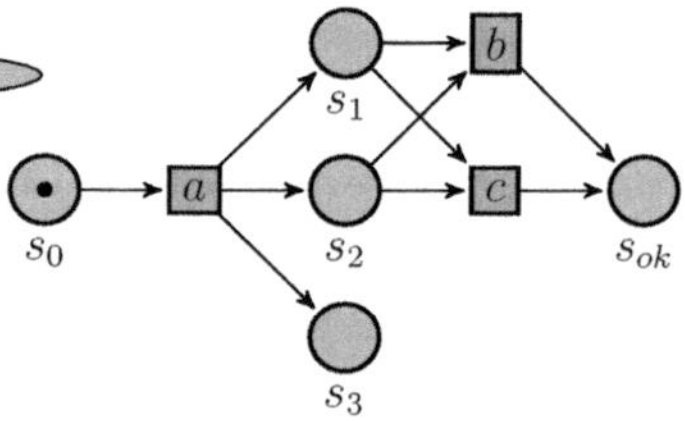

Fig. 4. CL Example as Petri Net

The architecture contains an *inductive learner* and a *deductive reasoner*: the queries (1) and (2) can be decided using a classical deductive reasoning system. The third type of query additionally needs a behavior learning mechanism. The deductive reasoner detects anomalies on context behavior. Its operations are based on deduction of contradictions from the context formulas by the context monitor, the implicit rules and explicit rules. A deducted contradiction results in an anomaly detection event, as the monitored context behavior contradicts the one which is formally stipulated by the rules (implicit and explicit ones). We suggest a mechanism based on Context Logic (CL), a formalism that features a syntax similar to Description Logics (DL) with a specific set of relations employed to describe contextual relations [10]. A detailed exposition of CL is beyond the scope of this paper and can be found in [9].

Table 1. Relations in Context Logic

Syntax	Example	Reading
$c \sqsubseteq_{\text{who}} d$	paul $\sqsubseteq_{\text{who}}$ admin	c is a sub-group of d
$c \sqsubseteq_{\text{what}} d$	car $\sqsubseteq_{\text{what}}$ smart-vehicle	c is a sub-class of d
$c \sqsubseteq_{\text{when}} d$	July.1.13:00 $\sqsubseteq_{\text{when}}$ Summer	c is during d
$c \sqsubseteq_{\text{where}} d$	geo4154N 1230E $\sqsubseteq_{\text{where}}$ Rome	c is (spatially) in d

Intuitively, atomic formulae of CL describe partial ordering relations between contexts, which can be atomic identifiers or complex expressions. In contrast to DL, the atomic formulae of CL can be combined with propositional logic conjunctives. Four fundamental relations of CL are shown in table 1. However, using additional relations $\sqsubseteq_{\text{how}}$, $\sqsubseteq_{\text{why}}$, basic condition/event structures as required for the DSI can be encoded. A condition/event Petri Net (PN) $\langle P, T, F, m_0 \rangle$ consists of a set of *places* P encoding *conditions* and a set T of *transitions* encoding *events*, where $F \subset (P \times T) \cup (T \times P)$ is the set of edges of the net and m_0 is the *initial marking*. Here a function $m_i : P \to \{0, 1\}$ is called a *marking*. A transition t is activated in a marking m_i iff for all p holds:

- if $(t, s) \in F$ then $m_i(p) = 0$
- if $(s, t) \in F$ then $m_i(p) = 1$.

We match the how-dimension to conditions, i.e. places, and the why-dimension to events, i.e. transitions. We can encode the edges in the net shown above (Fig. 4) with $c(i)$ representing the current context at time i by encoding pre-conditions and post-conditions:

$$[s_0 \sqsubseteq_{\text{how}} c(i)] \wedge \neg[s_1 \sqcup s_2 \sqcup s_3 \sqsubseteq_{\text{how}} c(i)] \to [c(i) \sqsubseteq_{\text{why}} a] \tag{1}$$

$$[s_1 \sqcup s_2 \sqsubseteq_{\text{how}} c(i)] \to [c(i) \sqsubseteq_{\text{why}} b] \vee [c(i) \sqsubseteq_{\text{why}} c] \tag{2}$$

$$[c(i) =_{\text{why}} a] \to [s_1 \sqcup s_2 \sqcup s_3 \sqsubseteq_{\text{how}} c(i+1)] \tag{3}$$

- If s_0 holds in $c(i)$ and s_1, s_2, and s_3 do not hold, then a fires in $c(i)$.
- If s_1 and s_2 hold in $c(i)$ and s_1, s_2, and s_3 do not, then c or d fires in $c(i)$.
- If a fires in $c(i)$, then s_1, s_2, and s_3 hold in $c(i+1)$.

3 Conclusion

We proposed a concept and methods for capturing contextual information, event causality and timing for DP of distributed business processes and services, which can track changes and generate decision events, so as to automatically trigger basic preservation steps or to notify a DP engineer. The architecture is derived from a concept for monitoring sensing systems. We added a deductive reasoner that can check processes for adherence to explicit contracts, and we sketch how an inductive learner can be used to detect anomalies not covered by these contracts.

Acknowledgments. The authors would like to acknowledge the funding by the European Commission under the ICT project "TIMBUS" (Project No. 269940, FP7-ICT-2009-6) within the 7th Framework Programme.

References

1. Bocchi, L., Honda, K., Tuosto, E., Yoshida, N.: A theory of design-by-contract for distributed multiparty interactions. In: Gastin, P., Laroussinie, F. (eds.) CONCUR 2010. LNCS, vol. 6269, pp. 162–176. Springer, Heidelberg (2010)
2. Cao, Q., Abdelzaher, T., Stankovic, J., Whitehouse, K., Luo, L.: Declarative tracepoints: a programmable and application independent debugging system for wireless sensor networks. In: Proceedings of SenSys 2008, pp. 85–98. ACM, New York (2008)
3. Chen, B.R., Peterson, G., Mainland, G., Welsh, M.: Livenet: Using passive monitoring to reconstruct sensor network dynamics. In: Nikoletseas, S.E., Chlebus, B.S., Johnson, D.B., Krishnamachari, B. (eds.) DCOSS 2008. LNCS, vol. 5067, pp. 79–98. Springer, Heidelberg (2008)
4. Krsul, I., Ganguly, A., Zhang, J., Fortes, J.A.B., Figueiredo, R.J.: VMPlants: Providing and Managing Virtual Machine Execution Environments for Grid Computing. In: Proceedings of SC 2004. IEEE, Washington, DC, USA (2004)
5. Lee, K.H., Slattery, O., Lu, R., Tang, X., Mccrary, V.: The state of the art and practice in digital preservation. Research of the National Institute of Standards and Technology 107(1), 93–106 (2002)
6. Li, P., Regehr, J.: T-check: bug finding for sensor networks. In: Proceedings of IPSN 2010, pp. 174–185. ACM, New York (2010)
7. Nycum, S.H., Kenfield, D.L., Keenan, M.: Debugging software escrow: Will it work when you need it? Computer Law 4(3), 441–463 (1984)
8. Römer, K., Ringwald, M.: Increasing the visibility of sensor networks with passive distributed assertions. In: Proceedings of REALWSN 2008, pp. 36–40. ACM, New York (2008)
9. Schmidtke, H.R., Hong, D., Woo, W.: Reasoning about models of context: A context-oriented logical language for knowledge-based context-aware applications. Revue d'Intelligence Artificielle 22(5), 589–608 (2008)
10. Schmidtke, H.R., Woo, W.: Towards ontology-based formal verification methods for context aware systems. In: Tokuda, H., Beigl, M., Friday, A., Brush, A.J.B., Tobe, Y. (eds.) Pervasive 2009. LNCS, vol. 5538, pp. 309–326. Springer, Heidelberg (2009)
11. Tolle, G., Culler, D.: Design of an application-cooperative management system for wireless sensor networks. In: Proceedings of EWSN 2005, pp. 121–132 (2005)
12. Woehrle, M., Plessl, C., Lim, R., Beutel, J., Thiele, L.: Evant: Analysis and checking of event traces for wireless sensor networks. In: Proceedings of SUTC 2008, pp. 201–208. IEEE, Washington, DC, USA (2008)
13. Wu, Y., Kapitanova, K., Li, J., Stankovic, J.A., Son, S.H., Whitehouse, K.: Run time assurance of application-level requirements in wireless sensor networks. In: Proceedings of IPSN 2010, pp. 197–208. ACM, New York (2010)
14. Yang, J., Soffa, M.L., Selavo, L., Whitehouse, K.: Clairvoyant: a comprehensive source-level debugger for wireless sensor networks. In: Proceedings of SenSys 2007, pp. 189–203. ACM, New York (2007)

Promoting Personalized Collaborative Distributed Learning through i-Collaboration 3.0

Eduardo A. Oliveira[1], Patricia Tedesco[1], Thun Pin T. F. Chiu[2], and Viviane Aureliano[1]

[1] Informatic Centre,
Federal University of Pernambuco (UFPE),
Recife – PE – Brazil
{eao,pcart,vcoa}@cin.ufpe.br
[2] Recife Center for Advanced Studies and Systems (C.E.S.A.R)
Recife – PE – Brazil
thunpin@cesar.org.br

Abstract. This article presents i-collaboration 3.0, a framework that supports the promotion of personalized distributed collaboration between students that collaborate to learn by using their Web 2.0 tools of choice (MSN, Twitter, Facebook,...). The framework is an extension of i-collaboration, a conceptual model that used Virtual Learning Companions (VLC) and the MBTI personality test to personalize learners' experience in VLE. I-Collaboration 3.0 has a conceptual model that includes the pedagogical objective of the framework, the VLC new responsibilities in the framework and the students' contextual information modeling in order to ensure a more interactive experience for the Learner. Moreover, it counts with an infrastructure already implemented that is compliant with the model and that includes the integration of the framework with Twitter (implementation of VLC as a Twitter user, where students can make questions by @mentions), MSN (implementation of VLC as a MSN user, where students can add him as a MSN contact and make questions) and Websites (implementation of VLC as a chatterbot - can be integrated with any website or blog).

Keywords: collaborative and group learning, ubiquitous learning environments, social recommendations.

1 Introduction

Although there is a large offer of Virtual Learning Environments (VLE) in the market, little has been done to motivate students to use them [1]. In fact, the available VLE have presented the same basic functionalities over the years, which have led to a general feeling of isolation, demotivation and high student evasion rates [2]. Current VLE still do not cater for the learner's individual needs.

According to Brooks and colleagues [5], nowadays, web-based learning systems face many of the challenges typical of the Semantic Web, namely: extensibility, interoperability, the use of domain ontologies, contextualization and consistence of

M. Beigl et al. (Eds.): CONTEXT 2011, LNAI 6967, pp. 221–225, 2011.

metadata, dynamic sequencing of learning and contents, integration and reuse of content, distribution of services and the need for new models of learning.

As a contribution to the challenges found in the Social Semantic Web, which we believe also contribute to reducing the number of problems currently found in distance learning, this article presents the i-Collaboration 3.0, a Adaptive Intelligent Collaborative Learning Support (AICLS) framework to support learning on Web 3.0. The framework is an extension of i-collaboration (v1.0) model [1,2,3] that is based in the use of Virtual Learning Companion (VLC) integrated with VLE collaborative tools, and supported by the use of the MBTI personality test [6].

This article is organized in 4 sections. Section 2 presents related works. Section 3 discusses the proposed i-collaboration 3.0 framework. Finally, Section 4 presents the conclusions and further work.

2 Related Works

Research related to Adaptive Educational Systems (AES) has identified that new challenges (extensibility, interoperability, contextualization and data reuse and integration) are related to the attempt to represent the information on the Web in a way that computers can understand and manipulate it [4, 11, 10].

Magnisalis and colleagues [7] propose that AICLS systems must better support adaptivity and intelligence in the context of computer-supported collaborative learning (CSCL) bringing together AESs and intelligent tutoring system (ITSs) on one hand and CSCL systems on the other. There is strong evidence that adaptation advances the learning effects of CSCL (e.g., [8], [9]). The AICLS can be classified and their design and operation can be analyzed in the following dimensions: Pedagogical objective (PO), Target of Intervention (TI), Modeling (M), Technology (T) Design space (DS). This classification scheme emerged from a systematic analysis of Magnisalis and colleagues [7] reviewed works, focusing on the key features of an AICLS system, as discussed or otherwise emphasized by the authors/designers in their articles. As a way of contribute to better represent, adapt, integrate and distribute the information on the AICLS systems, we present in this article the i-collaboration 3.0.

3 I-Collaboration 3.0

I-Collaboration 3.0 is an extension of i-collaboration (v1.0) model, a conceptual model that used Virtual Learning Companions (VLC) and the MBTI personality test to personalize learners' experience in VLE. The framework has a conceptual model that includes the pedagogical objective of the framework, the VLC new responsibilities in the framework and the students' contextual information modeling in order to ensure a more interactive experience for the Learner. Moreover, it counts with an infrastructure already implemented that is compliant with the model and that includes the integration of the framework with Twitter (implementation of VLC as a Twitter user, where students can make questions by @mentions), MSN (implementation of VLC as a MSN user, where students can add him as a MSN contact and make questions) and Websites (implementation of VLC as a chatterbot - can be integrated with any website or blog).

Conceptual Model

- **Pedagogical objective (PO)**

The intelligent collaboration 3.0 (or i-collaboration 3.0) aims to promote the collaboration between distributed students (the student doesn't need to access a VLE to learn, the learning objects must be find in the same Web 2.0 tools/social networks that student is – e.g: Twitter, MSN, Facebook, ... - the knowledge is distributed, decentralized) through content adaptation (based on students particular needs - context) and students recommendation.

- **Target of Intervention (TI)**

In i-collaboration 3.0 we needed to refine the initial model (i-collaboration 1.0) to support distributed students with personalized contents. In the proposed framework, the VLC was adapted to be responsible for keeping data integration between the different Web 2.0 tools/social networks. The VLC in the proposed framework has only one database (that contains domain content and integrated students' contextual information). With this approach, the VLC can, with context support, adapt contents, information and do recommendations, based on the student particular needs. Context is any information that can be used to characterize the situation of an entity, where an entity is a person, place, or object that is considered relevant to the interaction between a user and an application [12]. The VLC, that is part of the framework, is intended to run anywhere, without dependencies.

- **Modeling (M)**

I-Collaboration 3.0 was modeled to work in a way that each VLC client for a particular Web 2.0 tool (e.g. Twitter, MSN) is responsible for implementing an interface provided by the framework, which is transparent to the student who communicates with the VLC in the Web 2.0 tool. The framework considers a unique database with students' contextual information and a context module that is responsible for promoting the students' collaboration and content adaptation and personalization (through students' behavior and MBTI). Context module has students' information such as: knowledge that the student already has about a content, student MBTI profile, content that the student has seen in current course, what the student must study more... these information are considered in all the Web 2.0 tools where the student is found (to provide adapted content, based on his tastes).

- **Design space (DS)**

Based on Magnisalis [7] dimensions, i-collaboration 3.0 could be classified as implicit (the instructions implicitly arise as a result of students behaviors, platform and MBTI profile) and direct.

Infrastructure

- **Technology**

In i-collaboration 3.0 we propose an architecture that provides an easy interface to allow the use of a VLC in different Web 2.0 tools/social networks (each platform, such as Twitter and MSN, has access to the VLC, as a service, by implementing the provided i-collaboration 3.0 interface). The interface has the following signature: *public String getResponse(String receivedText, String userId, AmbientType ambientType).* Any client interested in using the framework must just call this method, informing the student text (first parameter), the student id (second parameter – student login), and the student environment (third parameter - value that represents the Web 2.0 tools/social networks and could be MSN, Twitter, Facebook,...).

4 Conclusions and Further Works

Through the use of i-collaboration 3.0, this paper presented a contribution solution to the problems that have made difficult the use of distributed personalized learning and collaboration. The framework seeks to deal with each student in a unique and personal way, in the environment that the user feels better, thus motivating these students to learn.

This work, currently implemented and available in Twitter (with Twitter4J API), Web chatterbot (for any website/blog) and MSN (with JML API) instances is being prepared for experiments in Introduction to Programming domain with a large number of students of science of computer in Federal Institution of Pernambuco (IFPE). The recommendation (to promote the collaboration) of students located in different Web 2.0 tools/social networks is being studied and analyzed. In the future, the framework will be integrated with Facebook and Gmail and will be available under GPL license for the scientific community.

References

1. Oliveira, E.A., Tedesco, P.: Putting the Intelligent Collaboration Model in practice within the Cleverpal Environment. In: 2009 International Conference of Soft Computing and Pattern Recognition, Malacca, Malaysia, pp. 687–690. IEEE, Los Alamitos (2009), doi:10.1109/SoCPaR.2009.13
2. Oliveira, E.A., Tedesco, P.: i-Collaboration in Practice: Results from our investigation within the Cleverpal Environment. In: 2009 IEEE International Conference on Intelligent Computing and Intelligent Systems (ICIS 2009), Shanghai, China, November, 20-22, pp. 347–351 (2009); 978-1-4244-4738-1/09
3. Oliveira, E., Tedesco, P.: i-collaboration: Um modelo de colaboração inteligente personalizada para ambientes de EAD. In: Anais do XVIII Simpósio Brasileiro de Informática na Educação - SBIE, São Paulo - SP, pp. 412–421 (2007); ISBN 978-85-7669-157-0
4. Isotani, S., Mizoguchi, R., Bittencourt, I.I.: E. - Estado da Arte em Web Semântica e Web 2.0: Potencialidades e Tendências da Nova Geração de Ambientes de Ensino na Internet. RBIE 17(1) (2009)
5. Brooks, C.H., Greer, J.E., Melis, E., Ullrich, C.: Combining ITS and eLearning technologies: Opportunities and challenges. In: Ikeda, M., Ashley, K.D., Chan, T.-W. (eds.) ITS 2006. LNCS, vol. 4053, pp. 278–287. Springer, Heidelberg (2006)
6. Myers & Briggs Foundation: About the MBTI Instrument, `http://www.myersbriggs.org`
7. Magnisalis, I., Stavros, D., Karakostas, A.: Adaptive and Intelligent Systems for Collaborative Learning Support: A Review of the Field. IEEE transactions on Learning Technologies 4(1) (January-March 2011), doi:10.1109/TLT.2011.2
8. Tsovaltzi, D., Rummel, N., Pinkwart, N., Scheuer, O., Harrer, A., Braun, I., McLaren, B.: CoChemEx: Supporting Conceptual Chemistry Learning via Computer-Mediated Collaboration Scripts. In: Proc. Third European Conf. Technology Enhanced Learning, pp. 437–448 (2008)
9. Chen, W.: "Supporting Teachers' Intervention in Collaborative Knowledge Building. J. Network and Computer Applications 29, 200–215 (2006)

10. Devedzic, V.: Semantic Web and Education. Springer, Heidelberg (2006)
11. Vouk, M.A., Bitzer, D.L., Klevans, R.L.: Workflow and end-user quality of service issues in web-based education. IEEE Transactions on Knowledge and Data Engineering 11(4), 673–687 (1999)
12. Dey, A.K.: Understanding and Using Context. Personal and Ubiquitous Computing 5(1), 4–7 (2001)

A Real-Time Living Activity Recognition System Using Off-the-Shelf Sensors on a Mobile Phone

Kazushige Ouchi and Miwako Doi

Corporate Research & Development Center, Toshiba Corporation
1, Komukai-Toshiba-cho, Saiwai-ku, Kawasaki 212-8582, Japan
{kazushige.ouchi,miwako.doi}@toshiba.co.jp

Abstract. We propose an in-home living activity recognition method using only off-the-shelf sensors, namely, an accelerometer and a microphone, which are commonly applied in mobile phones. The proposed method firstly estimates a user's movement condition roughly by acceleration sensing. Secondly, it classifies the working condition in detail by acoustic sensing when it estimates the condition to be working by acceleration sensing. We developed a prototype system to recognize the user's living activity in real time and conducted two experiments to confirm the feasibility of the proposed method. As a result of the first experiment, three movement conditions; quiet, walking, and working, are classified with more than 95% accuracy by acceleration sensing. And it classified working into seven conditions with 85.9% accuracy by acoustic sensing. Moreover, the result of the second experiment shows that it is effective to adopt instance-based recognition according to the assumed application.

Keywords: Living activity recognition, Accelerometer, Microphone, Mobile phone.

1 Introduction

Context-aware services are expected to become common with the spread of mobile phones equipped with an accelerometer, a GPS, and other built-in sensors. On the other hand, in aging societies, it is increasingly important to monitor the in-home daily living activities of the elderly. In regard to monitoring everyday living activities at home, various activities, such as walking, cleaning, cooking, washing dishes, and going to the lavatory, need to be monitored. It is hard, however, to use GPS in doors and to recognize these activities by using only a body-worn accelerometer. Therefore, approaches different from the above-mentioned context-aware services using mobile phones have been tried. For example, several behaviors can be recognized by using many ambient sensors [1]. Although applicable to special facilities, the cost of installing and operating the sensors is an obstacle to introduction of the service in typical homes. We consider in-home living activity recognition using only off-the-shelf sensors, namely, an accelerometer and a microphone, which are commonly applied in mobile phones, without installing equipment in the environment.

2 Related Works

Studies on activity recognition using an accelerometer and/or a GPS on mobile phones have been reported [2]-[4]. In such studies, several migration activities are

M. Beigl et al. (Eds.): CONTEXT 2011, LNAI 6967, pp. 226–232, 2011.

detectable by a mobile phone. It is difficult, however, to precisely recognize our target activities—in-home living activities, including not only migration but also housework and so on—by using an accelerometer and GPS.

A mobile phone naturally has a microphone for its primary function and it can also be used as an acoustic sensor. Some studies on context awareness by using an accelerometer and a microphone on a mobile phone have also been reported [5]-[7]. However, the previous studies focused to recognize migration activities precisely or rough status of the user, and have not tried to recognize in-home living activities.

On the other hand, [8] uses a special sensor device equipped with an accelerometer, a microphone, and a camera on the wrist to recognize 15 living activities. In contrast, we aim to recognize principal living activities by only a mobile phone without requiring any other devices.

3 Proposed Method

3.1 Target Living Activities

There are a large variety of daily living activities. They are classified into ADL (Activities of Daily Living) and IADL (Instrumental ADL) in the field of elderly care or rehabilitation. ADLs are the basic activities of daily living such as feeding ourselves, dressing, walking, using the lavatory, and bathing. Health professionals routinely refer to the ability or inability to perform ADLs as a measurement of the functional status of the elderly and people with disabilities. IADLs are more complicated and advanced activities such as housekeeping, taking medicine, managing one's money, and going on outings. Although IADLs are not necessary for fundamental functioning, they let an individual live independently in a community. In regard to the care of the elderly, independent living levels are evaluated in terms of both ADL and IADL. Thus we are endeavoring to take both of them into consideration.

3.2 Processing Flow

The proposed method consists of the two-step classification process shown in Fig. 1. Firstly, the 3-axis accelerometer is used to roughly classify the user's movement condition into "walking," "working," and "quiet." We defined "working" as the condition of doing certain kinds of living activities involving physical movement other than "walking." Running, climbing up stairs and climbing down stairs are included in "walking."

Secondly, when the movement condition is classified into "working," the microphone is activated and estimates the sort of living activities by analyzing the ambient sound. In the present work, in order to evaluate the feasibility of the proposed method, we selected the following living activities: walking, brushing teeth, shaving, drying the hair with a hairdryer and flushing a toilet, which are typical ADLs, and vacuuming, washing dishes and ironing, which are typical IADLs.

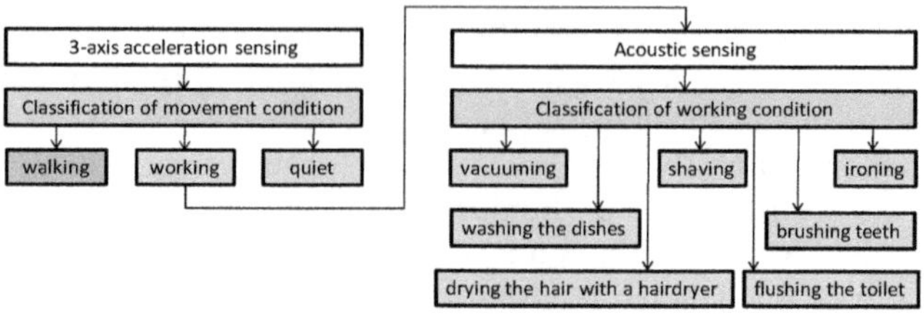

Fig. 1. Processing flow

3.3 Classification of Movement Condition by Acceleration

We propose a simple algorithm that roughly classifies the movement condition into "walking," "working," and "quiet" by using only variances of 1-sec data series from the 3-axis accelerometer. Since this paper focuses on verification of the proposed method's feasibility, we assume that a user has a mobile phone in his/her breast pocket. 3-axis accelerations on the chest are digitized at the rate of 10 bits every 50ms and 1-sec variance of vertical direction acceleration is calculated. We selected vertical direction acceleration for walking detection, because a striking change of acceleration occurred in the vertical direction during "walking." We set the threshold 0.05[G^2] experimentally.

When the above process determines that the movement condition is not "walking," the 1-sec variances of each-axis acceleration are calculated. Then "working" and "quiet" are distinguished by the maximum variance of 3 axes. We set the threshold at 0.0001[G^2]. Its square root, standard deviation, is 0.01[G], a value commonly used as a threshold of body-motion detection for sleep/wake identification [9].

3.4 Classification of Working Condition by Ambient Sound

When the movement condition is classified into "working," the microphone is activated and the working condition is classified by ambient sound as shown in Fig. 2. In this case, the ambient sound data of the user's own target working condition need to be trained beforehand, because target working conditions are different for every person and the ambient sound corresponding to each working condition varies among individuals, kinds of home electrical appliances used, and so on. From the viewpoint of actual use, the prior training should not be troublesome. So we use short-time, 10-second, training procedure for each "working" condition. We selected Support Vector Machine (SVM) as a classifier in anticipation of its high generalization capability.

We use not only Mel-Frequency Cepstral Coefficient (MFCC) as an acoustic feature, but also Root Mean Square (RMS) and Zero-Crossing Rate (ZCR). Previous studies on activity recognition from ambient sound [8][10] used MFCC as an acoustic feature. We also think that MFCC shows the feature of ambient sound most strikingly. RMS mainly shows the strength of the sound and ZCR is a feature of the pitch within the intervals. RMS and ZCR show features other than that of MFCC and we expect to raise the level of the classification accuracy by using them. In this paper, we use 16bit 16kHz sampling sound data and the acoustic features are calculated every 512 samples with no window overlap. Averages of each acoustic feature are output every 1 second. The classification into one of the trained working conditions is executed every 1 second while the classified movement condition by acceleration is "working."

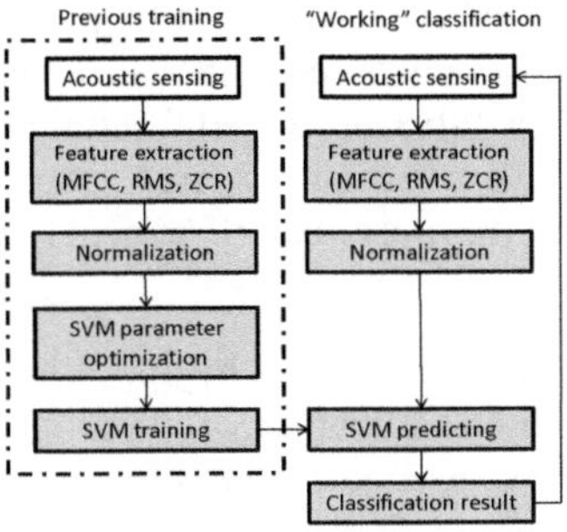

Fig. 2. Classification of working condition by ambient sound

4 Evaluation Experiments

4.1 Prototype System

Although the proposed method is supposed to be installed on a mobile phone, we used a prototype device as shown in Fig. 3 to record 3-axis acceleration and ambient sound simultaneously in order to collect data of actual living activity effectively. In the case of data collection, it records the synchronized data to the microSD card in stand-alone mode. It also has a communication mode to send the measured data to other device such as a laptop via Bluetooth. Moreover, we developed a windows application which classifies the user's current condition every second based on the received data from the prototype device in real time. Fig. 3 shows a result display example of real-time living activity classification. Using this prototype device, we conducted the 2 experiments described below.

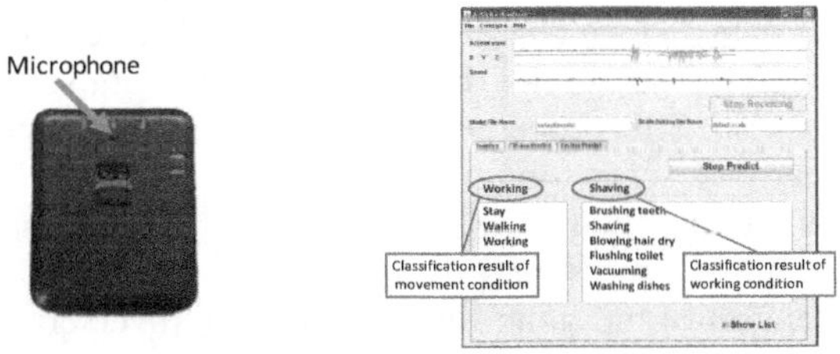

Fig. 3. A prototype device and a result display example of real-time activity classification

4.2 Basic Performance Evaluation

Experimental Setup. First, we conducted an evaluation experiment to assess the basic performance of the proposed method in a conventional home. 4 subjects (a man and a woman in their 60s, a man and a woman in their 30s) wore the prototype device in their breast pocket and acted all target activities in accordance with the task flow provided. We collected 2 data sets per subject, that is, a total of 8 data sets. The order of the flow was rearranged with each cycle. Collected target activities are "Walking," "Brushing teeth," "Shaving," "Drying the hair with a hairdryer," "Flushing the toilet," "Vacuuming," "Washing dishes," "Quiet (watching TV)."

Classification Accuracy of Movement Condition. Classification of movement condition by acceleration sensing was executed in every sampling. In this process, each working condition such as "Brushing teeth" should be classified into "Working." The movement conditions were classified into one of the categories, "Quiet," "Walking," and "Working," with more than 95% accuracy by using only variances of acceleration.

Classification Accuracy of Working Condition. When the movement condition is classified into "Working," the classification of working condition was executed at 1-sec interval when the averages of acoustic features are calculated. The classification accuracies (precision) are shown in Table 1.

Table 1. Classification accuracy of working condition (Left: by using every subject's data, Right: by using subject's own data)

Living activity (working)	Accuracy (%)
Brushing teeth	68.3
Shaving	91.4
Drying the hair with a hairdryer	91.6
Flushing the toilet	71.7
Vacuuming	70.2
Washing dishes	67.2
Ironing	70.3
Average	**75.8**

Living activity (working)	Accuracy (%)
Brushing teeth	73.0
Shaving	91.9
Drying the hair with a hairdryer	96.1
Flushing the toilet	94.5
Vacuuming	87.0
Washing dishes	81.9
Ironing	77.2
Average	**85.9**

The left shows the basic performance by following the evaluation procedure instead of leave-one-out cross-validation, which is commonly used in studies of this kind. First, we chose any 10-sec sound data of each working condition from 1 data set as training data and we classified the other 7 data sets by using the trained data. Then, we chose any 10-sec sound data from another data set for training and classified the others likewise. This procedure was executed 8 times per working condition in order to use every data set as training data.

Meanwhile, the right shows the accuracy by using the user's own data for training. We chose any 10-sec sound data for training from each subject and classified only another data set of the same subject, and then reversely classified the original data set by training another data set. By using only the subject's own data for training, the classification accuracy was improved to 85.9% from 75.8%.

4.3 Practical Performance Evaluation

Instance-Based Recognition. In the foregoing section, we evaluated the classification accuracy for each condition. Considering practical use, it is more important to recognize each overall condition correctly. In other words, a percentage of classification accuracy (likelihood) for each trained working condition might not be important for practical use, but it is especially significant whether each overall continuous working condition would be recognized correctly or not. So we propose an instance-based recognition procedure which is summarized as follows. If the maximum likelihood during the continuous working condition is more than 50%, it is considered to be the condition of the maximum likelihood. If the maximum likelihood is less than 50%, it is considered to be neither a trained condition nor a target working condition.

Experimental Setup. We conducted an additional evaluation experiment to assess the accuracy of the instance-based recognition. 10 subjects (five men and five women in their 60s) wore the prototype device in their breast pocket in an in-house mock living room. First of all, the subjects acted each activity for 10 seconds to collect training data. Then, they sequentially acted all target activities in accordance with a fixed task flow as in the previous experiment. In this experiment, we directed the subjects to act all the target activities in the order of "Washing dishes," "Vacuuming," "Ironing," "Flushing toilet," "Brushing teeth." However, we did not direct the subjects how to spend the intervals between target activities. So they acted freely during the intervals—chatting, stretching, and so on. Namely, an untrained working condition might occur during the intervals. In this case, the instance-based recognition should be considered to be an untrained condition. We collected 50 target working conditions (5 conditions per subject) and 50 interval conditions (5 conditions per subject).

Results and Discussions. Although the instance-based recognition could classify the trained condition with 98% accuracy (49/50), 9 instances (18%) of untrained conditions were wrongly classified into trained conditions such as "washing dishes," "ironing," and "flushing toilet." Given that the proposed method is applied to a watching-over service for single elderly people, this type of false recognition is undesirable, because a recognition-result recipient for the assumed service such as relatives or a care manager would misidentify the working condition as a false recognized target condition even if it were actually untrained condition. This may cause misunderstanding of the user's independent living level. We are considering the solution to the problem by adding some inquiry functions. Of course, the recognition method is applicable to some practical services for which false recognition of an untrained condition poses little problem.

5 Conclusion and Future Work

In this paper, we proposed an in-home living activity recognition method using only off-the-shelf sensors, namely, an accelerometer and a microphone, which are commonly applied in mobile phones. Moreover, we proposed the instance-based recognition method and evaluated the basic performance and the practical performance of the proposed method through two experiments.

We plan to develop a new application based on the proposed method available for mobile phones and to measure the actual power consumption on mobile phones. We also discuss the scheme of watching-over services for elderly people and evaluate the feasibility in an actual usage environment by using mobile phones.

Acknowledgements. This research was partly supported by the Ministry of Internal Affairs and Communications, Japan.

References

1. Fujii, et al.: Behavior description algorithm based on home sensor data using nonlinear transformations. In: International Conference on Networked Sensing Systems (INSS 2008), pp. 63–66 (2008)
2. Iso, T., Yamazaki, K.: Gait Analyzer based on a Cell Phone with a Single Three-axis Accelerometer. In: Proceedings of MobileHCI 2006, pp. 141–144 (2006)
3. Györbíró, N., et al.: An Activity Recognition System For Mobile Phones. Mobile Networks and Applications 14(1), 82–91 (2009)
4. Cho, K., et al.: Human Activity Recognizer for Mobile Devices with Multiple Sensors, uic-atc. In: Symposia and Workshops on Ubiquitous, Autonomic and Trusted Computing, pp. 114–119 (2009)
5. Kobayashi, A., et al.: Shaka: Method for Estimating User Movement Using Mobile Phone. Journal of the Information Processing Society of Japan 50(1), 193–208 (2009) (in Japanese)
6. Siewiorek, D., et al.: SenSay: A Context-Aware Mobile Phone. In: Poster of 7th IEEE International Symposium on Wearable Computers (ISWC 2003) (2003)
7. Miluzzo, E., et al.: Sensing Meets Mobile Social Networks: The Design, Implementation and Evaluation of the CenceMe Application. In: Proceedings of the 6th ACM Conference on Embedded Networked Sensor Systems (SenSys 2008), pp. 337–350 (2008)
8. Maekawa, T., et al.: Object-Based Activity Recognition with Heterogeneous Sensors on Wrist. In: Floréen, P., Krüger, A., Spasojevic, M. (eds.) Pervasive Computing. LNCS, vol. 6030, pp. 246–264. Springer, Heidelberg (2010)
9. Cole, R.J., et al.: Automatic sleep/wake identification from wrist actigraphy. Sleep 15, 461–469 (1992)
10. Chen, J., et al.: Bathroom Activity Monitoring Based on Sound. In: Gellersen, H.-W., Want, R., Schmidt, A. (eds.) PERVASIVE 2005. LNCS, vol. 3468, pp. 47–61. Springer, Heidelberg (2005)

An Empirical Study on Web Search Behavior through the Investigation of a User-Clustered Query Session

Hyun Kyu Park, In Ho Cho, Sook Young Ji, and Joong Seek Lee

Seoul National University, Department of Digital Contents Convergence, Seoul, Korea
{parktistuta9,myorion,purpler7,joonlee8}@snu.ac.kr

Abstract. Web search behavior is being diversified. And the diversification of web search behavior makes query both sporadic and non-sequential. In this case, it is difficult to understand why and how users search any information. Context of web search makes it possible to classify sporadic and non-sequential queries according to each interest. However, only the user him/herself can identify the context of web search behavior exactly. Hence, it is necessary to conduct a client-side research in which users are deeply engaged. The purpose of this research is to develop and apply the methodology that systematically examines the web search behavior and its context. To achieve this, (1) client-side log data is collected, then participants (2) clustered the queries based on context and (3) filled in a questionnaire as to each clustered queries. Also, interviews were conducted in each person. The finding of this study is that the features of UCQS are different from previous studies. Furthermore, we identified the flow of users' web search behavior.

Keywords: Web Search Behavior, User-Clustered Query Session, Context of Web Search Behavior.

1 Introduction

Web search behavior is being diversified. This is a result from the tendency that people often have multiple information problems at hand at the same time, and the increasing complexity of the information environment [1]. Moreover, as search services continue to develop by supporting such trends, the diversification is accelerating. To name a few, many people now use tabbed browsing, which allows multiple web pages to be opened concurrently, for multitasking [2]. And people are intrigued by the presented information from search services like 'real-time issues', while they seek certain information. Recently, users who seek information on YouTube or Twitter are increasing too.

Diversification of web search behavior makes queries both sporadic and non-sequential. Information seekers, of course, resolve their information problems in a single search episode frequently. However, users do not just refine queries. Rather, information seekers change their search strategies, aiming for places where they think the appropriate information is located [1]. Furthermore, users can have many pages

M. Beigl et al. (Eds.): CONTEXT 2011, LNAI 6967, pp. 233–245, 2011.

open concurrently and switch among them in any order, regardless of interest. Thus, if we look over certain parts of queries generated by an individual user, it may seem to be a combination of irrelevant words. In this case, it is difficult to understand why and how users search information.

The context of web searching makes it possible to classify sporadic and non-sequential queries according to each interest. For instance, when we look at the successive queries such as 'Soccer shoes, computer, e-bay, and Messi', each query seems unrelated. But if we know the context, we are able to understand that the user wishes to buy soccer shoes, especially the personal edition of Messi, from E-bay. Since the user's computer did not work well during this process, a need of buying a new computer may come into the user's mind suddenly. Namely, classifying queries based on context helps collecting rich information about web search behavior. Thus, the queries must be united into a single group according to the context of the search.

However, only the user him/herself can identify the context of web search behavior exactly. Hence, it is difficult to discover the detailed context from previous transaction log analyses. To be specific, as transaction log data typically consists of an electronic record of the user's information search requests of queries, and the system's response, it presents confined context information. The context enacted in a search is only exactly known by the user. This is not noticeable through the established server-side research, as well as the simple client-side research (directly extracting the log record of the user). Hence, it is necessary to conduct a client-side research in which users are deeply engaged.

In this respect, the purpose of this research is to develop and apply the methodology that systematically examines the web search behavior and its context. To achieve this, 1) client-side log data is collected, and then 2) participants cluster the queries based on their contexts and 3) fill in a questionnaire for each cluster. Also, interviews were conducted with every person.

2 Related Works

2.1 Transaction-Log Analysis (TLA)

Transaction log data typically consists of an electronic record of the user's information searching request of an information system, or query, and the system's response. Thus, most of them are inevitably server-sided. Jansen and Pooch [3] reviewed several transactional log analyses and proposed a research framework. Based on this review and by incorporating some additional information, representative works in this field include Hoelscher [4], Jansen, Spink, Bateman, and Saracevic [5], Jansen, Spink, and Saracevic [6], Silverstien, Marais, Henzinger, and Moricz [7] and Jansen, Spink, Pedersen [8], each study using server data of *Fireball* [4], *Excite* [6,7] and *AltaVista* [8,9]. Furthermore, Jansen and Spink [10] accumulated and comprehensively reviewed 9 researches on 5 search engines of the U.S. and Europe. And more recently, Orlando and Silvestri introduced the discipline of query log mining, its foundations, the basic algorithms and techniques in terms of the improvement of effectiveness and efficiency of the Web Search Engine (WSE) [4].

Among them, the work of Jasen et al. [6] is special, since it analyzed 51,473 'real' *Excite* logs with the systematic methodology. They adopted 'session', 'query' and 'term' as a unit of analysis from the fact that a number of previous researches commonly focused on how many terms consisted of queries submitted by the searcher. These notions affected other TLA studies and are also the core of the framework proposed by Jansen and Pooch [3].

However, as the log itself and the record on WSE are not privy, it could be treated as limited data from search engines that do not contain user profiles or context information except user IDs. To complement information on users, several studies have used client-side logs to study web seeking behaviors. Since client-side logs can be collected by using a custom extension or customized tool, some unique tools were developed. Among one of the earliest tools, Catledge and Pitkow [11] used an instrumented version of *XMosiac* to record the actions of 107 participants over the course of 21 days. Dubroy et al [2] investigated how and why users of Mozilla Firefox use multiple tabs by collecting click-stream logs. They were gathered from the study participants with the custom extension for Firefox.

Since transaction log data contain too many queries, a query 'session' was used as a unit of web search analysis. A 'session' is usually defined as the entire sequence of queries submitted by a user during one interaction with the WSE, and sometimes includes a certain range of time condition. According to previous researches, 25.5 minutes were claimed as the session interval [12] and, consequently, 30 minutes have become the usual temporal range for session cutoff. Besides, Silverstien et al. [7] and Anick [13] analyzed queries in each basis of 5 and 60 minutes of session intervals. However, despite the equivalent gravity, there has been little consideration on the concept of a 'session'. It is found that, as He and Göker pointed out, a lot of studies on transaction log lack user-oriented views [14]. Some previous studies, however, must be taken into account. Defining a session as a 'meaningful unit of user activities', He and Göker investigated *Excite* and *AltaVista* logs to find out the optimal session interval and suggested 10-15 minutes as a result [14]. Spink, Park, Jansen, and Pedersen [15] suggested that the research approach in a rough manner regarding a session should be modified, since multitasking is becoming a general feature of users' web search behavior. In this context, furthermore, Jansen, Spink, Blakely, and Koshman [16] examined the way of defining a 'session', comparing three different analyzing approaches on the same dataset. In the first case, they used only IP addresses and cookies, and in the other two cases they additionally considered a temporal cutoff or context changes. As a result, they reported that the best measure is the third case, in which they additionally considered the context changes, i.e. query reformulation patterns as a variable of defining a query session.

In this respect, recent researches deal with session and query clusters as a concept of the 'meaningful' flow on users' web search as a task-solving or goal-achieving process, mainly from the perspective of information seeking behavior. Boldi, Bonchi, Castillo, Donato, Gionis, and Vigna [17], through 'query-flow', represented a trace of related information-seeking queries, i.e. queries within the same 'search mission'. The notion of query-flow, in this perspective, implies a kind of 'logical session' and could be seen as search behavior patterns. Jones and Klinkner [18], for analyzing queries in web search, proposed a way of automatically segmenting user query streams into hierarchical task structures consisting of sessions, missions, and goals.

While transaction-log analysis and studies about session, like the ones mentioned above, can provide a great deal of insight, they do not capture why people use the web the way they do. Thus, many researchers employed multiple data-gathering methods to corroborate findings or enhance the understandings of web search behavior [2, 19, 20]. But, by not treating web search behavior as a linear process influenced by context, it will be difficult to acquire rich information. In short, it is necessary to gather client-side data and bring user engaged methods for investigating web seeking behavior. Besides, moving further from the formal analyzing of user queries, it is required to introduce more meaningful or semantic concepts of the query and session, which is discussed in recent researches in terms of query clusters and query flow [15, 16, 17].

2.2 Context of Web Search Behavior

Context is generally recognized to affect web search behavior in a variety of ways [21]. In this regard, there are many researches for understanding information seeking behavior operating within several kinds of contexts [22][23]. However, context has been, and remains an ineffable concept in information science [24].

Along this line, Kelly [19] tried operationalizing context to measure and make recommendations for measuring information seeking context. Kelly discussed descriptions of the relationships between situation and context, especially based on the study of Cool [25]. It is considered that the problematic situation, which requires the acquisition of new knowledge or a restructuring of the old to clarify unknown or ambiguous information, is a set of contextual elements with specific values. Following this line of thought, Kelly defined context as specific 8 variables from bigger variables (e.g., task, topic, usefulness). Then, 7 Ph.D. students used laptop computers equipped with a client-side logger to identify which aspects of context should be considered. It was reported that 5 variables, endurance, frequency, stage, persistence, and familiarity, were related to the tasks and topics of their web seeking behavior.

Furthermore, there are more particularly useful studies for conceptualizing context. To be specific, Vakkari [26] identified three types of tasks used in information seeking studies and defined task as a "piece of activity to be done in order to achieve a goal (416p.)". Also, several researches claim that topic knowledge on user affects the information seeking behavior [27]. Time concept which takes context as successive search episodes is noticeable too [28].

3 Methodology

In this paper, transaction logs were used to overcome limitations of previous researches and fill up the user context. We investigated web search behavior (1) using client-side logs and not server-side data and (2) adopted a more user-engaged query session called User Clustered Query Session (UCQS). To be specific, since log data lack semantic information, we made users cluster their queries and label each query session. Then, users were required to answer several questions on each self-clustered session by themselves based on context, such as motivations, triggers and actual interests of their search behavior and other channels which were used to get further information during or after the web search.

3.1 Participants

A total of 92 participants (45 female, 47 male; 51 in their 20s and 41 in their 30s) were recruited through the Internet. The following three rules were applied when recruiting participants. First, participants have to use the Internet over 2 hours a day. This time is based on the average web usage time of 20s and 30s in Korea, 18.6 and 15.6 hours per week, respectively [29]. Second, there is no constraint on the occupation of participants. This criterion is applied to avoid bias in terms of job characteristics. As a result, the pool of participants comprised of various occupations from self-employed persons, professors, white-collar workers, blue-collar workers, housewives, students, and so on. Finally, only Internet Explorer users were selected. As Internet Explorer is the most popular web browser in Korea, the instruments were optimized to it.

3.2 Instruments and Data Collection

Transaction log data was collected using the customized tool, '*LogCatcher*'. It gathers network events every 5 minutes and sends them to our server. To be specific, various data, such as access time, page title, URL, query, search engine, IP address, and names of web browser are gathered by this tool. *LogCatcher* was provided to participants via email and participants were asked to install it on their primary computer. Once installed, a small window is generated on the upper right corner and indicates that the web activity logs are being collected.

When *LogCatcher* is stabilized on the participants' computers, the participants are guided to explore the web in the same way as they did previously. The daily web activities are collected in the database and the participants visit the research website to do their assignment. The assignment is consisted of two parts: Cluster and Questionnaires for the Clustered-queries. Participants view their own web activity logs on the research website and cluster the queries in groups according to the rules that they learned. After the clustering is complete, the participants answer the questionnaires according to the clustered queries. The participants' transaction logs consist of all network events. Thus, for analyzing the web search behavior, they have to be transformed.

We showed the daily web behavior records to the participants. Hence, participants can connect to the *QueryCluster* and execute the following tasks after skimming over the logs. That is, participants are instructed to confirm the click stream logs, stacked during the day, and then cluster related queries, after naming each cluster. After doing that, they are supposed to reply to the questionnaire that follows. As depicted below, this process is done in a sequential way that comprises of three parts.

(a) 'Web activity logs' part. At the left side of the web page, the click stream logs are shown chronologically. In particular, queries are highlighted with gray lines among the logs because not all the logs, but only queries are required to be clustered.

(b) 'Clustered-query' part. Web searching is not linear. Instead, it is rather complicated since many queries have non-linear sequences. Therefore, participants themselves are instructed to drag and drop the related queries to the center pane after looking over the left pane. Then, when they finish naming, one UCQS comes out.

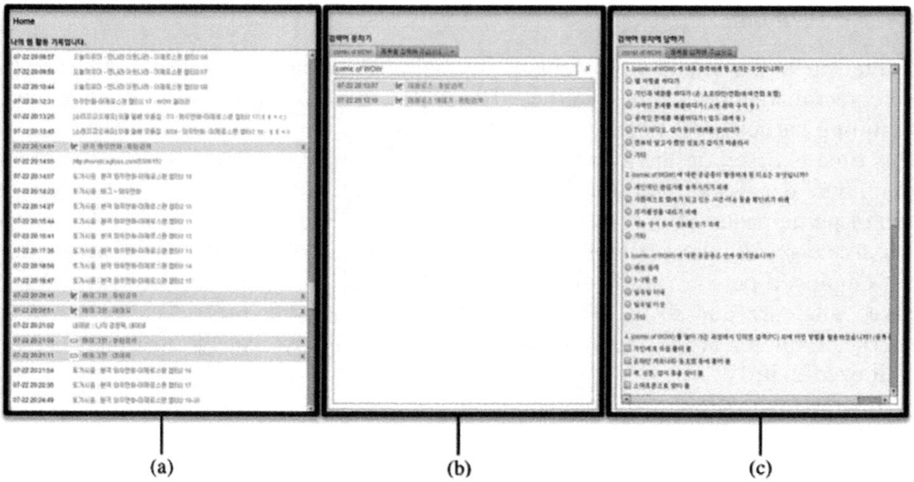

Fig. 1. Interface of the *QeuryCluster*

(c) 'Questionnaire' part. In this part, participants respond to the questionnaire according to each UCQS. The questionnaire consists of eight multiple-choice questions and one open-ended question for gaining more in-depth information about the context. To be specific, it investigated the flow of web search behavior according to motivation, trigger, using another source, self-diagnosing and using another source after finishing web search.

4 Results and Implications

4.1 Features of Web Search Behavior

After installing the program on their work computer, each participant was involved in our experiment for a week. At the end of the data collection period, 7996 queries were collected and 2712 UCQSs were clustered by participants. UCQS means continuous units that are concerned in participant's interests so we could figure out several features.

According to Table 1, participants typically generate 4.7 UCQS per day. The duration was defined as the time difference between the first query and last. That is, the UCQSs last 67.28 minutes on average. The median (6 minutes) and three quarter (37 minutes) implicate most of the interests are continued under one hour. As some interests last a long time, it produces a graph of a power function, as shown in Figure 2.

The graph in Fig. 2 represents 2,712 UCQSs by duration time, and displays 2175 UCQSs with 80.1% residing between 1-60 minutes. Other UCQSs were shown as types of long tail to maximum 1,368 minutes.

Back to Table 1, the number of queries in each UCQS showed 2.92 on average. But the maximum value is 65. These abnormal cases, with a long tail appearing in the duration, are possible because of the 'Real Time Issue' service, which displays the top search queries, a communized search assistant feature in Korean portal sites. Some participants spent a long time looking at these contents.

Table 1. The Main Features of UCQS

Mean	Quartiles			Duration of session in previous work
	25	50	75	
UCQS per day	4.70	3.825	4.28	12min(He, 2002)
Duration of UCQS (min.) (except single-query sessions)	67.28 (102)	2.92 (4.44)	6 (20)	26min(Jansen, 2000)
The number of queries per UCQS (except single-query sessions)	2.92 (4.44)	1 (2)	6 (20)	30min(Jones. R. et al., 2008)

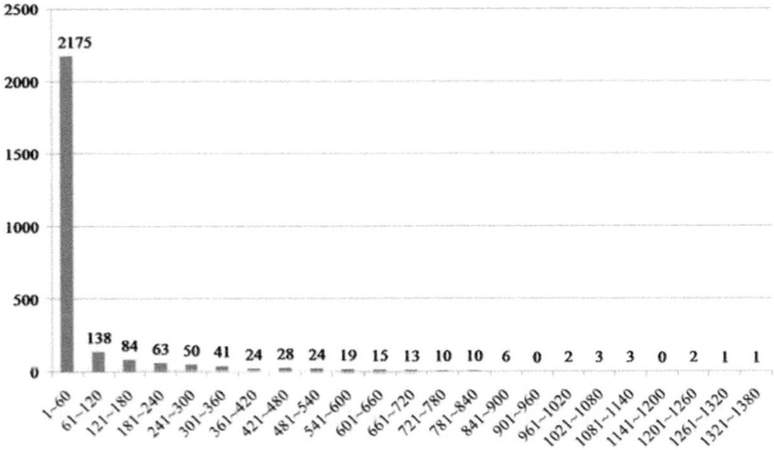

Fig. 2. The distribution of the durations of UCQS shows a power function. The x-axis of this graph is the time duration of USQS (minutes) and y-axis is the number of sessions.

Table 2. Independence of UCQS by demographic factors

	By gender		By age	
	Sig. (2-tailed)	Mean Difference	Sig. (2-tailed)	Mean Difference
UCQS per day	.181	-.629	.647	.215
Duration of UCQS (min.) (except single-query sessions)	.871 (.544)	-.768 (-5.99)	.361 (.438)	4.259 (7.50)
The number of queries per UCQS (except single-query sessions)	.127 (.189)	.161 (.296)	.067 (.515)	.106 (.148)

To get an idea of how the features are affected by demographic factors, Table 2 summarizes the differences between each variable. There exists no significant relation between the duration, the number of UCQS, and the number of queries by gender and age. In other words, gender and age do not influence UCQS.

4.2 Flow of Search Behavior

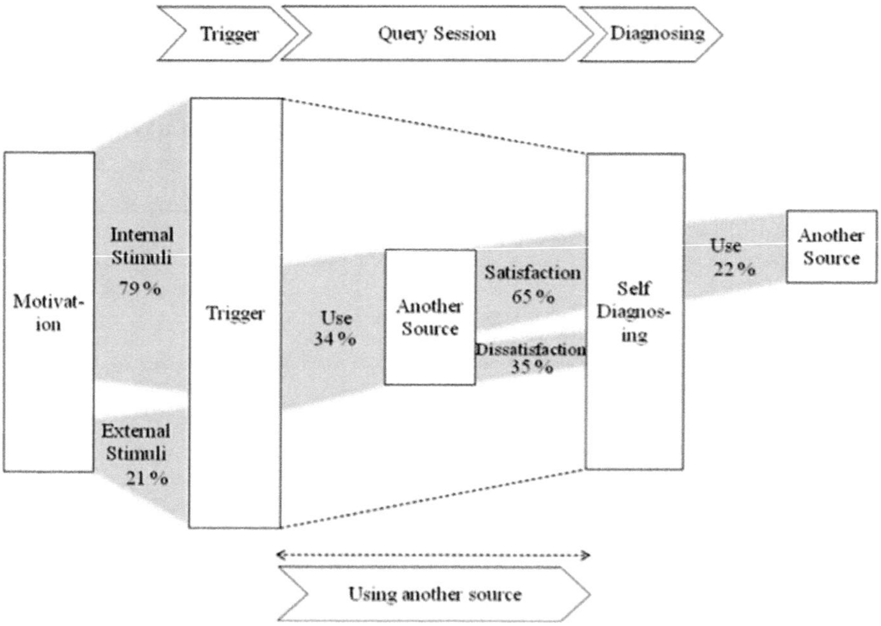

Fig. 3. The flow of search behavior; motivation, trigger, current usage of another source, self-diagnosing, and post-usage of another source

Fig. 3 shows the process when a web search occurs. First of all, the motivation, that could be divided into two classes, namely internal stimuli (79 percentile) and external stimuli (21 percentile), is born. Then the trigger causes searching to happen so that an actual web searching behavior has taken place accompanied with using another source, such as a newspaper. Through self-diagnosing, the results of searching are estimated as worthy or not. If someone concludes as worthy, the process is over. However, they will use another source that was not found in the result of web search, in reverse case. Among the data, 80 percentile of the participants, who were gratified with the results, did not proceed. In this flow, ‘using another source’ during or after the web search is interesting because it shows that many people do not fully depend on the Internet contents. Rather, they actively mobilize all sources that offer a solution. To be specific, they used an acquaintance (49%), on-line communities (32%), publications (15%), and smartphones (4%). Meanwhile, it is statistically verified, and shown below, that each stage of the web search behavior flow is not independent.

Table 3. Correlation of Each Stage (*p<.05, ** p<.01)

	Pearson Chi-square	Contingency coefficient
Motivation x Trigger	512.28**	.320**
Trigger x Another source	15.52*	.059*
Another source x Self diagnosing (It indicates 'during web search')	15.42*	.058**
Self diagnosing x Another source (It indicates 'after web search')	18.91*	.083**

Table 3 shows how the duration of UCQS and the number of queries are differentiated by each constructions of trigger. From Table 4, it can be observed that the longest duration appears when the user solves a personal problem. Contrary to this, during talking with an acquaintance, users spend a relatively short time to search for information on the web. Similarly, during solving a personal problem, users generate more queries. That is, 4.5 queries per UCQS are observed in this context. Through the interview, many participants reported on the importance of solving personal problems. For example:

"I used to spend much effort when I search for something on my personal problem. [...] Because it often affects important things like homework or tests and so on." (B2013)

Table 4. The Relationships among Trigger, Duration and the Number of Queries

	Trigger
Duration	- During web surfing (73.8min) > During talking with an acquaintance (45.3min)* - During talking with an acquaintance (45.3min) < During solving a personal problem (93.5min)* During solving a personal problem (93.5min) > During using media (44.2min)
The number of queries	- During web surfing (73.8min) > During talking with an acquaintance (45.3min)* - During talking with an acquaintance (45.3min) < During solving a personal problem (93.5min)* - During solving a personal problem (93.5min) > During using media (44.2min)

Characterizations of the information sources used for each trigger are displayed in Figure 4. There are, typically, more users who did not use other sources during or after web search. However, relatively conspicuous high rate of using other source is observed when they search information during talking with an acquaintance. It is easy to suppose that users can solve his/her curiosity between close friends and the Internet as information sources in conversations. On the other hand, users do not wander from information source to information source during web surfing. It may be caused by the reason that users generally do casual searching during web surfing:

"Web surfing is just web surfing. I mean, it is a kind of browsing for scanning articles about entertainment or movie stars. So I rarely search something in earnest during web surfing." (A2011)

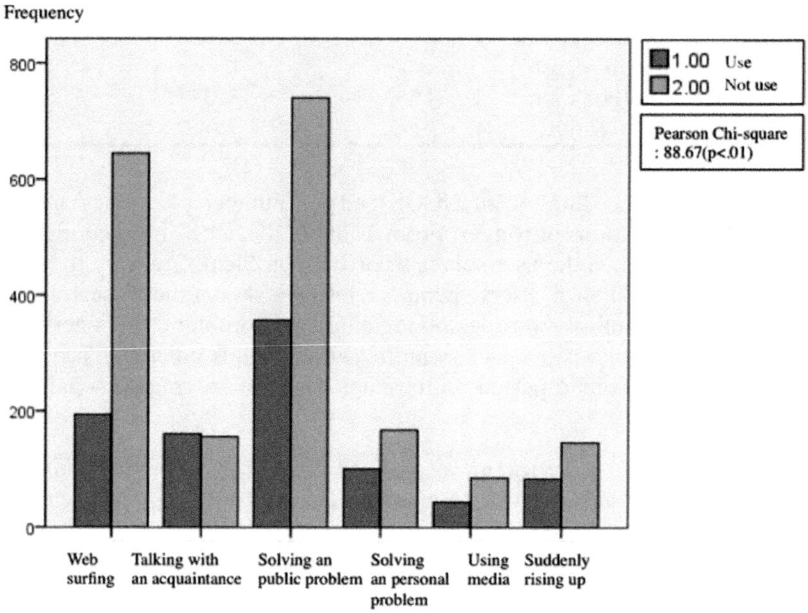

Fig. 4. The Relationships between Trigger and Other Sources for Improving Search Result

5 Conclusion

In this study, a sequence of queries in the same interest was defined as User-Clustered Query Session (UCQS). By adopting UCQS as a unit of analysis, the users' web search behaviors were examined, which were previously not ascertainable with server-side log research. As a result, some noticeable characteristics of UCQS were found, and a type of the web search flow of user was identified through the progress of UCQSs.

In short, it was found that the distribution graph of UCQSs by duration time had characteristics of the power function. Moreover, other features of USQS revealed extreme values too. These abnormal cases are caused by several factors, one of which is the 'Real Time Issue' service of Korean portal sites. The fact that there is no significant difference on the features of UCQS by gender and age implicates a generality of the web searching behavior.

Secondly, the flow that represents the pattern of users' search behavior was analyzed from the answers of questionnaires. In this experiment, the UCQS's flow was shown to be 'motivation → trigger → current usage of another source → self-diagnosis → post-usage of another source'. Of other sources, 'acquaintance and online-community' took the highest ratio and this implies that participants use social sources heavily and thus, it can be inferred that SNS may have a connection with evolution of search. The duration of UCQS and the number of queries are differentiated by each variable of trigger significantly.

Moreover, relatively conspicuous high rates of using other sources are observed when users search information while talking with an acquaintance. On the other hand, users do not wander from information source to information source during web surfing.

The findings of this study are of considerable significance due to the following two aspects. First, this study proposed the concept of UCQS, indicating a sequence of related interest, on Information Seeking behavior. Second, based on the proposed concept, this study conducted the first analysis reflecting the whole user context of search by examining participants' web search behavior beyond the limitations of server-side log researches. For realizing this, a system was developed to convert raw data into UCQSs.

Despite the contribution, this study is subject to some limitations. First, some participants had arbitrary behaviors on *QueryCluster*, even though they were asked to form UCQSs using the provided manual. Also, each process of UCQS flow was less semantically analyzed than the existing statistic results. Therefore, in addition to age and gender, the differences of demographic factors should be considered in further studies and more in-depth analysis will be needed to determine which effect each process of UCQS flow has on the following process.

References

1. Spink, A., Park, M., Jansen, J.B.: Multitasking during Web search sessions. Inf. Proc. Manage. 42(1), 264–275 (2006)
2. Patrick Dubroy, R.B.: A Study of Tabbed Browsing Among Mozilla Firefox Users. In: CHI 2010: Browsing, The research on the actual condition of the internet usage in Korea. KISA, Seoul, pp. 673–682 (2009)
3. Jansen, B.J., Pooch, U.: A review of Web searching studies and a framework for future research. Journal of the American Society for Information Science and Technology 52(3), 235–246 (2001)
4. Hoelscher, C.: How Internet experts search for information on the Web. In: World Conference of the World Wide Web, Internet, and Intranet, Association for the Advancement of Computing in Education, Orlando (1998); (Note: Published on CD-ROM with no page numbers)
5. Jansen, B.J., Spink, A., Bateman, J., Saracevic, T.: Real life information retrieval: A study of user queries on the web. SIGIR Forum 32(1), 5–17 (1998)
6. Jansen, B.J., Spink, A., Saracevic, T.: Real life, real users, and real needs: A study and analysis of user queries on the web. Information Processing and Management 36(2), 207–227 (2000)
7. Silverstein., C., Marais., H., Henzinger., M., Moricz, M.: Analysis of a very large web search engine query log. SIGIR Forum 33(1), 6–12 (1999)

8. Jansen, B.J., Spink, A., Pedersen, J.: A temporal comparison of AltaVista Web searching. Journal of the American Society for Information Science and Technology 56, 559–570 (2005)
9. Jansen, Spink: How are we searching the World Wide Web? A comparison of nine search engine transaction logs. Information Processing and Management 42(1), 248–263 (2006)
10. Zhang, M., Jansen, B.J., Spink, A.: Information Searching Tactics of Web Searchers. American Society for Information Science and Technology 43, 1–14 (2006)
11. Catledge, L.D., Pitkow, J.E.: Characterizing browsing strategies in the World-Wide Web. Computer Networks and ISDN System 27(6), 1065–1073 (1995)
12. Jones, R., Klinkner, K.L.: Beyond the Session Timeout: Automatic Hierarchical Segmentation of Search Topics in Query Logs. In: 17th ACM Conference on Information and knowledge Management, pp. 699–707. ACM, New York (2008)
13. Anick, P.: Using Terminological Feedback for Web Search Refinement – Alog-based Study. In: 26th Annual International ACM SIGIR Conference on Research and Development in Informaion Retrieval, pp. 88–95. ACM., New York (2003)
14. He, D., Göker, A.: Detecting session boundaries from Web user logs. In: 22nd Annual Colloquium on IR 5Research IRSG 2000, Cambridge, UK, pp. 57–66 (2000)
15. Spink, A., Park, M., Jansen, B.J., Pedersen, J.: Multitasking during Web search Sessions. Information Processing and Management 42(1), 264–275 (2006)
16. Jansen, B.J., Spink, A., Blakely, C., Koshman, S.: Defining a Session on Web Search Engines. JASIST 58, 862–871 (2007)
17. Boldi, P., Bonchi, F., Castillo, C., Donato, D., Gionis, A., Vigna, S.: The Query-flow Graph: Model and Applications. In: 17th
18. Jones, R., Klinkner, K.L.: Beyond the Session Timeout: Automatic Hierarchical Segmentation of Search Topics in Query Logs. In: 17th ACM conference on Information and knowledge management, pp. 699–707. ACM, New York (2008)
19. Kelly, D., Cool, C.: The effects of topic familiarity on information search behavior. In: Hersh, W., Marchionini, G. (eds.) Proceedings of the Second ACM/IEEE Joint Conference on Digital Libraries (JCDL 2002), pp. 74–75. ACM Press, New York (2002)
20. Kellar, M., Watters, C., Shepherd, M.: A field study characterizing Web-based information-seeking tasks. Journal of the American Society for Information Science and Technology 58, 999–1018 (2007)
21. Saracevic, T.: The stratified model of information retrieval interaction: Extension and applications. In: Schwartz, C.S. (ed.) Proceedings of the Annual Meeting of the American Society for Information Science (ASIS 1997), pp. 3–9. American Society for Information Science and Technology, MD (1997)
22. Ingwersen, P., Jarvelin, K.: Information retrieval in context. In: Ingwersen, P., Belkin, N.J. (eds.) Proceedings of the SIGIR 2004 Workshop on Information Retrieval in Context, pp. 6–9. ACM Press, New York (2004)
23. Belkin, N.J.: Ineffable concepts in information retrieval. In: Sparck Jones, K. (ed.) Information retrieval experiment, pp. 44–58. Butterworth, London (1981)
24. Cool, C.: The concept of situation in information science. Annual Review of Information Science and Technology 35, 5–42 (2001)
25. Vakkari, P.: Task-based information searching. Annual Review of Information Science and Technology 37, 413–464 (2003)
26. Choo, C., Detlor, B., Turnbull, D.: Information seeking on the web: An integrated model of browsing and searching. First Monday 5(2) (2000), http://www.firstmonday.org/ISSUES/issue5_2/choo/index.html

27. Lin, S.J., Belkin, N.J.: Modeling multiple information seeking episodes. In: Roderer, N. (ed.) Proceedings of the Annual Conference of the American Society for Information Science (ASIS 2000), pp. 133–146. American Society for Information Science and Technology, Silver Spring (2000)
28. InternetTrend, `http://trend.logger.co.kr/trendForward.tsp`
29. Fisher, K.E., Lynne, S.E., Mckechnie, E.F.: Theories of Information behavior. Information today (2005)

Indoor Localization Using Audio Features of FM Radio Signals

Andrei Popleteev, Venet Osmani, Oscar Mayora, and Aleksandar Matic

Create-Net, Via alla Cascata 56/D, 38123 Trento (TN), Italy
{andrei.popleteev,venet.osmani,oscar.mayora,
aleksandar.matic}@create-net.org

Abstract. Typical localization systems use various features of the signal to estimate the distance, including received signal strength indicator (RSSI), timing information or angle of arrival (AoA). However, there are a number of signal features of FM radio that may also be suitable for localization, namely stereo channel separation (SCS) and signal to noise ratio (SNR). This paper investigates the feasibility of indoor localization using fingerprinting of audio features of FM radio signals emitted by low-power FM transmitters using SNR and SCS values. The experimental results demonstrate the possibility of audio-based localization, when signal strength readings are not available.

1 Introduction

Majority of wireless localization systems estimate the distance to the positioning beacons using either timing information or properties of the received signal, with received signal strength indicator (RSSI) being most widely used signal-related feature. However, the RSSI readings are not always available from the hardware, or are reported with a very low granularity, which significantly limits the accuracy of the positioning system. To address this issue, other signal features might be used for estimating the distance between the mobile unit and the positioning beacons.

A promising technology for indoor localization is FM radio, which is widely available, power-effective and low-interference, and provides a positioning accuracy comparable to Wi-Fi based systems [1]. However, many FM receivers do not report any RSSI information to the software layer. At the same time, the FM signal carries an audio component; the received audio quality depends on the radio-frequency (RF) signal properties and thus it may be possible to utilize audio features for localization.

The aim of this paper is to evaluate the feasibility of RSSI-less indoor localization using audio features of the FM radio signals. To achieve this, we first estimate dependence of audio features on the transmitter-to-receiver distance. In this regard, two suitable audio features were identified, namely, signal-to-noise ratio (SNR) and stereo channel separation (SCS). Then, we evaluated the localization performance of the system using SNR, SCS and RSSI fingerprinting approaches.

2 Distance-Dependent Audio Features of FM Radio Signals

The relative position of the user with regard to a beacon can be characterized by the angle between directed antennas, signal propagation time and certain properties of the

M. Beigl et al. (Eds.): CONTEXT 2011, LNAI 6967, pp. 246–249, 2011.

received signal. For the FM radio, we have identified three distance-dependent features, namely: received signal strength (RSS), audio signal quality (represented by SNR), and stereo channels separation (SCS). As the RSS' dependence on distance has already been studied before [1], this paper focuses on the audio-related features.

The audio information is encoded in the RF signal by means of modulation, and the quality of extracted audio depends on the quality of the received RF signal that degrades with the distance due to path loss. Thus, it is reasonable to assume that audio signal quality depends on the distance between receiver and transmitter: as the signal strength decreases with the distance, the SNR for the RF signal drops, and the demodulated noise passes through to the audio part, thus affecting the audio SNR.

To test the feasibility of audio SNR method for FM positioning, a short-range FM transmitter (embedded into a König MP3 player) has been set to broadcast continuous dual-tone multi-frequency (DTMF) signal composed of 1209 Hz and 697 Hz sine waves [2]. This signal was received by Brando USB FM radio, with noise-reduction turned off. The audio signal, sampled at 44.1 kHz, was transformed using 8192-band FFT and the SNR was then calculated as follows:

$$SNR = \frac{band_{697Hz} + band_{1209Hz}}{mean(all\_bands)} . \tag{1}$$

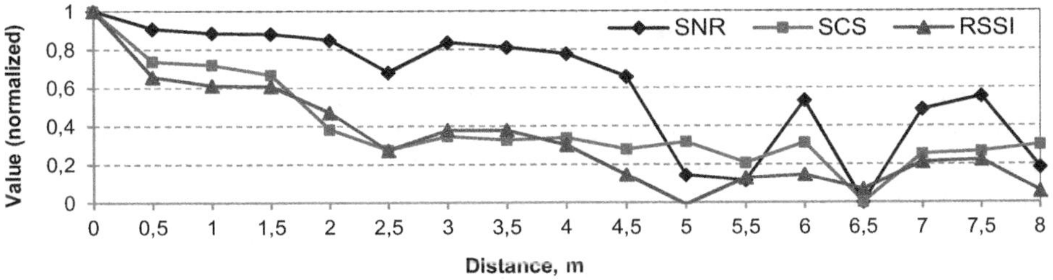

Fig. 1. SNR, SCS and RSSI dependence on distance

The results in Fig. 1 demonstrate that audio SNR does in fact reflect the distance from the signal source, even though the dependence is less smooth than in the case of RSSI. At short distances, the reception quality is high and the SNR value is limited only by the characteristics of the transmitter and receiver. As the distance increases, the SNR declines. Thus, audio SNR can be utilized as a distance-dependent feature (provided that audio quality augmentation features of the receiver are switched off).

The motivation for considering the stereo channel separation (SCS) as a measure of distance was two-fold. Firstly, the stereophonic signal is more sensitive to noise than the monophonic one [5]. The inherent white noise of the RF signal mostly affects the 19-kHz stereo pilot subcarrier and the differential L–R part of the encoded stereo signal [4, 5], where L and R denote the left and the right audio channels, respectively. The summary L+R signal, however, is less sensitive to the RF noise. Secondly, the distortions in the pilot subcarrier also affect the quality of the stereo signal. At longer distances, where the RF signal quality degrades, the receiver circuitry gradually combines the stereo channels to maintain the sound quality [6], and the L+R part starts to dominate in the output of the receiver, which results in the reduction of SCS.

In order to evaluate SCS feature, the transmitter was set to broadcast a stereophonic sound; each stereo channel contained a sinusoidal signal with DTMF [2] component frequencies (1209 Hz for the left channel and 697 Hz for the right one), which guaranteed no overlapping of signals of different channels, or their harmonics. Then, a 8192-band FFT was performed over the right channel of the received signal, and the SCS value was calculated as the difference between the 697 Hz band (the one transmitted on right channel) and the "ghost" 1209 Hz band (transmitted on the left channel, but appearing on the right one due to channel crosstalk). Thus, when the reception quality is high, only a minimal fraction of the left-channel signal appears on the right channel, resulting in a high SCS value. However, if the stereo separation is poor, the two frequency bands are almost equal and thus the SCS value is minimal. The experimental results in Fig. 1 confirm that, as the distance increases the SCS quickly deteriorates, reaches its minimum and remains constant thereafter. The minimum SCS corresponds to mono reception.

The use of stereo channel separation as a measure of distance is unique for FM positioning and, according to the literature, has never been evaluated before. However, it has certain limitations. Firstly, the transmitters must broadcast a known stereo signal, so that the client can estimate the channel cross-talk. Secondly, the SCS method is appropriate only for shorter distances than the RSSI since at long distances the RF signal is too weak and the stereo reception is not feasible.

3 Positioning Performance

An experimental evaluation of the audio-based FM positioning performance has been performed in the 12x6 m room described in [1]. Three short-range FM transmitters were setup to broadcast a stereophonic signal, as described above. The mobile client was a laptop equipped with a Brando USB FM Radio receiver. For each accessible point of a 1-m grid in the room, the laptop recorded a 5 second long audio sample from each transmitter and simultaneously acquired the RSSI values for the beacon being recorded (at 10 Hz rate). The recorded audio samples were processed to estimate the SNR and SCS values as described in previous section. Finally, the SNR, SCS and RSSI measurements for each point were averaged. The localization performance was evaluated using the fingerprinting approach with nearest neighbor classifier and leave-one-out evaluation [7]; the algorithm was implemented in R [8].

The results presented in Fig. 2a confirm the feasibility of FM positioning based on audio signal properties, as all methods perform better than the baseline (where the system returned a random training point for any input fingerprint). The SCS approach demonstrates a slightly better performance than the SNR approach, and provides the best median accuracy (2.1 m) over all competitors. However, the best 95th-percentile accuracy is demonstrated by the RSSI.

In order to understand the reasons behind the inferior performance of audio-based methods, let us consider the dependencies between the collected SNR, SCS and RSSI values (see Fig. 2b). For low RSSI values the SNR increases linearly or quasi-linearly; at certain point, however, it saturates to its maximum of about 50 dB. Thus, the SNR approach is usable for positioning only at relatively long distances (low RSSIs); at shorter ranges the SNR's dependence on the distance is weak. This explains why SNR demonstrated lower positioning accuracy than SCS: the power of the used

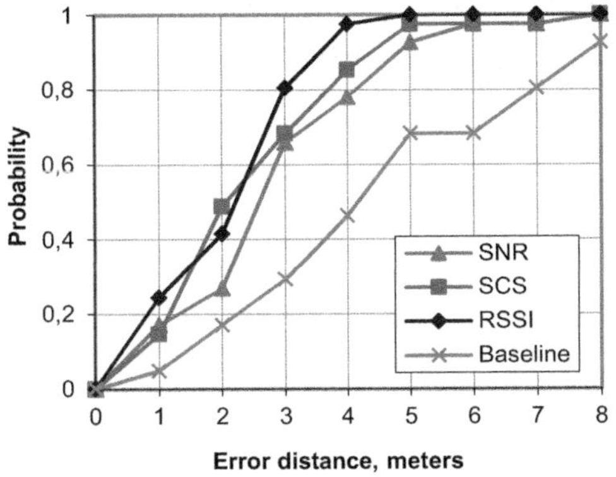

a) Positioning performance

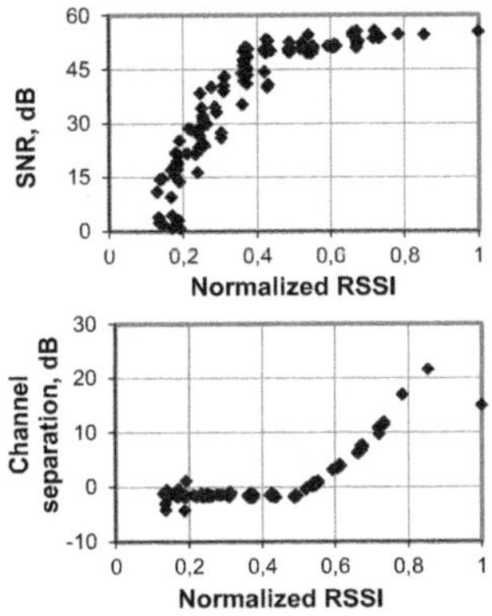

b) SNR and SCS vs. RSSI

Fig. 2. (a) Accuracy of FM positioning system using audio signal features. (b) Relationship between SNR, SCS and RSSI.

transmitters was sufficient to provide a good audio quality (that is, maximum SNR) in the whole test environment. For SCS, when the signal is weak, the reception is monophonic and the channel separation is low. As the RSSI increases, the receiver eventually switches to stereophonic mode, where the channel separation continues to improve (up to hardware capabilities) as the RSSI grows.

The experimental results demonstrate that audio features are suitable for localization. While the FM-specific SCS approach works only at shorter distances with high RSSI levels, the audio SNR method is more suitable at longer ranges with low RSSI values. The RSSI approach, in contrast, is applicable for all distance ranges and provides better accuracy. The audio-feature based localization may however prove useful when RSSI readings are imprecise or not available.

References

1. Matic, A., Popleteev, A., Osmani, V., Mayora, O.: FM radio for indoor localisation with spontaneous recalibration. J. of Pervasive and Mobile Computing 6(6), 642–656 (2010)
2. ITU Recommendation Q.23: Technical features of push-button telephone sets (1988)
3. Barry, J.R., Lee, E.A., Messerschmitt, D.G.: Digital Communication. Springer, Heidelberg (2003)
4. De Vries, A.J.: Stereo FM transmission system. US Patent 3133993 (1964)
5. Bose, A.G., Short, W.R.: A theoretical and experimental study of noise and distortion in the reception of FM signals. IEEE Trans. Broadcasting 47, 164–179 (2001)
6. Silicon Laboratories, Inc.: Si4702/03 datasheet (2008)
7. Bahl, P., Padmanabhan, V.N.: RADAR: An in-building RF-based user location and tracking system. In: IEEE INFOCOM, vol. 2, pp. 775–784 (2000)
8. R Development Core Team: R: A language and environment for statistical computing

SENST*: Approaches for Reducing the Energy Consumption of Smartphone-Based Context Recognition

Maximilian Schirmer and Hagen Höpfner

Bauhaus University of Weimar, Bauhausstr. 11, 99423 Weimar, Germany
maximilian.schirmer@uni-weimar.de, hoepfner@acm.org
http://www.mobile-media.eu

Abstract. Modern smartphones provide sensors that can be used to describe the current context of the device and its user. Contextual knowledge allows software systems to adapt to personal preferences of users and to make data processing context-aware. Different sensors or measurement approaches used for recognizing the values of particular context elements vary greatly in their energy consumption. This paper presents approaches for reducing the energy consumption of utilizing smartphone sensors. We discuss sensor substitution strategies as well as logical dependencies among sensor measurements. The paper describes the first milestone towards a generalization of such strategies. Furthermore, We show that energy awareness benefits from a more abstract view on context elements.

Keywords: Context Recognition, Energy Awareness, Smartphone Sensors, Sensor Triggering, Sensor Substitution.

1 Introduction and Motivation

Considering user contexts is an important issue for modern computer systems. In order to adaptively react on the individual needs of users under certain situations, context recognition is indispensable. Possible reactions reach from an adaptation of the availability settings (e.g., muting a device during a meeting) to complex adaptations in ubiquitous environments (e.g., darkening the room during a presentation). In our research, context primarily means the abstraction of ascendancies describing the actual situation of users. The literature in the area of ubiquitous computing provides various approaches for describing and modeling contexts [28,17,8,30]. These approaches strongly discriminate in the way they can be used for designing and realizing context-aware applications. However, they have in common that the status of the user and of the physical and technical environment as well as the history of interactions with the system are essential for modeling and recognizing contexts [23]. The description of the user status typically bases on a set of personal information on identity, current location, activities, or needs. In addition, information about the presence of other people in the vicinity might

* SENST is an acronym for sensor substitution and triggering

M. Beigl et al. (Eds.): CONTEXT 2011, LNAI 6967, pp. 250–263, 2011.

be important. Furthermore, a system can learn (and later on predict) preferences and requirements by analyzing a user's interaction history.

In general, it is required that context recognition is done automatically. Otherwise, the configuration efforts could overstrain users, as they would otherwise have to specify the parameters describing the context or even to manually "select" a context. However, automated context recognition requires sensors that measure the relevant data from the user's or device's surroundings. In our approach, we decided to use sensors in everyday objects instead of utilizing special hardware. We focus on smartphones, as it is possible to assign such devices directly to individual users. Furthermore, smartphones are widely-used and provide great computing power and comprehensive sets of sensors.

Unfortunately, recent developments regarding the performance and the sensor technology have a strong impact on the devices' energy consumption. In fact, heavily using all capabilities discharges the power supply within a few hours. Therefore, it is necessary to realize the smartphone-based context recognition in an energy-aware manner and to minimize the use of energy-intensive sensors. This approach is key for achieving user acceptance. Apple, e.g., recognized the importance of a long uptime of their iPhone devices and introduced techniques that reduce the energy consumptions of position determination. In this paper, we present a more generic approach for the energy-aware and smartphone-based recognition of context elements. We introduce two approaches, sensor substitution and sensor triggering, that can be used to balance the energy consumptions of various sensor-driven context recognition alternatives.

The remainder of this paper is structured as follows: Section 2 clarifies the terminology used in the paper. Section 3 discusses the related work. Section 4 analyzes sensors provided by smartphones. Section 5 introduces our strategies for reducing the energy consumptions of the context recognition. Section 6 contains the evaluation. Section 7 concludes the paper and gives an outlook on future research directions.

2 Context, Context Elements, and Sensors

In the research area of ubiquitous computing, the term "context" is associated with different meanings and interpretations. The most general (but not directly applicable or implementable) definition originates from Anind Kumar Dey. In [14], he wrote:

> "*Context* is any information that can be used to characterize the situation of an entity. An entity is a person, place or object that is considered relevant to the interaction between a user and an application, including the user and applications themselves."

In order to recognize contexts, it is important to model them properly. A number of different context models already exists [7]. Most of them agree on the fact that a simple listing of parameters like location, time, or information on activities is not sufficient to describe a context [13]. Hence, modern context models (e.g., [31,28]) also include social aspects of the users and human factors.

From a technical point of view, context-aware ubiquitous applications base on three core components: (1) sensors, (2) middleware, (3) actuators [4,5]; the order within this sequence also implies the direction of the data flow. Sensors are typically defined as devices that convert physical phenomena into electrical signals [22]. As discussed above, context is more than a simple concatenation of values. Hence, we can consider a more abstract definition of *sensors*. Hardware as well as software components can serve as sensors and measure raw data in the environment. In most cases, the middleware is realized in form of an event notification infrastructure system. Examples are Elvin [33,15], Hermes [27], and SIENA [12]. It provides a multilevel conversion and transformation process where sets of rules are applied on the raw data in order to infer *context elements*. These context elements can then be used to describe contexts. Finally, actuators react on a certain context in order to adapt the system accordingly.

In this paper we focus on (1) and (2). However, we do not discuss inference or machine learning strategies but aim on "calling" them in an energy-efficient way. In the course of this paper, we use the following formal definitions: Let $\mathcal{S}^{KE} = \{S_1^{KE}, \ldots, S_n^{KE}\}$ with $n \in \mathbb{N}$ be the set of all sensors measuring raw data that can be used to infer a context element *KE*. Furthermore, let $\mathbf{dom}(KE)$ be the domain of this context element. The function $w(v(S_x^{KE})) = \mathbf{dom}(S_x^{KE}) \rightarrow \mathbf{dom}(KE)$ maps a sensor value $v(S_x^{KE})$ from the domain of the sensor $\mathbf{dom}(S_x^{KE})$ with $S_x^{KE} \in \mathcal{S}^{KE}$ to the domain of the context element. Furthermore, we have to consider that not all sensors work in all environments (e.g., WIFI triangulation requires a WIFI infrastructure). Therefore, let $\mathcal{S}_U^{KE} = \{S_1^{KE,U}, \ldots, S_m^{KE,U}\}$ with $m \in \mathbb{N}, \mathcal{S}_U^{KE} \subseteq \mathcal{S}^{KE}$ be the subset of sensors available in a environment U. We are aware of the fact that this definition seems to exclude context elements that are inferable from combinations of various sensors. This issue is part of future work, but does not obliterate the results we achieved so far. Such a combination of sensors is considered as single (combined) sensor in this paper.

3 Related Work

Our energy-aware, smartphone-based context recognition approach overlaps with various related research areas. Besides the context recognition issues discussed in Section 2, energy awareness in computer systems as well as the use of sensors embedded into everyday objects are related research fields.

Energy-aware computer systems are becoming increasingly important. One reason is the need for reducing carbon dioxide emissions. Another more technical reason is the uptime of battery-powered mobile devices. Energy-aware hardware has already been under research for a couple of years. Approaches like sleep modes or performance scaling are state of the art. On the other hand, the research on energy-aware software is rather novel. However, first papers illustrate the importance of energy-aware software. The authors of [11] found out that alternative implementations of algorithms have a different energy consumption resulting from a different utilization of the underlying hardware. Recursive algorithms (e.g., merge sort) require much more memory than inline algorithms (e.g., insertion sort). However, both alternatives solve the same problem, the sorting of a list of values, but consume different amounts of energy. This example illustrates that it is possible to substitute hardware resources. Insertion sort saves memory accesses by increasing the number of comparisons (resource CPU). As discussed in [19], memory access consumes more energy than CPU calculations. Hence, resource substitution can be used in order to reduce energy consumption [10]. Other publications support this hypothesis. The authors of [36] show that a compression of data by a factor greater that 10% (CPU) reduces the energy consumption of data transmission (resource network). Regarding [21], a similar effect appears while storing data on hard disks.

Regarding the sensor-based context recognition, there is a need to balance energy consumption and accuracy. The authors of [24] analyzed various location determination approaches using smartphones. GPS supports the highest accuracy while alternative approaches (WIFI- or Bluetooth-based) consume less energy. The proposed a-Loc-algorithm predicts the probability of movements and queries the appropriate sensor only if it is required. a-Loc is an example for sensor substitution (cf. Section 5). The "Lucid Dreaming" system [20] utilizes different operation modes of sensors in order to save energy. The system utilizes a geophone [3] to observe vibrations within buildings. An analog circuit, which requires less energy, initiates (on demand) a more precise but more energy-intensive microcontroller-based measurement. In other words, the more energy-intensive and more accurate sensor logically depends on the less energy-intensive but also less accurate one. This approach is an example for sensor triggering (cf. Section 5).

Sensors in everyday objects (e.g., in smartphones) enable researchers to easily assign context-relevant data to individual users because everyday objects typically belong to a person. Furthermore, such items are frequently used [32]. For example, the "MediaCup" [6] is able to recognize its filling level by analyzing data from a temperature and an acceleration sensor. In addition, one can localize the cup in an ubiquitous environment and therefore determine the context of the user. The authors of [35] used such sensors for the "SenSay" system. They predict the reachability of smartphone users by analyzing the acceleration sensor. However, systems like MediaCup or SenSay use specialized sensors. We aim for utilizing standard sensors in smartphones (cf. Section 4). The "BreadCrumbs" system [26] uses WIFI sensors to determine the position of mobile devices in order to calculate movement profiles. These profiles are utilized for increasing the connectivity during movements. These examples illustrate the potential of the use of sensors in combination with smartphones but do neither provide a generalized approach nor focus on energy consumption.

4 Sensors in Mobile Devices

In the context of mobile devices (e.g., smartphones), sensors provide valuable interfaces from the physical world to the software systems on the devices. Nowadays, sensors in mobile devices are widely spread: according to a study conducted by ABIresearch [1], 85% of all smartphones sold worldwide will be equipped with a GPS sensor by the year 2013, 50% will include an accelerometer, and nearly 50% of the devices will feature a gyroscope. To date, these sensors are mainly used as input methods for controlling games, for the location-based adaption of applications, for augmented reality applications, or for movement-based commands (e.g., shaking the device triggers the undo command). Our approach aims at a more general, versatile and energy-aware use of the available sensors in order to determine context elements of smartphone users.

In this section, we present an overview of the most commonly used smartphone sensors using the example of the Apple iPhone 4. We categorize the sensors into four distinct groups: (1) technology that originally serves as communication interface; (2) environment sensors; (3) multimedia features of smartphones; and (4) software sensors.

Communication Interfaces as Sensors: Traditional communication interfaces in smartphones rely on technologies such as GSM/UMTS, Wireless LAN, and Bluetooth. Besides their intended type of use (data exchange and communication), these interfaces can also be used as sensors. They mainly substitute location sensors for the determination of the mobile device's current whereabouts. This is either realised by triangulation (based on cell towers in the vicinity of the device and their known location) [9,29]; or by assigning the known position of an access point with the highest signal strength to the smartphone. While the former approach reaches a greater accuracy, the computational effort for the positioning is increased as well. The low costs of Bluetooth devices provide interesting positioning opportunities in buildings.

Using communication interfaces as location sensors represents an alternative to the more obvious GPS technology when it can not or should not be used. The choice of the most suitable alternative depends on the desired accuracy (e.g., determining the current city does not require a positioning within 10 meters), available energy resources (e.g., repeated positioning over long periods of time draws large amounts of energy), and environment conditions (e.g., GPS will not work in buildings). In order to assess the energy consumption of the interfaces, their individual communication protocols should be considered, as well. As an example, the electronic components of the Bluetooth interface draw far less power than Wireless LAN components. However, the complex protocol for discovering nearby Bluetooth devices dampens this advantage as positioning will take longer and consume a comparable amount of energy over time [24].

Among all electronic components in smartphones, the communication interfaces have the highest energy consumption. In a recent experiment, the energy consumption of a Google G1 smartphone during the discovery process of nearby devices using different approaches was analyzed [24]. The communication interfaces were evaluated against the traditional GPS method. The results indicate that positioning using cell tower association has the lowest energy consumption (< 20mJ), followed by wireless LAN (545.07mJ) and Bluetooth ($1299.6 \cdot N(t) + 558$mJ; depends on the number of discoverable devices $N(t)$). GPS positioning requires 5700mJ for the first fix (cold start) and 1425mJ for each additional request.

Environment Sensors: Commonly found environment sensors in smartphones are the GPS sensor, ambient light sensor, proximity sensor, accelerometer, and the gyroscope. The Apple iPhone 4 smartphone contains the following environment sensors: (1) GPS and compass (Broadcom BCM4750); (2) ambient light and proximity (TAOS TSL2771); (3) acceleration (ST Micro LIS331DLH); and (4) gyroscope (ST Mirco L3G4200D). The GPS sensor allows a precise positioning outside of buildings, at the cost of a prolonged period of time for the location acquisition (and therefore a high energy consumption [24]). In order to accelerate the positioning process, additional data from the GSM communication network is used ("Assisted GPS" [16]).

The ambient light sensor (typically a photo diode) enables the smartphone to detect the current ambient light level in its environment. Typically, this sensor is used to adapt the brightness of the display to the ambient lighting conditions (full brightness for high environment light level, and vice versa). As a context element, the lighting conditions can be used in various ways. For example, a high level can indicate outdoor activity.

The proximity sensor is realized as a combination of an infrared emitter diode and a photo diode sensitive to infrared light. If an object is in close proximity to the emitter, its light is reflected back to the photo diode. This allows the smartphone to detect the presence of objects (maximum distance approx. 10 cm). The sensor is used to turn off the display while the user is holding the phone to her ear, in order to avoid unintended interactions. Besides this use case, other applications can be envisioned for this sensor, ranging from gesture recognition up to the use as an infrared communication interface.

The accelerometer measures the acceleration that affects the mobile device on three axes. This allows an approximation of the device's current orientation in space, based on changes in the acceleration. Modern smartphones use accelerometers realized as microelectrochemical systems (MEMS) made of silicon because of the devices' small case constraints. The sensor works like a spring pendulum with springs made from silicon studs. Typically, the sensor is used to adapt the display orientation to the current orientation of the device. However, there is also a great number of applications that use the sensor for motion control. As the sensor provides clues on the activity of the smartphone, it can be used as a trigger for sensors that logically depend on it (cf. Section 5).

The gyroscope sensor is often used in combination with the accelerometer. It is also a MEMS device and delivers more accurate values for the position of the mobile device in space. This allows a more precise reaction to changes in position or orientation.

Multimedia Features as Sensors: Every smartphone features means for recording audio signals (microphone) and video signals (camera). Nowadays, some devices even provide more than one microphone in order to reduce interferences or feature several cameras (e.g., on the device's front and back sides). Apart from their intended use as a recording device, there is a number of interesting ways to use these multimedia features as sensors. Sounds from the environment can be recorded and analyzed in order to draw conclusions about the current whereabouts of users (e.g., [2], cf. Section 5). Furthermore, a communication interface with a low energy footprint can be realized with a modulated audio signal as transfer method (e.g., [18])

The overwhelming amount of ways of use for cameras in smartphones induces some thinkable or already realised approaches for using cameras as sensors. Obviously, com puter vision algorithms can be applied to detect context elements. Among the possible scenarios are the identification of users or people in the vicinity, detecting and identifying known objects (e.g., for positioning [37]), or the more simple determination whether a user is near the device. However, processing camera images is energy-intensive because of the complexity of the algorithms and the prolonged use of the camera.

Software Sensors: Many utility or productivity applications on smartphones store and process large amounts of personal data. This data can be used for the determination of context elements, as well. For example, calendar data about a meeting that takes place at a given time and date can be sufficient for positioning a user (cf. Section 5). A great number of unread emails could indicate unattainability of the user, or data about the currently played music on the smartphone could allow to draw conclusions about a user's current mood.

5 Energy-Aware Determination of Context Elements

As described in Section 2, context comprises various context elements. The most popular context element is location. The authors of [34] define the location of an object as the objects position on earth, relative to a point of reference. However, there exist various measurable or inferable technical, physical, device specific, and social cultural context elements. Even a location might be determined in different ways, e.g. directly via GPS or by interpreting signal strengths of WIFI hotspots. As previously discussed, these techniques differ in their accuracy and their energy consumption. GPS is more precise than any triangulation approach, but requires more energy. However, certain applications do not require precise positions, but work perfectly with abstract (semantic) locations (e.g., the name of a city or the name of a point of interest). The appropriateness of a certain context elements' value depends on the probability that the value is correct for the given application. With this general criterion we can also use (energy-efficient) software sensors for location determination. For example, if entries in a calendar stored on a smartphone indicate that the user should be in a meeting, then the meeting location is likely to be the current location of the user (and of the device).

Taking the formal definitions from Section 2, we can include energy as a factor in the formalism. Let $e(S_x^{KE,U})$ with $S_x^{KE,U} \in \mathcal{S}_U^{KE}$ be the energy consumption of a measurement of sensor $S^{KE,U}$ in the given environment U. Furthermore, let $g(S_x^{KE,U})$ with $0 \leq g \leq 1$ be a measurement function returning the probability that a value of a context element is appropriate. We call g an appropriateness function. This function depends on the application scenario and on the granularity of sensor values. In general, it must be higher if only the name of a city is requested. In fact, GPS and triangulation methods would return an appropriateness value of 1 in this case. However, a detailed analysis on how to define g for various context elements and various application scenarios is subject to future work. In this paper, we follow the assumption that correct appropriateness functions exist.

Sensor substitution: The idea of sensor substitution bases on the observations from the resource substitution discussed in Section 3. Considering location as an example, we already know about different alternatives. These alternatives have different energy consumptions, but "solve" the same task (similar to the sorting algorithms, cf. Section 3). In order to choose the most energy-efficient alternative, we utilize Algorithm 1. The algorithm uses only one loop cycle and does not access any sensor. Hence, it requires only a little amount of energy to choose the appropriate ($g(S) \geq AV$) alternative. Please remember that detailed research on $g(S)$ is not in the focus of this paper.

The authors of [2] have shown that sensor substitution reduces the energy consumption for location determination. However, they did not consider software sensors.

Algorithm 1. *Sensor substitution*

Input:	$\mathcal{S}_U^{KE}$	// set of available sensors
	KE	// requested context element
	AV	// minimal accepted appropriateness
Output:	W^{KE}	// Context element value
	$FALSE$	// Notification in case of an error

```
def get_context_element_value_with_substitution(KE, S_U^KE, AV)
min_e_sensor=NULL // variable for storing "best" sensor
min_e=-1 // variable for keeping minimal required amount of energy
for each S ∈ S_U^KE do // loop through all alternatives
    if ((min_e == −1 ∨ (min_e > e(S)) ∧ g(S) ≤ AV))
        then {min_e_sensor=S; min_e=e(S);}
if min_e==-1 then return(FALSE) else return(w(v(min_e_sensor)))
```

Sensor triggering: In contrast to sensor substitution, sensor triggering aims at utilizing the different energy consumption characteristics of sensors in order to activate or inhibit the determination of context element values. The general idea is to measure environmental changes through sensors with a low energy consumption and to use energy-intensive methods only if changes imply an update. Formally, this means that we have a set of triggering sensors $\mathcal{S}_U^{T\rightarrow KE}$ consisting of two subsets $\mathcal{S}_U^{T+KE}$ (positive triggers) and $\mathcal{S}_U^{T\text{-}KE}$ (negative triggers). In the location example, a positive triggering sensor could be the acceleration sensor. If the device is not moving, then the location can not change; or—in other words—a new location determination is only necessary if the acceleration sensor measures movement. A negative trigger in this scenario could be a software sensor. If the smartphone indicates an incoming call or message, then a movement of the device is likely, but a location change does not have to take place. The realization of sensor triggering depends on the APIs provided by the smartphones' development kits. Some sensors must be frequently polled in order to monitor the trigger values. Other sensors use interrupts and notify the system about (significant) changes. While reacting to an interrupt is (by definition) energy-efficient as the smartphone would raise the flag anyway, polling sensor changes needs a deeper look into the energy consumption of the triggering sensors and the appropriate measurement frequency. Algorithm 2 illustrates a polling-based triggering. For now, we assume that the poll frequency is constant among the triggers and that negative trigger sensors return only *true* or *false* on request. However, we will generalize this idea in our future work.

Algorithm 2. *Sensor triggering using polling*

Input:	$\mathcal{S}_U^{KE}$	// set of available sensors
	$\mathcal{S}_U^{T+KE}$	// available positive triggers
	$\mathcal{S}_U^{T\text{-}KE}$	// available negative triggers
	KE	// requested context element
	x	// time to wait between loop cycles
Output:	W^{KE}	// Context element value
	FALSE	// Notification in case of an error

```
def get_context_element_value_with_polling(KE, S_U^KE, S_U^T+KE, S_U^T-KE, x)
min_e_sensor=NULL // variable for storing "best" positiv triggering sensor
min_e=-1 // variable for keeping minimal required amount of energy
for each ST ∈ S_U^T+KE do // loop through all alternatives
```

```
05     if ((min_e == −1 ∨ min_e > e(ST)))
06         then {min_e_sensor=ST; min_e=e(ST);}
07 if min_e==-1 then return(FALSE) // no positiv trigger available
08 else
09     trigger_value=v(min_e_sensor) // remember initial value
10     while TRUE do // start loop
11         wait x seconds
12         if (trigger_value <<>> v(ST)) ∧ (¬∃NST ∈ S_U^{T-KE}|v(NST)==TRUE)
13             MEASURE AND ANNOUNCE
14         trigger_value=v(min_e_sensor) // remember current value
15     done
```

The algorithm first selects the most energy efficient trigger *ST* (line 2 to 6). Afterwards, it starts looping and monitoring this sensor. If a change in the triggered sensor value is recognized (line 12) and no negative triggers are active, the context element is measured and notified (line 14). We can use Algorithm 1 for this, or resort to direct measurement. The authors of [25] have shown that an approach like this might reduce the energy consumption. However, we are not aware of any general framework or evaluation of sensor triggering approaches in the area of location (or even context).

6 Evaluation

We conducted a first evaluation of the trigger method in order to assess its potential to reduce the energy consumption for GPS positioning. In our evaluation, we analyzed energy consumption as well as the accuracy for the trigger method, a naïve polling method, and the suggested continuous positioning method of the Apple iOS 4 platform.

The evaluation system was implemented on the Apple iOS 4.3.1 platform, running on an Apple iPhone 3GS (cf. Figure 1). We conducted several walks with the smartphone on a predefined course with a length of 1.4km. The course contained two stops at traffic lights (between 1 and 2 minutes each) and two intentional periods of sitting (3 minutes each) on a park bench.

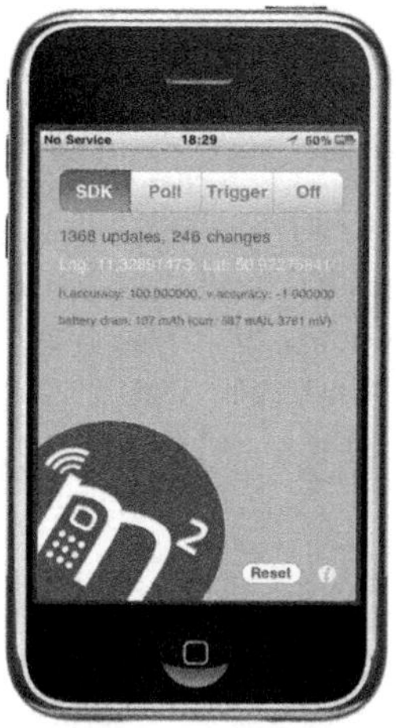

Fig. 1. SENST app on the Apple iPhone 3GS

Method: During these walks, the system acquired location data using one of these methods: (1) *Trigger*, the location request is triggered when a certain threshold value of the smartphone's accelerometer is reached (we experimentally determined this value so that the positioning is triggered every 10-20 steps during a normal walk), the system then waits for the first location with new coordinates and turns off until triggered again; (2) *Polling*, the location is requested periodically at a rate of 0.2Hz; (3) *SDK*, the location manager of the Apple iOS SDK was responsible for updating the location; and (4) *Off*, no GPS data was requested, but the display brightness settings, network and communication interfaces were configured in the same way as in the previous conditions. In order to minimise interference with alternative positioning methods of the iOS, the iPhone did not have a SIM card inserted and wireless LAN and Bluetooth were turned off in all conditions. Furthermore, we disregarded previously retrieved and cached location data.

In addition to the geographical location and GPS accuracy (horizontal and vertical), information about the iPhone's battery was logged as well. Using the device's internal registry of hardware components, we were able to read the remaining battery capacity $C_p(t)$ at a point in time t that was computed by the system's power management unit with an accuracy of 1mAh at a rate of 1Hz during all of the described conditions. The log was stored in the device's main memory until the walk was completed, and then transferred to the flash memory for later access during the analysis.

Results: In summary, our results indicate that a significant amount of energy can be preserved using the sensor trigger method introduced in this paper. However, the amount of coordinates collected during a defined period of time and the average accuracy across all coordinates is also lower compared to the Polling or SDK conditions.

Figure 2 illustrates the impact of the described methods on the iPhone's battery capacity. In Figure 2(a) we subtracted the remaining battery capacity at a time t from the baseline condition ("Off") in order to assess how much more energy the other methods draw: $\triangle C_{p_{\text{Trigger}\,|\text{Poll}\,|\text{SDK}}}(t) = C_{p_{\text{Off}}}(t) - C_{p_{\text{Trigger}\,|\text{Poll}\,|\text{SDK}}}(t)$. This normalized analysis indicates that the difference in power consumption of the SDK and polling methods grows linear over time, while the triggering method shows periods where the difference to the "Off" condition remains constant. These are the periods of time where no GPS positioning is requested.

Figure 2(b) shows that the triggering method still consumes more energy than the "Off" condition (because the GPS sensor is still used), although the other methods

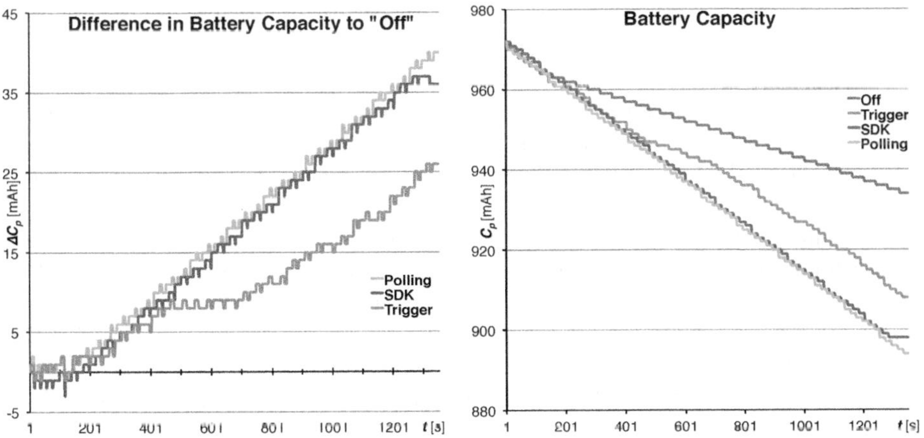

(a) (b)

Fig. 2. Energy evaluation charts

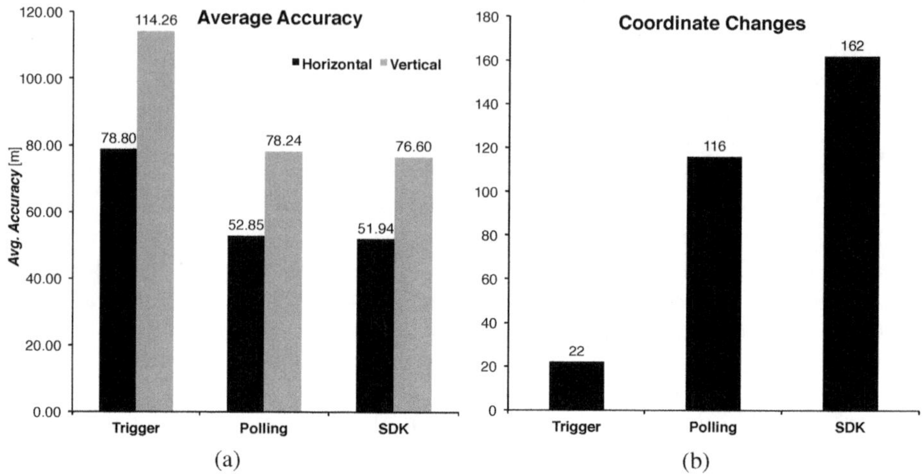

Fig. 3. Accuracy charts

require even more energy. The advantage in power consumption of the triggering method, compared to the SDK and polling conditions, grows over time.

Concerning the accuracy of the acquired geographical location data, the triggering method gathered a smaller amount of coordinates, and these coordinates also had a smaller horizontal and vertical accuracy. This can be explained with the fact that the accuracy increases with repeated requests, but in the triggering condition our system stopped inquiring location data after the first new location data was retrieved. The polling and SDK methods had the chance to repeatedly query the GPS system for new coordinates in a short period of time, which results in a smaller error.

As Figure 3(a) indicates, the average accuracy does not differ significantly between the polling and SDK conditions, but the trigger method performs worse. Figure 3(b) shows that the amount of coordinate changes is also greatly reduced by the triggering. The naïve polling method performs worse than the SDK method, probably due to the fact that the SDK method utilizes undocumented internal optimizations and adapts the polling frequency. The smaller amount of coordinate changes in the trigger condition shows that the method effectively influences the GPS positioning process and reduces the number of GPS requests.

All conditions allow a reconstruction of the walk route. In Figure 4, we have plotted the coordinates that were gathered using the different methods on a map. A red line between the coordinates illustrates the route, the green circles illustrate the accuracy (in meters) at the coordinate point. This visualization shows that the polling and SDK methods produce overlapping coordinates at several positions while the trigger method shows few overlaps and includes the most important turns, although the number of coordinates is rather small.

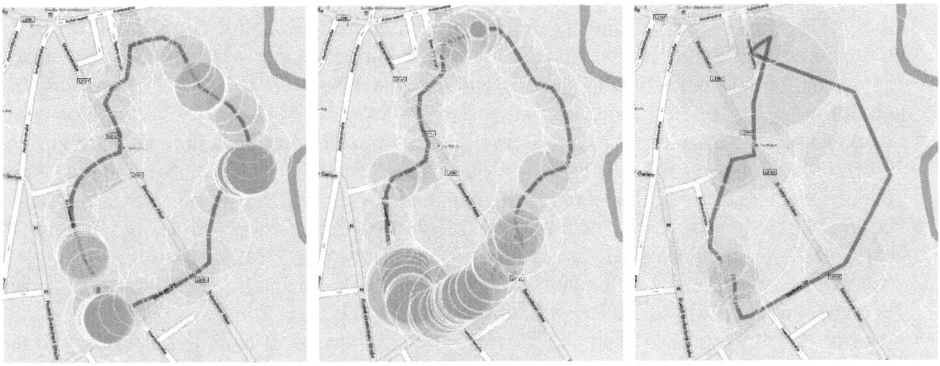

(a) Polling route. (b) SDK route. (c) Triggering route.

Fig. 4. Reconstructed routes

7 Summary, Conclusions, and Outlook

In this paper, we presented first ideas for energy-aware, smartphone-based context recognition. We have shown the importance of context-aware systems and addressed a novel direction within this research area. We suggest the use of sensors embedded into smartphones for the recognition of user contexts as such devices are widely spread and typically assigned to a particular user. Furthermore, the available APIs enable an easy access to the available sensors. We have shown that using these sensors requires additional energy and discussed approaches for reducing the energy consumption of their use. We introduced two concepts: sensor substitution and sensor triggering. In our evaluation, we have shown that an early prototypical implementation of the triggering method effectively reduces the energy consumption of GPS positioning.

We have used location as one example for a context element. However, both presented strategies aim to be or become generic approaches. However, we just started the research in this area and already pointed out certain future research directions in the paper. Hence, it is necessary to take a deeper look into the context recognition process as sensor measurements, context element determination, and context determination are interrelated and depend on each other. Furthermore, we will conduct research on the appropriateness of context element values while considering user requirements as well as application scenarios. Furthermore, we recognized a lack of support from existing context models regarding energy awareness. Besides the approaches discussed in this paper, we are currently working on sensor data measurement distribution strategies.

References

1. ABIresearch: Abiresearch mobile device user interfaces report. Website (September 2010), `http://www.abiresearch.com/research/1003813`
2. Azizyan, M., Constandache, I., Choudhury, R.R.: Surroundsense: Mobile phone localization via ambience fingerprinting. In: Proc. of the 15th Annual Int. Conference on Mobile Computing and Networking, pp. 261–272. ACM Press, New York (2009)

3. Barzilai, A.: Improving a Geophone to Produce an Affordable Broadband Seisometer. Ph.D. thesis, Department of Mechanical Engineeering, Stanford University (January 2000)
4. Baumgarten, U., Schmohl, R.: Context-aware computing: a survey preparing a generalized approach. Lecture Notes in Engineering and Computer Science, vol. 2168(1), pp. 744–750 (2008)
5. Beckmann, C., Schirmer, M., Paul-Stueve, T., Gross, T.: Sensation: Eine plattform zur entwicklung ubiquitärer umgebungen. In: Mensch & Computer - 7. Fachübergreifende Konferenz für interaktive und kooperative Medien, Oldenbourg, München, pp. 273–276 (2007)
6. Beigl, M., Gellersen, H.-W., Schmidt, A.: Mediacups: Experience with design and use of computer-augmented everyday artefacts. Computer Networks 35(4), 401–409 (2001)
7. Bolchini, C., Curino, C.A., Quintarelli, E., Schreiber, F.A., Tanca, L.: A data-oriented survey of context models. SIGMOD Record 36(4), 19–26 (2007)
8. Brown, P.J., Bovey, J.D., Chen, X.: Context-aware applications: from the laboratory to the marketplace. IEEE Pers. Comm. 4(5), 58–64 (1997), `http://www.cs.kent.ac.uk/pubs/1997/395`
9. Bulusu, N., Heidemann, J., Estrin, D.: Gps-less low cost outdoor localization for very small devices. IEEE Pers. Comm. 7(5), 28–34 (2000)
10. Bunse, C., Höpfner, H.: Resource substitution with components — optimizing energy consumption. In: Cordeiro, J., Shishkov, B., Ranchordas, A.K., Helfert, M. (eds.) Proc. of the 3rd Int. Conference on Software and Data Technologie, vol. SE/GSDCA/MUSE, pp. 28–35. INSTICC Press, Setúbal (2008)
11. Bunse, C., Höpfner, H., Roychoudhury, S., Mansour, E.: Energy efficient data sorting using standard sorting algorithms. In: Cordeiro, J., Ranchordas, A., Shishkov, B. (eds.) Software and Data Technologies. CCIS, vol. 50, pp. 247–260. Springer, Heidelberg (2011)
12. Carzaniga, A., Rosenblum, D.S., Wolf, A.L.: Design and evaluation of a wide-area event notification service. ACM Transactions on Computer Systems 19(3), 332–383 (2001)
13. Dey, A.K.: Understanding and using context. Pers. Ubiquitous Computing 5(1), 4–7 (2001)
14. Dey, A.K.: Providing Architectural Support for Building Context-Aware Applications. Ph.D. thesis, College of Computing, Georgia Institute of Technology (December 2000)
15. Fitzpatrick, G., Mansfield, T., Kaplan, S., Arnold, D., Phelps, T., Segall, B.: Augmenting the workaday world with elvin. In: Proc. of the Sixth European Conference on Computer-Supported Cooperative Work, pp. 431–450. Kluwer Academic Publishers, Dordrecht (1999)
16. Garin, L.J., Chansarkar, M.M., Miocinovic, S., Norman, C., Hilgenberg, D.: Wireless assisted gps-sirf architecture and field test results. In: Proc. of the 12th Int. Technical Meeting of the Satellite Division of The Institute of Navigation, pp. 489–498. The Institute of Navigation, Inc, Manassas (1999)
17. Gross, T., Prinz, W.: Awareness in context: A lightweight approach. In: Proc. of the 8th European Conference on Computer-Supported Cooperative Work, pp. 295–314. Kluwer Academic Publishers, Dordrecht (2003)
18. Honan, M.: iphone credit card reader lets you accept plastic anywhere. Website (Februar 2010), `http://www.wired.com/reviews/2010/02/pr_square_iphone`
19. Höpfner, H., Bunse, C.: Towards an energy-consumption based complexity classification for resource substitution strategies. In: Proc. of the 22. Workshop on Foundations of Databases. CEUR Workshop Proceeding, CEUR-WS.org, vol. 581 (May 2010), `http://ceur-ws.org/Vol-581/`
20. Jevtic, S., Kotowsky, M., Dick, R.P., Dinda, P.A., Dowding, C.: Lucid dreaming: Reliable analog event detection for energy-constrained applications. In: Proc. of the 6th Int. Conference on Information Processing in Sensor Networks, pp. 350–359. ACM Press, New York (2007)
21. Kansal, A., Zhao, F.: Fine-grained energy profiling for power-aware application design. ACM SIGMETRICS Performance Evaluation Review 36(2), 26–31 (2008)

22. Kenny, T.: Sensor Fundamentals. In: Wilson, J.S. (ed.) Sensor Technology Handbook, Newnes, ch. 1 (December 2004)
23. Lieberman, H., Selker, T.: Out of context: Computer systems that adapt to, and learn from, context. IBM Systems Journal 39(3&4), 617–632 (2000)
24. Lin, K., Kansal, A., Lymberopoulos, D., Zhao, F.: Energy-accuracy trade-off for continuous mobile device location. In: Proc. of the 8th Int. Conference on Mobile Systems, Applications, and Services, pp. 285–297. ACM Press, New York (2010)
25. Mohan, P., Padmanabhan, V.N., Ramjee, R.: Nericell: Rich monitoring of road and traffic conditions using mobile smartphones. In: Proc. of the 6th ACM Conference on Embedded Network Sensor Systems, pp. 323–336. ACM Press, New York (2008)
26. Nicholson, A.J., Noble, B.D.: Breadcrumbs: Forecasting mobile connectivity. In: Proc. of the 14th ACM Int. Conf. on Mobile Computing and Networking, pp. 46–57. ACM Press, New York (2008)
27. Pietzuch, P.R., Bacon, J.: Hermes: A distributed event-based middleware architecture. In: Proc. of the 22nd Int. Conference on Distributed Computing Systems, pp. 611–618. IEEE Computer Society, Los Alamitos (2002)
28. Rittenbruch, M.: Atmosphere: A framework for contextual awareness. Int. Journal of Human-Computer Interaction 14(2), 159–180 (2002)
29. Roos, T., Myllymäku, P., Tirri, H., Misikangas, P., Sievänen, J.: A probabilistic approach to wlan user location estimation. Int. Jrnl. Wireless Information Networks 9(3), 155–164 (2002)
30. Schilit, B.N., Adams, N., Want, R.: Context-aware computing applications. In: Proc. of the 1st IEEE Workshop on Mobile Computing Systems and Applications, pp. 85–90. IEEE Computer Society, Los Alamitos (1994), `http://citeseer.nj.nec.com/schilit94contextaware.html`
31. Schmidt, A., Beigl, M., Gellersen, H.-W.: There is more to context than location. Elsevier Computer & Graphics Journal 23(6) (December 1999)
32. Schmidt, A., Laerhoven, K.V.: How to build smart appliances? IEEE Pers. Comm. 8(4), 66–71 (2001)
33. Segal, B., Arnold, D.: Elvin has left the building: A publish/subscriber notification service with quenching. In: Proc. of the 1997 Australian Open Systems Users Group Conference – AUUG (1997)
34. Seydim, A.Y., Dunham, M.H., Kumar, V.: Location-Dependent Query Processing. In: Proc. of the 2nd ACM Int. Workshop on Data Engineering for Wireless and Mobile Access, pp. 47–53. ACM Press, New York (2001)
35. Siewiorek, D., Smailagic, A., Furukawa, J., Moraveji, N., Reiger, K., Shaffer, J.: Sensay: A context-aware mobile phone. In: Proc. of the 7th IEEE Int. Symposium on Wearable Computers, pp. 248–257. IEEE Computer Society, Los Alamitos (2003)
36. Veijalainen, J., Ojanen, E., Haq, M.A., Vahteala, V.-P., Matsumoto, M.: Energy Consumption Tradeoffs for Compressed Wireless Data at a Mobile Terminal. IEICE Transactions on Communications E87-B(5), 1123–1130 (2004)
37. Ye, Z., Chen, X., Li, Z.: Video based mobile location search with large set of sift points in cloud. In: Proc. of the 2010 Multimedia Workshop on Mobile Cloud Media Computing, pp. 25–30. ACM Press, New York (2010)

Distributed Spatial Reasoning for Wireless Sensor Networks*

Hedda R. Schmidtke and Michael Beigl

Pervasive Computing Systems, TecO,
Vincenz-Priessnitz-Strasse 3, 76131 Karlsruhe, Germany
{hedda.schmidtke,michael.beigl}@kit.edu
http://www.teco.edu

Abstract. Location-aware systems are mobile or spatially distributed computing systems, such as smart phones or sensor nodes in wireless sensor networks, enabled to react flexibly to changing environments. Due to severe restrictions of computational power on these platforms and real-time demands, most current solutions do not support advanced spatial reasoning. Qualitative Spatial Reasoning (QSR) and granularity are two mechanisms that have been suggested in order to make reasoning about spatial environments tractable. We propose an approach for combining these two techniques, so as to obtain a light-weight QSR mechanism, called *partial order QSR* (for brevity: PQSR), that is fast enough to allow application on small, low-cost computing devices. The key idea of PQSR is to use a core fragment of typical QSR relations, which can be expressed with partial orders and their linearizations, and to additionally delimit reasoning about these relations with a size-based granularity mechanism.

Keywords: Partial order reasoning, contextual reasoning, qualitative spatial reasoning, context-aware computing, distributed reasoning.

1 Introduction

Relational reasoning about parameters of context, such as location, time, agents, objects, events and conditions in an environment [19] can have a high complexity. However, efficient methods for handling the parameter of location have been studied extensively in the area of Qualitative Spatial Reasoning (QSR). QSR has been proposed to allow efficient reasoning about spatial relations [5], e.g. for autonomous mobile robots.

Two classes of relation systems have received particular attention: directional relation systems, which regard cardinal direction relations, such as *north-of*, or relative direction relations, such as *left-of*, and mereotopological relation systems, which describe relations of spatial containment or *spatial part-of* and *overlap*. The classical model for cardinal direction relations [13,8], which is appropriate with respect to a broad range of application scenarios, interprets the directional

* This research was partially supported by the Deutsche Forschungsgemeinschaft (DFG) in the project *SenseCast* (BE4319/1).

M. Beigl et al. (Eds.): CONTEXT 2011, LNAI 6967, pp. 264–277, 2011.

relations in terms of points in an absolute coordinate system. When we combine directional and mereological reasoning however, the spatial entities under consideration have to be regions, since points are spatial entities that do not have parts. Two types of combined calculi have been suggested to address this problem: several calculi [11,8,10] distinguish between an inner region within which mereotopological reasoning takes place, and an outer region within which directional relations are resolved; another approach [15,4] is to generalize directional relations to apply to extended regions by detailing possible types of directional relations between parts. The second variant has been argued [15] to have higher expressive power, but also comes at the cost of lower inferential power.

The aim of this paper is to explore how far the limitations of expressive power in a variant of the classical, light-weight approaches [11,8,13] can be extended without sacrificing inferential power. We discuss the proposed calculus with a focus on applications in the area of *location-aware systems*: computationally restricted devices with sensors – such as *smart phones* or *sensor nodes* in wireless sensor networks – that can adapt their functions to dynamically changing spatial conditions. In order to realize intelligent location-aware systems, an expressive, flexible, and particularly light-weight representation of spatial knowledge is required. Current location-aware systems can react to a known location but cannot yet process spatial relations [3].

We show that a variant of the classical, light-weight QSR approach can be a building block for relational reasoning in this application domain, and we illustrate our claim with a simple example of a distributed mechanism for sending notifications about traffic conditions *along a certain direction* and *within a certain region around a landmark* on a highway. This scenario is prototypical for a location-aware system insofar as it employs a typical mixture of coordinate information and spatial containment information to trigger an application. However, our scenario is novel as it involves processing and distribution of relational spatial information.

The classical model [13,8] for cardinal direction relations, which interprets the directional relations in terms of relations between points in an absolute coordinate system, is sufficient for such scenarios: a broad range of location measurement technologies, such as GPS, yield a coordinate with a certain fixed accuracy. As we want to also include mereological relations however, we require a model, such as [8], that explains how to link regions and point coordinate abstractions. The choice of this operation has far-reaching implications for the appropriateness with respect to common sense and the interpretability, and thus usefulness, of inferences obtained from the reasoning system as a whole.

We use a solution that is based on concepts of size-based granularity [20]. Granularity was introduced [12] as a means to organize and cluster knowledge into manageable portions that can then be handled efficiently. Spatial granularity has been applied successfully as a means to model and resolve inconsistencies between different representations, e.g. for ontology integration [7], and has also been shown to be useful in the representation of vague concepts [18].

The resulting relation system, *partial order QSR* (for brevity: PQSR), consists of mereological and directional partial ordering relations together with granularity and uncertainty relations. We explore the expressiveness of two particular relation systems that are able to distinguish 54 and 704 classes of spatial relations, respectively. The corresponding inferential method is similarly efficient as the bipath-consistency method [9], in which relations are also computed separately, and yields a light-weight yet expressive reasoning framework.

The main part of this paper is organized into three sections. The first section discusses partial ordering relations, linear ordering relations, and size-based granularity as forming the core of efficient qualitative spatial reasoning. In the second section, we present the directional and mereological relations in the relation system R54 and the additional granularity relations that yield the relation system R704. In the third section, we evaluate our approach with respect to inferential properties and expressive power, and discuss implications for time and space complexity in a distributed application scenario. In the conclusions, we discuss how the proposed approach can be generalized to other parameters of context.

2 Ordering Relations and Granularity

The general idea of our PQSR approach is to use a core of partial order relations to efficiently store and reason about spatial relationships. We introduce two sets of core relations: partial orders and their linearizations provide the basic reasoning power, and granularity and indistinguishability extend this set with additional expressiveness for modeling uncertainty and for filtering out irrelevant details.

2.1 Partial Orders and Linearizations

A partial order P is a relation that has the properties of antisymmetry (A1) and transitivity (A2). It is called *strict* if it is asymmetric (A3).

$$\forall x, y : P(x, y) \wedge P(y, x) \rightarrow x = y \quad \text{(A1)}$$

$$\forall x, y, z : P(x, y) \wedge P(y, z) \rightarrow P(x, z) \quad \text{(A2)}$$

$$\forall x, y : P^s(x, y) \rightarrow \neg P^s(y, x) \quad \text{(A3)}$$

An example of a partial order is is the mereological *part-of* relation, which we denote as M_P.[1] The axiom (A1) for M_P reads: if x is part of y and y is part of x, then x and y are identical. Axiom (A1) for M_P reads: if x is part of y and y is part of z, then x is part of z. Another example is the cardinal direction relation *directly to the north-of* N_P^S, which is intuitively a strict relation: a city is not to the north of itself. However, for the purposes of this paper, we consider the non-strict variant of this relation N_P.

[1] The subscript P indicates a relation for which the axioms (A1) and (A2) hold.

We call a relation L *linearization* of a partial order P, if and only if L is a transitive (A5), linear (A4) relation that contains P (A6):

$$\forall x, y : L(x, y) \vee L(y, x) \tag{A4}$$

$$\forall x, y, z : L(x, y) \wedge L(y, z) \rightarrow L(x, z) \tag{A5}$$

$$\forall x, y : P(x, y) \rightarrow L(x, y) \tag{A6}$$

$$\forall x, y : L(x, y) \wedge L(y, x) \rightarrow \forall z : (L(x, z) \leftrightarrow L(y, z)) \wedge (L(z, x) \leftrightarrow L(z, y)) \tag{1}$$

$$Q(x, y) \Leftrightarrow L(x, y) \wedge L(y, x) \tag{D1}$$

By transitivity, such a relation orders its elements in a consistent way (1). We further define a relation Q (D1) that identifies the equivalence classes generated by L. Many relations that have been used for QSR are (strict) partial orders that have meaningful linearizations. In particular, we study in this article the mereological *part-of* M_P between spatial regions with its linearization *smaller-than* M_L and the cardinal direction relations *north-of* N_L and *east-of* E_L as linearizations of corresponding underlying partial order relations N_P and E_P.

We generally use the following notation: with respect to a given partial order X_P, we indicate a relation for which the axioms (A5)-(A6) hold as X_L. Therefore the linearization *smaller-than* of M_P is written as M_L. The equivalence relation that is defined (D1) from a linearization is indicated with the subscript Q. For M_L (*smaller-than*) for instance, we thus obtain M_Q (*same-size as*).

For any relation X we indicate the inverse relation as iX (D2), i.e.: *south-of* as iN_L and *west-of* as iE_L.

$$\forall x, y : iX(x, y) \Leftrightarrow X(y, x) \tag{D2}$$

We can compute a generic composition table for a partial order P, its linearization L, and their inverses iP and iL as shown in table 1. Note that $=$ implies P, and that P implies L (A6). The relation system therefore is not mutually exclusive. However, the system is jointly exhaustive, since L is a total relation (A4). Table 1 shows that inference yields either a single resulting relation or no information (*any*). We call this property *uniqueness*. All informative entries can be proved by transitivity (A2,A5). Uniqueness is an important property

Table 1. Composition table for a partial order P, its linearization L, and their inverses iP and iL. The entry *any* indicates a situation, in which no information can be inferred.

	P	$=$	iP	L	Q	iL
P	P	P	any	L	L	any
$=$	P	$=$	iP	L	Q	iL
iP	any	iP	iP	any	iL	iL
L	L	L	any	L	L	any
Q	L	Q	iL	L	Q	iL
iL	any	iL	iL	any	iL	iL

insofar as it always gives us a unique answer to any query that can be answered at all. However, it is obvious that composition tables having this property can be generated for any set of relations if mutual exclusiveness is not required.

2.2 Size-Based Granularity

Size-based granularity is a representational mechanism that can be used to handle differences in sizes and to model uncertainty. We follow the axiomatic characterization of [18], which describes granularity based on context regions with a restricted grain-size. Granularity here is determined by the concept of the grain-size for a context region: parts of an object that are smaller than the grain-size can be disregarded as unimportant details; objects beyond the range of the context region are not in the focus of current considerations. We generalize the approach [18] in two ways: we intend the axiomatization to apply to arbitrary partial order relations, not only to the mereological part-of relation; and we allow any region to serve as a context region and impose no further restrictions. As above, we use P as a placeholder for a partial order relation, and L, for a corresponding linearization.

The relation of being a *grain region relative to a context region* is characterized using a relation G, with $G(x, y)$ denoting that x is a *grain* of the *context region* y. *Coarsening* then is an operation of changing from a context region c_1 to a larger region c_2 containing c_1, with the grains of c_2 also being larger than the grains of c_1. Axiom A7 formally characterizes this property: grains are ordered by size (Q) in the same way as their respective context regions and vice versa. All regions can serve as grains and context regions (A8), and all parts of a region c that have the same size as a grain of c are also grains of c (A9). The last axiom (A10) states that the grains of a context are proper parts of the context.

$$\forall c_1, c_2, g_1, g_2 : G(g_1, c_1) \wedge G(g_2, c_2) \rightarrow [Q(c_1, c_2) \leftrightarrow Q(g_1, g_2)] \qquad \text{(A7)}$$

$$\forall x \exists c, g : G(g, x) \wedge G(x, c) \qquad \text{(A8)}$$

$$\forall c, x : P(x, c) \wedge G(g, c) \wedge Q(x, g) \rightarrow G(x, c) \qquad \text{(A9)}$$

$$\forall c, g : G(g, c) \rightarrow P(g, c) \wedge g \neq c \qquad \text{(A10)}$$

This concept of granularity allows us to reason about levels of granularity based on any partial order P and linearization L. Intuitively, the level of granularity of a context can then be understood as the interval of sizes between the size of the context region and that of its grains. The advantage of this notion is that it neither imposes a partitioning of the underlying domain of regions nor of the derived domain of sizes.[2] Two regions can then be compared with respect to the layers of granularity for which they are context regions:

---

[2] Cf. [18] for a more detailed discussion of size-based granularity and its implications in comparison to partitioning approaches, and [17] for a discussion of its plausibility as a cognitive concept.

$$F(x,y) \Leftrightarrow \exists g : G(g,y) \wedge L(x,g) \tag{D3}$$

$$I(x,y) \Leftrightarrow (\exists g : G(g,y) \wedge L(g,x) \wedge L(x,y)) \vee (\exists g : G(g,x) \wedge L(g,y) \wedge L(y,x)) \tag{D4}$$

$$\forall x,y : [F(x,y) \rightarrow L(x,y)] \tag{2}$$

$$\forall x,y : F(x,y) \vee I(x,y) \vee F(y,x) \tag{3}$$

$$R(x,y) \Leftrightarrow I(x,y) \vee L(x,y) \tag{D5}$$

We call a region x *finer* than a region y, if y has a grain that is larger than x (D3). Two regions are *indistinguishable*, if one is smaller than the other, but not smaller than a grain of the other region (D4). We obtain by the transitivity of L, that L contains F (2) and that F, iF, and I together are jointly exhaustive. In order to obtain a composition table with the uniqueness property, we add relations R (D5) and iR for expressing the disjunction $I \vee L$ and its inverse $I \vee iL$ (table 2). As the table shows, the relations R, I, and iR introduce a high degree of uncertainty into the reasoning system.

Table 2. Composition table for F, L, and I extended with a relation R (indistingushable or smaller) yields a table having the uniqueness property

	F	L	R	I	iR	iL	iF
F	F	F	L	L	any	any	any
L	F	L	R	R	any	any	any
R	L	R	any	any	any	any	any
I	L	R	any	any	any	iR	iL
iR	any	any	any	any	any	iR	iL
iL	any	any	any	iR	iR	iL	iF
iF	any	any	any	iL	iL	iF	iF

Given any two relations X_P and X_Q, we indicate a relation that fulfills (A7)-(A10) by X_G and we can derive relations X_F, X_I, and X_R using (D3), (D4), and (D5), respectively.

3 Directional and Mereological Relations

We now illustrate more closely, how directional and mereological reasoning can be interpreted as partial order reasoning and derive two relation systems R54, containing 54 directional and mereological relations, and R704, a relation system extended with additional granularity relations. A detailed discussion of a possible model, however, is beyond the scope of this paper and can be found in [20].

3.1 Directional Reasoning

Local inference about eight cardinal directions (*north*, *northeast*, *east*, etc) in the so-called *projection-based* relation system [8] can be generated [13] from combinations of two independent strict linear ordering relations (*more-to-the-north-than* and *more-to-the-east-than*) together with their two inverses and two additional equivalence relations (*same-wrt-north-south* and *same-wrt-east-west*).

We can understand the projection-based relation system as spanned by two partial orders *directly to the north of* (N_P) and *directly to the east of* (E_P), reflecting the orderings on north-south-axes and east-west-axes. These relations are not linear orders, since two points that do not lie on the same north-south-axis, for instance, are not ordered by the *north*-relation.

We can obtain the relations of the Ligozat calculus as the corresponding linearization relations (*more-to-the-north-than* N_L and *more-to-the-east-than* E_L) that compare points that do not necessarily lie on the same axis. We can then restrict the discussion to the relations N_L and E_L and the nine cardinal direction relations that can be defined as combinations of one of the three relations N_L, iN_L, N_Q with one of the three relations E_L, iE_L, E_Q, such as

$$\text{exact North: } N_L E_Q(x,y) \Leftrightarrow N_L(x,y) \wedge E_Q(x,y)$$
$$\text{Northeast: } N_L E_L(x,y) \Leftrightarrow N_L(x,y) \wedge E_L(x,y)$$
$$\text{Northwest: } N_L iE_L(x,y) \Leftrightarrow N_L(x,y) \wedge iE_L(x,y).$$

The composition table for these relations can directly be derived from table 1. Like the relation system of table 1, the resulting relation system is not mutually exclusive, relations overlap for boundary cases, but it is jointly exhaustive. The combined composition table retains the uniqueness property in the following sense: it contains precise entries, entries that are precise for one direction and non-informative for the other, and completely non-informative entries.

For the directional relations, the granularity relations derivable from the basic size relations N_L, E_L, and inverses, represent distances into the respective directions. The statement $N_F(x,y)$ could be read as x is distinguishably to the north of y; $N_I(x,y)$, as x is indistinguishable with respect to the north direction from y.

The notions of granularity and uncertainty in the case of directional relations can be identified with a positional uncertainty ϵ of a given type of location device [20]. An interpretation of $G(g,c)$ for N_F and N_I can then be derived: a region r_1 is minimally to the north of a region r_2, iff it is exactly ϵ measurement units to the north. The relation N_F expresses that the distance towards the north is at least ϵ measurement units, whereas N_I represents a case in which the distance is no more than ϵ measurement units. All relations taken together, we obtain a sum of eight relations along the north-south axis (N_L, N_Q, N_F, N_R, N_I, iN_L, iN_F, iN_R) and another eight relations along the east-west axis (E_L, E_Q, E_F, E_R, E_I, iE_L, iE_F, iE_R). Note that the parameter ϵ is a fixed parameter of the model, e.g. representing the accuracy of a certain type of positioning device. We can model multiple positioning devices using multiple sets of granularity relations.

3.2 Mereological Reasoning

A mereological *part-of* relation M_P can be used to reason about spatial regions, that is, spatially extended objects. This fundamental relation is widely used in

QSR, e.g. in [14]. It is obvious that *part-of* is a partial order. A meaningful relation M_L that is a linearization for *part-of* is the comparison of sizes. Axiom A6 then reads: if x is a part of y, then x is smaller than y. The size of a region can be interpreted as maximal extension [16], geometrically, for instance, the radius of the smallest disc enclosing a region: M_L orders two regions according to the radius of the smallest discs containing the regions. The notions of granularity and uncertainty in the case of mereological relations can be interpreted as in the models of [18,20]: the grains of a region are parts whose size is below a certain percentage of the whole.

As we view mereological reasoning and directional reasoning as independent types of reasoning, the connection between the relations does not have to be specified for the purpose of reasoning, and accordingly inference can be carried out in separate steps using three relatively small composition tables. For instance, we would infer (figure 1 and figure 2, respectively):

$$M_P N_L E_L(a,b) \wedge M_P N_Q E_L(b,c) \Rightarrow M_P N_L E_L(a,c), \tag{4}$$

$$M_P N_L E_L(a,b) \wedge M_Q N_L E_L(b,c) \Rightarrow M_L N_L E_L(a,c) \tag{5}$$

Although however reasoning is resolved in this simple manner, the combined relations considerably expand the range of spatial situations expressible with the relation system.

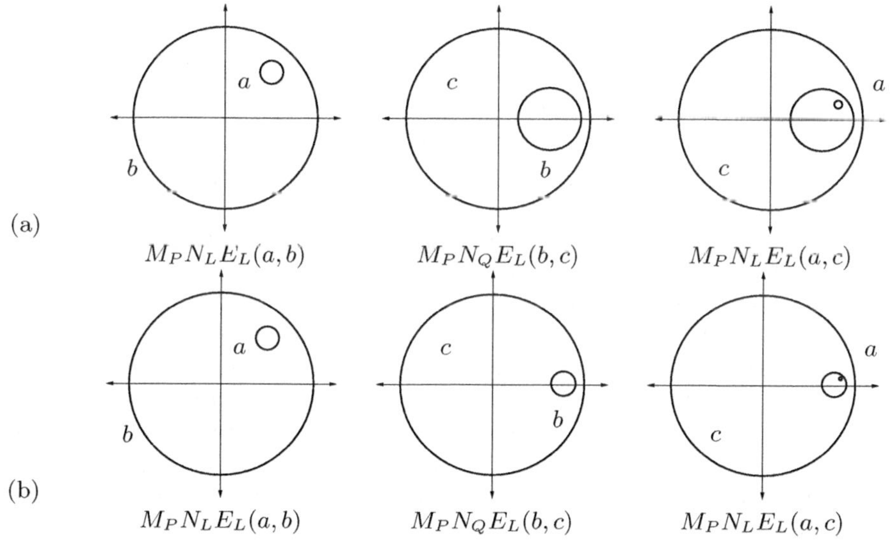

Fig. 1. Two interpretations of the inference scheme (4)

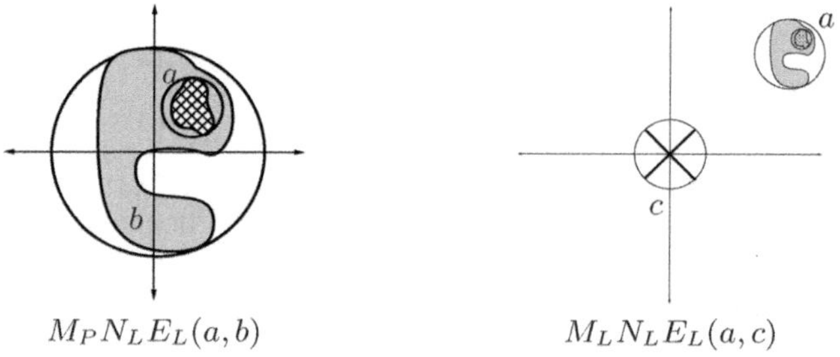

Fig. 2. Inference about sizes and directions (5)

4 Evaluation

In this section, we evaluate our approach concerning expressiveness and inferential properties, and we discuss implementation for distributed reasoning with respect to an application scenario.

4.1 Expressiveness and Inferential Properties

The directional component of the relation system, that is, the compound relations consisting of combinations of N_L, N_Q, iN_L with E_L, E_Q, iE_L can be compared with the composition tables in [8,13]. We translate four prototypical cases of composition table entries of [8] into PQSR.

$$N_L E_Q(x,y) \wedge N_Q E_L(y,z) \Rightarrow N_L E_L(x,z) \quad (6)$$
$$N_L E_Q(x,y) \wedge iN_L E_Q(y,z) \Rightarrow E_Q(x,z) \quad (7)$$
$$N_L E_L(x,y) \wedge N_L iE_L(y,z) \Rightarrow N_L(x,z) \quad (8)$$
$$N_L E_L(x,y) \wedge N_Q E_L(y,z) \Rightarrow N_L E_L(x,z). \quad (9)$$

It is obvious, that all four inferences follow from table 1. This illustrates that our composition table corresponds to that of [8,13].

For the mereological relation system, we have 6 (M_P, $M_=$, iM_P, M_L, M_Q, iM_L) or 11 (adding M_F, M_R, M_I, iM_R, iM_F) relations, respectively; and for the directional relation system, 9 (combinations of N_L, N_Q, iN_L with E_L, E_Q, iE_L) and 64 relations (adding N_F, N_R, N_I, iN_F, iN_R and corresponding E-relations). Inference in PQSR works by lookup in three tables instead of by lookup in one complete table, so as to reduce space requirements. The complete relation system of combined relations $M_x N_y E_z$ contains $6 * 3 * 3 = 54$ relations without uncertainty relations (called R54 in the following), and $11 * 8 * 8 = 704$ relations with uncertainty relations (called R704). By carrying out the lookup procedure in three steps, space requirements can be reduced considerably: for R54 a $6 * 6$-table is sufficient, for R704, a table containing all $11 * 11$ basic relations can be used, and further compressions would be possible. The full composition tables, in contrast, would contain $2,916$ (R54) and $495,616$ entries (R704), respectively.

When we study the properties of entries, we can see that there are 8 entries for which no information can be inferred in table 1 and 15 additional entries (not counting those of L and iL, which are already included in table 1) in table 2 for uncertainty relations. The composition table spanned by the six M-relations without uncertainty thus contains 8 non-informative and 28 precise entries, whereas the extended set of 11 M-relations contains 77 non-informative entries (non-informative entries for M_P, $M_=$, iM_P and additional $25 * 3$ non-informative entries in combination with the five uncertainty relations) and 44 precise entries. For the N-relations, we get 2 non-informative out of of 9 entries without uncertainty, and 25 non-informative out of 64 entries with uncertainty; and likewise for the E-relations.

As every individual lookup for the three components of a combined relation has the uniqueness property, that is, either a single entry is inferred or there is no information at all, we obtain that the combined composition table retains a weakened uniqueness property in the following sense: it contains a) precise entries, b) entries that are precise for some components but non-informative for others, and c) completely non-informative entries. The complete table for R54 has 1,372 (47%) entries of category (a), 1,515 (52%) for (b), and 32 (1%) for (c). For R704, we obtain 66,924 (13%) entries for (a), 280,467 (57%) for (b), and 148,225 (30%) for (c).

PQRS R54 is a powerful inference mechanism with a table of 99% informative entries. For the extended set of relations R704, these results do not carry over. However, the considerably increased expressive power of R704 and the fact that it can be used to express restrictions with respect to context and granularity, make it an ideal tool for pre-filtering information before reasoning, so as to further speed up R54. Furthermore, the modeling of uncertainty allows expressing context quality, an important aspect in location-aware computing [2].

4.2 Application Scenario: Location-Awareness

Location-awareness has been an important research topic in the field of Ubiquitous and Pervasive Computing for a decade [1]. Location-aware systems are computing systems that are designed to adapt their behavior to their spatial surroundings. E.g. in wireless sensor networks, location-awareness is a key property for self-organization and location-based routing. Typically the devices used in these settings are small sensor nodes with only about 1-128k of RAM (used for volatile data), about 5-256k of ROM (used for program and constant data) and 1-100 MIPS of computing power. This is a very ambitious setting for reasoning systems and requires us to minimize resource consumption especially regarding RAM and ROM. However, first experiments [6] indicate that partial order reasoning is feasible on this platform.

We can illustrate the gain in efficiency and robustness with respect to an example that is similar to the non-spatial reasoning implemented in [6]. The description of the example is simplified in terms of technical operation, and focuses on selected reasoning aspects. Consider a row of cars traveling along a highway. A typical scenario used in research in car-to-car communication is the road condition or road block example.

Figure 3 shows a car a moving towards the north, and a road block – e.g. an accident – before exit $N38$ in terms of the driving direction. In the example, car a detects the road block and communicates this information to all other cars "behind" it. We can show now how this task can be implemented using PQSR. The distributed implementation does not depend on the complexity of the setting, e.g. the number of cars on the road or on the availability of a central service.

In our example, cars are equipped with rather simple relative positioning techniques using peer-to-peer ultrasound measurement between cars, acceleration sensors, a processing unit and wireless communication between cars. Using this sensor system, we can determine if cars are directly aligned to each other, i.e. driving in the same direction on the same road. Detection of alignment is even possible if roads are multi-lane. All cars that are aligned share the highway as a common reference system, even if far away cars might not be aligned directly with respect to measurement from a car several hundred meters in front or back. This ensures that their cardinal direction relations are consistent with each other, so that the axioms for N_L or E_L are fulfilled.

Exits are global landmarks along a highway, and their numbering can be used to generate a directional linear ordering on which to base a granularity representation. The cars then use two directional measurement systems and accordingly two sets of granularity systems can be employed: indistinguishability N_{I1} in the first granularity system depends on the accuracy of the sensor system, whereas it depends on the ordering of exits in the second case (N_{I2}).

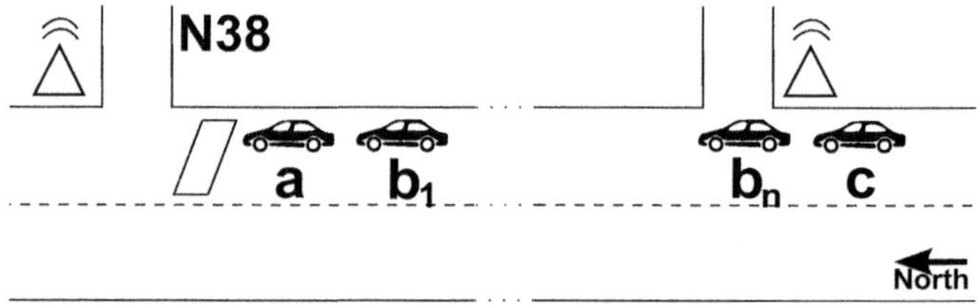

Fig. 3. Sending a notification along the highway: the driver of car c is informed about the road block detected by a via cars b_1 to b_n and can thus avoid the obstructed path

Using the PQSR mechanism, cars can infer their relative position and communicate information along the highway. Consider the example of a car a moving towards the north, encountering a road block before exit N38. This car could send this information to cars and other participants in the network "behind" it. To implement this as a distributed mechanism, we send the information to cars x that fulfill $iN_L(x, a)$. The following packet would convey all necessary information:

from: aID
via: none
to x**:** $iN_L(x, \text{aID})$ in context $iN_{I2}(x, \text{exitN38})$
do: forward, warning: road block

A car b_1 that receives the packet, first finds out whether it is a proper recipient (**to** x**:**): b_1 first checks the contextual condition $iN_{I2}(b_1, \text{exitN38})$, that is, whether it is close enough to *exitN38*. As noted above, we use the contextual conditions expressible in R704 for pre-filtering, not for reasoning. Only if the condition is a known fact, b_1 starts to check whether $iN_L(b_1, a)$ holds using R54 reasoning and then executes the applications *forward* and *warning*. Application *forward* broadcasts the message again but with a modified via-field: it needs to indicate that b_1 sent the message and what its relation to the original sender was, e.g. by specifying additionally:

via: b1ID, $iN_L(\text{b1ID}, \text{aID})$.

A car c that receives the packet from a car b_n, but does not have a direct connection to a, can then infer whether it is a recipient or not by checking whether $iN_L(c, a)$. By measurement, c knows its relation to cars in its immediate vicinity, that is, it knows whether $iN_L(c, b_n)$. From $iN_L(c, b_n)$ and $iN_L(b_n, a)$ (the via-statement) follows $iN_L(c, a)$; and c again warns and forwards the information (replacing the via-part), otherwise it ignores it. In this way, information can be broadcast along the highway, until cars are met that lie outside the context of *exitN38*.

The example illustrates how inference in PQSR can be automatically distributed over a range of interested sensor nodes in a network. Each node only needs to reason about nodes in its direct vicinity and about local landmarks. The local model consist only of local nodes, the remote original sender, and landmarks. In clear contrast to a centralized location model, e.g. with geo-information services, the computational effort for finding recipients is restricted to, and distributed among, participating nodes. The effort for each node in every step consists of a) establishing a fact base of knowledge from current measurement and received packets, b) filtering for relevant objects using R704 relations, c) removing non-R54 information and performing R54 reasoning to determine locations, and d) triggering services. The fact base established in (a) regards mainly local information: as the message is forwarded from a to c, each node needs to consider only the sender a and nodes within its direct communication range. Global information comes in only with the landmark in the contextual condition in our example scenario. Information about remote landmarks is removed in the filtering step (b). Thus, the complexity of reasoning for each sensor node is physically restricted by a constant maximally possible number of nodes in its proximity. The amount of lookups in (c) is therefore determined solely by the length of the transmitted descriptions, but independent of the amount of cars and other participants of the network that are not within the restricted context.

5 Conclusions

We presented PQSR, a light-weight QSR approach for mereological and directional reasoning. PQSR was designed as a QSR mechanism for location-awareness in WSN applications. It is tailored to be efficiently applicable on sensor nodes with restricted computational power. For fast inference, PQSR combines partial order reasoning and granularity-dependent inference. In PQSR, size and distance are represented qualitatively with relation systems of size-based granularity. The combined relation system is highly expressive, distinguishing 704 relations, and has an inferentially powerful fragment (R54) with a composition table containing 99% informative entries.

We illustrated the benefits of the overall system with an integrating application scenario of reasoning for location-awareness in a car-to-car navigation scenario. We showed that reasoning in PQSR can be performed in a manner exploiting the spatial distribution of sensor networks for spatial reasoning.

Partial ordering relations have been argued to play a key role for context-aware computing systems [19]. The reasoning mechanism we proposed can be easily extended to cover not only spatial relations but the whole range of partial order relations described in [19], including temporal relations, the sub-class relation, and set-containment relations.

References

1. Beigl, M., Gray, P., Salber, D. (eds.): Workshop on Location Modeling for Ubiquitous Computing (2001), `http://www.teco.edu/locationws/`
2. Berchtold, M., Riedel, T., Decker, C., Beigl, M., Bittel, C.: Quality of location: estimation, system integration and application. In: INSS. IEEE, Los Alamitos (2008)
3. Choudhury, T., Quigley, A.J., Strang, T., Suginuma, K. (eds.): LoCA 2009. LNCS, vol. 5561. Springer, Heidelberg (2009)
4. Clementini, E., Billen, R.: Modeling and computing ternary projective relations between regions. IEEE Transactions on Knowledge and Data Engineering 18(6), 799–814 (2006)
5. Cohn, A.G., Hazarika, S.M.: Qualitative spatial representation and reasoning: An overview. Fundamenta Informaticae 46(1-2), 1–29 (2001)
6. Ding, Y., Laue, F., Schmidtke, H.R., Beigl, M.: Sensing spaces: Light-weight monitoring of industrial facilities. In: 5th Workshop on Behaviour Monitoring and Interpretation (2010)
7. Euzenat, J.: Granularity in relational formalisms - with application to time and space representation. Computational Intelligence 17(3), 703–737 (2001)
8. Frank, A.: Qualitative spatial reasoning about distances and directions in geographic space. Journal of Visual Languages and Computing 3, 343–371 (1992)
9. Gerevini, A., Renz, J.: Combining topological and size information for spatial reasoning. Artif. Intell. 137(1-2), 1–42 (2002)
10. Goyal, R., Egenhofer, M.: Consistent queries over cardinal directions across different levels of detail. In: 11th International Workshop on Database and Expert Systems Applications, pp. 876–880. IEEE Computer Society, Los Alamitos (2000)
11. Hernández, D.: Qualitative Representation of Spatial Knowledge. LNCS, vol. 804. Springer, Heidelberg (1994)

12. Hobbs, J.: Granularity. In: Josh, A.K. (ed.) Ninth International Joint Conference on Artificial Intelligence, pp. 432–435. Morgan Kaufmann, Los Angeles (1985)
13. Ligozat, G.: Reasoning about cardinal directions. Journal of Visual Languages and Computing 9, 23–44 (1998)
14. Randell, D., Cui, Z., Cohn, A.: A spatial logic based on region and connection. In: Knowledge Representation and Reasoning, pp. 165–176. Morgan Kaufmann, San Francisco (1992)
15. Schmidtke, H.R.: The house is north of the river: Relative localization of extended objects. In: Montello, D. (ed.) COSIT 2001. LNCS, vol. 2205, pp. 415–430. Springer, Heidelberg (2001)
16. Schmidtke, H.R.: A geometry for places: Representing extension and extended objects. In: Kuhn, W., Worboys, M., Timpf, S. (eds.) COSIT 2003. LNCS, vol. 2825, pp. 235–252. Springer, Heidelberg (2003)
17. Schmidtke, H.R.: Granularity as a parameter of context. In: Dey, A.K., Kokinov, B., Leake, D.B., Turner, R. (eds.) CONTEXT 2005. LNCS (LNAI), vol. 3554, pp. 450–463. Springer, Heidelberg (2005)
18. Schmidtke, H.R., Woo, W.: A size-based qualitative approach to the representation of spatial granularity. In: Veloso, M.M. (ed.) International Joint Conference on Artificial Intelligence, pp. 563–568 (2007)
19. Schmidtke, H.R., Woo, W.: Towards ontology-based formal verification methods for context aware systems. In: Tokuda, H., Beigl, M., Friday, A., Brush, A.J.B., Tobe, Y. (eds.) Pervasive 2009. LNCS, vol. 5538, pp. 309–326. Springer, Heidelberg (2009)
20. Schmidtke, H.R., Beigl, M.: Positions, regions, and clusters: Strata of granularity in location modelling. In: Dillmann, R., Beyerer, J., Hanebeck, U.D., Schultz, T. (eds.) KI 2010. LNCS (LNAI), vol. 6359, pp. 272–279. Springer, Heidelberg (2010)

Mental Models of Ambient Systems: A Modular Research Framework

Felix Schmitt, Jörg Cassens, Martin Christof Kindsmüller, and Michael Herczeg

Institute for Multimedia and Interactive Systems
Ratzeburger Allee 160, D–23562 Lübeck, Germany
{schmitt,cassens,mck,herczeg}@imis.uni-luebeck.de

Abstract. This paper outlines our current research program in the fields of ambient intelligence and context-aware computing and the tools we are building to accomplish this research program. From a discussion of our conception of mental models in the domain of ambient context-aware computer systems we derive hypotheses which we intend to test empirically. A modular framework for implementing and assessing situation awareness in humans and computers is introduced. We describe the framework's architecture and illustrate its suitability for its intended purpose. Finally, we present an outline of our next steps towards real world application systems for our research.

Keywords: Context awareness, ambient intelligence, mental models.

1 Introduction

During the last few decades, computers have taken on an increasingly important role in our lives. Most households do not only own a PC for Internet access and word processing; dedicated gaming consoles or smartphones are also used on a regular basis. Most of these devices are not commonly associated with the word "computer" although they are computing devices in the strongest sense. Today, computational power sees its most widespread use in embedded platforms. Washing machines, refrigerators, television sets, alarm clocks, audio components, cars, cameras, and many more classes of technical artifacts that surround us every day contain a large amount of hard- and software.

In many of these appliances, networking with other devices is either already implemented or can be accomplished with little effort. This allows not only to harvest computational power from already existing sources, but also to access a multitude of environmental sensors and actuators already connected to the embedded network nodes.

For this mesh of embedded computers that has the potential to enhance the usefulness of technical devices, Weiser [1] coined the term *ubiquitous computing*. Your digital photo camera might send the photos you have just taken to your TV set once you put them close to each other. Your MP3 player might offer its songs to your car's audio system once you are seated.

M. Beigl et al. (Eds.): CONTEXT 2011, LNAI 6967, pp. 278–291, 2011.

This scenario gets even more attractive when one thinks of linking these input and output channels with knowledge representations and reasoning mechanisms in order to offer novel context adapted services from a combination of all devices' capabilities. This is what we mean when we are talking about *ambient intelligence* and *context aware computing*. Context awareness of digital artifacts or networks of such needs more than massive amounts of sensor input and distributed output channels. First and foremost, it implies a semantically rich representation of the context, i.e. deeper insight into the situation that is unfolding and its meaning to the persons that are present (and maybe even to absent ones).

What we like to accomplish within technical artifacts is a concept that originates in human beings. People are context aware, and they should be able to be so even when interacting with ubiquitous and ambient computer systems of high complexity. Users should be given a chance to understand what their systems' state is, why the state is as it is, and what will likely happen next. Failure to provide this insight will hinder the applicability of ambient intelligent systems and their acceptance among users in real life applications.

2 Research Program

The concept of context awareness is relevant with regard to ambient intelligent computer systems as well as to their users. The former need context awareness to provide their services in a ways that are unobtrusive and adequate to the situation at hand while the latter depend on the same concept in order to interact with the systems in satisfying and confident ways. It is this double meaning of context awareness that caught our interest in this kind of systems. As our research group is inherently interdisciplinary, our interest in the field of ambient, context aware computing is threefold. In this section, we will outline how these three streaks of our work contribute to our view on the topic.

Regarding ambient, intelligent, and context aware systems, we are particularly interested in:

- the *cognitive science perspective*: how users build, refine, change, and discard their mental models of ambient intelligent systems,
- the *artificial intelligence perspective*: how to build context aware systems, and
- the *HCI perspective*: how to foster the construction of adequate mental models in users of ambient intelligent systems.

We found that current theories of mental models have critical shortcomings when applying them to ambient intelligent systems. To target our research interests mentioned above, we chose a twofold approach. We want to explore the concepts of context and awareness in order to understand the situatedness of users' perception of and interaction with ambient intelligent computer systems. The theoretical concepts form the backdrop for our development of real systems with which we can test our hypotheses. Users' difficulties in constructing appropriate mental models of ambient intelligent systems emerge along two dimensions. First, the supply of good affordances to highlight interaction possibilities becomes difficult when the human-computer interface blends with the physical environment and artifacts. Second, intelligent systems might produce seemingly unforeseeable behavior, possibly without direct user interaction.

3 Theoretical Foundations

To illustrate our point and to motivate the development of our awareness framework, we will outline our theoretical understanding of the domain in this section. First, we will define a taxonomy of common conceptions of mental models and derive a pragmatic working definition. Then we will introduce our understanding of situation awareness and context awareness.

3.1 Mental Models: A Taxonomy and a Pragmatic Approach

The term *mental model* does not refer to a single well defined psychological construct. Various research traditions have coined the term in various ways, emphasizing different aspects in accordance with their respective subject. Each of these conceptions has its purpose in a specific field of research, and before we start discussing mental models, we have to make clear, in which sense we are using the term. It will become obvious that some of the available definitions highlight very different aspects of mental models; one single well-defined concept is not sufficient explaining all empirical findings and relevant concepts in our field of work. Therefore we will point out some of these definitions important to our work and derive a pragmatic working definition.

Modern conceptions of mental models found in literature can often be attributed to one of three lines of research: cognitive science, engineering psychology, and supervisory control. We will describe the former two traditions in more detail. It is important to note that the contribution of the latter can be seen, e.g., through cognitive psychologists like Johnson-Laird [2] interpreting Craik [3] or through engineers and engineering psychologists like Endsley et al. [4] relating their concept of situational awareness to the mental model approach in the supervisory control tradition. Thus, it contributes to our understanding as well. After introducing the basic concepts of mental models defined by cognitive science and engineering psychology respectively, we take a step back and derive a pragmatic definition that satisfies the needs of our work.

The Cognitive Science Tradition. From a cognitive science point of view, mental models are the part of the dynamic knowledge representation structures that is mainly dealing with the *where* information. In terms of Baddeley's [5] working memory model, the structure where mental models are represented is called visuo-spatial sketchpad. The "*where system*" is the structure where mental models of spatial and temporal aspects of the situation at hand are represented. This structure is interconnected with the "*what system*" containing propositional facts.

The term "*mental model*" denotes a specific level of knowledge representation. *Schemata* describe the structure and content of generic knowledge. *Production systems* define declarative and procedural knowledge as well as the processes that transfer one into the other. Mental models can be seen as the highest level representation, namely a dynamically updated image of the actual situation, to which it has a homomorphous mapping. Within this tradition, *reasoning* is regarded as the construction of such models. Cognitive Psychologists dealing with human reasoning like Johnson-Laird [2] or dealing with language comprehension like Van Dijk and Kintsch [6] operate close to this conception of the term.

The Engineering Psychology Tradition. Gentner and Stevens [7] as well as Wilson and Rutherford [8] focus on the fields of engineering of technical artifacts, human-machine interaction and human factors. In this area, it is necessary to distinguish several levels of mental models in several groups of stakeholders that are related to one artifact. According to Norman [9] these are:

1. the *user's conceptual model* of the artifact – the representation of the artifact,
2. the *user's mental model* – the internal representation (cf. prev. sect.), and
3. the *designer's conceptual model* of the artifact.

Conceptual models are mental models as well, and the nomenclature is only to distinguish them from the cognitive science style mental models. Note, though, that mental models in the engineering psychology tradition refer to long term memory structures rather than to working memory representations.

To describe the process of a user's construction of his or her (conceptual) mental model, Kindsmüller [10] coined the term *model induction*. This refers to the fact that mental models are progressively constructed from observations, assumptions and pieces of external information by the user herself. The process can only be fostered by inducing these building blocks in the user, since mental models cannot be "uploaded" to the user's mind as a whole. We use this concept when it comes to identifying design rules for ambient systems.

A Pragmatic Approach to Mental Models. As stated above, these three disciplines (cognitive science, engineering psychology, and supervisory control) have quite different conceptions of mental models. Unfortunately it is sometimes unclear which of these conceptions authors are relating the term mental model to. We basically agree with the notion of Rouse and Morris [11] that detailed understanding of the different concepts may help pushing basic science as well as applications further. Moreover, Rouse and Morris propose a common functional definition of mental models that we deem useful for our field of work, namely the design of complex technical systems: *"Mental models are mechanisms whereby humans are able to generate descriptions of system purpose and form, explanations of system functioning and observed system states, and predictions of future system states."* This definition does not limit the scope of "systems", so that it generalizes upon all three notions of mental models found in literature. Nevertheless most applications of the concept mental models in designing and introducing systems can benefit from narrowing down the fuzzy term mental model to one of these specific notions, in order to avoid confusion.

Building on the previously laid out conceptions and connotations of mental models, we can state the following with respect to our research:

1. When talking about mental models, we hereafter refer to what engineering psychologists would call the user's conceptual model of a system. This includes the users' abilities

   a. to *describe* the system's working mechanisms in their own, albeit simplifying manner,
   b. to *explain* the interaction with the system, i.e. effective actions with regard to certain interfaces and the system's reaction to those, and
   c. to *formulate expectations* with regard to the system, that means anticipation of the system's behavior in a given context or situation.
2. The users' mental model in the sense of their internal knowledge representation is also of interest, since understanding the circumstances of its construction, modification, or refusal will help us to formulate rules and guidelines for the design of ambient intelligent systems.
3. These rules are then supposed to influence the designers' conceptual models of the systems they construct, but this construction process is not in the focus of our research.

3.2 Situation Awareness and Context Awareness

When talking about awareness, we need to understand what this term actually means. The concept of *situation awareness* originates in human factors research. As Endsley, Bolté, and Jones [4] put it, situation awareness (SA) means *"being aware of what is happening around you and understanding what that information means to you now and in the future"*. This short definition already identifies three so-called "SA-levels" of mental activity that build on top of each other to constitute situation awareness:

1. *perception* of the environment,
2. *comprehension* of the situation at hand, and
3. *projection* into the future.

These three elements show very clearly how closely interconnected situation awareness and mental models are (see our pragmatic approach to mental models in Sect. 3.1).

Apart from *situation awareness*, another related term that can be found in literature is *context awareness*. Although both concepts are closely related, we see differences with regard to the level of semantic interpretation of the situation at hand. Turner [12] has defined *situation* as the entire set of circumstances and *context* as those identifiable features that have predictive power for the behavior of an agent. This correlates with our understanding of the term *situation* denoting a particular combination of circumstances at a given time, whereas *context* relates to a generalized class of situations (cf. Halliday and Hasan [13]). In a hospital, updating a patient's fever chart might happen in the context of the daily ward round which is instantiated by Dr. Miller and Dr. Bower standing at Mrs. Smith's bedside. Abstracting situations into contexts helps people to cognitively master the manifold of situations they encounter all the time: they have mental models of certain contexts, which in turn enable them to retrieve scripts and schemas that propose default interpretations, behavior and expected outcomes.

"Becoming aware of", that is: identifying, a certain context requires a semantically rich representation of the situation at hand. Since semantics of real world situations are quite hard to model computationally, the question arises to which extent we need these semantics in order to provide useful awareness services to the user. We believe that for most tasks usually targeted with contemporary awareness technologies full context awareness is not necessary, but much simpler inferences will suffice. Despite their lack of a semantic representation of the situation, these systems can nevertheless foster situation awareness in their users. The unique properties of ambient systems, which we mentioned in Sect. 1 as well as in [14], however, require more complex semantic models to account for the sheer variety of possible inputs as well as the implicitness of their interactions with users.

From the conception of awareness outlined above, we can derive the following hypotheses about ambient computer systems and their users:

1. Appropriate mental models of a system are necessary prerequisites for the user's context awareness when interacting with the system.
2. Helping users to build an appropriate mental model of situations can improve the users' situation awareness.
3. A system that is supposed to be context aware with regard to certain interactions (even if they are distributed in space and/or time) needs some sort of "mental model", i.e. a semantically rich representation of the situation at hand.

4 Software Framework

Based on our previously laid out concepts of context awareness and mental models, we have been developing a framework for the engineering of context aware systems. Applications built on top of this framework will help us to understand the implications of ambient intelligence on human-computer interaction. We also use the framework to empirically test our theoretical understanding outlined above.

The design of the architecture is based on several principles to connect with this understanding:

- It facilitates prototype-based, feature-driven development processes for rapid deploy-test cycles.
- It allows generating models of context based on current practice in a user-centered development process.
- It allows to use sensors and actuators which connect to users' existing mental models as well as facilitate the generation of new mental models based on metaphors and current practice.
- The system can give enough explanatory feedback so that the user is aware of the system state.

Ultimately, software engineers who want to equip their system with context awareness will be able to implement our *Modular Awareness Construction Kit*'s (MACK) interfaces and install the desired MACK components along with their software. Manufacturers of, e.g., ambient assisted living solutions or interactive guides for museums can thus offer context aware systems with less development effort, just like they would include interfaces to third-party media servers or communication systems.

The MACK framework's architecture is comprised of several functional components that can be modularly combined to provide the required input and output channels as well as domain knowledge and computation thereupon. The architecture also reflects our approach that users' mental models of MACK-based systems are subject to model induction as introduced in Sect. 3.1 and may thus profit from a variety of media types and modalities, i.e. human-computer interfaces.

4.1 Overview

In Fig. 1, the left- and rightmost columns denote the various sensors and actuators, i.e. the system's input and output channels. These need to implement various properties such as the internal XMPP-based protocol. All information is gathered and distributed via the Awareness Hub, which in turn asks the Reasoning Manager's AI engines for interpretation of the information. User data and settings are kept by a separate component for greater modularity and adaptability. Generic sensors and actuators that are not inherently MACK-enabled are driven by a gateway component.

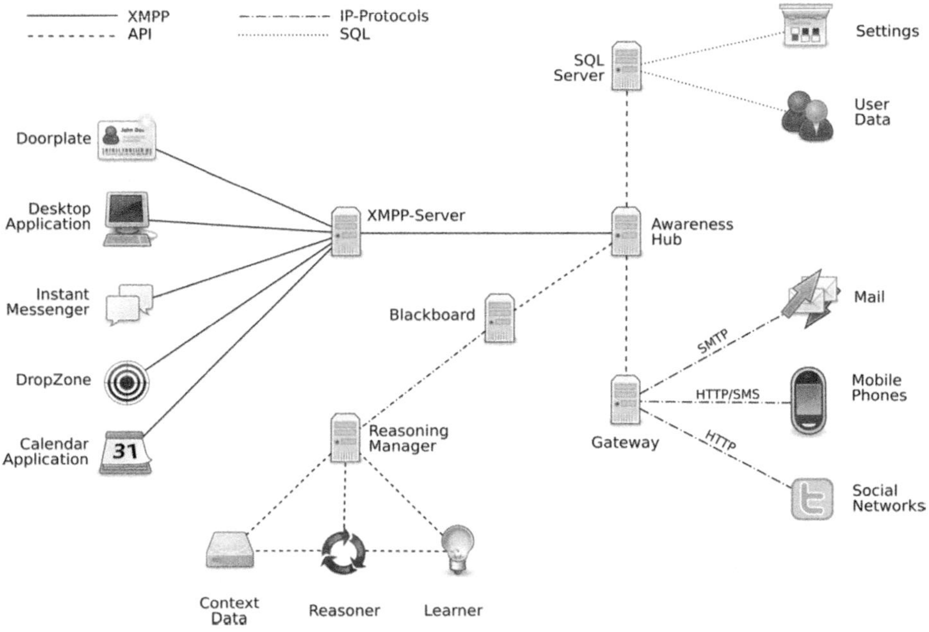

Fig. 1. Architectural overview of the MACK framework

The interfaces between these components are well-defined for interoperability, extensible for future enhancements, and based on standardized open protocols such as TCP/IP and XMPP. Usage of proprietary APIs is kept minimal.

MACK's origin lies in our development of the MATe office awareness system (cf. [14]), of which MACK can be seen as a generalization and abstraction suitable for various types of application systems. Many of the currently implemented peripherals still show MACK's ancestry in that they are primarily targeted at determining and communicating a knowledge worker's interruptibility. The underlying infrastructure and controller logic can be easily used to drive other sensors and actuators though. From the framework perspective, MATe can be seen as an application system which is heavily based upon a MACK infrastructure.

4.2 Sensors

Context-aware systems do not necessarily need to employ a large number of sensors (cf. [15, 16]). On the other hand, we argue that the actual number and types of sensors necessary is depending on the application domain. Our intention to provide a generic framework leads us to create a multitude of sensor modules so that MACK-based application systems can target a multitude of usage scenarios. We will describe two of our peripherals as examples for the inputs our system is able to deal with. The information gathered from some of the sensors does not seem to be valuable by itself. The AwarenessHub will, however, try to relate as many of these inputs as possible to enable the reasoning component to draw semantically rich inferences.

The DropZone is a marked area on the user's desk. People are asked to place a personal token in this area as soon as they enter the room. Despite this explicit interaction, we see the DropZone as an ambient interface, because the tokens are to be carried on the users' key rings. Just like hanging your keys on the key hooks in your hallway when you return home, dropping them in the DropBox area will be highly automatized after only a short period of usage. In our prototype, the token is an optical 2D marker which can be recognized via a camera. This presence information is then forwarded to the AwarenessHub.

With MikeRofone, we aim to identify the number of speakers in a given environment and, via voice signatures taken from individual speech samples, which persons are present. Speech content is not analyzed. The DropZone's camera comes with an integrated microphone which we use to analyze background noise in the room. Due to the large amount of processing power necessary for the analysis, MikeRofone runs on the user's desktop PC.

4.3 Actuators

The ambient character of our system does not only become manifest in its input channels, i.e., sensors, but also with respect to its output channels in the form of various actuators.

One actuator that highlights the ambient nature of our system is the so-called DoorLight. Office doors at our institute have four frosted glass panels of which one can be equipped with LED strips running along two of its edges. A microcontroller evaluates the AwarenessHub's messages and can illuminate the glass panel in either green, yellow, or red color to indicate the user's current interruptibility status. Due to the relatively large area of the "display", co-workers can notice their colleague's status from the corner of their eye while passing down the hallway. For the same reason, the illumination can be dim enough to not draw one's explicit attention.

Another peripheral, the DeskCube, is a combination of actuator and sensor. It consists of a 9x9x9 cm^3 plastic cube, which bears a 8x8 LED matrix on each side. A microcontroller inside the cube uses the matrices to display iconic representations of the six most probable interpretations of the user's current context, the most probable pointing upwards. Thus, the user becomes aware of the system's beliefs. If the system is wrong, the user can simply turn the cube to display the correct context on top. A 3-axis accelerometer within the cube detects the new position and feeds the corrective value back to the AwarenessHub, thereby offering learning input to our reasoners.

4.4 Gateway

The Gateway component allows for the integration of services and devices that are not MACK-enabled. The Gateway's connectivity and functionality can be extended by plug-ins that implement foreign APIs. Currently, this is demonstrated by an SMS service that can be used by the AwarenessHub to notify users of other users' availability or to forward them messages that someone else left on their interactive DoorPlate (cf. [14]).

4.5 AwarenessHub

The AwarenessHub forms the central component of the MACK architecture. It mainly acts as a message passing hub, hence the name. The AwarenessHub keeps track of all other MACK devices including the various peripherals as well as of the user accounts and settings. It forwards messages and retrieves information on behalf of other components while enforcing the users' preference and privacy settings.

The AwarenessHub does not act as a server in the sense that other components log into it to become part of the installation. Instead, the AwarenessHub itself is implemented as an XMPP client. This allows the developers of MACK-enabled application systems to reuse an existing private or even publicly available XMPP server. XMPP supports encrypted connections, so this approach does not in itself imply data protection concerns.

4.6 Reasoning

Since the reasoners are integrated with the rest of the system through a well defined interface they can be easily extended and replaced. For bootstrapping the development, we used only one reasoner for a couple of defined areas of competence each (interruptibility, location of the user, etc.). The reasoners were simple production systems. For empirical testing of our theoretical hypotheses, however, greater flexibility and expressive power is required.

Reasoner. In 2010, Ruge [17] implemented a first reasoner for assessing the interruptibility status of users. This reasoner is based on a domain ontology written in OWL (see below) and the description logics reasoner Pellet [18]. Since this reasoner is based on an open-world assumption, which makes certain inferences impossible, we use an additional close-world reasoner for processing the world model.

For the future, the use of other reasoning paradigms is planned as well, for example using a case-based approach [19]. Compared to other paradigms, case-based reasoning (CBR) suits MACK's needs particularly well for two reasons: First, our system should be able to operate in weak theory domains. The second reason is the relative sparseness of instances of these contexts, i.e. situations that are available to learn from. Both reasons make CBR an especially promising extension of MACK's reasoning subsystem.

Ontology. Ontology development is a highly complex and error-prone task, so it is beneficial to recycle already existing work in the field. Analysis of existing solutions revealed none that would fit our needs, though. Development of Chen et. al.'s [20, 21] *CoBrA-ONT* has been discontinued, and current software tools cannot be used on it. The *CoCa Service Platform* [22] is more up-to-date, but its *Generic Context Management Model* (GCoM) is not freely available. *ONTONYM* [23] provides an extensive model of persons with their respective personal and professional environment, including sensors and properties of technical artifacts. Its structure and handling, however, seemed overly complex for our current state of work, so we opted for an in-house development.

Ruge [17] implemented BOWIE, the *Basic Ontology for Work Information Exchange*. We opted for OWL as the description language, because it is a standard representation for which reasoners exist and which can be used for exchange purposes. In order to work on a unified knowledge model, BOWIE assumes that all information about the world is provided by sensors. Instead of modeling a place's size as an attribute to the `Place` class, a (virtual) `Size` sensor monitors all places and delivers a value upon request. Sub-class axioms and conditional object properties allow for set-based logic operations on the ontology.

Blackboard. MACK's initial reasoning architecture has two main drawbacks. First, several of the different reasoners operate at least partly on the same world model. For example, both the location and the interruptibility reasoner need information on whether the user has placed her personal token in the DropZone (cf. [14]). Second, since the envisioned usage scenarios are in weak theory domains, we deem it beneficial to use different reasoners for the same question and combine their results, for example by using ensemble reasoning [24].

To address these two drawbacks, we are currently restructuring MACK's reasoning subsystem to employ a blackboard architecture [25]. The idea behind blackboards can be understood with the metaphor of a group of human experts who collaboratively solve a problem. The initial problem and world model are written on a blackboard. Whenever one of the experts sees a question he can answer using the known information, he will contribute his results to the blackboard, in the hope that this helps other experts to solve their own tasks.

Our blackboard component uses the same principle: new information from the sensors is written on a shared model in a shared representation language. The different reasoners act upon changed information and write their results to the same model. In our example, the location reasoner could update a user's whereabouts after the DropZone in an office registered the personal token. The updated location information is then used by several interruptibility reasoners who, in turn, update the interruptibility information of the given user.

5 Empirical Evaluation

As we already stated in Sect. 4, MACK is being developed in order to test the viability of our theoretical conceptualizations of mental models and context awareness. From the framework application systems are derived which are deployed among actual end users. One example for the type of systems that can be built on top of the MACK architecture is our office awareness support system MATe. Empirical studies conducted among these application systems' users help us to evaluate to which degree our hypotheses hold in practice. Based on the results we will further refine our theoretical understanding of mental models and context awareness.

Methods used to gain insight into the construction process and structure of users' mental models related to our systems include qualitative interviews and a newly adopted version of the structure-formation-technique by Scheele and Groeben [26] using concept maps (cf. Novak and Cañas [27]) drawn by the users.

Since our software is still considered work in progress, no summative evaluation has been conducted so far. However, since we are using an entangled combination of User-Centered Design (cf. [28]), and Feature-Driven Development [29] we have (bi-) weekly formative evaluations in our development process to make sure that short-coming are detected and repaired early in MATe's/MACK's evolution. These formative evaluations helped us to optimize the common usability of the input and output devices. This is important because we do not want handling problems to interfere with our test results regarding the construction of users' mental models later on.

6 Conclusions and Future Work

In the preceding sections, we have given an introduction to basic concepts that are relevant when dealing with ambient intelligent computer systems. Operating close to the pragmatic definition by Rouse and Morris [11], we conceive mental models as a particular type of long-term memory contents that enable people to describe a system's working mechanisms, to explain their interaction with the system and to anticipate future system behavior. Context is defined as an abstract classification of particular situations, helping people to cognitively master situational challenges by fostering the retrieval of applicable mental models and the knowledge they consist of.

We argue that context awareness (as opposed to situation awareness) requires semantically rich representations and abstractions of the relevant features of a situation at hand. While innate to the human mind, representations of this kind are hard to model computationally. Our *Modular Awareness Construction Kit* (MACK) is intended to implement a software framework for this task. Because of its open architecture, it can be used to construct applications systems in a wide variety of domains.

In the course of our research on ambient, context-aware computing we will use systems built on top of MACK to test our hypotheses which we presented in Sect. 3. For this purpose, though, MACK needs further enhancement with regard to some of its properties and components.

6.1 Reasoning

Most of the existing reasoners are simple production systems, and are linked to the office awareness domain, We plan to both introduce new reasoners suitable in other fields of application and to augment the existing ones with other paradigms.

With more than one reasoner available in the MACK framework, the question arises which of them is right in case they disagree with regard to a question posed by the AwarenessHub. Thus, we need an *Arbiter*. We are currently considering different decision strategies:

- If the different reasoners perform basic ensemble reasoning, its task would be to simply count votes for each outcome and let the majority win.
- If the other reasoners not only deliver their vote, but also an estimate of their own confidence in their decision, it has to calculate the most probably correct decision.

Within MACK's architecture (cf. Fig. 1), the Arbiter will probably not be implemented as another reasoner, but as part of the Reasoning Manager that controls and monitors the various reasoners' access to the blackboard.

6.2 Mobile Client

To leverage more information to reason upon, we will introduce a mobile MACK client for Android-based smartphones. Since users often carry these devices with them, we expect more frequent information updates compared to stationary sensors. The software will evaluate data from acceleration sensors (walking) as well as location data from GPS and WiFi connections. Furthermore, we can get information on appointments and tasks from other Android apps. As a frontend, the MACK client will allow querying the AwarenessHub for the status of fellow users.

6.3 Evaluation

As soon as the current iteration of code and hardware development is finished, an instance of MACK in the form of the MATe system will be installed on the premises of our research group. In a first step, we will equip several offices with the various components and put the system into everyday use. This will enable us to leverage sufficient log data as well as user experience to conduct a summative evaluation of the system's status quo as well as its ability to support our theoretical understanding of context awareness and users' mental models of ambient computer systems.

References

1. Weiser, M.: The Computer for the Twenty-First Century. Scientific American 265, 94–100 (1991)
2. Johnson-Laird, P.N.: Mental Models: Towards a Cognitive Science of Language, Inference, and Consciousness. Harvard University Press, Cambridge (1983)
3. Craik, K.J.W.: Theory of the human operator in control systems. I. The operator as an engineerig system. British Journal of Psychology 38, 56–61 (1947)
4. Endsley, M.R., Bolté, B., Jones, D.G.: Designing for Situation Awareness. Taylor & Francis, London (2003)
5. Baddeley, A.D.: The episodic buffer. A new component of working memory? Trends in Cognitive Sciences 4(11), 418–423 (2000)
6. Van Dijk, T.A., Kintsch, W.: Strategies of discourse comprehension. Academic Press, New York (1983)

7. Gentner, D., Stevens, A.L.: Mental Models. Lawrence Erlbaum Associates, Hillsdale (1983)
8. Wilson, J.R., Rutherford, A.: Mental models: theory and application in human factors. Human Factors 31(6), 617–634 (1989)
9. Norman, D.A.: Some Observations on Mental Models. In: Gentner, D., Stevens, A.L. (eds.) Mental Models, pp. 7–14. Lawrence Erlbaum Associates, Hillsdale (1983)
10. Kindsmüller, M.C.: Trend-Literacy. In: Zur Interpretation von Kurvendarstellungen in der Prozessführung. Shaker Verlag, Aachen (2006)
11. Rouse, W.B., Morris, N.: On looking into the black box: Prospects and limits in the search for mental models. Psychological Bulletin 100(3), 349–363 (1986)
12. Turner, R.: Context-mediated behavior for intelligent agents. International Journal of Human-Computer Studies 48(3), 307–330 (1998)
13. Halliday, M.A.K., Hasan, R.: Language, Context, and Text: Aspects of Language in a Social-semiotic perspective. Deakin University, Victoria (1985)
14. Schmitt, F., Cassens, J., Kindsmüller, M.C., Herczeg, M.: Mental Models of Disappearing Systems: Challenges for a Better Understanding. In: Cassens, J., Kofod-Petersen, A., Zacarias, M., Wegener, R. (eds.) Proceedings of the Sixth International Workshop on Modelling and Reasoning in Context, Lisbon, CEUR-WS.org (2010)
15. Fogarty, J., Hudson, S.E., Lai, J.: Examining the robustness of sensor-based statistical models of human interruptibility. In: Dykstra-Erickson, E., Tscheligi, M. (eds.) CHI 2004: Proceedings of the SIGCHI Conference on Human Factors in Computing Systems, pp. 207–214. ACM, New York (2004)
16. Hudson, S.E., Fogarty, J., Atkeson, C.G., Avrahami, D., Forlizzi, J., Kiesler, S., Lee, J.C., Yang, J.: Predicting Human Interruptibility with Sensors: A Wizard of Oz Feasibility Study. In: Cockton, G., Korhonen, P. (eds.) CHI 2003: Proceedings of the SIGCHI Conference on Human Factors in Computing Systems, pp. 257–264. ACM, New York (2003)
17. Ruge, L.: Koordinierung von Inferenz- und Lernprozessen für Pervasive-Computing-Anwendungen. Diploma thesis, University of Lübeck (2010)
18. Sirin, E., Parsia, B.: Pellet: An OWL DL reasoner. In: Haarslev, V., Möller, R. (eds.) 2004 International Workshop on Description Logics, pp. 212–213 (2004)
19. Aamodt, A., Plaza, E.: Case-Based Reasoning: Foundational Issues, Methodological Variations, and System Approaches. AI Communications 7(1), 39–59 (1994)
20. Chen, H.: An Intelligent Broker Architecture for Pervasive Context-Aware Systems. PhD thesis, University of Maryland, Baltimore County (2004)
21. Chen, H., Finin, T., Joshi, A.: The soupa ontology for pervasive computing. In: Calisti, M., Walliser, M., Brantschen, S., Herbstritt, M., Tamma, V., Cranefield, S., Finin, T., Willmott, S. (eds.) Ontologies for Agents: Theory and Experiences. Whitestein Series in Software Agent Technologies and Autonomic Computing, pp. 233–258. Birkhäuser, Basel (2005)
22. Ejigu, D., Scuturici, M., Brunie, L.: CoCA: A Collaborative Context-Aware Service Platform for Pervasive Computing. In: Latifi, S. (ed.) ITNG 2007: Proceedings of the International Conference on Information Technology, pp. 297–302. IEEE Computer Society, Washington, DC (2007)
23. Stevenson, G., Knox, S., Dobson, S., Nixon, P.: Ontonym: a collection of upper ontologies for developing pervasive systems. In: Gomez-Perez, J. (ed.) CIAO 2009: Proceedings of the 1st Workshop on Context, Information and Ontologies, pp. 1–8. ACM, New York (2009)

24. Plaza, E., Ontañón, S.: Ensemble Case-Based Reasoning: Collaboration Policies for Multiagent Cooperative CBR. In: Aha, D.W., Watson, I. (eds.) ICCBR 2001. LNCS (LNAI), vol. 2080, pp. 437–451. Springer, Heidelberg (2001)
25. Jagannathan, V., Dodhiawala, R., Baum, L.S. (eds.): Blackboard Architectures and Applications. Academic Press, Orlando (1989)
26. Scheele, B., Groeben, N.: Die Heidelberger Struktur-Lege-Technik (SLT). Eine Dialog-Konsens-Methode zur Erhebung subjektiver Theorien mittlerer Reichweite. Beltz, Weinheim (1984)
27. Novak, J.D., Cañas, A.J.: The theory underlying concept maps and how to construct and use them. Tech. rep., Florida Institute for Human and Machine Cognition, IHMC (2008)
28. Norman, D.A., Draper, S.W.: User Centered System Design: New Perspectives on Human-Computer Interaction. Lawrence Erlbaum, Hillsdale (1986)
29. Palmer, S.R., Felsing, J.M.: A Practical Guide to Feature-Driven Development. Prentice Hall, Upper Saddle River (2002)

LiCoRMS – Towards a Resource Management System Based on Lifecycle and Content Information

Axel Schulz[1,2], Benedikt Schmidt[2], and Heiko Paulheim[3]

[1] Technische Universität Darmstadt, Telecooperation Group,
Hochschulstraße 10, 64289 Darmstadt, Germany
[2] SAP Research, Bleichstrasse 8, 64283 Darmstadt
{axel.schulz,benedikt.schmidt}@sap.com
[3] Technische Universität Darmstadt, Knowledge Engineering Group,
Hochschulstraße 10, 64289 Darmstadt, Germany
paulheim@ke.tu-darmstadt.de

Abstract. Knowledge intensive work is characterized by dealing with an increasing amount of resources, like documents or e-mails. To increase efficiency, users frequently reuse existing resources, e.g., create new documents by using existing ones as a template. This paper introduces *LiCoRMS*[1], a lightweight system for supporting the reuse of resources by capturing and managing relationships between resources using lifecycle *and* content information in resource-centered metadata as well as in an ontology.

Keywords: Metadata, Lifecycle, Resource Management, Ontology.

1 Introduction

In modern knowledge-intensive working environments, the knowledge worker performs a lot of tasks to acquire, to distribute and to create new knowledge. Especially linking resources is one of the main objectives of a knowledge worker [1]. Such links can be created implicitly, e.g., by reusing existing resources (which relates the original reused resource to the newly created one), or by explicitly creating links between information sources.

A study of Ravasio et al. [2] shows that, while users have to deal with an increasing amount of resources, they generally have problems to find related resources, since links between resources are often not explicit, e.g., between a document attached to an e-mail and the detached document stored in a local folder.

Fig. 1 shows an example of collaborative work on a document, where authors exchange different versions of the document via e-mail. In the example, user 1 creates a new document, edits it, and sends it to users 2 and 3 via mail. Users 2 and 3 edit the document and resend the edited versions to user 1. User 1 saves the attachments on his desktop. During these external editing processes, user 1 has also changed her local version.

[1] Lifecycle and Content-based Resource Management System.

M. Beigl et al. (Eds.): CONTEXT 2011, LNAI 6967, pp. 292–295, 2011.

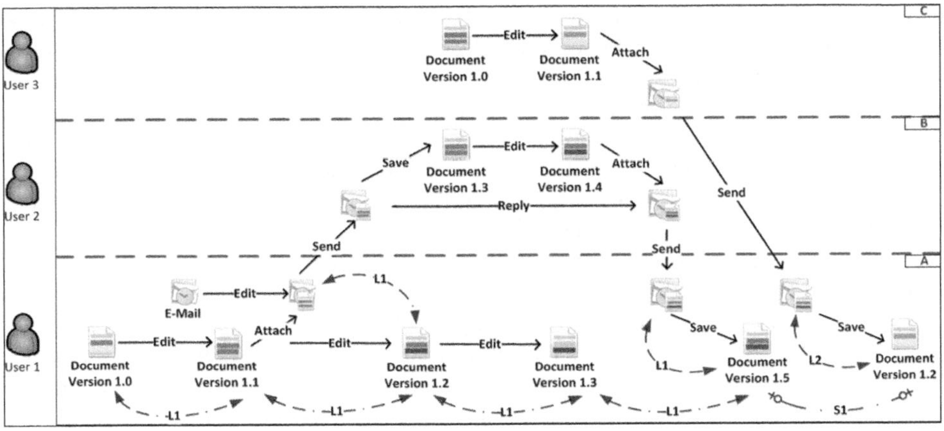

Fig. 1. Example lifecycle for the collaborative creation of documents, involving several related versions of the same document

This collaborative scenario shows that highly complex, distributed activities on resources can lead to an increased number of implicitly related resources on the local desktop. To address these local resource management problems shown in the example, the reuse of resources can be supported by capturing, managing and explicating such implicit relationships between resources.

In order to help user 1 to identify and manage the different versions of the document, it is necessary to capture lifecycle information (L1,L2), which may be distributed across different systems. Relationships between resources may also exist because of the semantic relationship of resources (S1). For example, a document is related to an e-mail it is attached to because of the contents of the document and the e-mail. Furthermore, there may be relationships to additional documents on the user's system.

This paper introduces the *LiCoRMS* system, which captures the user's actions on his local system to describe resources by using *both* lifecycle and content metadata (as opposed to existing systems, which typically only use one of the two) and to provide related resources based on this metadata. The system is robust against loss of information when collaborating with users who do not use LiCoRMS.

2 Management of Lifecycle and Content Metadata

In LiCoRMS, we store lifecycle and content metadata in a resource-centered manner as well as in an ontology-based repository. Thus, we combine the advantages of a decentralized storage, which supports distributed processing of documents, with the power of ontology-based reasoning on resources; their contents, and their usage. For resource-centered metadata, there are formats commonly used, like IEEE LOM[2],

[2] http://ltsc.ieee.org/wg12/

Dublin Core[3] and CAM [3]. We decided to use an adaptation of the CAM format, because it allows an efficient representation of metadata and enables the description of lifecycle information.

Besides general information about a document (such as title, type, creation date, etc.), we store lifecycle information as a series of events (including pointers to other resources that were included in the event, e.g., when a document is attached to an e-mail), as well as content information about the document (stored as a set of keywords with their frequency of occurrence).

In the context of a resource management system, the identifiers of documents and events are of special importance. First, references to resources must be uniquely identifiable. Second, for a decentralized management of resources, these values are stored as part of the resources in a way that they are also preserved when processing a document on external systems. Thus, the direct reference between the metadata and the resource remains existent. This enables the bridging of systems without context monitors. Each version of a document has its own ID, which makes it possible to capture and to differentiate lifecycle metadata for every version of a document.

3 Central Concepts of the Resource Lifecycle Ontology

The metadata format is represented using a Resource Lifecycle Ontology (RLO), which is built upon the widely adopted DOLCE top level ontology [4]. Using an ontology allows for providing metadata information in a standardized format, such as RDF.

In the RLO, we have defined a number of central concepts for formalizing content and lifecycle information of documents. A resource, which is present as a file in the file system, is represented by the `CWO:File` concept, using the corresponding concepts from the Computer Work Ontology (CWO) [5].

The lifecycle information through the changing of resources by user activities are represented in the `RLO:InformationTransformationActivity` concept. Every `RLO:InformationTransformationActivity` is related to a `CWO:File`, because the activity changes the file. For representing this relationship, we have defined the `RLO:transforms` association. Thus, a direct relationship between an activity and the corresponding resource can be described. For describing the different activities on resources, several concepts have been introduced. For example, a `RLO:Mail-send-activity` describes the sending of e-mails. Transformation activities may also `DnS:use` (for concepts and relations of the Descriptions & Situations (DnS) Ontology and the Ontology of Plans (OOP) see [4]) other files, e.g., the file attached to an e-mail. The executing user can be defined using the `OoP:Activity` and the related `DnS:Agent`.

A `RLO:File` can be changed by several transformations. Therefore relationships between the transformations have to be described. These are defined using the `DnS:successor` and `DnS:predecessor` relationships between the transformations. This allows for tracking the lifecycle information of a document.

---

[3] http://dublincore.org/

In addition to the lifecycle information described in the transformation activities, the ontology allows for defining content information to allow for finding related resources based on the content information for resources without lifecycle information. Those connections are established using text-based similarity, using the `RLO:DescriptiveStatistic` concept, which is an `OIO:InformationObject` [6] and describes another `OIO:InformationObject`. The `RLO:DescriptiveStatistic` references a set of `OIO:Word`.

4 Conclusion

In this paper, we have introduced the LiCoRMS system for capturing and managing lifecycle and content metadata for resources. While most existing systems concentrate either on lifecycle or on content metadata, our system combines both variants and preserves metadata when processing resources on systems without LiCoRMS. We have implemented a prototype of LiCoRMS, consisting of a context monitor, a centralized ontology-based storage, a visualization module for resource lifecycle information, and slots for several usage modules.

The simultaneous capturing of lifecycle and content information as resource metadata and in an ontology-based repository allows for a number of possible applications, such as proactive user assistance or decentralized collaborative document editing. While the resource-centered storing enables the exchange of resources with external systems, the ontology-based storage enables the fast discovery of related resources through lifecycle information, which would be difficult using only a resource-centered metadata format.

References

1. Davenport, T.H.: Thinking for a living. In: How to Get Better Performance and Results from Knowledge Workers. Harvard Business School Press, Boston (2005)
2. Ravasio, P., Schär, S.G., Krueger, H.: In pursuit of desktop evolution: User problems and practices with modern desktop systems. ACM Transactions on Computer-Human Interaction 11, 156–180 (2004)
3. Wolpers, M., Martin, G., Najjar, J., Duval, E.: Attention metadata in knowledge and learning management. In: Tochtermann, K., Maurer, H. (eds.) Proceedings of I-Know 2006: 6th International Conference on Knowledge Management, Graz, Austria, pp. 1–8 (2006)
4. Gangemi, A., Borgo, S., Catenacci, C., Lehmann, J.: Task Taxonomies for Knowledge Content D07 (2004)
5. Schmidt, B., Paulheim, H., Stoitsev, T., Mühlhäuser, M.: Towards a Formalization of Individual Work Execution at Computer Workplaces. In: Andrews, S., Polovina, S., Hill, R., Akhgar, B. (eds.) ICCS-ConceptStruct 2011. LNCS (LNAI), vol. 6828, pp. 270–283. Springer, Heidelberg (to appear, 2011)
6. Oberle, D., Lamparter, S., Grimm, S., Vrandečić, D., Staab, S., Gangemi, A.: Towards ontologies for formalizing modularization and communication in large software systems. Applied Ontology 1, 163–202 (2006)

Entropy of Audio Fingerprints for Unobtrusive Device Authentication

Stephan Sigg[1], Matthias Budde[2], Yusheng Ji[1], and Michael Beigl[2]

[1] National Institute of Informatics, Tokyo, Japan
{sigg,kei}@nii.ac.jp
http://www.nii.ac.jp
[2] KIT, TecO, Karlsruhe, Germany
{budde,michael}@teco.edu
http://www.teco.edu

Abstract. Context-based authentication methods enable the unobtrusive establishment of authentication or even secure keys. While several context-based authentication methods have been proposed recently, often the entropy of the seed for the cryptographic keys is not exploited. We study the entropy of audio fingerprints which can be utilized to pair devices in close proximity. In this work, for 600 audio fingerprints from five distinct audio classes recorded at three different locations, we applied 7490 statistical tests from the dieHarder battery of statistical tests.

Keywords: Audio fingerprinting, Entropy, Pervasive computing, Unobtrusive device authentication.

Secure communication is an important issue in pervasive environments. It is required to prevent an adversary from entering a network, to protect confidential information, or to prevent an adversary from manipulating network operations. With mobile devices, communicating entities might change frequently. Also, communications are frequently conducted with previously unknown devices. This makes it complicated to provide a mostly unobtrusive security mechanism.

We exploit ambient audio as a seed for the creation of shared cryptographic keys among devices in physical proximity. Two devices willing to establish a secure channel take a synchronized audio recording and compute audio fingerprints based on this sample. We show how secure key exchange is possible with fuzzy cryptography schemes and that the entropy of audio fingerprints is high.

The establishing of a secure communication channel between devices has been studied by several authors in the literature [1]. In [2], for instance, the authors propose two protocols for secure authentication that utilize accelerometer data on devices that are shaken together. For sufficient entropy in the generated feature vectors that are utilized as a basis to the key generation, the devices have to be shaken together for a sufficiently long time [3]. This procedure is feasible only for small mobile devices and requires direct access to both devices in order to pair them. Furthermore, the shaking of devices can not be considered

M. Beigl et al. (Eds.): CONTEXT 2011, LNAI 6967, pp. 296–299, 2011.

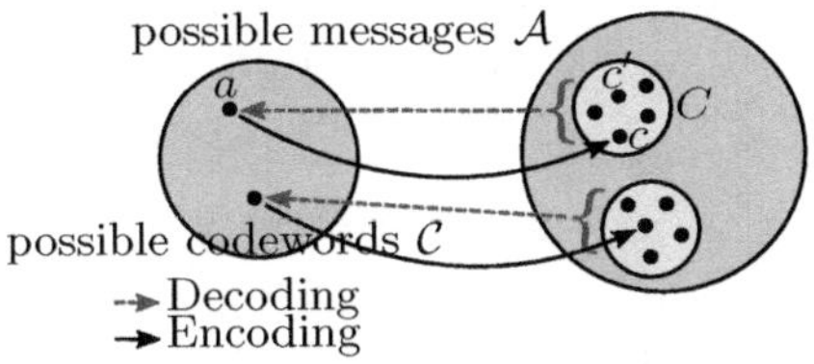

(a) Encoding maps message $a \in \mathcal{A}$ to codeword $c \in \mathcal{C}$. Decoding maps several $\tilde{c} \in C, C = \{c, c', c'', \dots\}$ to one $a \in \mathcal{A}$

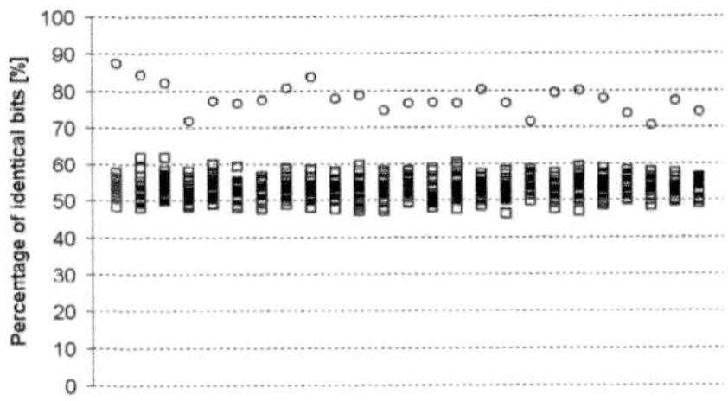

(b) Similarity of fingerprints from different (squares) and identical (circles) audio

Fig. 1. Fuzzy cryptography to correct errors in audio fingerprints of distinct devices

unobtrusive. This Candidate Key Protocol generates feature sets with identical hash values on both devices and concatenates them to create a shared secret key among devices [4]. In [5], a false negative rate of more than 11 percent was reported for this approach and for features extracted from accelerometer data.

1 Key Generation by Audio Fingerprinting

Through audio fingerprinting short characteristic bit sequences of an audio stream are created [6,7]. We propose to extract audio fingerprints from synchronized recordings on mobile devices, possibly correct their Hamming distance with fuzzy cryptography schemes, and then to utilize these fingerprints as the seeds for cryptographic keys among devices.

Figure 1(a) illustrates this concept. A message a of length m is mapped uniquely to a specific codeword c of length n: $a \mapsto c : a \in \mathcal{A}, c \in \mathcal{C}$. We utilize error correcting codes for this mapping, so that similar codewords c' are decoded to the same massage a.

The protocol is able to generate secure keys based on ambient audio if and only if the audio samples are synchronized and taken in close proximity. In various case studies we experienced a good performance and robustness against differing noise levels for this protocol. It was implemented using parts of the Fuzzy Commitment scheme detailed in [8] together with Reed-Solomon codes [9]. The codes were applied in conjunction with the Secure Hash Algorithm with 256 bit (SHA-256).

However, a possible weakness are the audio fingerprints that are used as seeds for the secret keys. Clearly, if the entropy of the audio fingerprints were low, an adversary could use additional knowledge to increase the probability to correctly guess the secret key.

1.1 Similarity of Audio Fingerprints

In our implementation we split $r = 44100$Hz audio recordings of 6.375 seconds into $n = 17$ frames of identical length of 0.375 seconds. On each frame a discrete Fourier transformation weighted by a Hann window is applied. Frames are divided into $m = 33$ frequency bands on which the sum of the energy values is calculated and saved in an energy matrix E with energy per frame per frequency band. Using E, a 512 bit fingerprint f is generated, where every bit is calculated as $\forall i \in \{1, \dots, n-1\}, \forall j \in \{0, \dots, m-2\}$

$$f(i,j) = \begin{cases} 1 & \text{if } E(i,j) - E(i,j+1) - \\ & (E(i-1,j) - E(i-1,j+1)) > 0, \\ 0 & \text{otherwise.} \end{cases}$$

To classify the suitability of audio fingerprints as the basis for a classical key generation scheme we recorded 25 different samples with five samples for five distinct activities each. The activities considered are a music sample, a person clapping her hands, snipping, speaking and whistling. These samples were played back by an audio source and sampled again through two microphones in various distances from the source. We installed the microphones at 1.5m, 3m, 4.5m and 6m distances. The similarity of fingerprints is depicted in figure 1(b) exemplary for microphones at 1.5m and 3m distance. The image clearly shows, that the similarity is higher for identical audio samples (circles) than for dissimilar samples (squares). However, also identical samples produce fingerprints that differ in a considerable number of bits. These errors are then corrected by Reed-Solomon error correcting codes.

1.2 Entropy of Audio Fingerprints

In order to test the entropy of generated fingerprints we applied the dieHarder [10] set of statistical tests. This battery of tests calculates the p-value of a given random sequence with respect to several statistical tests. The p-value denotes the probability to obtain the provided input sequence given a truly random bit generator. We applied all 24 statistical tests in the set on fingerprints of 480 bits length. In 7490 test-batches of 100 repeated applications of one specific test each, only 173 batches, or about 2.31% resulted in a p-value of less than 0.05.[1] Each specific statistical test was repeated at least 70 times. The p-values are calculated according to the statistical test of Kuiper [11].

Figure 2 depicts the proportion of p-values that pass a sequence of tests and an exemplary histogram for the RGB bit distribution test.

For each of the 34 test series conducted, figure 2(b) depicts the fraction of tests that did not pass a sequence of 100 consecutive runs for all 107 distinct tests in the DieHarder battery of statistical tests.

2 Conclusion

We detailed the unobtrusive creation of audio-fingerprint based cryptographic keys and presented a subset of our results achieved on the entropy of audio

[1] All results are available at `http://www.ibr.cs.tu-bs.de/users/sigg/StatisticalTests/TestsFingerprints_110601.tar.gz`

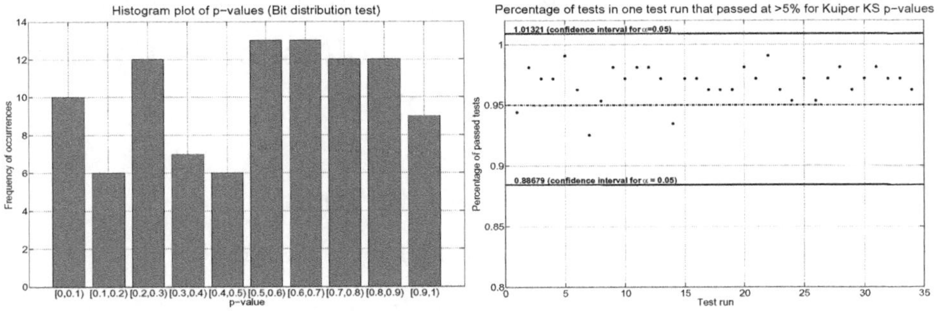

(a) Histogram plot of p-values for the RGB Bit Distribution test (b) Proportion of sequences passing a test

Fig. 2. P-Values for the fingerprints obtained

fingerprints. Generally, we observed that no significant weakness could be observed for any of the 24 different statistical tests utilized.

Acknowledgments. This work was supported by a fellowship within the Postdoc-Program of the German Academic Exchange Service (DAAD)

References

1. Mayrhofer, R., Gellersen, H.: Spontaneous mobile device authentication based on sensor data. Information Security Technical Report 13(3), 136–150 (2008)
2. Mayrhofer, R., Gellersen, H.: Shake well before use: Intuitive and secure pairing of mobile devices. IEEE Transactions on Mobile Computing 8(6) (2009)
3. Mayrhofer, R.: The Candidate Key Protocol for Generating Secret Shared Keys from Similar Sensor Data Streams. In: Stajano, F., Meadows, C., Capkun, S., Moore, T. (eds.) ESAS 2007. LNCS, vol. 4572, pp. 1–15. Springer, Heidelberg (2007)
4. Mayrhofer, R., Gellersen, H.: Shake well before use: Authentication based on accelerometer data. In: LaMarca, A., Langheinrich, M., Truong, K.N. (eds.) Pervasive 2007. LNCS, vol. 4480, pp. 144–161. Springer, Heidelberg (2007)
5. Bichler, D., Stromberg, G., Huemer, M., Loew, M.: Key generation based on acceleration data of shaking processes. In: Krumm, J., Abowd, G.D., Seneviratne, A., Strang, T. (eds.) UbiComp 2007. LNCS, vol. 4717, pp. 304–317. Springer, Heidelberg (2007)
6. Wang, A.: An Industrial Strength Audio Search Algorithm. In: International Conference on Music Information Retrieval, ISMIR (2003)
7. Wang, A.: The Shazam music recognition service. Communications of the ACM 49(8), 48 (2006)
8. Juels, A., Wattenberg, M.: A Fuzzy Commitment Scheme. In: Sixth ACM Conference on Computer and Communications Security, pp. 28–36 (1999)
9. Reed, I., Solomon, G.: Polynomial codes over certain finite fields. Journal of the Society for Industrial and Applied Mathematics, 300–304 (1960)
10. Brown, R.G.: Dieharder: A random number test suite (2011), `http://www.phy.duke.edu/~rgb/General/dieharder.php`
11. Kuiper, N.: Tests concerning random points on a circle. In: Proceedings of the Koinklijke Nederlandse Akademie van Wetenschappen, vol. Series a 63, pp. 38–47 (1962)

A Context-Based Approach to Detecting Miscreant Behavior and Collusion in Open Multiagent Systems

Larry Whitsel and Roy Turner

School of Computing and Information Science
University of Maine
Orono, ME 04469–5752 USA
{lwhitsel,rmt}@cs.umaine.edu

Abstract. Most multiagent systems (MAS) either assume cooperation on the part of the agents or assume that the agents are completely self-interested, for example, in the case of bidding and other market-based approaches. However, an interesting class of MAS is one that is fundamentally cooperative, yet open, and in which one or more of the agents may be self-interested. In such systems, there is the potential for agents to misbehave, i.e., to be *miscreants*. Detecting this is tricky and context-dependent. Even more difficult is the problem of detecting collusion between agents.

In this paper, we report on a project that is beginning to address this problem using a context-based approach. Features of the MAS' situation are used by a subset of the agents to identify it as an instance of one or more known contexts. Knowledge the agent(s) have about those contexts can then be used to directly detect miscreant behavior or collusion or to select the appropriate technique for the context with which to do so. The work is based on context-mediated behavior (CoMB), and it develops a new form of collusion detection called society-level analysis of motives (SLAM).

Most work on multiagent systems (MAS) has either assumed that the agents are all cooperative (e.g., in cooperative distributed problem solving approaches [1]) or all self-interested (e.g., in contracting and bidding approaches [7]). An interesting case, however, is a MAS where the fundamental intent is for it to be cooperative, but which may include self-interested agents. This class of MAS corresponds to many real-world systems, for example open client-server networks such as the Web, Wi-Fi networks, and so forth. In this kind of system, it is important to recognize when agents are at odds, either intentionally or unintentionally, with the goals of the system—when they are, as we term them, *miscreants*.

Detecting miscreant agents is difficult. It essentially is a problem of trust: Do we trust a particular agent (1) to be able to abide by the rules of the society, as well as the spirit of those rules (*capability*), and (2) to be willing to do so (*trustworthiness*)?

M. Beigl et al. (Eds.): CONTEXT 2011, LNAI 6967, pp. 300–306, 2011.

A very important kind of miscreant behavior is *collusion*: multiple agents either acting in unison or according to a secret agreement that in either case violates the intention of the society. It is essentially unsanctioned coalitions among agents.

Collusion detection is difficult due to the variety of ways in which it can manifest. For example, explicit collusion often occurs with the fact of the collusion itself being hidden, for example, by a priori agreements, by using covert communication channels, or by masking any communication over shared channels. The agents involved may act differently under different circumstances, and the time course of their collusive behavior can vary, sometimes to intentionally mask the collusion. Implicit collusion can occur without any communication between the agents involved at all, and it is ephemeral: agents that collude in one situation may compete in another.

Even though in general there is great variation in miscreant behavior and collusion, in many domains there will be patterns that, if identified, can help detect the behavior. A simple example of this is the case in which two agents are known to have explicitly colluded in the past. When an agent observes these two agents entering the MAS, then this defines a context in which it should suspect collusion to be likely. There are other, society-level features as well that define contexts where miscreant behavior or collusion is likely. For example, in a MAS where there is some competition between agents for rewards (e.g., some types of contracting systems), there is adequate motive for self-interested agents to cheat, and implicit collusion should be watched for in which two agents "gang up" on a leader.

To capitalize on these patterns of features, we are developing an approach to handling miscreant agent behavior and collusion based on our prior work in context-mediated behavior (CoMB) for intelligent agent control [9,8]. This approach explicitly represents contexts that are important from the standpoint of detecting miscreant behavior. These are represented as knowledge structures called *contextual schemas* (c-schemas), which in addition to describing contexts, also contain prescriptive knowledge about how to behave while in the context. One or more trusted agents in the MAS monitor the situation, constantly attempting to diagnose it as an instance of one or more contexts it knows. When this is possible, then the c-schemas representing the contexts can directly provide hypotheses about possible miscreant behavior and collusion as well as suggestions for techniques to detect or confirm such behavior.

1 Detecting Miscreant Behavior and Collusion

Previous work on detecting miscreant behavior generally treats the problem as one of making social trust decisions. Work has typically focused on three approaches, based on either: socio-cognitive trust utility (e.g., [2]), primarily cast in terms of game theory; reputation-based approaches (e.g., ([6]); or machine-learning approaches (e.g., [3]). Each of these approaches has its own strengths and weaknesses that determine for which situations it is appropriate. Elsewhere, we report on simulation experiments that compare the techniques in our test domain [10] under different circumstances. While no single technique is appropriate for all situations, the group of techniques can be thought of as a toolbox from which a MAS can, once the context is known, select the appropriate response.

Detecting collusion is difficult, and it varies based on whether the collusion is implicit or explicit. Implicit collusion is difficult to detect because it can arise without any formal agreement between the agents or even without any communication (in-channel or out-of-channel) between the agents at all. For example, two agents may independently realize that a third is close to a victory in a game or close to winning a bid and begin to tacitly cooperate to bring the agent back into parity or to defeat it.

Detecting explicit collusion may be as simple as intercepting communication between the colluding agents, but even this is likely to be difficult. Communication can be encoded, with even the fact of the encoding be masked, or the communication may be covert (out-of-channel) communication. For example, an agent might communicate with another by a particular agreed-upon pattern of movements (for physical agents) that look innocent to others, or by taking actions to modify some system-level parameter, such as paging rate, I/O rate, or the availability of some resource [5] (for software agents).

2 Identifying Important Situational/Societal Features

In our approach, agents use features of the situation as well as society-level features to determine what the context is, which then allows the agent to identify or predict miscreant behavior or collusion. Here, we briefly discuss some of these important features.

Some features of the overall situation—for example, the potential existence of rewards for cheating—can predict the presence of miscreant agents. Features of the agents participating in the MAS are also important. Obviously, if all the agents are designed by the MAS' designers, then trust can increase, but the MAS may be able to reason about the likelihood of cheating even if this is not the case. For example, if the MAS knows the reasoning abilities of an agent, it may in some cases be able to predict its responses to the ongoing situation, and so predict whether or not it will behave. Even when the reasoning processes may not be so transparent, the MAS may be able to reason about an agent's likely behavior based on what it knows in general about the class of agent or about the particular agent, e.g., from past interactions or other sources of reputation data.

Features of the society can also give clues about the presence collusion. We use the term *society-level analysis of motive* (SLAM) for the process of using such features to detect collusion or other forms of miscreant behavior.

One such feature has to do with agent actions. Each action can be characterized as being beneficial, neutral, or harmful to each other agent in the system, as well as to the system as a whole. If an agent's actions give a disproportionate benefit to another agent, then collusion between the two should be suspected.

Disproportionate benefit analysis can be used to detect possible collusion between agents. Actions are labeled as beneficial, neutral, or harmful by summing their effects over time on each other agent and comparing the effects to the average level of benefit of all actions in the society. A side-effect of this analysis will be to also identify an agent's aggressiveness even if collusion is not present. For example, we may find that some agent is always more harmful or more helpful than is the norm to all other agents, or some particular class of agents. This can be used to help detect non-collusive miscreants at the society level, and at the individual agent level, it can be used to adjust an agent's responses to the aggressive or altruistic agent.

Another feature that can indicate collusion is uncharacteristic behavior by one or more agents, particularly when paired with other changes in the situation. For example, if a normally neutral agent suddenly becomes more aggressive or docile when a new agent enters the system, then a reasonable hypothesis is that the two occurrences are linked, possibly due to collusion between the agents.

Other features that could be indicative of collusion have to do with detecting paired features of agents. For example, implicit collusion could be found by measuring the correlation between actions and comparing that correlation with the societal mean, say by "ganging up on" an opponent, making similar bids, or paired postures (e.g., aggressive/submissive). Although this can happen in explicit collusion as well, here there is a richer set of behavior available due to the ability of the colluding agents to agree on their roles and the ability to arrange to share risks and rewards. This might allow agents to agree to take complementary actions, for example. Of course, sophisticated agents might attempt to obfuscate collusion, and consequently any pairing of actions or postures would have to be detected statistically, over time.

Other attributes of the MAS agents can also serve as features predictive of possible collusion. For example, agents owned by the same organization or even arriving together into society might be worth watching for signs of collusion.

3 Using Contextual Knowledge

Miscreant behavior, including collusion, is more likely in some situations than others, and it presents differently in different situations as well. Consequently, the approach we take to miscreant detection is based on context-mediated behavior (CoMB), which uses a priori contextual knowledge to determine appropriate behavior in a particular situation. Here, that behavior is the process of detecting miscreants.

For now, we assume that there are one or more trusted agents in the multi-agent system that are tasked with (or at least capable of) detecting miscreant behavior. Since these agents primarily use a society-level analysis of motive, we call them SLAM agents. When a SLAM agent detects such behavior, its responsibility is to alert the rest of the MAS or in some other way take action. What action to take, while itself context-dependent, is MAS-dependent. Consequently, it is not the focus of this paper.

In our approach, a SLAM agent makes use of knowledge about the context to detect miscreant behavior. We make a distinction between a *situation* and a *context*. For a MAS, its situation is the sum total of all features, observable or otherwise, of itself, others, and its environment. Situations can be grouped, with the members of each group all having the same or nearly the same implications for the MAS in terms of predictions about outcomes of actions or events, likelihood of miscreant behavior and the type of that behavior, its agents' appropriate behavior, and other inferences that can be made about it, its agents, or its environment.

These groups of situations are what we mean by *context*: A context is a class of situation with important implications for a MAS or its agents. In our example contexts might be: detecting an aggressive agent, recognizing when two known compatriots are present, interacting when there is a reputation system in place, and so forth. Note that a given situation may be an instance of more than one context; for example, the MAS might be in the context in which two known compatriots are present and there is also a reputation system in place.

Our approach explicitly represents known contexts as knowledge structures called *contextual schemas* (c-schemas). A c-schema describes a class of situation as well as provides predictions about possibly unseen features of the situation which can help the MAS or its agents appropriately disambiguate new information. The features we discussed above define the space of contexts that are important, and they form the basis for the representation of the c-schemas.

Context assessment is the process of determining of which contexts a given situation is an instance. It is a diagnostic process, with features of the situation playing the role of signs and symptoms and contexts playing the role of "diseases". The descriptive knowledge contained in c-schemas is used to diagnose the situation as being an instance of one or more contexts the c-schemas represent. In past work, we have used an abductive diagnostic process based on the work of Miller, Pople, and Myers [4].

The c-schemas comprising the context assessment help the agent or MAS decide how to behave. In general, we are interested in using context to help agents in the MAS decide how to participate in the society as well as how to detect miscreant behavior. Our prior work in CoMB addresses the former; here, we focus on the latter.

A particular context assessment can directly serve as a hypothesis that miscreant behavior is occurring. That is, the context might be, essentially, "a miscreant agent is present" or "collusion is occurring". Depending on the degree of belief associated with the hypothesis, which will depend both on how strongly the agent believes its assessment and how strongly the c-schema in question predicts the offending behavior, it may or may not need to gather additional evidence to confirm the hypothesis.

Context can also focus attention on salient features of the situation, for example, unusual communication or the possibility of a covert channel. Although these might be noticed otherwise with additional reasoning, using c-schemas allows the features to be noticed automatically as a side-effect of context assessment.

C-schemas can also tailor an agent's reasoning techniques to fit the situation. For example, in our current work on SLAM, we intend to build a dynamic decision network (DDN) for each other agent in the system, adjusting its belief about their attitudes each time an action is observed. Instead of building these structures from scratch when a new agent enters the system, we can store parameters of the networks in c-schemas representing contexts involving the agents. Then, when the agent is seen again, the c-schemas will be retrieved and will allow the networks to be immediately re-instantiated.

It is important for an agent to always maintain an accurate view of the context, even as the situation changes. This can be done in several ways. First, the agent can re-assess its context on a regular basis, and when the assessment produces a new set of c-schemas, the new merged c-schemas become the new context representation and behavior changes automatically. Second, we can identify a set of context change-inducing events (CCIE) that agents should look for. When these are detected, then context assessment would be done. Examples of CCIEs we have so far identified include: detection of collusion; change in composition of the MAS due to an agent entering or exiting; detection of unusual message traffic or covert channels; and, for some kinds of domains, temporal characteristics, such as immediately following startup or at a critical stage of a game or problem-solving session. Finally, c-schemas can themselves suggest when the context should change by predicting features or events that indicate the c-schema is no longer a good fit for the situation or that suggest other c-schemas that are better.

While we have not yet addressed the question of the origin of c-schemas, CoMB itself has the position that c-schemas are actually generalized cases of problem solving and that they can be learned from experience via similarity-based or other kinds of learning. Learning is not the focus of this work, however, and we anticipate, initially at least, hand-crafting c-schemas for our agents to use.

4 Conclusion and Future Work

In this paper, we have described a context-based approach to the problem of miscreant behavior detection that is being developed, in which known contexts are explicitly represented and reasoned about, and in which the context representations (c-schemas) contain context-appropriate knowledge the agents can use to guide their decision making. We believe that this approach will allow agents to more easily detect such behavior by using knowledge that is appropriate to the current context.

Although work on context-mediated behavior, on which this work is based, is somewhat mature, the work reported in this paper is still in the early stages and is the subject of a PhD dissertation that is in progress. The short term will see a more complete design and implementation of the context-based SLAM approach described.

In the longer term, we anticipate this approach being the basis for more general context-aware multiagent systems. In such systems, context would itself be a first-class object for discussion and reasoning about by the agents, and context assessment would be a shared activity among at least a subset of the agents. Such systems would be able to adjust their behavior and possibly their form to fit their evolving context.

References

1. Durfee, E.H.: Distributed problem solving and planning. In: Weiss, G. (ed.) Multiagent Systems: A Modern Approach to Distributed Artificial Intelligence. The MIT Press, Cambridge (1999)
2. Falcone, R., Castelfranchi, C.: Social trust: A cognitive approach. In: Castelfranchi, C., Tan, Y. (eds.) Trust and Deception in Virtual Societies, pp. 55–90. Kluwer Academic Publishers, Dordrecht (2001)
3. Iszuierdo, L., Izquierdo, S.: Dynamics of the Bush–Mosteller learning algorithm in 2x2 games. In: Weber, C., Elshaw, M., Mayer, N. (eds.) Reinforcement Learning: Theory and Applications, p. 424. I-Tech Education and Publishing, Vienna (2008)
4. Miller, R.A., Pople, H.E., Myers, J.D.: INTERNIST–1, an experimental computer-based diagnostic consultant for general internal medicine. New England Journal of Medicine 307, 468–476 (1982)
5. Moskowitz, I., Kang, M.: Covert channels-here to stay? In: Reggio, G., Astesiano, E., Tarlecki, A. (eds.) Abstract Data Types 1994 and COMPASS 1994. LNCS, vol. 906, pp. 235–243. Springer, Heidelberg (1995)
6. Mui, L., Mohtashemi, M., Halberstadt, A.: Notions of reputation in multi-agents systems: a review. In: Proceedings of the First International Joint Conference on Autonomous Agents and Multiagent Systems, AAMAS 2002, Part 1, pp. 280–287. ACM, New York (2002), http://doi.acm.org/10.1145/544741.544807
7. Sandholm, T.: Distributed rational decision making. In: Weiss, G. (ed.) Multiagent Systems: A Modern Approach to Distributed Artificial Intelligence. The MIT Press, Cambridge (1999)
8. Turner, R.M.: Adaptive Reasoning for Real-World Problems: A Schema-Based Approach. Lawrence Erlbaum Associates, Hillsdale (1994)
9. Turner, R.M.: Context-mediated behavior for intelligent agents. International Journal of Human–Computer Studies 48(3), 307–330 (1998)
10. Whitsel, L.T.: A Simulator for Rule-based Agent Trust Decisions. Master's thesis, University of Maine, Department of Computer Science, Orono, Maine (2010)

A Notion of Event Quality for Contextualized Planning and Decision Support Systems

Leendert W.M. Wienhofen[1], Davy Preuveneers[2], Andreas D. Landmark[1], Pieter J. Toussaint[1], and Yolande Berbers[2]

[1] Department of Computer and Information Science,
Norwegian University of Science and Technology
Sem Sælandsv 7-9, NO-7489 Trondheim, Norway
{leendert.wienhofen,andreala,pieter}@idi.ntnu.no
[2] Department of Computer Science, K.U.Leuven
Celestijnenlaan 200A, B-3001 Leuven, Belgium
{davy.preuveneers,yolande.berbers}@cs.kuleuven.be

Abstract. This paper presents an approach for contextualizing an event-based decision support system for scheduling patient assessments in a hospital. To cope with unexpected delays, patient coordinators often pursue a worst case scenario when scheduling patient assessments, leading to an underutilization of human resources and equipment when the procedure went without complications. We present a context-based decision support system for patient planning that helps the patient coordinator with taking well-informed rescheduling decisions and anticipating changes in other patients' schedules. The system uses information and events produced by medical equipment. As these events can be non-deterministic, we demonstrate how our domain specific context model can be used to contextualize events to enhance their quality and ascertain their meaning.

1 Introduction

In this paper, we focus on the planning tasks of healthcare professionals and the coordination of the flow of patient assessments in a hospital. A lot of data is collected during these assessments for the primary purpose of creating a human-oriented decision support system for patient treatment. Secondary objectives such as improved planning, coordination and rescheduling support for medical resources are generally not implemented because there are no explicit and all-encompassing guidelines describing every step of the activity in detail. Additionally *all patients are different*, even with the same diagnosis. That is why patient assessment schedules often pursue a worst case scenario to cope with their non-deterministic nature and unexpected delays. This leads to two problems:

1. An underutilization of resources when the assessment went without problems
2. A lack of information to reschedule patients on-demand more effectively

Our goal is to look for ways to (1) alleviate some of the pressure on the patient coordinator at peak times, (2) to improve the utilization of resources, and (3) to

M. Beigl et al. (Eds.): CONTEXT 2011, LNAI 6967, pp. 307–320, 2011.

enable a more pro-active behavior by all the medical stakeholders involved in the patient assessment flow. Trying to create a software support system for such a decision process then entails support for aggregating and combining heterogeneous knowledge from a variety of sources. This ensures a proper flow of information to the patient coordinator so that he can take well-informed rescheduling decisions and anticipate changes in other patients' schedules. We use system events (e.g. sensor readings) and information (e.g. changes in the Electronic Patient Record (EPR)) produced by medical resources as a way to recognize ongoing patient assessments. However, these events are an *incomplete*, *uncertain* and sometimes *ambiguous* representation of the activity. The research challenge that we face is that *due to non-deterministic human behavior and with legacy medical equipment not designed for this purpose, it is impossible to assume a one-on-one mapping of system events onto patient assessment activities.* This discrepancy can impact the quality assurance of a medical decision support system if one relies on particular event patterns being analyzed by event processing systems.

To ascertain the meaning of the events, we introduce a notion of event quality and a way to contextualize events in order to bridge this gap between system events and patient assessment activities. This way, the coordinator can improve the scheduling process of patient assessments by taking well-informed decisions and anticipate consequences with other patient assessments in case unexpected events occur. The key contributions of this paper are as follows:

1. We present a domain specific context model used in our decision support system for contextualized (re)scheduling of patient assessments.
2. We introduce the notion of Quality of Event (QoE) as a measure to describe how well events characterize activities in real life, and to improve the confidence in the data obtained through event processing.
3. We demonstrate how the domain specific context model can be used to contextualize events and influence their quality.

The paper is organized as follows. In section 2 we discuss the context of this research and present a typical patient assessment scenario in section 3. We motivate the need for quality assurance in context-aware and event-based decision support systems, discuss our approach towards contextualizing events, and present our domain specific context model in section 4. Section 5 evaluates these concepts with several events throughout a patient flow in a pre-operative hospital setting. We end with conclusions and further work in section 6.

2 Background and Related Work

The underlying presumption for the challenges presented in this paper is an intrinsic variability in clinical work [1,2,3]. This variation is due to multiple factors. Hospitals have increased in size and complexity in terms of architecture, organizational structure, new technology and treatments. Additionally the central piece of the puzzle, the human body, acts as both recipient and deliverer of care. Compared to the more traditional industrial processes, the human agent might appear highly irrational. On top of these constraints, most major hospitals also deal with a continuous stream of unforeseen, though somehow expected interruptions to their routine work in the form of incoming emergency cases preempting planned work as well as the outcome of treatment not going according to expectations. To cope with these variations, health care professionals need, at times detailed information about the state of the processes in their immediacy. The flipside of the increasing use of technology is a growing availability of streams of events from the equipment becoming available for secondary purposes such as reasoning. However, given the ambiguous nature of raw data taken out if its context, increasing the amount of data available introduces a new set of challenges.

Lee et al. [4] discuss concerns with data fusion in healthcare environments, and more particularly in pervasive healthcare monitoring systems (PHMS). The software challenges they identified regarding collecting and aggregating events from body sensor networks, wireless sensor networks and mobile devices are similar to ours. The rate of collected data in medical sensor networks is increasing, and so is the complexity to produce high confidence data for medical diagnosis and treatment. They address the reliability of measured data by body sensors and communicating the data over heterogeneous wireless networks.

Similar work on uncertainty in complex event streams was demonstrated in [5]. Wasserkrug et al. confirm that most contemporary event composition systems are unable to handle incomplete or uncertain information. Their framework not only handles uncertain events, but also the uncertainty in the inference process. They consider a temporal context and which events are relevant to the inference of other events. Compared to their work, the uncertainty on the occurrence of events in our application scenario is much more dynamic.

Schwiderski-Grosche et al. propose in [6] a composite event language for spatio-temporal reasoning. Time and space are also important for our work to contextualize events. The authors acknowledge the problems of estimating location and the uncertainty it creates to synchronize events in both the time and space domain. The authors go to great lengths to formalize the event operators, the composite event expressions, and the semantics of the spatio-temporal model of the events. However, for the application domain we consider, we would also need expressive power to infer the overall quality of an event pattern when the spatial and temporal characteristics of its constituents are uncertain. Such information is critical to ascertain the trustworthiness of certain complex events happening and the medical decision process that depends on them.

3 Use Case Scenario of Patient Assessment Activities

The domain knowledge and the concrete use case behind this article was acquired through observations of a pre-operative medical evaluation for cardiac patients in a Norwegian University Hospital Clinic (though do note that we have tried to keep the scenario at a level understandable for an audience without any form of medical training and therefore we needed to make some simplifications or minor

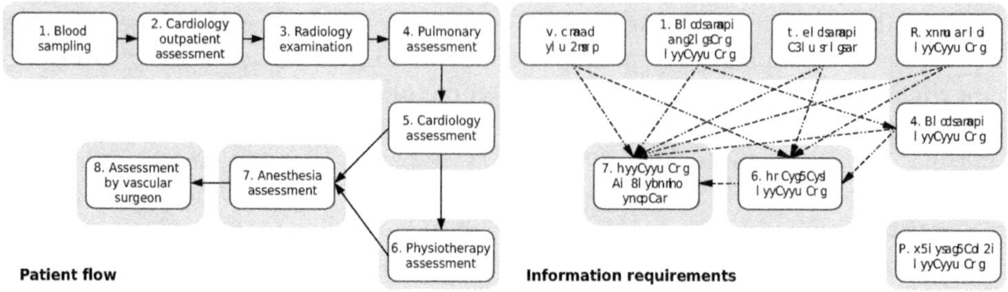

Fig. 1. Typical flow of patient activities (left) and information requirements (right)

changes to the scenario). To reduce the inconvenience for the patients, what used to be 7 examinations over several visits to the hospital has been compressed into one full day of examination activities. While this is beneficial to the patient, it increases the complexity on behalf of the hospital by increasing the need for timely coordination and communication in order to execute this plan. Problems that earlier could be sorted out between visits, will now have to be coordinated on the spot.

During the examination day, the patient has to undergo a number of standardized tests (e.g. laboratory tests, radiologic exam, ECG) in a more or less pre-determined chronological order, see Figure 1 (some deviations to the regular order are possible). While the patient traverses the activities according to the plan (see Table 1), the information dependencies between the activities are slightly decoupled from the ordering of work. For some of these activities it is both crucial that the right information is tied to the right patient, but also that the information from prior steps is available for later activities to proceed. Below, we have described the main activities over the course of such a day.

1. **Blood samples** are obtained for screening blood values, which could indicate patient conditions that need to be controlled to mitigate risk and ensure safe surgery.
2. **Cardiology outpatient assessment** to assess the suitability of the patient for surgical intervention with respect to the functioning of the patient's circulatory system. This includes an income interview and an *echo-Doppler* examination.
3. **Radiology examination** where x-ray imagery is used to help assess the suitability for operation. This also serves as input for the anaesthetist assessment later in the day.
4. **Pulmonary assessment** including a spirometry test. This is in essence a measurement of the amount (volume) and/or speed (flow) of air that can be inhaled and exhaled, and used to assess lung function. This is input for the anaesthetists and vascular surgeon's assessment.
5. **Cardiology assessment** to assess the heart function of the patient with respects to suitability for operation.

Table 1. Typical schedule for the examination day

	A_1	A_2	A_3	A_4	A_5	A_6	A_7	A_8
p_1	07:50	08:30	09:15	09:30	10:00	11:45	12:00	13:45
p_2	08:15	09:00	09:45	10:15	11:00	-	13:00	14:15
p_3	08:45	09:30	10:15	10:45	13:00	14:30	14:45	15:00

6. **Physiotherapy assessment** is undertaken for some specific diagnoses. The patient sees a cardiopulmonary physiotherapist for an assessment.
7. **Anesthesia assessment** is conducted to evaluate and score, the patient according to a standardized set of criteria, partly based on the information collected throughout the day. It is also meant to give the patient an opportunity to ask questions to ease any discomfort the patient has about being anesthetized and allow the anesthesiologist to make an evaluation of which form of anesthesia is to be used.
8. **Assessment by vascular surgeon** is the final point of the day where the patient has a consultation with a vascular surgeon. This gives the surgeon a last opportunity to make any additional examinations and the final evaluation based on all the data gathered during the day as well as an opportunity for the patient to ask questions about his or hers own illness and any discomfort about undergoing surgery.

Table 1 presents a typical schedule of an examination day of 3 different patients. It represents 3 patient flows p_i with various activities A_j (i.e. the assessments and examinations) taking place at a pre-defined timeslot. Though each activity can generate events, the clinical systems triggering events are not integrated and are largely unaware of each other. Hence it is not directly possible to automatically gather all this information across multiple sources. For a detailed explanation, see the next section.

4 Events in a Medical Application

Tables 2 and 3 present an overview of the events that can occur throughout the various patient assessment activities. Table 2 characterizes activities as a combination of events, whereas table 3 offers a more detailed description of the events.

Combinations of the events listed at the bottom lead to the activity representations at the top. In our notation, the ";" operator denotes a sequence of events, and "?" the presence of an optional event.

4.1 Ordering of Events

The order in which events occur often follows a predefined business logic or workflow path, which could be seen as an event pattern. The order in which events occur can differ based on the workflow path chosen.

Table 2. Activities and their underlying events

A1	BloodTest(p) = als ;gbc ;dbt	A5	CardiologyAssessment(p) = ae ;ce ;dr
A2	CardiologyOutpatientAssessment(p) = ae ;dr	A6	PhysiotherapyAssessment(p) = (ae)?
A3	RadiologyExamination(p) = ar (;cr?) ;sp ;er ;rr	A7	AnesthesiaAssessment(p) = ae ;dr
A4	PulmonaryAssessment(p) = (ae)?	A8	VascularSurgeonAssessment(p) = ae

Table 3. Capturable events

ae	AccessEPR(role, p)	dr	DictateResult(role, p)
als	AccessLabSystem(p)	er	ExaminationReady(role, p)
ar	AccessRIS(role, p)	gbc	GenerateBarCode(p)
ce	CardioEcho(p)	rr	ReportReady(role, p)
cr	ChangeRIS(role, p)	sp	StoreInPACS(role, p)
dbt	DispatchBloodTest(p)		

The ideal ordering of standard tests a patient typically has to undergo during the examination day (due the information dependencies of the medical stakeholders - see Figure 1) can be represented as follows:

$$A_2; A_5 \tag{1}$$

$$\{A_1, A_2, A_3, A_4, A_5\} \quad (; A_6)? \quad ; A_7 \quad ; A_8 \tag{2}$$

It shows that the first 5 activities can be carried out in any order, except for step 2 (*cardiology outpatient assessment*) that must precede step 5 (*cardiology assessment*). The sixth step (*physiotherapy assessment*) is optional, and the flow ends with steps 7 (*anesthesia assessment*) and 8 (*assessment by vascular surgeon*) in that order.

The ordering of activities in the patient workflow may change due to resource constraints or interference with other patients. For example, whereas the logical consequence of activities would be A_1, A_2, A_3, A_4, A_5, the order of activities A_2 and A_3 for a particular patient might be altered if there is there is currently no free slot in the radiology department.

4.2 Quality Concerns for Correlating Non-deterministic Events

The crux of the problem of event-based human-oriented decision support systems lies in the volatility and massiveness of the different event streams [7] being produced for each stakeholder in every patient flow. To properly interpret events and detect complex event patterns, we need sufficient expressive power to correlate events when attempting to reliably recognize a situation of interest. The following aspects are critical for measuring the relevance of events and the quality of the inferred knowledge.

- **Temporal locality:** Aggregating events implicitly introduces a notion of time, since the most common operators to relate events to one another explicitly deal with the order in which they occur [8]. The relevance of events may also be limited in time.

- **Spatial locality:** In addition to temporal locality, events can also be correlated in the space domain. Spatial correlations between event producers (e.g. location sensors and body sensors) may determine the outcome of making a correct decision.
- **Non-deterministic ordering and causality:** The event-condition-action (ECA) paradigm is often used to model causality between on the one hand events that occurred and on the other hand actions that have to be carried out or decisions that have be taken. Non-determinism is caused by (E) the indirect observations of real life events, (C) an incomplete representation of the situation due to some real life events not having a digital counterpart, and (A) the contextual dependency on any action or decision to be pursued.
- **Ambiguity and incompleteness:** Events can be periodic, stochastic or sporadic in nature. This complicates the process of defining and interpreting relevant event patterns as some situations of interest become very hard to represent as a single series of events.

To address these quality concerns, our goal is to contextualize events in order to influence their quality and to make sure that event streams are correctly interpreted.

Quality of Event (QoE): QoE is a quality measure for the validity of events of how well they characterize activities in the real world. The measure combines the following quality attributes: (1) q_p, the *probability* that the related activity has occurred, (2) q_r, the *reliability* that the order and the information the individual events carry are correct, (3) q_c, the *contextual relevance* (e.g. time, space, semantics) for being retained as a significant constituent in a complex event pattern (representing an activity).

All these aspects contribute to the confidence when interpreting event streams and to the ability to gain a better insight in the medical decision process. We formalize the notion of event quality with the following three metrics:

$$QoE_{min}(e) = min|q_p, q_r, q_c| \tag{3}$$

$$QoE_{a.avg}(e) = \frac{q_p + q_r + q_c}{3} \tag{4}$$

$$QoE_{m.avg}(e) = q_p * q_r * q_c \tag{5}$$

The three quality attributes q_p, q_r and q_c have a value between 0 and 1. The first quality metric QoE_{min} is the most strict for quality assurance and ensures that all quality attributes are above a certain threshold. The second metric $QoE_{a.avg}$ is the additive average. The third metric is a multiplicative average $QoE_{m.avg}$ that provides a measure of how the overall quality degrades or improves when one of the quality attributes changes. The advantage over an additive average is that if one of the quality attributes has a low score, then so does the overall quality of the event. With the additive average, a low score for one of the quality attributes can be averaged out with good scores for the other quality averages.

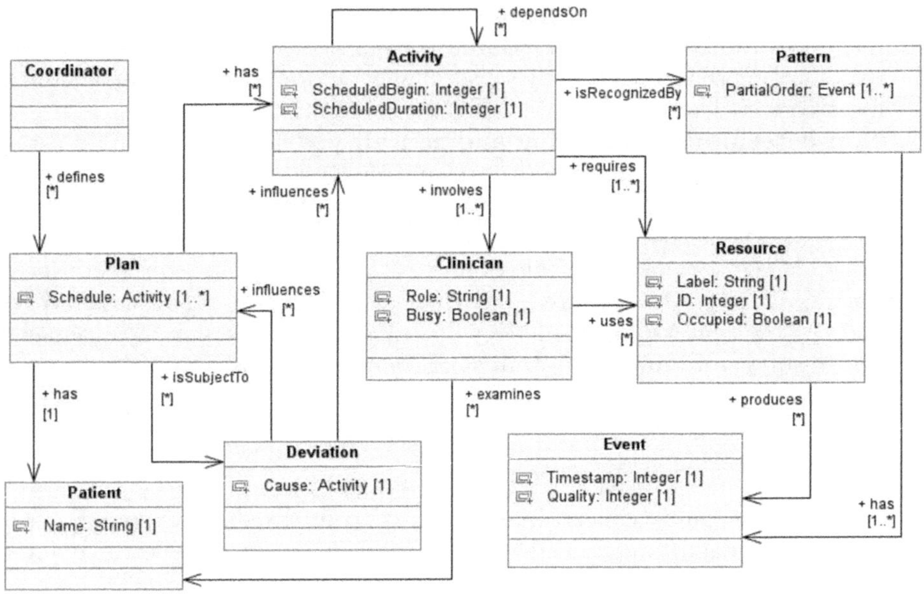

Fig. 2. Domain specific context model for patient assessment planning

More domain specific quality attributes can be added to these definitions when appropriate.

For activities A, we use similar metrics but then based on the QoE of the constituent events e_i rather than the quality attributes:

$$QoE_{min}(A) = min|QoE_{min}(e_1), ..., QoE_{min}(e_n)| \tag{6}$$

$$QoE_{a.avg}(A) = \frac{QoE_{a.avg}(e_1) + ... + QoE_{a.avg}(e_n)}{n} \tag{7}$$

$$QoE_{m.avg}(A) = QoE_{m.avg}(e_1) * ... * QoE_{m.avg}(e_n) \tag{8}$$

4.3 Domain Specific Context Model for Patient Assessments

The scheduling and coordination of patient assessment flows heavily relies on the coordinator's expertise and past experiences in similar situations. As such, context lives in the mind of the coordinator. Decision support systems that offer information that the coordinator already knows, are of no use. Therefore, the goal of our context model is not to offer an all-encompassing model that documents all concepts, but to offer the minimal amount of relevant information that can raise the attention of the coordinator about information he was unaware off or that somehow contradicts his assumptions.

Fig. 2 presents the major concepts of our domain specific context model that we use to contextualize events. It only offers a high-level overview and complements prior work on context modeling by the authors [9]. Concepts like *Resource* can be further specialized into various categories (*RadiologyRoom, HeartRate-Monitor, SpirometrySystem,* etc.).

Every patient is scheduled to undergo various assessment activities according to a plan. Each activity requires the attention of one or more clinicians who have medical equipment at their disposal. Through interaction with these resources, events are being produced. Patterns of these events can be used to characterize and recognize a particular patient assessment, and as such can be leveraged by an event-based decision support system to improve the on-demand (re)scheduling of patients. Note that multiple patients can undergo assessments in parallel. A deviation in one patient assessment plan cannot only influence the following activities in the patient assessment plan, but also have repercussions on other patient assessment plans due to resource allocation restrictions.

5 Contextualizing Events, an Example

As patients in our scenario undergo the same examinations by the same medical stakeholders, a variation in the time used versus the time planned will impact the consultation of the other patients. General event patterns can be created (see Section 4.1), though the temporal order may vary from patient to patient. As each of the activities generate events that map to the temporal ordering and the pattern, one can get a fair impression of the progress of a patient while he/she traverses all activities. For some of the activities, the events cannot be guaranteed to be caught, so assumptions need to be made. These assumptions build on two core notions: *contextualisation* and *quality.*

Quality has been described in Section 4.2 and in this section we will, by means of examples building on the scenario as previously described in Section 3, explain the concept of contextualisation of events. The quality attributes of each of the events depends on in which activity this event is being used and in order to cater for the quality, we propose to define an event quality indicator per event. The event quality is initially based ('seeded')on observations of the scenario and the activity quality indicator is calculated.

The EPR events are numerous, as the EPR system is being used throughout (and beyond) the hospital. EPR events of the type ae event consist of two parameters, *role* and *patient* (the parameter *role* is derived from the name of a HCP (Health Care Professional), which is listed with assigned roles, in our example, for simplicity, we only work with one role per HCP).

First, the filter only selects the ae events that contain a patient identifier equal to one of the three patients that are scheduled for the examination day. For simplicity, we limit the number of the patients to 3 and call these patients p_1, p_2 and p_3.

The ae event occurs in most of the activities, and to find out to which activity it belongs, we need to investigate the second of the event's parameters, *role.* As different examinations are carried out by different HCPs, one can get a sense of to which activity the event belongs. In total, the scenario contains 6 different HCPs, whom we call HCP_1 through HCP_6. All can access the EPR system:

A_2 (HCP_1 or HCP_3), A_4 (HCP_2), A_5 (HCP_3), A_6 (HCP_4), A_7 (HCP_5), A_8 (HCP_6) Note that A_1 and A_3 do not include EPR access, and that A_2 can be done by either HCP_1 or HCP_3 (HCP_1 is a junior HCP, HCP_3 a senior, ergo HCP_3 can do the work of HCP_1 but not the other way around).

Up to now, the described situation is relatively simple event filtering and matching. However, when an ae event arrives with the parameters HCP_3 and p_3, it would not be possible to find out whether the event belongs to A_2 or A_5. Even when the dr event comes after, it could still belong to both activities as these also share that event as it matches both patterns.

Instead of making a definitive decision on where to allocate the event, we propose to label the events with quality identifiers introduced in Section 4.2 and let the stakeholder decide whether the quality is satisfactory. For some HCPs even a low $QoEmin(A)$, $QoEa.avg(A)$ or $QoEm.avg(A)$ might still be sufficient to take action. The main point is that the system only supports a decision making process, it is not meant to replace it. For the coordinator in our scenario it is important to know where the patients are. The quality attributes in the example below pertain this situation: the quality of the event regarding the whereabouts of the patient (as mentioned, the attributes are 'seeds' based on actual observations).

A2: CardiologyOutpatientAssessment(patient) $=$ ae ;dr
  A2.ae($q_p = 1.0$, $q_r = 1.0$, $q_c = 0.8$)
  A2.dr($q_p = 1.0$, $q_r = 1.0$, $q_c = 0.5$)

A5: CardiologyAssessment(patient) $=$ ae ;ce ;dr
  A5.ae($q_p = 1.0$, $q_r = 1.0$, $q_c = 0.2$)
  A5.ce($q_p = 1.0$, $q_r = 1.0$, $q_c = 1.0$)
  A5.dr($q_p = 1.0$, $q_r = 1.0$, $q_c = 0.5$)

This gives the following initial values for the events related to A2:

$$QoE_{min}(A2.ae) = 0.8 \tag{9}$$

$$QoE_{a.avg}(A2.ae) = 0.93 \tag{10}$$

$$QoE_{m.avg}(A2.ae) = 0.8 \tag{11}$$

$$QoE_{min}(A2.dr) = 0.5 \tag{12}$$

$$QoE_{a.avg}(A2.dr) = 0.83 \tag{13}$$

$$QoE_{m.avg}(A2.dr) = 0.5 \tag{14}$$

When combined, it gives the following initial values for the activity A2:

$$QoE_{min}(A2) = 0.5 \tag{15}$$

$$QoE_{a.avg}(A2) = 0.88 \tag{16}$$

$$QoE_{m.avg}(A2) = 0.4 \tag{17}$$

For space saving reasons we do not present all calculations, as they are relatively straight forward. From this point forward, we only show the a.avg. This gives the following initial values for the events related to A5:

$$QoE_{a.avg}(A5.ae) = 0.73 \tag{18}$$

$$QoE_{a.avg}(A5.ce) = 1.0 \tag{19}$$

$$QoE_{a.avg}(A5.dr) = 0.83 \tag{20}$$

When combined, it gives the following initial value for the activity A5:

$$QoE_{a.avg}(A5) = 0.85 \tag{21}$$

From the scenario we learned that: For A_2, the ae event has a very high temporal and spatial meaning, as the patient is looked up in the EPR system just before the consultation and with the patient present.

For A_5 however, the very same ae event does not have the same meaning as the HCP can decide to access the EPR system at any time of the day and well before the patient's arrival.

Therefore, the q_c values for the ae event are different. The q_c values for the dr event are the same, and the reason that the value is set to 0.5 is that HCPs do not always dictate the finding right after the patient is done with the consultation. There might be a timespan upto multiple hours in between the consultation and dictation.

5.1 Event Contextualisation

Event contextualisation is the process of obtaining additional information surrounding an event in order to infer missing events or low-quality events. The goal of contextualising is to increase the event quality. In our example, the q_c values for the ae event and dr event are lower than 1.0 and could therefore benefit from contextualising. In order for a contextualisation engine to be useful, we have identified the following sources for our scenario:

- A list of existing events (see Section 4)
- Temporal constraints/ordering pattern (see Section 4.1)
- Probability of the actual temporal occurrence of events (ref. events that happen and a registered early or late)
- Number of times the specific pattern is instantiated (meaning that resources get occupied)
- Planned time schedule
- Resource constraints
- Event history over time (from a repository)

In our example we use 3 patients, p_1, p_2 and p_3. The capacity of the resources associated to the events is as follows: Blood sampling and radiology have a high parallel capacity and generally do not form a bottleneck. The other resources are limited to 1 patient at a time. In addition to the scenario described here, the resources are occupied by patients other than p_1, p_2 and p_3, meaning that capacity problems can emerge from outside of our scope.

Recall that the initial values are $QoE_{a.avg}(A2) = 0.88$ and $QoE_{a.avg}(A5) = 0.85$.

In order to adjust the q_c values of event ae(HCP_3, p_3), the first checkpoint is the planned time schedule (see Table 1) and the ordering pattern (see Section 4.1). From this we learn that that, for p_3, A_2 is scheduled at 09:30 and that A_2 always precedes A_5 (scheduled at 13:00).

The current time is 08:30. By checking the schedule and the ordering alone, we can still not increase the confidence. Therefore, we need to check the events for other patients and find: ae(HCP$_3$, p_1) at 08:28, ae(HCP$_3$, p_2) at 08:29, as well as ae(HCP$_1$, p_1). From this we can infer that HCP3 simply opened the EPRs of all patients in order to prepare for the day. Also, we learn that HCP$_1$ accessed p_1's EPR details. From this we can deduce that HCP$_1$ is the junior cardiologist on duty this day and therewith increase the q_c value for $A_2.ae$ by 0.1 and decrease the q_c value for $A_5.ae$ by 0.1.

The adjusted $QoE_{a.avg}(A2)$ is now 0.9 and $QoE_{a.avg}(A5)$ is now 0.84.

Find below another, more complex, example to illustrate the contextualisation of passed events based on the inferencing of new events. At 11:40 an ae(HCP$_4$, p_1) event arrives. First, we confirm that we have a p_1, and secondly we find that HCP$_4$ belongs to activity A_6, thirdly, we confirm that p_1 was scheduled to be consulted by HCP$_4$ at approximately the same timeslot as planned.

A6: PhysiotherapyAssessment(patient) = (ae)?
  A6.ae(q_p = 0.5, q_r = 1.0, q_c = 1.0)

This gives a $QoE_{a.avg}(A6.ae) = 0.83$ and $QoE_{a.avg}(A6)$=0.83

A7: AnesthesiaAssessment(patient) = ae ;dr
  A7.ae(q_p = 1.0, q_r = 1.0, q_c = 0.5)
  A7.dr(q_p = 1.0, q_r = 1.0, q_c = 0.5)

This gives a $QoE_{a.avg}(A7.ae) = 0.83$, $QoE_{a.avg}(A7.dr) = 0.83$, and $QoE_{a.avg}(A6) = 0.83$. The activity A_6 only consist of one event which may or not occur. Therefore, if the event occurs and matches to A_6, we can adjust q_p to 1.0 and in addition we can assure that event A_1 through A_5 have occured (based on the ordering as depicted in Section 4.1), we can now re-adjust the quality values of all previous events to 1.0 as we are certain that all have been carried out.

In case A_7 is triggered, for p_1 we can reason that the patient has been to A_6 even if no A_6 event has been caught, based on the schedule. For p_2 we can reason that event A_1 through A_5 have occured and for p_3, see the example above.

In case every patient meets for their first test on time, and the plan is kept, the coordinator has an easy day. However, the real-life situation is that the plan is hardly ever kept, and deviations occur throughout the day. Some of the reasons for deviations are that the consult time takes longer than planned, or the HCP needs to help patients outside of the scope of this application. By providing the quality of the inferenced events, the coordinator will better be able to re-schedule appointments when needed.

6 Conclusions and Further Work

Complex event processing for real world decision support systems, like health-care applications or other human-in-the-loop systems, must account for inherent uncertain and non-deterministic nature of event occurrences. The major cause of this concern is the gap that exists between the events that happen in real life, and their often incomplete or inaccurate representation with digital event patterns that are being processed by the event based systems.

In this paper, we attempt to bridge this gap by introducing the notion of quality of events (QoE) as a quality measure to characterize how well digital events represent events in the real world. The analysis presented in this paper provides insight into the diversity of quality requirements that we have to deal with when implementing such a system in medical pre-operative environment. These assessments and requirements are based on real life use cases obtained through various observations and discussions with medical stakeholders in the field.

The key contributions of this paper are (1) a requirements elicitation from a real world medical pre-operative use case through collaborations with medical stakeholders and experts in the field. These case studies served as a basis to identify shortcomings in the current state-of-the-art event based systems to identify the technical barriers to implement support for quality assurance demands, (2) the introduction of the concept Quality of Event (QoE) that represents the discrepancy between digital events and real world events, and (3) a novel approach to contextualize events to improve the event quality and the confidence in the data when used in the medical decision support system.

As part of our further work, we will continue to formalize the notion of quality for aggregated events and review the outcome with medical experts to ensure high confidence information is obtained and quality assurance is ensured.

Furthermore, we link this model to well-known specifications such as the Health Level 7 standard[1] to further reuse predefined and established concepts.

Additionally, further research should lead to continuous improvements of the quality metrics through feeding the correctness of the inference engine back into the system as input to the original quality metrics. Certain situations can confirm or refute previously recognized situations, thus leading to an improved set of quality metrics based on empirical data, improving upon any statically assigned quality metrics.

Acknowledgments. This research is partially funded by the VerdIKT-programme of the Research Council of Norway (grant no. 187854/S10), and partially funded by the Interuniversity Attraction Poles Programme Belgian State,

[1] `http://www.hl7.org`

Belgian Science Policy, and by the Research Fund K.U.Leuven. We would like to thank all our medical and non-medical colleagues from the COSTT project for sharing domain knowledge acquired through observations when studying the preoperative medical evaluation for cardiac patients at the university hospital.

References

1. Tucker, A.L.: The impact of operational failures on hospital nurses and their patients. Journal of Operations Management 22, 151–169 (2004)
2. Bardram, J.E., Hansen, T.R.: Why the plan doesn't hold: a study of situated planning, articulation and coordination work in a surgical ward. In: CSCW 2010: Proceedings of the 2010 ACM Conference on Computer Supported Cooperative Work, pp. 331–340. ACM, New York (2010)
3. Aaserud, M., Trommald, M., Boynton, J.: Elective surgery - cancellations, ring fencing and efficiency. Journal of the Norwegian Medical Association 1, 2516–2519 (2001)
4. Lee, H., Park, K., Lee, B., Choi, J., Elmasri, R.: Issues in data fusion for healthcare monitoring. In: Proceedings of the 1st International Conference on Pervasive Technologies Related to Assistive Environments, PETRA 2008, pp. 3:1–3:8. ACM, New York (2008)
5. Wasserkrug, S., Gal, A., Turchin, Y., Etzion, O.: Efficient uncertainty management in complex event systems: saving the witch from Henzel & Gretel. In: Proceedings of the Second International Conference on Distributed Event-Based Systems, DEBS 2008, pp. 305–308. ACM, New York (2008)
6. Schwiderski-Grosche, S., Moody, K.: The SpaTeC composite event language for spatio-temporal reasoning in mobile systems. In: Proceedings of the Third ACM International Conference on Distributed Event-Based Systems, DEBS 2009, pp. 11:1–11:12. ACM, New York (2009)
7. Banavar, G., Kaplan, M., Shaw, K., Strom, R., Sturman, D., Tao, W.: Information flow based event distribution middleware. In: Proceedings of 19th IEEE International Conference on Distributed Computing Systems Workshops on Electronic Commerce and Web-based Applications/Middleware, pp. 114–121 (1999)
8. Mühl, G., Fiege, L., Pietzuch, P.: Distributed Event-Based Systems, 1st edn. Springer, Heidelberg (2006)
9. Preuveneers, D., et al.: Towards an extensible context ontology for Ambient Intelligence. In: Markopoulos, P., Eggen, B., Aarts, E., Crowley, J.L. (eds.) EUSAI 2004. LNCS, vol. 3295, pp. 148–159. Springer, Heidelberg (2004)

An Architecture and a Prototype for Querying and Visualising Recorded Context Information

Erqiang Zhou, Bing Wu, Jianfeng Wu, and Yi Ding

School of Computing, Dublin Institute of Technology
Kevin St., Dublin 8, Ireland
{erqiang.zhou,bing.wu}@dit.ie, {jianfeng.wu,yi.ding}@mydit.ie

Abstract. This paper presents an architecture and a prototype for querying and visualising context information. The COINS modelling approach is employed to define and record the target information and its context information of an application domain. Two querying methods are provided for retrieving the recorded information: 1) natural language query which targets at physical context information and; 2) visual query environment which aims at logical context information. A knowledge representation model, master dictionary, is employed to facilitate the analyses of natural language queries. A prototype system based on the puzzle game Sudoku is used to illustrate the visual querying method, which integrates a replaying mechanism for the recorded context information.

1 Introduction

Context information can be classified into two categories when considering its dimensions: the physical (external) dimension (such as location, temperature) and the logical (internal) dimension (such as user's goals, business processes) [3]. Most of research mainly addressed one dimension of the context information, few research took both dimensions into account in one application domain. Generally only one dimension of the context information, usually the physical information, is used to facilitate the interaction between users and applications. One possible cause of such situation is that the physical context information can be obtained by sensors and it is domain-independent, while the logical context information is difficult to obtain and it is generally domain-dependent.

The acquirability of context information is another challenge for context-aware applications. According to Choujaa & Dulay [5], gathering real-life context information involves at least two[1] major issues: 1) technical difficulties in both hardware and software; 2) the expensive cost of hiring a cohort of test users.

This paper focuses on the logical dimension of context information while taking into account the physical dimension. It presents an architecture which addresses the issues of handling context information from the following three aspects:

[1] Choujaa & Dulay [5] listed four issues and the other two are: "*gathering subjective context information such as activity labels requires considerable user involvement and reporting*" and "*some pieces of context information are personal*".

M. Beigl et al. (Eds.): CONTEXT 2011, LNAI 6967, pp. 321–334, 2011.

– to obtain context information by integrating a recording mechanism into information systems so as to provide a live interactive record of context information that then can be queried and replayed;
– to query the physical context information, which is recorded by the recording mechanism, by using natural language and;
– to query the logical context information by implementing a relaying mechanism which visualises the logical context information so as to reproduce the interactions between users and information systems.

The rest of the paper is organised as follows: Section 2 presents the related work. Section 3 presents an architecture for querying and visualising context information. Section 4 outlines the authors' approaches about natural language query. Section 5 outlines the visualisation techniques for representing context information. Section 6 concludes this paper.

2 Related Work

Context information, such as users' activities, locations and environmental conditions or any information that can be used to characterise the situation of a person, place, or an object that is relevant to the interaction between an user and an application, is widely used to improve the intelligibility of information systems [6,10].

For example, Holmes & Murphy [9] proposed an approach to use structural context information to recommend source code in software developing process. Bai et al. [2] proposed to use *query-specific contexts*, which specifies the environment of a query such as the domain of interest, to improve the effectiveness of information retrieval. Sondhi et al. [11] described an approach to improve search experience by altering ambiguous topic related queries with additional contextual keywords derived from (topic-specific) query logs. Finkelstein et al. [7] utilised contexts information (such as profile, his/her interests, past searching experiences) to personalise web search and to achieve more relevant search results. Adomavicius & Tuzhilin [1] discussed how contextual information, such as time, location, can be modelled in recommender systems. Choi & Yoon [4] presented a meta-data model of context information so as to increase the richness of communication in human computer interactions.

In addition to research which focused on the "usage" of context information, there are research that addressed the quality and availability of context information. Henricksen & Indulska [8] pointed out that "*sensed context information is often inaccurate or unavailable as a result of noise or sensor failures, while user-supplied information is subject to problems such as human error and staleness*". Realising the difficulties of gathering real world context information, Choujaa & Dulay [5] investigated the possibility to use context data extracted from screenplays in certain context-aware applications when real-life data is not available.

3 The System Architecture

Context information is generally used as *additional* or *complementary* information for improving the intelligibility of information systems. Instead of considering how to use context information, this paper targets on the context information itself. More specifically, this paper presents an architecture which focuses on how to retrieve and present context information, addressing the problem of availability of context information by employing the COINS modelling approach [12].

3.1 The COINS Modelling Approach

The COINS modelling approach [12] manages complex information within the paradigm of recording live interactive records of information so that the recorded information can be queried and replayed.

The COINS model consists of three components: 1) a structure model employing Entity Relationship (ER) approach; 2) a rule mechanism which deals with logic constraints among attributes, entities and relationships and; 3) a recorder component which supports a mechanism of recoding and replaying the history of evolving information. Three kinds of recorders are provided in the COINS model: value recorders, rule recorders, and scene recorders, targeting at different type of information to be recorded respectively.

In the structure model, related entities are connected by relationships. At any given time unit, these connected entities and their attributes form a cluster of complex information within which atomic information units hold some logic connections with each other. This paper refers such a cluster of complex information as an information scene, which is a snapshot of linking-relations among certain entities and relationships at a given time unit. When such entities and relationships are of concrete value/contents for an information scene, it yields an instance of the information scene.

From COINS' perspective, a target information unit together with its context form an information scene. Accordingly, for an application domain, contexts can be modelled and defined with a context (scene) recorder in a COINS model, and then the context recorder can be implemented within the given domain. Once the context recorder is integrated into an information system, the defined context information can be automatically recorded when users interact with the system.

3.2 The Replaying Mechanism

Generally an information/database system responses to queries with static information. The ability of such an information/database system to responses to queries on past history with dynamic and evolving information has not been fully developed. Based on the recording mechanism of the COINS modelling approach, a replaying mechanism providing such an ability can be developed.

A simple way for replaying recorded instances of information scenes is to present them based on time order. That is, the changing history of the recorded information will be shown with the time that changes occur. A recorded instance of information scene can also be taken as a reference for displaying records of other scenes. In other words, the representation of the replaying history will focus on evolution of one scene, therefore its changing history will be shown sequentially, while other scenes whose time-stamps matches the time-stamp of the focused information scene can also be displayed accordingly. A more complex way to replay recorded information is to display designated scenes within a time interval or more generally, under given conditions. Such an approach would integrate the query mechanism and the visualisation techniques into the replaying process so as to facilitate the examination or inspection of the archived information.

3.3 An Architecture for Querying and Visualising Recorded Context Information

As shown in Figure 1, there are four main components in the system architecture: 1) an user interface; 2) a replaying component; 3) a recording component and; 4) a natural language query component. It is worth noticing that the user interface overlaps with the replaying component.

The *User Interface* component provides users with the functionalities for creating and updating domain models, it also enables users to query and replay the recorded information scenes with natural language as well as visual query mechanism. The *Query Input* module lists supported sample queries for physical context information while the *Query Results Representation* module presents the translating results as well as the querying results.

The *Natural Language Query* component provides services for processing natural language queries for physical context information. In the architecture, the

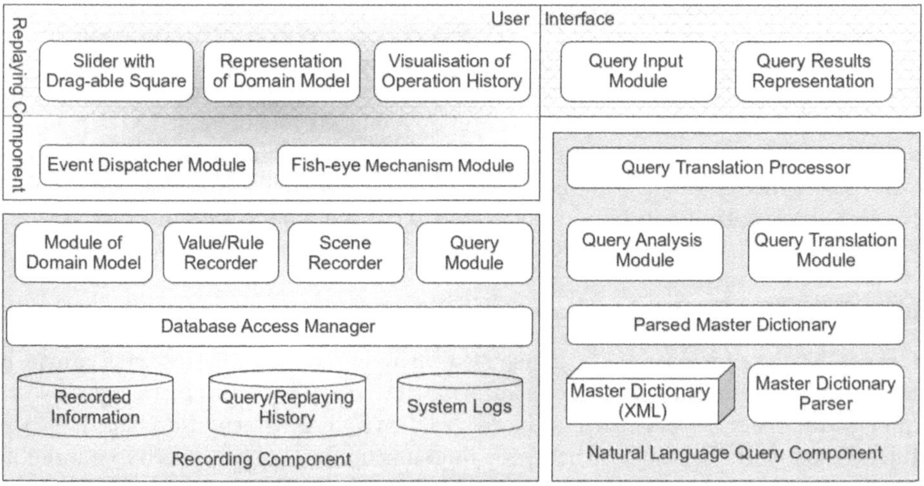

Fig. 1. The system architecture for querying and visualising recorded context information

Master Dictionary (*MD*), which will be introduced in Section 4, is realised in the form of an XML document. Therefore an *MD* parser is needed to parse the XML document. After that, the parsed *MD* acts as a knowledge base for analysing and translating given queries. The *Query Translation Processor* integrates the whole component into the prototype system by encapsulating the analysis and translation modules.

The *Recording* component implements the recording mechanism for the application of updating domain models. In detail, this component offers two main services for others: 1) to capture and generate information units which are specified by the COINS model, and thereafter store the information units into a database; 2) to retrieve the recorded information units and then reorganise (reproduce) them so as to facilitate the replaying process. In the architecture, one database is used to store the domain information and the recorded operating histories. For certain domains, the querying histories themselves are worthy to be saved for mining hidden patterns, which can be further used for optimising the system. In addition, system logs are also useful for finding errors and exceptions.

The *Replaying* component provides interfaces not only for creating and updating domain models, but also for visualising the updating processes so that users can query the operations of each process with visual facts (such as shapes) by using a mouse pointer.

4 Natural Language Query

Generally, the context information of the physical dimension is easier to be understood than that of the logical dimension. This is caused by the fact that certain physical context information can be directly sensed by humans' sensory organs or hardware sensors, while the logical context information usually involves domain knowledge or business processes.

A related fact is that physical context information is easier to be described with natural language, while the description of logical context information often needs the help of diagrams, colours, figures, etc..

Accordingly, when retrieving information with physical context information, natural language is a better option for describing the context; when retrieving information with the help of logical context information, the predefined artifacts are more suitable than natural language.

4.1 The Master Dictionary

In order to express the knowledge piece that a word conveys, this research employs '*category*' to express the knowledge that a group of words belongs to a particular category. For example, a grammatical category "Noun" includes the knowledge that if a word is a noun (the word belongs to the category "Noun"), then the word refers to a person, a place or something else. We define that a '*relation*' is a usage-relationship among words and categories. Thus such usage-relationships can be used to specify how a word can be used with other words or categories. We define an '*abstraction*' as a defining-relationship among words and categories. That is, an abstraction is a defining-relationship in which some words and categories are used to define a new meaning of a particular word.

A Master Dictionary (*MD*) is defined as a 4-tuple (W, C, R, A). Here W is a set of words; C is a set of categories; R is a set of relations and A is a set of abstractions. Once an *MD* is built for a specific domain, the context information described with natural languages can be analysed and processed by utilising the *MD*. It is beyond the scope of this paper to explain how to build such an *MD*.

4.2 Steps of Analysing a Natural Language Sentence

The overall strategy of the approach for analysing a natural language query is a kind of "bottom-up" processing. It starts from the analysis of each word to phrase units, such as noun phrases, time phrases and positional phrases; then to functional units from a sentence's perspective, such as subjects, predicates and clauses; and finally to the whole sentence.

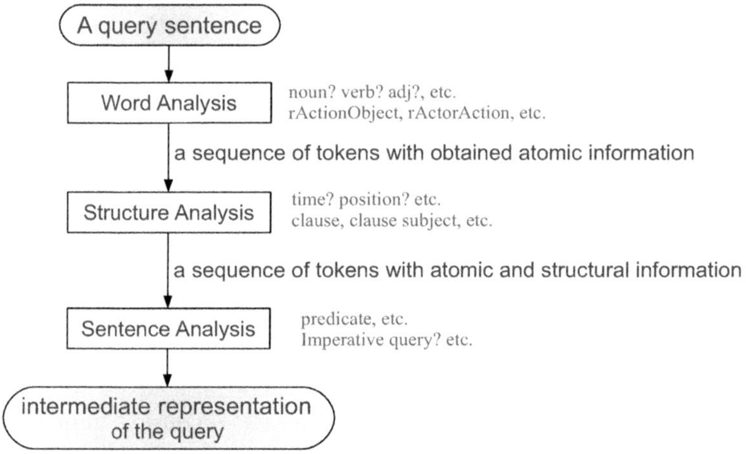

Fig. 2. The flow chart for analysing a query sentence

Figure 2 presents a flow chart for analysing a querying sentence. The whole process consists of three steps: 1) word analysis; 2) structure analysis and; 3) sentence analysis.

The word analysis takes a query as an input and gives an output of a sequence of tokens with obtained atomic information (which can be directly obtained from the *MD*).

The structure analysis determines the boundary of each functional unit in a sentence by taking advantage of the obtained information in word analysis as well as the *MD*. The output of structure analysis is a sequence of tokens with atomic information and structure information.

The sentence analysis takes the output of structure analysis as input and determines the types of the query: whether it is an *imperative query* or an *interrogative query*. Its output as a whole is an intermediate representation of the querying sentence. Such intermediate representation can then be converted to formal queries (such as SQL statements). Due to the page limitation, the translation approaches will be discussed in other papers.

5 Visualising Context Information

The puzzle game Sudoku is employed as the testbed for illustrating the replaying mechanism. A classical Sudoku puzzle is a Sudoku skeleton being filled with numbers for its cells in such a way that each of its 81 cells can either be blank, or contain a number within the range of 1 to 9. The key constraint for such Sudoku puzzles is that the number of a cell in 1) each row, 2) each column and, 3) each square must be unique within its corresponding row, column and square, respectively. The purpose the Sudoku Game is to solve a given Sudoku puzzle by filling all its blank cells under such a constraint. A valid Sudoku puzzle must have and only have one solution.

Physical Context Information in Sudoku. In the Sudoku example, physical context information involves four basic elements: time, location, user and puzzle. When users sign in the system and play a puzzle, their physical context information can be described as natural language queries. For example: "*who is online*"; "*when/where does Tom sign in the system*"; "*who solve the puzzle in ten minutes*"; "*which puzzle did Tom play more than 3 times*".

Logical Context Information in Sudoku. When playing Sudoku, users select a blank cell and fill it with a number. In such a move, some strategies of the Sudoku game may determine which number(s) the cell can be filled into. If the selected cell, say the focus cell, is treated as the target information, then the cells (reason cells) and rules involved in the strategy are the logical context of the target information. Accordingly, the target information (focus cell) and the its context information (reason cells and rules) consist of an information scene. This information scene grasps the reasons why only a certain number can be filled into a particular cell and others cannot.

In order to illustrate the relations between a focus cell and its reason cells, Figure 3 presents two examples. In Figure 3a, integers from 1 to 8 have appeared in the row, the column and the square that the focus cell belongs to; therefore only number 9 can be set to the focus cell, and integers from 1 to 8 are the reasons why the focus cell is 9.

In Figure 3b, four integers have appeared and they convey the information that no same numbers can be filled in the rows, columns and squares that they occupy. This leads to a result that only one cell in the middle square can be filled with the number 1. Therefore, the appeared numbers are the reason cells for filling number 1 into the focus cell.

The prototype system implements a scene recorder so as to automatically capture the described information scene instances when users play puzzles. Other

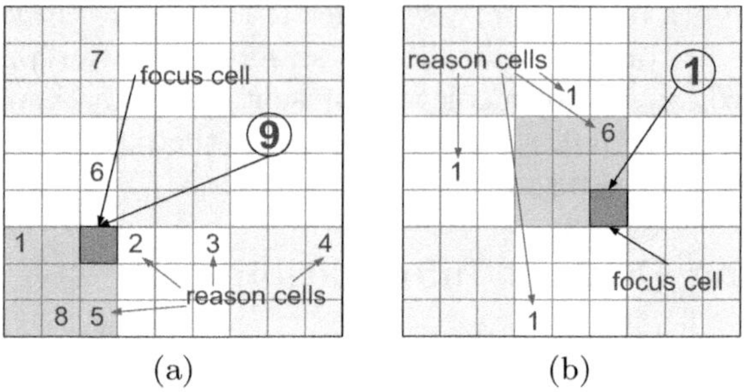

Fig. 3. Relations between a focus cell and its reason cells

necessary recorders (value recorder for cells and rule recorder for Sudoku rules) are also implemented. An *MD* is built to capture semantics of natural language words in the domain.

Two ways are provided in the prototype system for retrieving logic context information: 1) natural language query and; 2) visual query. Examples of using natural language are: "*replay the difficult puzzle which was played by Tom yesterday*"; "*why cell (4,5) is filled with 3*" or simply "*why cell 4 5*".

5.1 The Function Panels

The overall goal of the visualisation component is to facilitate the querying process by extracting and presenting the recorded information units that an user wants to know. The prototype system satisfies this need through a replaying mechanism, which treats a solving process as a sequence of information scenes, just as a media player treats a video as a sequence of images.

Three main panels are designed in the prototype system: 1) a puzzle panel, which is the main area for displaying the recorded information units; 2) an index panel, where each operation is visualised as a shape and the detail information about the operation can be retrieved by interacting with the shape; 3) a control panel, which not only provides buttons for replaying a solving process, but also offers a slider with a drag-able square so as to enhance the replaying experience.

Figure 4 shows three screen-shots of the play panel when replaying a solving process. Each screen-shot presents an information scene, which consists of a focus cell (the target information which is marked with a diamond) and several reason cells (the context information which is marked with circles). These information scenes are recorded automatically when users solve puzzles.

The help numbers shown on the right of the play panel not only emphases the row index in the panel, but also presents the distribution of the determined numbers[2] in the current puzzle layout. The more the number is determined in a puzzle layout, the lighter the colour of the number on the right will be.

[2] A determined number is a puzzle number, or a number (from 1 to 9) that an user gives to a cell and it does not cause any error under the current puzzle layout.

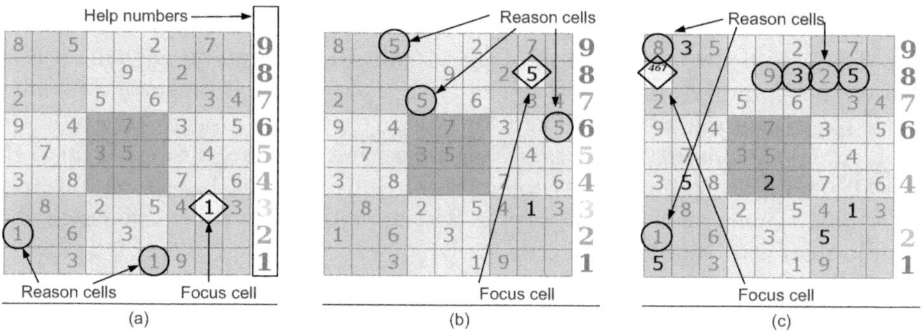

Fig. 4. The screen-shots of the play panel

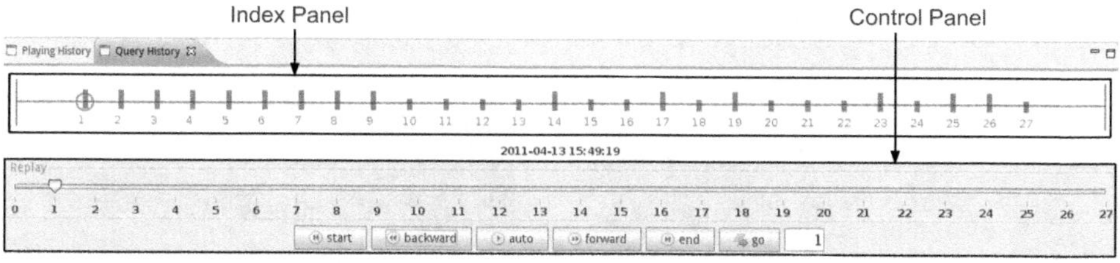

Fig. 5. The screen-shot of the index/control panel

The control panel, which consists of a slider panel and a button panel, is used to control the process of replaying the recorded information scenes. Figure 5 presents the screen shots of the index panel and the control panel.

In the index panel, each square represents an operation, which may be a normal operation, or a sub-operation (of a normal operation). Comparing to an normal operation, a sub-operation is represented as a shorter square. A square with a circle represents the focus operation, that means the corresponding puzzle layout of the operation is currently presented in the puzzle panel.

Three ways are provided in the control panel for controlling how the recorded information can be replayed. The tick on the slider can be dragged forward or backward for displaying the solving process. The control buttons can also be used to replay the history step by step whether manually or automatically. Users can also give an index number so as to show the corresponding recorded information by pressing the "go" button.

When users give orders in the control panel, the corresponding information scenes will be displayed in the puzzle panel. Three kinds of cells are distinguished in a replaying process: the focus cell that users updated in the given index; the error cells which violates the Sudoku rules; and the reason cells that compose a scene defined by rules. The replaying process is dynamically changing with different solving steps. Figure 4 and Figure 5 only show some static image in this process.

5.2 Fish-Eye Mechanism

For the index panel, one problem of the visualisation method is that if a solving process has hundreds of operations, the index panel then does not have enough space for presenting all these operations altogether. Two aspects involve in this problem: 1) the minimal space between shapes that users are interested in; 2) the overall number of the presented operations. A fish-eye mechanism and a dragable square (which will be discussed in Section 5.3) on the slider are designed to handle these two aspects respectively.

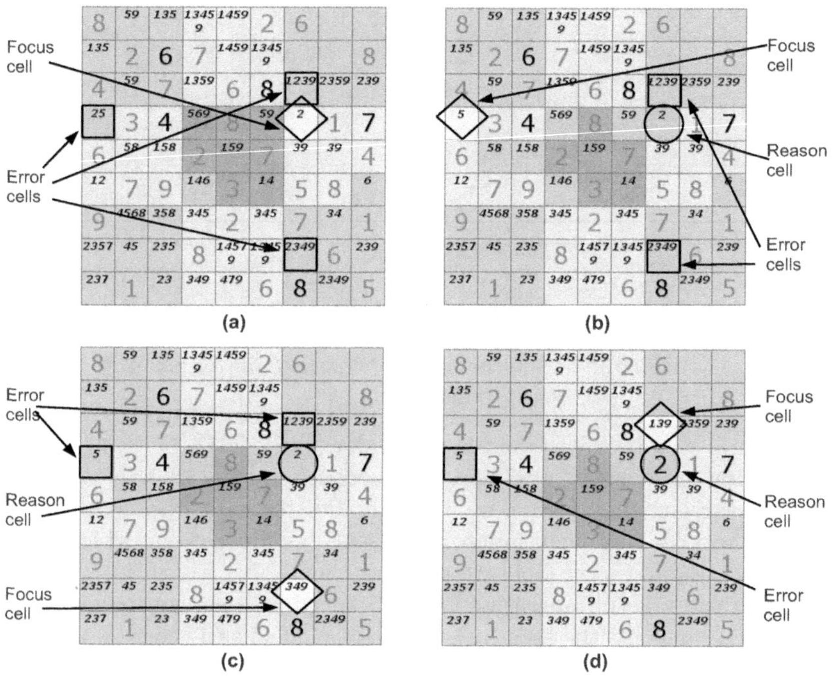

Fig. 6. Screen-shots of the puzzle panel for "auto-clean" operation

Consider the puzzle layout shown in Figure 6a, the three cells with a black rectangle are error cells because the focus cell (which is marked with a black diamond) has been set to number 2, while each of the three error cells has an optional number 2. In this situation, users can simply execute an "auto clean" operation by double click the diamond cell so as to remove the number 2 from the error cells. In the prototype system, the "auto clean" involves two additional sub-operations. Figure 6b, 6c and 6d present the screen-shots of the cleaning process. In each operation, the focus cell, which is marked with a black diamond, is the cell with new numbers; the reason cell, which is marked with a black circle, is the cell with a unique number 2.

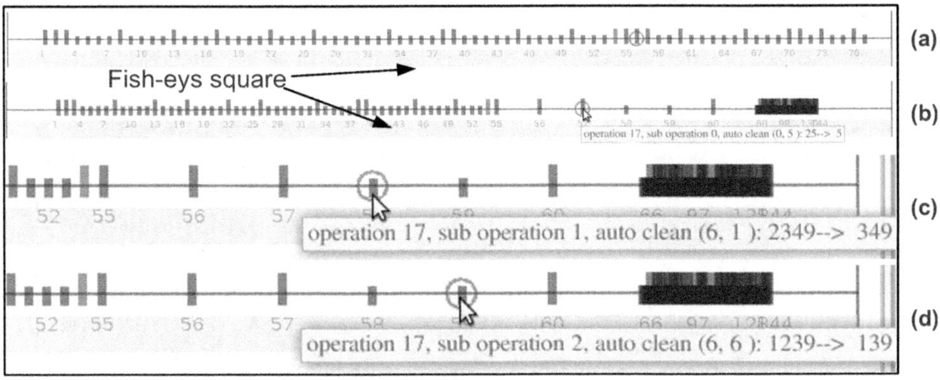

Fig. 7. Screen-shots of the index panel for "auto-clean" operation

For the index panel, the fish-eye mechanism will be automatically activated when the space between two operation squares is less than a pre-defined threshold value. In the index panel, this mechanism is represented as a square area just below the operation shapes. When an user moves a mouse pointer over the fish-eye area, the spaces between the five most nearest shapes to the mouse pointer will become larger, while the spaces between other shapes will become smaller.

Figure 7a illustrates the situation that a mouse pointer is outside of the fish-eye area. Figure 7b illustrates the situation that a mouse pointer first moves inside the fish-eye area and then moves to the operation shapes so that the detail about the operation will be displayed. While Figure 7a and Figure 7b give overall pictures about fish-eye mechanism of the index panel, Figure 7c and Figure 7d, which are the counterparts of Figure 6c and Figure 6d, present the details about the activated fish-eye areas.

5.3 The Drag-Able Square

While the fish-eye mechanism controls the spaces between operations, the drag-able square on the slider panel specifies the total number of the operations that will be drawn in the index panel. Just as the fish-eye mechanism, the drag-able square will be also automatically activated when the total number of the operations is greater than a pre-defined threshold value.

Initially, the drag-able square appears on the most left of the slider panel, as shown in Figure 8a. The covered indexes on the slider panel indicate that the operations of these indexes are now displayed in the index panel. If an user drags the square along the slider panel, the corresponding operations in the index panel will be automatically updated, as shown in Figure 8b.

For the index panel, if the fish-eye mechanism is also activated, then all operations will be displayed. In this case, although some parts of the operations overlap with each other, the operations near the mouse point are clear to users. This feature is shown in Figure 8c. The advantages of showing all operations in the index panel when the fish-eye mechanism is activated are that users can

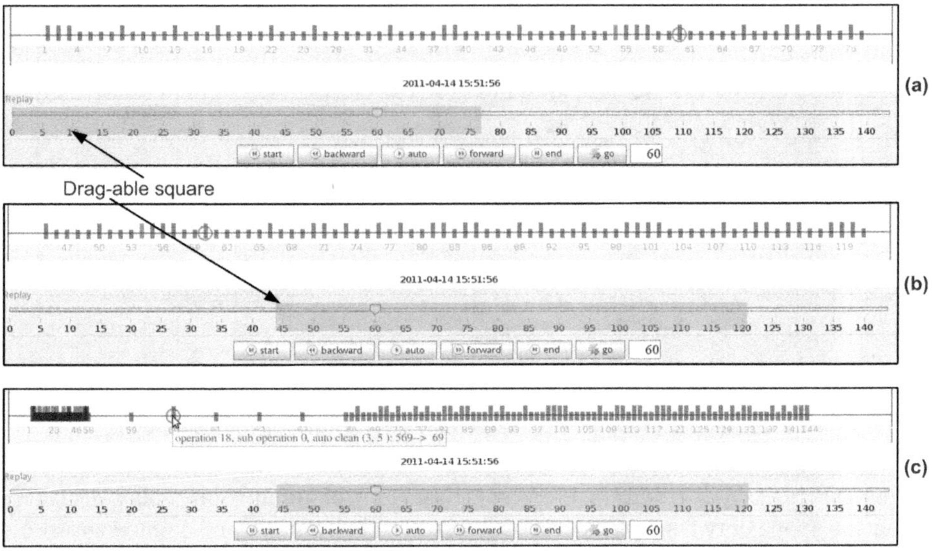

Fig. 8. Screen-shots of the drag-able square and the index panel

access all the operations only through the index panel and therefore do not need to move the mouse pointer to the control panel and click the traditional buttons.

5.4 Enhancement of the Index Panel

Initially, the fish-eye mechanism in the index panel is activated only when a mouse pointer moves inside the fish-eye square. That is, whenever a mouse pointer moves above or below the fish-eye square, the operation squares on the index panel will be restored to their normal positions. One drawback of this design is that when an user moves a mouse pointer to an operation square so as to retrieve the details of the operation, once the mouse pointer is moved outside the fish-eye square, the position of the operation square will change because of the restoring process of the whole index panel. Therefore, a re-search progress is needed for the user.

In order to provide a smooth visual query experience, the index panel is redesigned as follows: the index panel consists of three areas: 1) the fish-eye square; 2) the area below the square (normal area) and; 3) the area above the square (frozen area). When a mouse pointer moves inside the fish-eye square, the fish-eye mechanism is activated as normal; when a mouse pointer moves from the fish-eye square up to the frozen area, the operations squares remains frozen; when a mouse pointer moves from the fish-eye square down to the normal area, the operations squares will be restored to their normal positions.

The enhanced index panel is illustrate in Figure 9. In Figure 9a, the three screen-shots of the index panel demonstrate the moving of a mouse pointer in the frozen area when the fish-eye mechanism is activated. And when the mouse pointer moves back to the fish-eye square, the operation shapes are redrawn so

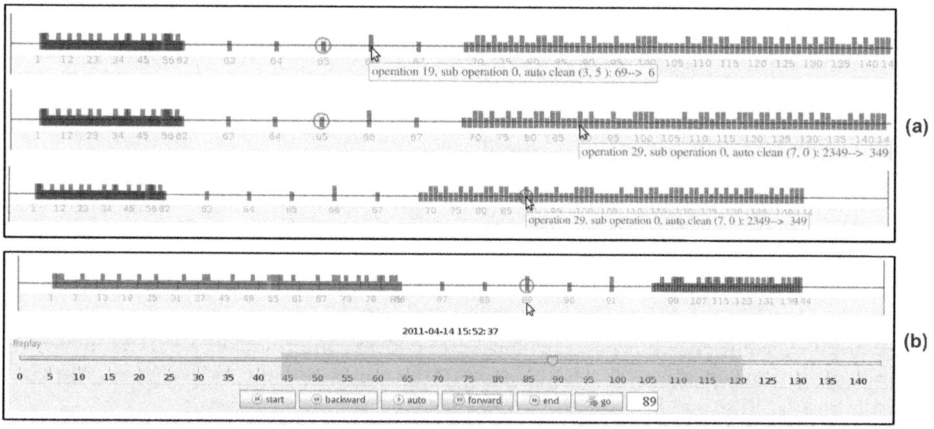

Fig. 9. Screen-shots for illustrating the enhanced index panel

that the operations near the mouse pointer are clear to users, as shown in Figure 9b. It is worthy to be mentioned that users can query the information scene of an operation by double clicking the corresponding shape drawn in the index panel.

6 Conclusion

This paper presented an architecture and a prototype system for querying and visualising recorded context information. In the architecture, domain knowledge is modelled by using the COINS modelling approach; the target information as well as its logical context information is treated as information scenes. One of the benefits of this architecture is that context information, especially those of logical dimension can be automatically recorded once the corresponding information scenes and scene recorders are defined and implemented.

In addition to addressing the acquirability of context information, two querying methods, which target for physical context information and logical context information respectively, are provided in the architecture. A prototype system has been developed by adopting the proposed architecture. The prototype system shows that the combination of natural language query and visual query techniques can facilitate the retrieving processes of physical context information as well as logical context information.

The future work will involve two main directions: 1) the improvement of the natural language part, such as to support more grammars of the supported language (currently English); 2) the support and integration of more context information, such as users' profiles and interests, so that the prototype system can automatically recommend related information to user.

Acknowledgement. The authors would like to thank the China Scholarship Council (CSC) and Dublin Institute of Technology (DIT) for their funding and support.

References

1. Adomavicius, G., Tuzhilin, A.: Context-aware recommender systems. In: Ricci, F., Rokach, L., Shapira, B., Kantor, P.B. (eds.) Recommender Systems Handbook, pp. 217–253. Springer, Heidelberg (2011)
2. Bai, J., Nie, J., Cao, G., Bouchard, H.: Using query contexts in information retrieval. In: Proceedings of the 30th Annual International ACM SIGIR Conference on Research and Development in Information Retrieval, pp. 15–22. ACM, New York (2007)
3. Baldauf, M., Dustdar, S., Rosenberg, F.: A survey on context-aware systems. Int. J. Ad Hoc Ubiquitous Comput. 2, 263–277 (2007)
4. Choi, O., Yoon, Y.: A meta data model of context information for dynamic service adaptation on user centric environment. In: International Conference on Multimedia and Ubiquitous Engineering, pp. 108–113 (2007)
5. Choujaa, D., Dulay, N.: Using screenplays as a source of context data. In: Proceeding of the 2nd ACM International Workshop on Story Representation, Mechanism and Context, pp. 13–20. ACM, New York (2008)
6. Dey, A.K.: Understanding and using context. Personal Ubiquitous Comput. 5, 4–7 (2001)
7. Finkelstein, L., Gabrilovich, E., Matias, Y., Rivlin, E., Solan, Z., Wolfman, G., Ruppin, E.: Placing search in context: the concept revisited. In: Proceedings of the 10th International Conference on World Wide Web, pp. 406–414. ACM, New York (2001)
8. Henricksen, K., Indulska, J.: Modelling and using imperfect context information. In: Proceedings of the Second IEEE Annual Conference on Pervasive Computing and Communications Workshops, pp. 33–37. IEEE, Los Alamitos (2004)
9. Holmes, R., Murphy, G.C.: Using structural context to recommend source code examples. In: Proceedings of the 27th International Conference on Software Engineering, pp. 117–125. ACM, New York (2005)
10. Lim, B.Y., Dey, A.K., Avrahami, D.: Why and why not explanations improve the intelligibility of context-aware intelligent systems. In: Proceedings of the 27th International Conference on Human Factors in Computing Systems, pp. 2119–2128. ACM, New York (2009)
11. Sondhi, P., Chandrasekar, R., Rounthwaite, R.: Using query context models to construct topical search engines. In: Proceeding of the Third Symposium on Information Interaction in Context, pp. 75–84. ACM, New York (2010)
12. Zhou, E., Wu, B., Ding, Y., Wu, J.: Coins: A modelling approach for recording & replaying complex information. In: Proceedings of the IADIS International Conference Information Systems 2011, Avila, Spain, pp. 37–44 (2011)

Author Index

Akrawi, Narin 97
Apolinarski, Wolfgang 18
Aureliano, Viviane 221

Beigl, Michael 104, 108, 214, 264, 296
Benotti, Luciana 26
Berbers, Yolande 307
Berchtold, Martin 104
Blackburn, Patrick 26
Brezillon, Patrick 40
Bucur, Doina 54
Budde, Matthias 296

Cassens, Jörg 145, 278
Ceusters, Werner 119
Chaker, Hamdi 67
Chevalier, Max 67
Chiu, Thun Pin T.F. 221
Cho, In Ho 233
Cruciani, Marco 71

David, Klaus 159
Ding, Yi 321
Ding, Yong 108
Doi, Miwako 226
Dumitrache, Anca 82

Edman, Anneli 97
Eriksson Lundström, Jenny 97

Friel, Owen 82

Geierhos, Michaela 173
Gordon, Dawud 104, 108
Grill, Thomas 115

Handte, Marcus 18
Hanne, Jan-Hendrik 104
Hastings, Janna 119
Herczeg, Michael 278
Holleis, Paul 5
Höpfner, Hagen 250

Ismail, Haythem O. 124

Jakimovski, Predrag 138
Ji, Sook Young 233
Ji, Yusheng 296

Kempson, Ruth 1
Kindsmüller, Martin Christof 278
Kishino, Yasue 185
Klein, Bernd Niklas 159
Kofod-Petersen, Anders 145
König, Immanuel 159

Landmark, Andreas D. 307
Lee, Joong Seek 233
Lee, Yeong Su 173
Le Phuoc, Danh 18

Maekawa, Takuya 185
Mahfouz, Aya S. 124
Marrón, Pedro José 18
Matic, Aleksandar 200, 246
Mayora-Ibarra, Oscar 200, 246
Mileo, Alessandra 82
Miyaki, Takashi 104
Mulligan, Kevin 119

Neumann, Martin Alexander 214

Obermeier, Philipp 82
Oliveira, Eduardo A. 221
Osmani, Venet 200, 246
Ouchi, Kazushige 226

Park, Hyun Kyu 233
Paulheim, Heiko 292
Polleres, Axel 82
Popleteev, Andrei 200, 246
Preuveneers, Davy 307

Riedel, Till 214

Sahami, Alireza 5
Sakurai, Yasushi 185
Schirmer, Maximilian 250
Schmidt, Albrecht 5

Schmidt, Benedikt 292
Schmidtke, Hedda R. 138, 214, 264
Schmitt, Felix 278
Scholz, Markus 108
Schulz, Axel 292
Sigg, Stephan 296
Smith, Barry 119
Soulé-Dupuy, Chantal 67

Taylor, Philip 214
Tedesco, Patricia 221
Toussaint, Pieter J. 307
Tricot, André 67
Tscheligi, Manfred 115
Turner, Roy 300

Voigtmann, Christian 159

Whitsel, Larry 300
Wienhofen, Leendert W.M. 307
Wu, Bing 321
Wu, Jianfeng 321

Yanagisawa, Yutaka 185

Zhou, Erqiang 321
Zimmermann, Antoine 82

GPSR Compliance

The European Union's (EU) General Product Safety Regulation (GPSR) is a set of rules that requires consumer products to be safe and our obligations to ensure this.

If you have any concerns about our products, you can contact us on ProductSafety@springernature.com

In case Publisher is established outside the EU, the EU authorized representative is:

Springer Nature Customer Service Center GmbH
Europaplatz 3
69115 Heidelberg, Germany

Batch number: 10844619

Printed by Printforce, the Netherlands